*"Clarity. Conscience. Convicting. These three words su~~m~~_____ ~~, experience~~ with Tony Evans. He never fails to speak with clarity to \_\_\_onscience—convicting of both God's love and my response."*

MAX LUCADO
Preacher/Teacher, Oak Hills Church of Christ

*"Tony Evans has hit a spiritual bull's-eye by showing in such a powerful way how to model the kingdom of God on earth, as it already is in heaven, in all areas of life. He makes it clear that nonbelievers will not be attracted to the Good News of the kingdom of God by what we say, but by what they see in our lives."*

BARBARA WILLIAMS SKINNER
President, Skinner Farm Leadership Institute

*"Lots of people in our messed-up nation are dispensing good advice, but good advice has never changed the human heart. Only the Good News of the gospel of Jesus Christ and the eternal truths of God's Word will fix America's families and communities. That's what the reader will find in the pages of this book written by one of America's best preachers and communicators, Dr. Tony Evans."*

LUIS PALAU
International Evangelist

*"The Kingdom Agenda is the most significant book my friend Tony Evans has ever written. It is 'must reading' for every believer who wants to live an authentic Christian life."*

JOHN PERKINS
The John Perkins Foundation

*"Dr. Tony Evans has successfully laid out a strategic discipline of living according to God's agenda. I would encourage anyone who wishes to make an impact for the kingdom of God to read this book, and take a serious look at God's Word, which will enable you to live your life as God intended you to live it in all areas of your life."*

CHARLES STANLEY
Senior Pastor, First Baptist Church of Atlanta

*Living all of life by ...*

# The KINGDOM Agenda

*What a way to live!*

# TONY EVANS

**MOODY PUBLISHERS**

CHICAGO

Cover Design: DesignWorks Group, Inc.
Cover Image: Henrik Weis
Editor: Jim Vincent


Library of Congress Cataloging-in-Publication Data

Evans, Anthony T.
    Kingdom agenda : what a way to live! / by Tony Evans.
        p. cm.
    Originally published : Nashville : Word Pub., c1999.
    Includes bibliographical references and index.
    ISBN-13: 978-0-8024-5123-1
    1. Christian life. I. Title.
    BV4501.3.E927 2006
    248.4—dc22
                                2005037116


We hope you enjoy this book from Moody Publishers. Our goal is to provide high quality, thought-provoking books and publications that connect truth to your real needs and challenges. For more information on other books and products written and produced from a biblical perspective, go to www.moodypublishers.com or write to:

Moody Publishers
820 N. LaSalle Blvd.
Chicago, IL 60610


7 9 10 8


*Printed in the United States of America*

*This book is dedicated to the late Tom Skinner,*
*whose life, ministry, and legacy*
*continue to inspire me greatly*
*and who clearly demonstrated*
*that there can be no distinction between*
*the sacred and the secular; and that the kingdom*
*of God must be brought to bear and integrated into all of life.*

# CONTENTS

# *Preface*

The *Kingdom Agenda* is my fourteenth book. I also consider it my magnum opus. Not simply because it is larger than my previous works nor because it necessarily outweighs the truths I've attempted to communicate in the past.

Rather, this book uniquely expresses my comprehensive worldview and philosophy of life and ministry. It is a worldview that I believe is solidly based on the authority of Scripture, and yet one I hope is communicated in a way that relates to the everyday realities of life.

This is fundamentally a book about the kingdom of God and His agenda for our lives. It is my conviction that the message of the kingdom is sorely lacking today. This is not because people don't speak of the kingdom but because far too much of their speech is in esoteric, theological "code words" that seem unrelated to the realities of life in the here and now.

The absence of a comprehensive agenda for life has led to deterioration in our world of cosmic proportions. People live segmented, compartmentalized lives because they lack a kingdom worldview. Families disintegrate because they exist for their own fulfillment rather than for the kingdom.

Churches are having a limited impact on society because they fail to understand that the goal of the church is not the church itself but the kingdom. This myopic perspective keeps the church divided, ingrown, and unable to transform the cultural landscape in any significant way.

And because this is so, society at large has nowhere to turn to find solid solutions to the perplexing challenges that confront us today—troubling problems such as crime, racism, poverty, and a myriad of other ills.

It is time for Christians to set forth a kingdom agenda! We need to set forth an agenda that is a comprehensive demonstration of the way our Creator intended every area of life to be lived. An agenda big enough to include both individuals and societal structures, clear enough to be understood and appropriated by the average person on the street, yet flexible enough to allow for the considerable differences among peoples and societies.

This book is my humble attempt as a covenantal and progressive dispensationalist to contribute to this exercise. I believe that Christianity offers not only a clear message for eternity but also a message that is workable in time. I believe it provides food for the soul but also a solid foundation for civilization.

I believe that a kingdom agenda provides another option, another way to see and live life in this world. It transcends the politics of men and offers the solutions of heaven. Such an agenda can hold its own against any of the humanistic worldviews of our day.

While I am certain that many will challenge some of my assumptions, I welcome those challenges because they will make me a sharper thinker and a more strategic biblicist. The Christian message, when communicated from a comprehensive, kingdom perspective, provides an agenda that can stand next to and above all other attempts to define the meaning of life, whether it be the individual, the family, the church, or the community.

A kingdom agenda based on God's Word, rather than a secular agenda based on man's word, is the best way to make all of life work as our Creator intended.

Everyone has an idea and a viewpoint, but I believe God has spoken and He has not stuttered. There are two answers to every question: God's answer and everyone else's. And everyone else is wrong! Thus it behooves us to bring our lives under God's rule and passionately pursue the kingdom agenda.

# A World Off Target

One day a man was on his way to spend the day with a good friend who lived on a farm.

When the man reached the farm, he turned onto the long, winding road that led to the farmhouse. On the way, he had to pass by the barn. But as he drove by the barn, he stopped and got out because he saw something that both amazed and stupefied him.

Drawn on the side of the barn were twenty targets. Each target had a hole right through the center of its bull's-eye. There were no other holes anywhere on the barn. Whoever had been using the barn for target practice was definitely a crack shot.

The visitor couldn't believe it. He got back in his car, drove up to his friend's farmhouse, and said, "John, before we do anything else, I've just got to ask you. Who in the world did the shooting on the side of your barn?"

John said, "Oh, that was me."

His friend replied, "I can't believe anybody can shoot that well! We're talking about twenty targets with twenty dead-center bull's-eye shots. You mean to tell me you did that?"

John said, "Made every shot."

"Where in the world did you learn to shoot like that?" John's friend asked.

"It was easy. I shot first; then I drew a target around the bullet hole."

## LEARNING TO PAINT BULL'S-EYES

That humorous story illustrates the situation our society is facing today. We do everything we can to give the impression that our lives are on target when in reality all we have done is learn to paint well!

We have sought to camouflage our emptiness and failure with materialism, the scramble for success and significance, and other pursuits. Some people even try to fill their emptiness through religious activities such as church membership. They have learned how to look, talk, and act like Christians, but all of these things, in and of themselves, are simply "paint jobs" that try to obscure the fact that we are a culture and a people tragically off target. We only have to look at the indicators to see that far too many individuals, families, and churches are missing the mark. And the results are seen in a society that is living by an agenda of madness.

## PERSONAL CHAOS

All we have to do is look at the indicators that tell us we are missing the target. Judging by the meteoric rise in popular psychology books, clinics, and programs, it would seem that personal lack of meaning and fulfillment is at an all-time high. If I were not in the ministry, I would become a psychologist so I could charge people two hundred dollars an hour to tell them why they need to come back next week!

But let me give you the real deal on this. The fact is that if you're a messed-up person and you have a family, you are going to contribute to a messed-up family, and if your family goes to church, then your messed-up family will contribute to a messed-up church.

And if you're a messed-up person contributing to a messed-up family contributing to a messed-up church, and your church is in a neighborhood, then your messed-up church will lead to a messed-up neighborhood.

And if you're a messed-up person contributing to a messed-up family contributing to a messed-up church leading to a messed-up neighborhood, and your neighborhood resides in a city, then your messed-up neighborhood will result in a messed-up city.

Now if you're a messed-up person contributing to a messed-up family contributing to a messed-up church leading to a messed-up neighborhood resulting in a messed-up city, and your city resides in a county, then your messed-up city will cause a messed-up county.

And if you're a messed-up person contributing to a messed-up family contributing to a messed-up church leading to a messed-up neighborhood resulting in a messed-up city residing in a messed-up county, and your county is part of a state, then your county will help create a messed-up state.

But that's not all. If you're a messed-up person contributing to a messed-up family contributing to a messed-up church leading to a messed-up neighborhood resulting in a messed-up city residing in a messed-up county helping to create a messed-up state, and your state is part of a country, then your messed-up state helps produce a messed-up nation.

Now if you're a messed-up person contributing to a messed-up family contributing to a messed-up church leading to a messed-up neighborhood resulting in a messed-up city helping to create a messed-up state that helps produce a messed-up nation, and your nation is part of the world, your messed-up country will leave us with a messed-up world!

So if we want a better world composed of better countries, inhabited by better states, made up of better counties, composed of better cities, inhabited by better neighborhoods, illuminated by better churches, made up of better families, we need to become better people. It all starts with personal responsibility!

## FAMILY CHAOS

This breakdown at the personal level has had devastating effects on the American family. After more than thirty years of failed social programs, the once-stable American family is rapidly deteriorating. Couples live as if they were wed by the secretary of war rather than by the justice of the peace! We are still hearing the figure of a 50 percent failure rate for new marriages. Materialism has become more important than maintaining marriages, and personal happiness has taken priority over family unity.

In the inner city, the disintegration of the family is even greater. More than six out of ten black children are born to unwed mothers. Two-parent families are now the exception in the inner city. The social implications of these statistics are nothing short of staggering.

The devaluation of women through the curse of pornography and the glorification of violence on television and in the movies have fueled family breakdown. In such an environment, it is no wonder that gangs flourish in our cities—and yes, they have moved to the suburbs too. There is no longer any such thing as fleeing the problem.

One reason gangs are popular is that they are substitute families. In a gang, young people can find the acceptance and sense of self-worth and accountability they aren't getting at home. Sadly, the gang provides that self-esteem in the context of horrible violence and crime.

## CHURCH CHAOS

All of these indicators clearly show how far our American culture has wandered from its moral moorings. And what about the church? What kind of influence has the church been able to assert in the midst of this personal and family breakdown? A rapidly declining influence.

Today the church and what it represents are all too often ridiculed, criticized, rejected outright, or simply ignored in the public square. And this is happening at the same time as acceptance for humanistic and non-Christian religious worldviews is growing, a concern we will address in this book.

The non-Christian society at large has failed to take the person and Word of God seriously. And the church has been ineffective in its efforts to impact our culture for Christ at the deepest levels.

Thus the church has contributed to the spiritual decline of American culture by failing to produce kingdom people who are accomplishing Christ's kingdom agenda and by failing to manifest and illustrate clearly the solutions of the kingdom for the critical issues of our day. We have done an admirable job of cursing the darkness. But we have done a poor job of spreading the light.

While we have talked about being the family of God, we have been a family in crisis, unable to provide spiritual leadership to our fledgling culture. Rather than being the church in the world, we have allowed the world and its agenda to invade the church and help shape our thinking and our actions. The result has been what I call a drive-through "McChristian" spirituality.

This has led to weak Christians leading weak families bringing about weak churches resulting in a weak nation. I believe the church's greatest need today is not for sinners to accept our worldview but for us to accept our worldview—our agenda—and make it the modus operandi of our daily lives.

It is not until the church reclaims its rightful position in society that the culture will have something to follow. By the power and grace of God, we can be instruments in His hands to salvage our culture. If we don't, I don't see anyone else around able to do the job.

## SOCIETAL CHAOS

Virtually every institution in our culture is revealing how far off target we have become.

The criminal justice system cannot begin to handle the increase in crime that keeps the general urban population living behind barred windows and doors while gangs, criminals, and drug dealers control the streets. Prisons can't be built fast enough to house the number of criminals the system seeks to incarcerate.

Neither has increased education stemmed the tide of moral decay now engulfing us. Metal detectors are now common at many high schools, and in some cities students must pass breath tests to be admitted to their school proms. All of this demonstrates graphically what happens when a society tries to teach information without ethics.

The popularity of television and radio talk shows is another indicator of how far we have missed the target of a holistic, well-balanced spiritual life. The babble by the hour that these shows offer, with their hosts parading all manner of maladjusted people before the public in the name of information and entertainment, reveals how misguided our society has become.

Not only is it shameful that these people hold up their sins to public exposure; it is equally shameful that a confused public is entertained by such nonsense. What used to be disgusting and embarrassing is now titillating.

A multitude of books, seminars, workshops, and symposia have not enabled us to bridge the racial, class, and cultural divides that separate us. Our technological advances have far outpaced our sense of community. We can send a robotic probe to examine the surface of Mars, but we cannot manage our relationships.

Add to these issues the growing awareness that government is unable to fix the problems of poverty and social decay, and it quickly becomes apparent that all the king's horses and all the king's men cannot spend enough money or create enough programs to put the Humpty Dumpty of our culture together again. As we will see later in this book, at the heart of our societal chaos and breakdown is a clash of worldviews, those presuppositions that determine how we look at and interpret life.

The worldview of humanism puts man at the center of the universe so that he attempts to define man and his relationships solely from naturalistic presuppositions. Theism, on the other hand, puts God in His rightful place at the center of the universe as life's highest Authority, by whom everything else must be measured. Both of these worldviews are religious in nature since both require faith—faith in man or faith in God. Both views also produce a set of principles and standards—an agenda—to be used in determining how life is to be lived. The direction of a society is decided by which worldview prevails. It should be obvious, judging by the way our society makes decisions, which worldview prevails. It should be obvious, judging by the direction our society is heading, that we need another agenda!

When people talk about what's wrong with the world, the problem is the government, the media, my boss, my parents, my children—anyone or anything but me. The refusal of people to take personal responsibility for their actions has become a national epidemic. Everyone is playing the blame game.

## SPIRITUAL AIDS

So the question is, What really is wrong with us as individuals, as families, as the church, and as a society? I believe that when you put all our problems on the examining table and shine the light of God's Word on them, it becomes painfully clear that what is happening to us is a lot like the beginning of the disease called AIDS. We are suffering from a case of spiritual AIDS.

As we know, AIDS is a breakdown in the body's immune system. As the HIV virus attacks and incapacitates the immune system, the body is rendered vulnerable to a host of other diseases. A cold can become pneumonia. An otherwise minor infection can become life-threatening. In fact, an AIDS sufferer usually does not die of the disease itself but of AIDS-related complications.

What is true of the AIDS virus is true on every level of our society. Our spiritual immune system has been badly damaged, with the result that cultural colds have become societal pneumonia, and minor cultural infections have now become life-threatening. And none of the medications being applied is correcting the problem. At best, they may simply suppress some of the symptoms temporarily.

Call-in counseling is not filling our personal sense of emptiness. Workshops, conferences, and even presidential calls for renewed harmony are not solving our crime problem. More condoms and sex education are not solving our moral problem. And more activism is not solving our social problems. What in the world is wrong with this world?

I believe that the heart of our problem is captured and summarized in these verses from 2 Chronicles 15, a passage talking about ancient Israel:

> *And for many days Israel was without the true God and without a teaching priest and without law . . . And in those times there was no peace to him who went out or to him who came in, for many disturbances afflicted all the inhabitants of the lands. And nation was crushed by nation, and city by city, for God troubled them with every kind of distress. (vv. 3,5–6)*

Scan these few verses, and you will see a picture of great spiritual and social chaos, the breakdown of a society. What was wrong? Three crucial things were missing in Israel's national life, and I believe they are missing today in American life too.

The first thing missing was "the true God."

Now the chronicler was not saying that the Israelites had become atheists or no longer believed in God. He wasn't saying that attendance at the temple was down. The sacrificial fires at the temple were still smoking. But Israel had lost a correct view of God, and the nation was no longer accomplishing His agenda.

The Israelites wanted a convenient God, one they could control. But if you have a God you can control, then you're god instead of Him. Any god you can boss around isn't the true God. The true God does not adjust to you. You adjust to Him.

The Israelites didn't want the true God messing around in their national life, reminding them that He had an agenda greater than their personal interests and desires. Our culture doesn't want a God like that either.

The world wants a nice little prayer before public meetings, but its people don't want to hear about the true God. And I'm afraid that sometimes the church isn't very interested in the true God either, because we have our own agenda.

But any time we do that we are helping to reinforce our culture's false view of God as a harmless deity who doesn't have anything significant to say about the educational, scientific, entertainment, civic, political, familial, legal, or racial issues of the day.

The second problem in Israel was a loss of teaching priests.

Again, the text doesn't say there were no priests. But the priests had stopped teaching the truth. They had traded enlightenment for entertainment. Worship had degenerated into a social club. The church was no longer the epicenter of all life and conscience of the culture, calling people to take God seriously.

I'm not saying we cannot or should not enjoy worship. There's nothing wrong with celebrating God and expressing our emotions in worship. But emotion is never to replace truth.

Israel was suffering from an absence of spiritual leaders who took seriously the authority of Scripture for all of life.

Have you ever wondered how we can have all these churches on all these corners with all these preachers and all these choirs and all these deacons and all these ministries—and still have all this mess? There's a dead monkey on the line somewhere!

Someone will say, "Well, I didn't like that sermon." Wrong response. The issue is whether it was true, not whether it was popular. Politicians need to be popular. Preachers need to tell the truth.

The issue of truth is all-important, as we will see in the pages that follow. Our society is schizophrenic because people want certainty in the important, everyday stuff, but nobody wants to admit that there is such a thing as a reliable body of truth; so relativism rules.

This lack of truth has led to a "conscienceless" society, in which people can sin big-time and feel no emotional or spiritual pain. God created pain, whether physical or spiritual, to tell us something is wrong and to keep us from going as far as we could go.

But when people do not have truth, they do not have anything to give them pain when they make wrong decisions. They become "seared in their own conscience as with a branding iron" (1 Timothy 4:2). They become anesthetized, losing their sense of right and wrong. In such a society every person becomes a law unto himself or herself, so chaos rules.

The process starts early these days. It used to be that most people's consciences didn't get anesthetized until college, where the professor in Philosophy 101 was at best an agnostic, or even worse, an atheist. So he would announce, "There are no absolutes."

But now kids in middle school and high school are learning that one person's answers and ideas are just as good as anyone else's, as we will see in a later chapter.

But in a world where everybody's answers are right, nobody's answers wind up being right. When a society loses truth, it loses meaning, because people are never really sure about anything.

So that's the mess we are in as a culture. But where do we go to find truth? There's only one standard of truth, the changeless Word of the one true God.

The third missing ingredient in Israel was God's law.

When a culture has a false view of God built on bad information, God begins to remove the restraint of His law, and evil begins to grow unbridled. What you and I are witnessing today in the rapid deterioration of our culture is the reality that God is removing more and more of His restraint.

Even sinners who respect God won't do certain things. But once God is removed from or marginalized in a culture, then the standard for a society is gone and God becomes one's worst enemy and worst nightmare. That's what had happened in Israel.

When the rule of God's law is missing, chaos replaces community. You cannot have order and structure in society without God. Men become enslaved by the very freedom they seek.

We have ungodly people in our culture who don't want any divine standard to which they must be held accountable. But when God leaves a society, hope goes with Him.

See, as long as you have God, you always have hope. He's the one thing you can bank on. If God is still in the picture, and as long as His agenda is on the table, it's not over until it's over.

Even if circumstances collapse, God will keep you. As long as God is front and center in a culture, there's hope. But when He is removed, just like people and their taxes leave the city and go to the suburbs, God goes to the spiritual suburbs, and the city's cultures deteriorate.

Actually, there is a law at work in our culture—the law of unrighteousness. It's become so strong that it almost seems as natural as the law of gravity.

Now if you're going to buck the law of gravity, you'd better have a law more powerful than gravity going for you. Well, the law of gravity can be "bucked" by the law of aerodynamics in flight.

In the same way, the law of unrighteousness can be bucked by the law of God if the church will power up the engine of God and start soaring. If we don't, this plane called American culture is going down—and we'll crash with it because we're on board.

## THE REAL PROBLEM

The stunning thing about the situation in 2 Chronicles 15 is that God was the cause of Israel's distress, not the sinners in that culture or the Devil.

Now when God is your problem, then only God is your solution. If God is ticked off, it doesn't matter whom you elect or what programs you initiate. Until His anger is assuaged, you won't be able to fix what's wrong or spend enough money to buy your way out of your dilemma.

This is the heart of our problems today. Too many individuals, families, churches, and communities want to keep God on the fringes of our lives. There He can be accessible if we have a need, but we can keep Him far enough away from the center of our lives that He doesn't start messing with our agendas.

As long as we keep God at a distance He will not take over the control center of our world, and thus unrighteousness will rule. He will be close enough for invocations and benedictions but not part of the debate in between.

The net result of all this is that we are seeing the "devolution" of mankind. The more we marginalize God, the worse things get. This is what Paul said in Romans 1:18 when he wrote, "The wrath of God is revealed from heaven against all ungodliness and unrighteousness of men." Then in verses 19–31, Paul traced the downward spiral of a culture that excludes God.

## TIME FOR AN ALTERNATIVE

What then must we do to reverse this downward spiral of our lives at all four of these levels? It is time for an alternative, a new agenda, that transcends human politics, secular social movements, and religious traditions. I would like to suggest an alternative, using a familiar analogy from my days as chaplain of the Dallas Cowboys football team.

One pass play involved a fly pattern run by Drew Pearson, a great Cowboy of that era. The idea was simple. Drew would run as fast as possible down the sideline, looking for a long pass from Roger Staubach in the hopes of scoring a touchdown.

However, sometimes the defense would blitz, rushing the quarterback before he had time to set up, look downfield, and throw the long pass. So on this play, Tony Dorsett was to peel, or waggle, off to the side and become Roger's safety valve or alternative receiver.

If the defense blitzed and Roger didn't have time to throw the long pass, he would toss a soft, short pass over to Tony as he peeled off on the side.

My friend, God has called for us to score a touchdown. He wants us to live life in the most meaningful, dynamic, and significant way possible. He has a play, an agenda, that will enable individuals, families, the church, and society to function properly if we will just follow that play.

But we keep allowing blitzing linebackers of humanism and defensive backs of secularism to penetrate our backfield, seeking to disrupt and detour the agenda God has set for us.

In the pages that follow, I have sought to "peel off to the side and offer an alternative," a biblically based kingdom agenda. I will attempt to demonstrate that God's Holy Book, the Bible, has provided us with a clear authority and a comprehensive, dynamic approach to all of life. I want to show you this through the four areas that God has given us to order all of life: personal, family, church, and community.

I believe that when these areas are lived out in proper relationship to God and to each other, He will enable us to live life as it was meant to be lived. The kingdom agenda—what a way to live!

# PART ONE

# THE KINGDOM
# AGENDA IN BIBLICAL
# PERSPECTIVE

# The Concept of a
# Kingdom Agenda

Everybody, it seems, has an agenda today. People have plans, pro-grams, things they want to accomplish, and specific ways they want to accomplish them.

God has an agenda, too; something He wants to accomplish in His way. The Bible calls this agenda God's *kingdom*. I like to think of the kingdom of God as the alternative, because that word says there is another way, another idea on the floor. As God's people, we are not limited by the choices this world offers us. God has an alternative plan for us—His kingdom.

Throughout the Bible, the kingdom of God is His rule, His plan, His program. God's kingdom is all-embracing. It covers everything in the universe. In fact, we can define God's kingdom as His comprehensive rule over all creation. It is the rule of God (theocracy) and not the rule of man (homocracy) that is paramount.

Now if God's kingdom is comprehensive, so is His kingdom agenda. The kingdom agenda, then, may be defined as *the visible demonstration of the comprehensive rule of God over every area of life.*

That has some serious implications for us. The reason so many of us believers are struggling is that we want God to bless our plans rather than our fulfilling His agenda. We want God to OK our plans rather than our fulfilling His plans. We want God to bring us glory rather than our bringing Him glory.

But it doesn't work that way. God has only one plan, one alternative, and it's His kingdom agenda. We need to find out what that is so we can make sure we're working on God's plan, not ours.

The Greek word the Bible uses for kingdom is *basileia*, which means basically a "rule" or "authority." Included in this definition is the idea of power. So when we talk about a kingdom, we're talking first about a king, a ruler, someone who calls the shots.

Now if there's a ruler, there also have to be "rulees," or kingdom subjects. And a kingdom also includes a realm; that is, a sphere over which the king rules. Finally, if you're going to have a ruler, rulees, and a realm, you also need kingdom regulations, guidelines that govern the relationship between the ruler and the subjects. These are necessary so the rulees will know whether they are doing what the ruler wants done.

God's kingdom includes all of these elements. He is the absolute Ruler of His domain, which encompasses all of creation. And His authority is total. Everything God rules, He runs—even when it doesn't look like He's running it. Even when life looks like it's out of control, God is running its "out-of-controlness."

God's kingdom also has its "rulees." Colossians 1:13 says that everybody who has trusted the Lord Jesus Christ as Savior has been transferred from the kingdom of darkness to the kingdom of light. If you are a believer in Jesus Christ, your allegiance has been changed. You no longer follow Satan but Christ.

And just in case there's any doubt, let me say right now that there are no in-between kingdoms, no gray areas here. There are only two realms in creation: the kingdom of God and the kingdom of Satan. We are subjects of one or the other.

## GOD'S KINGDOM AGENDA IS NOT . . .

The problem we have in the church today is that people misdefine God's kingdom. Some people secularize and politicize the kingdom, which means they think the solutions to our problems are going to fly into town on *Air Force One*.

These people believe that political involvement or social action will by themselves bring in the kingdom. Historically, this has been a liberal way of thinking.

But today, evangelicals have also entered the political arena. There's nothing wrong with that, but we need to remember that God's kingdom is not political. As I often say, God is neither Democrat nor Republican, and He doesn't ride the backs of donkeys or elephants.

At the other extreme are those Christians who overspiritualize the kingdom. In contrast to their politically active brothers and sisters, these are the folks who are so heavenly minded they're no earthly good. They live with their heads in the clouds, and the kingdom of God never moves beyond the esoteric stage with them. They're not able to put feet to the spiritual reality of the kingdom.

God's kingdom alternative is much bigger than the political and social realm; neither is it limited to the walls of the church. We need to clarify the kingdom as a foundation for everything we are going to talk about in this book.

This is crucial because when you were saved, the kingdom of God was set up in your heart so that it might reach to and direct the circumference of your life.

Having Jesus in your heart will get you to heaven. But having Jesus in your heart won't get heaven down into history. The Jesus in your heart must also be the Jesus who rules in the kingdom of which you are a part. So in this chapter I want us to see four basic truths about God's kingdom.

## GOD'S KINGDOM AGENDA ORIGINATES FROM HIS REALM

First of all, we need to see that God's kingdom originates from His realm, which is spiritual.

Now when I say that, I'm not denying what we said above, that the whole universe constitutes the realm of God's kingdom. What I'm talking about is the origin of God's kingdom. It is from above, not from the earth.

### Of Another Realm

We can see this in John 18:28–40, where Jesus appears before the Roman governor Pilate. The Jews want Jesus put to death, but they don't have the authority to carry out capital punishment. Only Rome can do that, so the Jews have to bring Jesus to Pilate to get his approval.

The Jews know exactly what accusation it will take to get Jesus executed by Rome. If He claims to be a king, He will be committing treason against Caesar (see John 19:12). So the charge against Jesus is that He made Himself out to be a king.

Now, if you call yourself a king, that implies you have a kingdom somewhere. So the first question Pilate asked Jesus was, "Are You the King of the Jews?" (John 18:33).

Notice Jesus' answer in verse 36: "My kingdom is not of this world. If My kingdom were of this world, then My servants would be fighting, that I might not be delivered up to the Jews; but as it is, My kingdom is not of this realm."

Now don't misread that. Jesus was not saying His kingdom is not *in* this world. He was saying His kingdom is not *of* this world. His kingdom does not originate from earth but from heaven. It is not derived from history but from a wholly different realm. Jesus' servants weren't up in military arms about His arrest because He was not trying to overthrow the Romans militarily.

When you have a kingdom agenda, it affects what you do and how you do it. Jesus was explaining to Pilate, "If My kingdom were of this world, My servants would be out there with their swords cutting off more than ears. They would be going to war. If My kingdom were man-made, I would not be going to the cross without a fight."

If you want to carry out God's alternative agenda, you have to do so His way rather than everybody else's way. To have a kingdom agenda affects your methodology. It means that you do what you do in a way that God approves of. His kingdom is worked out and applied on earth but from a divine frame of reference.

Too many believers are trying to have a happy marriage the human way. Too many are trying to find a fulfilled life using human methods. But you can't adopt man's methods to accomplish God's goals. That's not adopting a kingdom agenda. Jesus told Pilate, in essence, "My method reflects My source."

## A Body of Truth

In verse 37 Jesus said something else very significant: "Everyone who is of the truth hears My voice." A kingdom agenda assumes the existence of a body of truth. This puts us in conflict with our culture, because we live in a world where a commitment to truth no longer exists. People want convenience, not an absolute standard that says what is right and wrong, good and bad.

If you're going to be on God's agenda, you must believe in truth: an absolute, governing standard that is transcultural, transracial, and trans-situational. For believers, of course, this standard is the Word of God.

Our problem is that we have too many opinions and not enough truth. Even among Christians, absolute truth isn't always the governing standard. We say, "Well, this is how I feel," "This is what I think," "This is what my mama taught me." There's nothing necessarily wrong with thoughts or feelings, but they are not the deciding factors in discovering truth.

In the place of absolute truth we have substituted relativism, pragmatism, existentialism, pantheism, and many other "isms" that will become "was-isms" when confronted with God's absolute truth.

Jesus was saying in John 18:37, "If you understand My kingdom, you would know the truth." The only lasting solutions to life are biblical solutions, because only biblical solutions are derived from a heavenly source and can address the cause-effect relationship.

## Cause and Effect

Here's what I mean by cause and effect when it comes to the kingdom. Everything visible and physical is always controlled or derived from that which is invisible and spiritual. So if you want to fix the visible and physical problems, you've got to address the spiritual and invisible issues first.

Why? Because if you don't address the spiritual and invisible, then you will not have a divine reference point from which to solve the visible and physical mess. What you can see, hear, touch, taste, and smell must first be addressed from God's viewpoint before you can make any difference on the human level.

Satan wants to get us to skip the divine aspect because he knows we'll never solve our visible and physical problems until we address them from the divine realm. We need to understand that heaven rules earth. What happens up there determines what goes on down here. So if you're not in contact with heaven, don't be surprised if you're in a mess down here on earth.

One of the greatest kings in history, Nebuchadnezzar of Babylon, learned this truth the hard way. Old Nebby had a dream that disturbed him, so he asked the prophet Daniel to interpret for him.

Daniel told the king he would lose his kingdom and be driven into insanity until he learned that "it is Heaven that rules" (Daniel 4:26).

Then we are told that what Daniel prophesied came to pass (see v. 28).

## The Right Perspective

God's kingdom is lived from the perspective of heaven, not earth. That's why Jesus said, "Seek first His kingdom and His righteousness; and all these things shall be added to you" (Matthew 6:33). The pagans may run after the physical, visible stuff (see v. 32), but we are called to prioritize God's kingdom.

See, if we lose sight of the kingdom, God's realm gets lost and we start going after the physical things. When that happens, we're going to be skewed in our judgment.

Jesus said earlier in Matthew 6 that if you are not clear on the kingdom—the things of God—then you are spiritually blind (see vv. 22–23). And if you're spiritually blind, then your feet won't know which way to go. Spiritual blindness affects not only your eyes but all your life.

I will never forget one particular morning when I got soap in my eye in the shower. My eye started burning, so I began to rub it with my hand. The problem was, I had soap on my hands. So not only did I not get the soap out of my eye, I managed to get more soap in my eye—and soap in the other eye. Then I had two burning eyes!

I couldn't see, so I reached for the towel to fix this mess. But because I couldn't see, I hit my head on the soap dish sticking out of the wall. When I did that, I knocked the soap off the dish onto the shower floor. You can probably guess what happened next.

As I groped around for the towel in my blindness, I stepped on the bar of soap and went flying, hurting my back. There I was, flailing around in the shower with a headache and a backache and burning eyes, all because something blinded me.

Let me tell you, when you are spiritually blind you'll wind up with a headache and a backache and a "life ache," because the spiritual realm affects everything else in life. God's kingdom operates from the realm of heaven. The only way you will be able to see life with 20/20 vision is when you look at life from a kingdom perspective.

## GOD'S KINGDOM AGENDA REFLECTS HIS SOVEREIGNTY

Here's a second truth about God's kingdom I want us to consider. When you adopt God's kingdom agenda, you come under His sovereign rule. Sovereignty refers to God's supremacy over all of His creation—visible and invisible. His rules are universal, absolute, and comprehensive. God, therefore, is accountable to no one.

*Sovereignty* is a word many people don't like. But it's the only way God does business. In Psalm 103:19, David wrote, "The Lord has established His throne in the heavens; and His sovereignty rules over all." In other words, God is not operating by your permission.

Look at Psalm 115:3: "Our God is in the heavens; He does whatever He pleases." Lots of people don't want to hear that. Too bad. David also said, "Thy kingdom is an everlasting kingdom, and Thy dominion endures throughout all generations" (Psalm 145:13).

The claim of absolute sovereignty is the claim of deity, and God alone has the right to such a claim. All other such claims are idolatrous.

## Living by the Rules

There are certain rules you will have to follow if you come into my house. If you smoke, you will have to put it out before you come in, because the rule is no smoking in my house. If you swear, you'll have to use some mouthwash before you come into my house, because in my house we don't allow profanity.

If someone were to come into my house and say, "Evans, I hate this furniture. The colors on the walls are all wrong. I think they're horrible," well, so what? That person's opinion is irrelevant, because last time I checked he or she didn't pay for the furniture or the paint on the walls.

It's OK for someone to have an opinion about my house, but that opinion doesn't carry much weight with me for one simple reason: It's my house, not his.

So when you come to my house, you have two choices. You can either stay and adjust to my furniture and my color scheme, or you can leave. And I'm sure I would have the same two choices if I came to your house.

God says, "This world is My house, operating by My rules." That means unless you and I want to go out and create our own universe, we must adjust to the rules of God's house or suffer the consequences of our rebellion. To acknowledge God's sovereignty is to acknowledge His jurisdiction over every sphere of life, and to acknowledge His jurisdiction is to acknowledge the validity of His legislation in and over every area of life.

But like stubborn teenagers, we say to God, "Not only am I going to stay in Your house, God, I'm going to bring in my own rules. I'm going to complain about the furniture in Your house, but I'm still going to come to church and tell You to feed me, clothe me, and bless me. I want Your goodness in Your house, but excuse me if I give You a hard time."

## A Discount God

It took a recent trip to a discount department store to help me see all of this in a new light.

My wife, Lois, asked me to pick up a few things for her. You need to know that shopping and standing in checkout lines are not among my favorite things to do. And as things worked out, this particular day was not a good day for me to go shopping. The weather was nice, so everyone in Dallas apparently decided to go to this store. There were people everywhere. The checkout lines were all the way down the aisles.

So I got my stuff and went to the express checkout line, but it was even longer than the other lines. I was stuck, but as I stood there something dawned on me. The store I was in is famous for its discount prices. People come there and stand in long lines because they can purchase items for less than the full price.

It occurred to me, that's what a lot of people do on Sunday. They come to church looking for a "discount God." They want God on sale. They come saying, "God, I want You and Your kingdom, but I want it at a discount. Give me a sale price on Your kingdom; I want it at a discount. I want a little of this and a little of that but not the whole package. So give me 30 percent off the ticketed price."

People don't want a God who is sovereign, a God who says, "This is the package. When you get Me, you get My kingdom. And when you get My kingdom, you get My rules." There are no discounts in God's kingdom. He is sovereign. He rules over all. Psalm 24 teaches that so clearly:

> The earth is the Lord's, and all it contains,
> The world, and those who dwell in it.
> For He has founded it upon the seas,
> And established it upon the rivers.
> Who may ascend into the hill of the Lord?
> And who may stand in His holy place?

*He who has clean hands and a pure heart,*
*Who has not lifted up his soul to falsehood,*
*And has not sworn deceitfully.*
*He shall receive a blessing from the Lord. (vv. 1–5a)*

Verses 1–2 make it clear that everything on planet Earth belongs to God. Now, if everything belongs to God, how much belongs to us? Nothing. We may use the things of earth, but we don't own them.

That's good, because God's sovereignty means He is responsible if something breaks down. If you try to own your life, when something goes wrong you get to fix it. But if God owns your life, when something goes wrong He fixes it. I'd rather be under God's ownership any day!

Living in God's kingdom brings blessings, but you don't get the blessings of the King if you're not willing to live for His kingdom. You don't get to enjoy the blessings of the King if the King cannot have you. You don't get the King who owns everything if you keep demanding a spiritual discount.

Until we become kingdom people with a kingdom agenda, we will miss much of the blessing God has for us. To show up at church on Sunday when God doesn't own our Monday through Saturday is a waste of time.

It is a false dualism to say, "Lord, You can have Sunday, but don't bother me on Monday, because I have to go back to the real world." No, no. On Sunday you're in the presence of the God who made everything. He says, "Take Me with you. Don't leave Me in the pew."

## Sovereignty and Our Choices

God's sovereignty also means that He either causes all that happens, or He permits all that happens. But whether He causes it or permits it, when everything is finished it will come out the way He wants it to come out.

This helps to answer the question, Why is so much out of whack and out of control in our world? God's sovereignty doesn't mean there won't be any problems. It doesn't mean Satan won't rebel, or that people won't say no to His will. Sovereignty says this is God's house, and when it's all said and done, it's going to come out His way.

For us, the question is not whether God is sovereign. This issue is how we relate to His sovereignty. He can execute His kingdom agenda with or without us. I want to go with Him joyfully as He unfolds His plan rather than stand in His way and have Him have to go through me or over me.

But either way, God is going to get where He's going. God's kingdom agenda cannot be thwarted. Now that's good news for those of us who are committed to Him and His kingdom, because there's a promise involved here for us. That promise is found in a very familiar verse, Romans 8:28: "We know that God causes all things to work together for good to those who love God, to those who are called according to His purpose."

Paul is talking about committed Christians, those who are living for God's kingdom. If you are living on a kingdom agenda, your life may seem like a wreck, but Paul said that believers know something important.

The Greek word here for "know" is *oida*, which means intuitive knowledge. It means we know even when it doesn't look like we know. We know when it doesn't feel like we know. We know when everything says we don't know.

What do we know? We know that God causes all things to work together for our good. You say things are falling apart. People are putting you down. You got laid off from your job. The doctors say they don't know if you're going to make it.

God can cause all of these things to work together because He is sovereign. We can know intuitively, despite circumstances, that God is in control, working things together that look out of control. He orchestrates everything so that His divine purpose is worked out.

Sometimes I walk into the kitchen to see what Lois is cooking. She may be putting together a meal that does not look to me like it's going anywhere. It's a little of this and a little of that and a little of the other. I'll say, "What are you making?"

Lois will answer, "Wait and see."

And if I have the patience to wait while she puts the master's touch to that meal, when it comes to the table all I can say is, "Mm, mm good!"

That's how God works. He can take a little of this and a little of that and a little of the other stuff that doesn't look tasty, mix it up by His sovereignty, stir in a little omnipresence, add a little omnipotence, stir in a little grace, throw in a little goodness, mix in a little mercy, and stir it all together. When it comes out of the oven, all you can say is, "This is good."

But the only ones who can say that are those who love God and are committed to His purpose. You've got to be on His plan, not on your plan. You've got to be following His agenda, not your agenda. It's not, "Lord, this is what I want," but, "Lord, what do You want?" That's a kingdom agenda.

## GOD'S KINGDOM AGENDA OPERATES FOR HIS GLORY

A third fact I want you to understand about a kingdom agenda is that it operates for God's glory.

Romans 11:36 says, "For from Him and through Him and to Him are all things. To Him be the glory forever. Amen." Of course, *amen* means "so be it." There it is. That's it. God's glory is the bottom line in His kingdom.

### For His Pleasure

Paul said everything is *from* God. He is the First Cause, the source. Then Paul said *through* Him everything is. God is also the effective cause of everything in creation. And everything is to Him. He is the final cause. It all returns to Him to bring Him glory forever.

It is crucial that we understand that God created the universe for His pleasure and His glory (see Revelation 4:11). That includes us (see Isaiah 43:7). God did not make the world first and foremost for us but for Himself. Everything is created to bring God glory.

*Glory* is a sweet word. It comes from a Greek word that means "to be heavy" or "to have weight." When we say, "This dude is heavy," we're giving significance to him. We're adding weight to his person. That's what glory is.

To understand this concept, you must understand the difference between intrinsic glory and ascribed glory. Most of us are only familiar with ascribed glory. This is the glory we assign to people because of who they are, what they do, or how much they make.

For example, when we put a black robe on a man or woman, we call that person "Your Honor" because we ascribe glory to the role of judge. When someone pulls up in a limousine, we stop to see who it is, because we assume anyone riding in a limousine has to be significant.

That's ascribed or assigned glory, meaning that if you take away the black robe or the limo, the people involved lose their glory. Human beings can only have ascribed glory.

Not so with God. People can ascribe glory to God, but even if we refuse to glorify Him He hasn't lost anything, because God has intrinsic glory.

The sun does not have to try to be hot. Even on a cloudy day, the sun is hot. The sun doesn't have to try to be bright. Even when it's dark outside, the other half of the world is seeing the brightness of the sun.

What heat and brightness are to the sun, glory is to God. It's part of who He is. You can go into your house and pull all your blinds, but you haven't diminished the sun one bit. No matter what you and I do, we can't mess with the glory of God. Everything in His kingdom is designed to bring Him glory. And this is how it should be since there is nothing and no one greater than God for Him to give glory to. Thus, if God is to give glory to someone, He is limited to Himself since there is none greater than He to receive glory.

## Holding It Together

Now let me show you a tremendous implication of this for those of us who will adopt a kingdom agenda. In Colossians 1:15–17, Paul wrote:

> And [Jesus] is the image of the invisible God, the first-born of all creation.
> For by Him all things were created, both in the heavens and on earth,
> visible and invisible, whether thrones or dominions or rulers or authorities—
> all things have been created by Him and for Him. And He is before all
> things, and in Him all things hold together.

This is deep. Let me tell you, if you adopt God's kingdom agenda, Christ will bring together the things in your life that are falling apart. He will either fix the situation, fix you in the situation, or fix you in spite of the situation.

Jesus Christ can do that because He is the One who holds all things together. But you must decide to live for His glory. You must say, "Lord, my goal today is to make You significant. I want to ascribe to You the glory that already belongs to You. I want to radiate, reflect, demonstrate, magnify, and illustrate Your glory." That's a kingdom agenda.

Most of our insurance policies call a natural disaster an "act of God." If a storm blows your roof off, that's an act of God. But we don't give Him glory when He keeps the roof on. It's an act of God if it rains and floods the crops, but we ought to give Him glory that we eat every day. Lots of people run to church when something goes wrong. But people on a kingdom agenda come into God's presence to give Him glory no matter what.

## GOD'S KINGDOM AGENDA OPERATES ACCORDING TO HIS WILL

We've come to the fourth and final truth I want us to consider concerning God's kingdom agenda. It is this: A kingdom agenda operates in accordance with God's will.

"Thy kingdom come," the Lord's Prayer says. "Thy will be done." You cannot have the kingdom if you're not willing to submit to the King's will.

### God-in-the-Box

One of the first toys I remember playing with was that little jack-in-the-box clown that pops up to the tune "Pop Goes the Weasel." That's how many people try to treat God—a clown in a box who pops up whenever we want Him to appear and do our bidding.

"Bless me now, Lord. I'm turning the handle. Come on, pop up." Then we stuff Him back down in the box and close the top when we don't see Him anymore. God-in-the-box. Don't pop up yet because I haven't played Your tune.

But a kingdom person says, "Not my will, but Thy will be done." Jesus said in Matthew 13:11 that the kingdom is a mystery to those who aren't willing to hear and see and understand what God is doing. Jesus would not reveal His Father's will to people who were not willing to obey it.

### God's Kingdom Will

Let me show you why God has you and me in His kingdom. In Daniel 7:13–14, the prophet wrote:

> *I kept looking in the night visions, and behold, with the clouds*
> *of heaven one like a Son of Man was coming, and He came*
> *up to the Ancient of Days and was presented before Him.*
> *And to Him was given dominion, glory and a kingdom, that all the*

*peoples, nations, and men of every language might serve Him. His*
*dominion is an everlasting dominion which will not pass away; and*
*His kingdom is one which will not be destroyed.*

You were brought into God's kingdom to serve Him, to do His will, and to confiscate from Satan that which belongs to God.

The prophet Isaiah also learned that the kingdom of God operates according to His will. In probably the most famous passage in the book of Isaiah, the prophet said, "In the year of King Uzziah's death, I saw the Lord sitting on a throne, lofty and exalted" (6:1).

Isaiah had just experienced a tragedy. The king who had brought Israel a long way back toward God had just died. So what's the point? After all, Isaiah knew the Lord before King Uzziah died.

The point is that Isaiah didn't really see the Lord until Uzziah died. He needed to learn that although a king was dead, the King was fine.

Sometimes it takes a tragedy or other negative circumstances for us to see God. Now we may know Him in terms of being our Savior. But a lot of us won't really say, "God, I want to see You; I want to experience You," until our "King Uzziah" dies. That's often why God allows tragedy to come into our lives.

He's not just interested in getting us to heaven. He wants us to see Him here on earth. Sometimes God is most clearly seen in the midst of bad situations. When we're in a crisis, it's not enough to say, "Lord, why am I in this mess?" We need to be praying, "Lord, help me to see You the way those three Hebrew boys saw You in the midst of the fiery furnace" (see Daniel 3).

What did Isaiah see? He saw a God who is holy to the third power. "Holy, Holy, Holy, is the Lord of hosts, the whole earth is full of His glory" (Isaiah 6:3). The prophet saw a God who rules over all the affairs of life.

What did Isaiah do when he saw God? He cried out, "Woe is me, for I am ruined!" (v. 5). The word *ruined* means "coming unstitched." Isaiah felt like he was falling apart, unraveling before a holy God. "I am a man of unclean lips," Isaiah continued.

But Isaiah experienced grace. He saw one of the seraphim come to him with a hot coal from the altar, and he touched Isaiah's lips with this announcement, "Your sin is forgiven" (vv. 6–7). The lips are the most sensitive part of the human face. The angel touched Isaiah's lips with a hot coal, which meant there was pain. Isaiah needed to get his life cleansed, but when he did, he discovered God's will for him.

That's the point. "Then I heard the voice of the Lord, saying, 'Whom shall I send, and who will go for Us?' Then I said, 'Here am I. Send me!'" (v. 8). There it is. Isaiah got to know the will of God, and he got the power to do the will of God when he saw God. The prophet got plugged into God's kingdom agenda when he responded to God's will.

## BECOMING A KINGDOM PERSON

Do you want to be a kingdom person? Do you want to discover God's alternative, His agenda, for your life? He's waiting to reveal it to you. But you must make the decision. If you want to know which way to go, just ask. If you don't know the way, come to the One who knows the way. Seek God by restructuring your thoughts, words, and deeds to conform to the standards of His righteousness.

I can't tell you what following God's kingdom agenda will mean for you. I just know that whatever it is, you must be willing to do His will. You must be able to pray, "Thine is the kingdom, and the power, and the glory, forever. Amen" (Matthew 6:13). It is God's program, God's agenda, that we want.

If that means being single, we're ready to do that for His sake. If that means staying in this marriage even though right now we're not happy in it, we're ready to do that. If that means staying on this job we don't like, we're ready. If that means we don't reach all our goals, that's OK as long as we can say, as Paul did, "I have finished the course" (2 Timothy 4:7).

We used to have two dogs at our house. They belonged to my son, but when he wasn't home, I had to take care of them. These dogs had a good life, as dog lives go. Those bad boys came out and found food just sitting on their plates. They got fresh water every day. They had a warm spot to sleep. My son sent me to a special store to buy special food for those dogs.

One day I was trying to get one of the dogs to move while I fed it, and the dog growled at me. I looked at the brother and thought, *You're a fool. I'm here feeding and watering you at no cost to you. I don't want to do it, don't need to do it, don't feel like doing it. And you're growling at me?*

That dog didn't understand that he ate by grace. He drank by grace. He had a place to sleep by grace. The only thing that dog should have said to me when I came out was, "Thank you, bowwow," because everything he had was by grace.

When you decide to live by a kingdom agenda, you no longer say,

"This is my food, and You'd better give it to me, God. You'd better supply my drink. This is my house, and You'd better keep it covered and paid for. And You'd better keep clothes on my back." You don't say that. The only thing you say when you get up in the morning is, "Thank You, God, bowwow."

Our desire should be to give God the glory and live for His will, because we're on His agenda. In the chapters that follow, I want to challenge you to follow a kingdom agenda, to live life for the King and His kingdom. He's the source. He's in charge. He's sovereign. When we do His will, we become His alternatives in a world that needs to see a better way to live.

And when we live for God, we can look back on each day and say, "Lord, I did Your will as best I knew it." Then and only then will we begin to live. Are you ready to discover God's alternative? Let's get after it! (See this author's comprehensive teaching on the doctrine of God in *Our God Is Awesome*, Moody Publishers.)

# The Necessity of a Kingdom Agenda

In part 1 we are looking at God's kingdom agenda from a biblical perspective before we begin applying it to the various areas of our lives. We need to get the foundation laid before we begin raising the walls.

The title of this chapter may seem puzzling. But it will soon become clear why I use the word *necessity* in this case. In a word, a kingdom agenda is a necessity because another kingdom has been set up that rivals God's kingdom. A rebellion has been perpetrated against God's rule. Let's talk about that, and then I want to consider mankind's role in this drama.

The Bible clearly teaches a rebellion took place in heaven. The "star of the morning" (Isaiah 14:12), the beautiful and powerful angel once known as Lucifer, raised his head and his hand in an attempt to take God's throne from Him (see vv. 13–14).

Lucifer was defeated and kicked out of heaven. Now he is Satan, "the prince of the power of the air" (Ephesians 2:2). For a short time, God has permitted Satan to become the ruler of a rival kingdom, the world of unsaved humanity and the demons of hell.

So Satan has his own kingdom, and we can see and feel its effect everywhere. I want to make four observations about Satan's kingdom so that we can see the necessity of making God's kingdom agenda our priority.

## SATAN'S KINGDOM IS MARKED BY REBELLION

Whenever you see rebellion to legitimate authority, you are seeing Satan at work. The thing that characterizes him and his kingdom is rebellion against divine authority.

Satan's exalted place among the angels in heaven and his rebellion against God are clearly spelled out in Scripture. He was the "anointed cherub who covers" (Ezekiel 28:14), occupying a special place around the throne of God. This probably had to do with overseeing the worship and service of God by the millions of angels God created. Lucifer was God's "chief lieutenant."

But one day, Satan looked into the mirror and said, "Mirror, mirror on the wall, who's the fairest of them all?" He got what we would call the "big head," a "theo ego," or a "God complex." He became dissatisfied with his position. He looked at God's throne and thought, *Maybe there's room for two.* Isaiah explains Lucifer's thinking: "How you have fallen from heaven, O star of the morning, son of the dawn! You have been cut down to the earth, you who have weakened the nations! But you said in your heart, 'I will . . .'" (14:12–13a).

Now we come to the five times Satan explained his haughtiness by boasting, "I will." Maybe that's why the Bible says pride is first on God's "hate list" (see Proverbs 6:16–17). God hates pride because it is the fundamental attitude of the kingdom that rivals His. Let's look at these five *I wills.*

### *"I Will Ascend to Heaven."*

In Isaiah 14:13, Satan said, "I will ascend to heaven." Now Satan was not talking about being a tourist. He already had access to God's throne. We know that because in Isaiah 6 we see the angels worshiping God in the heavenly temple in His presence. In fact, Satan had access to God after his fall (see Job 1:6; 2:1).

So Satan could go into heaven anytime he wanted. Getting there was not what he had on his mind in Isaiah 14. He was talking about an invasion, a direct attack designed to unseat God from His throne.

Now you can see why every time you try to run your own life, be your own boss, and act like you are your own god, you are saying, "Satan, I agree with you. Get God out of here!"

Whenever God looks on human independence—which is living as if He doesn't exist—it reminds Him of the rebellion in heaven that took place in eternity past. And He hates it. Here's why we need to live on a kingdom agenda.

## "I Will Raise My Throne."

Satan's second boast in Isaiah 14:13 was also a whopper: "I will raise my throne above the stars of God." He wanted to push God off His throne and take His place.

This one is interesting because Satan had his eye on rising above "the stars of God." We've already said Satan's own name was "star of the morning" (v. 12). The stars of God are His angels (see Job 38:7). Satan wanted to usurp God's authority over the angelic creation.

In other words, Satan was saying, "I'm tired of this. Every day I've got to lead all these millions of angels in worshiping God. Every day I've got to make sure they are obeying God. I've got to check the rolls to make sure they are at their stations on time. I'd rather have them worship and honor *me*."

Are you getting the picture so far that Satan did not have small plans for his rebellion? This is not some evil-looking little guy with horns, a pitchfork, and a red jumpsuit, trying to find something to do. He wanted all of God's angels to follow him.

Revelation 12:4 indicates that Satan was partially successful. One-third of the angels joined his coup d'état. One-third said to Satan, "We like your agenda. We are going to follow you." These angels are now called demons.

## "I Will Sit on the Mount of Assembly."

The word *mountain* is used in the Bible as a symbol of authority or rule (see Isaiah 2:2 and Daniel 2:35). So by this boast, Satan was saying he wanted to control the affairs of the universe. He did not want to be handed a program. He wanted to write his own program.

In the Lord's Prayer, we say, "Thy kingdom come. Thy will be done" (Matthew 6:10). Satan is saying, "My plan." The angels made their choice between those options. We have to make that choice again and again as we decide whose agenda we will follow.

## "I Will Ascend."

Satan's fourth boast is found in the first half of Isaiah 14:14: "I will ascend above the heights of the clouds." In the Bible, clouds are used to reflect the glory of God. Often when God revealed Himself, it was in a cloud (see Exodus 13:21; 40:34).

What Satan wanted here was to receive greater glory than God. *Glory* means to put someone on display. Satan wants us to put him on display, to show him off.

Unfortunately, many times we do a bang-up job of that. Whenever we rebel against God, we bring glory to Satan and support his desire to displace God. Satan wanted the glory that belongs to God alone.

## "I Will Make Myself Like the Most High."

Now we come to the bottom line. Satan saved his biggest brag for last. This is crazy thinking.

It is impossible for Satan to be like God because he has none of God's attributes. God is eternal; Satan is a created being. God is omnipresent; Satan can only be in one place at a time. God is omniscient; Satan does not know the future unless it is revealed to him.

Since Satan could never be like God, what could he have had in mind in his fifth "I will"? There's only one thing he could have had that God has. If Satan had been successful in pulling off his coup, he would have had no authority outside of himself to whom he would have to answer.

See, the one thing Satan hated about God was that God never has to answer to anyone. God never has to say, "May I? Can I? Should I?" God never has to make a request, because God is totally autonomous. He has self-contained authority.

Satan had to get permission to act, and he no longer wanted to have to get permission. He wanted to be his own authority. That is precisely why, when people do not obey legitimate authority over them, they act in rebellion against God.

Before we go on, let me drop something on you that we'll deal with later in the book. One reason so many Christians miss out on the blessings of God in their lives is that they are rebelling against God's ordained authority.

The Bible uses the word *obey* a lot. God is into obedience for His children. So whether it's in the home, the church, or the community, we are called to obey those whom God has set over us. We will explore these issues later on.

So here was Satan, overcome by pride, initiating a rebellion to try to unseat God from His throne.

## SATAN'S KINGDOM IS SPIRITUAL

This is a second characteristic of Satan's kingdom: It is spiritual, just as God's kingdom is spiritual. So it shouldn't surprise us that these two kingdoms clash in the spiritual realm.

You don't have to be a Christian for long to learn that the Christian life is a battleground, not a playground. The reason this is true is that we are in conflict with a spiritual foe. Paul gives us the classic description of the battle:

> Finally, be strong in the Lord, and in the strength of His might. Put on the full armor of God, that you may be able to stand firm against the schemes of the devil. For our struggle is not against flesh and blood, but against the rulers, against the powers, against the world forces of this darkness, against the spiritual forces of wickedness in the heavenly places.
> (Ephesians 6:10–12)

### The Real Enemy

Our real problem is not "flesh-and-blood" people. They are only the vehicles Satan works through to carry out his agenda. So unless you are living on God's kingdom agenda, getting mad at other people won't solve your problem. All Satan has to do is find the right person, and you will get all messed up again.

That's why just getting a new wife or a new husband won't necessarily solve your problem. If Satan gets hold of your new spouse, you are going to react the same old way and move on to someone new. We have to understand that the real battle is spiritual, because that's the realm in which Satan operates. Now don't get me wrong. I am not saying that the physical isn't real or that a person or circumstance controlled by Satan shouldn't be dealt with. It's just that addressing these things will only work if you are also addressing the cause behind the problem.

We can't be strong in our own power to fight Satan. The Bible never tells us just to be strong. Paul said, "Be strong in the Lord." We need that because Satan has all manner of evil spiritual forces lined up against us. This is why it is absolutely crucial that we live life in the Spirit by prioritizing the spiritual aspects of life if we are going to experience victory in all aspects of our lives (see Ephesians 5:18; Galatians 5:16).

### Heavenly Places

These forces are in "heavenly places" (Ephesians 6:12). This expression is used several times in the book of Ephesians (see 1:3; 2:6; 3:10). The phrase "heavenly places" does not refer to heaven. It describes a sphere of authority where God and Satan do battle for our allegiance and obedience and where spiritual decisions are made.

There is a lot happening in this realm. So if you don't know how to function in heavenly places, you are going to be messed up in your earthly places. See, many of us believers are trying to "live heavenly" without living in the heavenly places.

The best way to illustrate this is to think about Capitol Hill in Washington, D.C., where the laws that govern our country are written.

There are two warring factions on the Hill: Democrats and Republicans. The two parties have different philosophies and different agendas, and each side wants to win each issue. So the laws that are passed to govern us are often based on which party wins the day on Capitol Hill.

Something similar happens in heavenly places. God and Satan are at war to see who will establish the rules that govern earth. The nature of Satan's kingdom makes it imperative that we learn to think spiritually. Why? Because if you are not thinking spiritually, you won't be in tune with what is happening in the heavenly realms. You won't recognize Satan's agenda when you see it, so you won't be able to say no to it.

Living in the heavenly places means identifying with a spiritual worldview and participating in a divine frame of reference. We need to learn to put the spiritual ahead of the physical, because our real battle is against a kingdom that seeks to influence and dominate us spiritually.

Satan knows that if he can get us hooked into his way of thinking spiritually, the physical will follow.

## THE CHARACTER OF SATAN'S KINGDOM IS DECEPTION

Anyone who hangs around church knows what doctrine is. It's a system of teaching designed to instruct you. Bible doctrine is the teaching of what the Word of God says. When we learn Bible doctrine, we are engaging in the study of God's system of truth.

Did you know that Satan has a system of doctrine too? Paul said in 1 Timothy 4:1, "The Spirit explicitly says that in later times some will fall away from the faith, paying attention to deceitful spirits and doctrines of demons."

Knowing what we know of Satan, it isn't surprising that his system of doctrine is designed to mislead us. After all, his kingdom is built on lies and deceit. We are seeing a lot of his "doctrine" in our world today. Many people don't recognize it because demonic doctrines don't always come across as demonic.

For example, people will say, "Out of concern for our children, we must hand out condoms." What they really mean is, "Let's help our kids become more immoral." But they are not going to say that. That's how Satan is. He doesn't want the truth to come out. He wants to deceive and trick.

Satan works hard to come up with doctrines that deceive. And he has some pretty good helpers here on earth, people known as false teachers who seek to deceive others by teaching Satan's lies as God's truth. Paul said in 1 Timothy 4:2 that they are "seared in their own conscience as with a branding iron."

That means they have no feeling about what they are doing. There are plenty of people in our society who can commit all kinds of sin without showing any feeling. But Paul is not talking about wicked people in general. He's talking about people who are mishandling the Word of God while passing themselves off as Christian preachers and teachers.

There are all kinds of people out there operating in the name of God and His Word, telling folks how to make a lot of money in God's name and other things that the Bible does not teach.

The problem is people believe these heresies. People are following doctrines of demons, thinking they are acting in the name of God. You have to know the Word of God to know the difference. Satan's kingdom is built on deception because he is the "granddaddy" of all liars (see John 8:44).

## THE EFFECT OF SATAN'S
## KINGDOM IS DEATH

Satan's kingdom is a kingdom of spiritual death. The subjects of Satan's kingdom are walking dead people. Paul describes these people this way:

> *And you were dead in your trespasses and sins, in which you formerly walked according to the course of this world, according to the prince of the power of the air, of the spirit that is now working in the sons of disobedience. Among them we too all formerly lived in the lusts of our flesh, indulging the desires of the flesh and of the mind, and were by nature children of wrath, even as the rest. (Ephesians 2:1–3)*

Paul said that people who are outside of God are spiritually dead. That is, they are unable to respond to spiritual stimuli. Corpses don't listen to conversations in funeral homes. They have no appetite for food, and they feel no pain. They cannot function at all.

In the same way, people without God cannot function spiritually. The only difference between "good" sinners and "bad" sinners is the state of their decay and decomposition. The bum on skid row and the non-Christian uptown are equally dead. One is dressed better, but both are dead without the life of God.

Satan's kingdom not only produces the environment of spiritually dead people. It produces disobedient people (see Ephesians 2:2). When men and women begin operating on Satan's kingdom agenda, they set out on a course that brings them in direct conflict with the kingdom of God. That's what Satan delights in, of course, because he is not only the granddaddy of all liars, he is the original "son of disobedience."

The tragedy of people who are serving Satan's agenda is that they are under the judgment of God. They are living on borrowed time, and hell is their destiny. This is all the reason we need to reach out and snatch people from Satan's grasp. They are destined for eternal death without Christ.

Have you ever come out to your kitchen at night and seen a roach? Tell the truth and shame the devil! What is your first inclination when you see a roach? To step on it. You don't stop to examine a roach to see whether he might be a good-looking insect who deserves to live. A roach is an unclean creature that deserves to die, period!

Well, when God sees people functioning in the kingdom of Satan, they look like roaches to Him. Some are nice roaches. Some are roaches with perms. Some are Neiman-Marcus roaches. Some are K-Mart roaches.

But it doesn't matter how nice they look. All people living outside of God's kingdom are marked for death. We as believers can praise God that even though we were once destined for death as members of Satan's kingdom, God saved us by His mercy (see Ephesians 2:4–5). Everything Satan touches turns rotten. Death is the inevitable product of his kingdom.

So that's Satan's kingdom. Since everything about the devil is unalterably opposed to God, you can see why it is necessary that God establish the agenda of His kingdom for His people.

## MANKIND AS MANAGER OF GOD'S KINGDOM

Now let's follow up our study of Satan's rebellion by considering where *we*, as God's people, come into the kingdom picture. God has appointed us as managers or stewards of His kingdom in this age. And someday we will rule with Him in the ultimate expression of His kingdom, the millennial reign of Jesus Christ on earth.

### Created for God's Glory

How did this come about? I want to demonstrate that mankind was created and appointed a place of service in God's kingdom to demonstrate His glory, His power, and His ultimate triumph to all of creation.

Like all created beings, Satan was created to bring God glory. But Satan rebelled and abdicated his role, and God judged him. For His own reasons, God has given Satan enough "leash" to go about building a rival kingdom. And even though Satan is already thoroughly defeated and his kingdom is destined for destruction, he is working furiously to thwart God's plan.

Now, God will always have His glory. And since Lucifer, His highest created being and "manager" of the heavenly kingdom, failed to glorify Him, God has entrusted the management of His kingdom to another part of His creation, mankind.

This is, in fact, the very reason God created mankind. Our creation was God's response to the angelic rebellion. God purposed to demonstrate to the angelic realm what He can do with a creature lower than the angels (see Psalm 8:3–8) who yielded to Him, over against the higher creature that rebelled against Him (see Ephesians 3:10). This amazing plan preserved God's glory.

## Created to Rule

What I'm saying is that when Satan rebelled, God did something amazing. He created the human race to rule over His created order. We see this in Psalm 8:

> When I consider Thy heavens, the work of Thy fingers, the moon and the stars, which Thou hast ordained; what is man, that Thou dost take thought of him? And the son of man, that Thou dost care for him? Yet Thou hast made him a little lower than God, and dost crown him with glory and majesty! Thou dost make him to rule over the works of Thy hands; Thou hast put all things under his feet. (vv. 3–6)

This is why, when God created Adam and Eve, He said, "Let them rule over the fish of the sea and over the birds of the sky and over the cattle and over all the earth" (Genesis 1:26). Then God told our first parents to "subdue" the earth (v. 28).

That's the same concept we just read about in Psalm 8. God created someone "a little lower" than Himself, and even lower than the angels (see Hebrew 2:7), who would have management responsibility in light of the angels' failure.

When the book of Genesis opens, we see chaos that was set in motion by Satan's rebellion (1:2). We know that Satan thought so much of himself he wanted to be like God. But God created someone who ranks beneath the angelic realm in order to demonstrate to the angels and to Satan and his demons God's incredible power and glory.

In other words, it was impossible that God would not have a kingdom that would rule over and defeat the kingdom of Satan. And as I said above, when Jesus Christ sets up His millennial kingdom, it will be the final, triumphant declaration of God's glory. Satan will then be chained up during that time to demonstrate his utter defeat and judgment (see Revelation 20:1–3).

God created you and me to harness a part of His creation. Every person was created with that divine intent. The tragedy is that mankind went after Satan, stopped trying to be a manager, and started trying to be an owner, thus parroting Satan's sin.

## ABDICATING OUR
## MANAGEMENT RESPONSIBILITY

Genesis 3 outlines the fall of mankind for us. While God created us to manage His creation and demonstrate His glory to the angelic realm, Satan sought to dismantle that commitment to God and transfer it to himself.

The question is often asked, "When Satan sinned, why didn't God just destroy him and keep on trucking?" If God had just destroyed Satan, He would never have demonstrated to Satan His power, His wisdom, His glory, and all of His other divine attributes working together to accomplish His intended plan (see Ephesians 3:10).

So God created man and woman and gave them the right of rulership, as we saw above (see Genesis 1:26–28). But Satan interfered with that plan:

> *Now the serpent was more crafty than any beast of the field which the Lord God had made. And he said to the woman, "Indeed, has God said, 'You shall not eat from any tree of the garden'?" And the woman said to the serpent, "From the fruit of the trees of the garden we may eat; but from the fruit of the tree which is in the middle of the garden, God has said, 'You shall not eat from it or touch it, lest you die.'" And the serpent said to the woman, "You surely shall not die!" (Genesis 3:1–4)*

### Challenging the Owner

God had left clear instructions to His managers about how He wanted them to manage His creation. But Satan called into question the Owner's right to set the rules and regulations of His creation. Satan has been doing it ever since, and managers of God's kingdom have been falling by the wayside ever since.

Whenever we allow the Evil One to dictate how we are to function under the rule of God, we jeopardize our management position. That is precisely why many Christians never fully realize their calling or their purpose for living.

You were not designed to live a purposeless life. God has given you a responsible position to fill as manager in His kingdom. But if you don't realize that role, you will never know your purpose for being born.

In the garden of Eden, Satan challenged God's authority as the

Ruler of His kingdom. His strategy is revealed in Genesis 3:5, where the serpent told Eve, "God knows that in the day you eat from it your eyes will be opened, and you will be like God, knowing good and evil."

Eve went for the lie, and Adam fell in with the rebellion too (see vv. 6–7).

## Living Beyond Our Privileges

Satan tried to make Eve think that God was being jealous of His deity. But Satan knew no one could be like God. How did he know? Because he tried it himself and got booted out of heaven!

God created us for His glory. So whenever we try to take glory unto ourselves and live independently of God, we are living well beyond our management privileges.

When I was a student at Dallas Seminary, Lois and I used to house-sit for people in an exclusive section of Dallas. These houses were something else, a real contrast to my little 1968 Chevy Nova parked in "our" house's circular, sophisticated driveway.

Our job was to watch over one house, keep things going, and keep it clean. In exchange we got to live like a king and queen. The home's owners would stock the refrigerator and pay us for staying there while they went away on business or vacation.

I used to tell the guys at the seminary, "Look, come to my pad this afternoon." I mean, I played with that thing!

But Lois was always careful to remind me, "Don't touch this. Don't touch that. Don't go there."

I would say, "Why?"

"Because this is not our house."

Lois was saying that we had to be careful about what we did because the owners were only letting us use the house.

You are only here because God is letting you be here. You are only serving God because He allows you to serve. What Satan wants to do is make you think you can do all of this independently of God.

## The Great Sin

That's why the great sin isn't adultery or homosexuality. The great sin of the Bible is to live independently of God, to try to live as if God does not exist. Satan wants you to become like him—not under God's authority but in rebellion against God.

Let me put it another way. Satan wants you to stop thinking like a manager and start thinking like an owner. If you have ever rented somewhere and then owned a home, you know the difference between being a manager and an owner.

When you rent a home or an apartment, your landlord takes responsibility for most of the building's upkeep because you don't own it. But if you own the house, when the roof goes bad, you get to fix it. When the water heater goes out, you must buy a new one. There are responsibilities that come with ownership.

That's also true in life. If you want to be the owner of your life and live as though God has no say over you, He is going to respond, "You want to own your life? OK, when it breaks down, you get to fix it."

I don't know about you, but I would prefer to be a "renter" under God's ownership. That way if something breaks down, I can go to the Owner and say, "Lord, this is Your property, Your body, Your money. I have given everything over to You. I'm just the renter here, so I ask You to take care of things."

When we abdicate our management role in God's kingdom and start acting like the owner, we bring a lot of headaches on ourselves. His agenda does not include our ownership.

## RECOVERING OUR MANAGEMENT RESPONSIBILITY

Psalm 8 shows us God's intention for our role in His kingdom. But we have also seen that mankind abdicated his responsibility by yielding to Satan's temptation and by mimicking Satan's rebellion. As a result of Adam and Eve's sin, they lost out on God's intent for their work in His kingdom (see Genesis 3:8–24). They got booted out of Eden, much like Satan got booted out of heaven.

But even in the midst of His judgment, God let Adam and Eve know it would not always be like this. He gave them the promise of a Redeemer who would reverse the curse of sin (see Genesis 3:15). Jesus will also reverse the effects of Satan's and mankind's rebellion against God's kingdom when He comes to rule in His kingdom.

### Reversing the Curse

God is not going to leave things in their state of being cursed. Satan will never have the last word. As we said above, it is impossible for God's plan to be thwarted. Psalm 8 was the plan for our management of God's kingdom. In Hebrews 2, we find a restatement of that plan, showing that salvation is the means by which we recover our management status under God.

The author of Hebrews asks an important question in verse 3 of this text: "How shall we escape if we neglect so great a salvation?" Now, he is not talking about losing your salvation. He is talking about neglecting the salvation you already have.

One reason we must not neglect our salvation, in terms of being all that God wants us to be, is found in Hebrews 2:5. God has subjected "the world to come" to us. This is the one-thousand-year reign of Christ on His earthly throne in the millennium.

It's in this context that the writer of Hebrews records verses 6–8, a quotation from Psalm 8:4–6. These are key verses referring to our position as managers of God's kingdom. Then Hebrews 2:9 refers to Jesus coming to earth to die for our sins and the glory He received at His resurrection.

## New Managers

What Hebrews 2 is saying is phenomenal. The first Adam was created to manage God's creation, but he blew it by yielding to Satan. But the Bible says that the earth, both in this present age and in the age to come, will be managed by humans, not angels.

So what God did was become a man in the person of Jesus Christ, whom the Bible calls the "last Adam" (1 Corinthians 15:45). As the new Adam, Christ is calling to Himself a new humanity, redeemed people we call Christians, who will manage His kingdom the way it was meant to be managed.

Now it's true that we will only become perfect managers in the future kingdom age. But it is also true that when Jesus saved us, He recovered for us the kingdom management position we forfeited in Adam.

## What It Means

So what does all of this mean for you today? It means that when God saved you, He gave you a new life based on what He wants you to be and where He wants you to go.

You may say, "Wait a minute, Tony. You can't tell me the dead-end job I'm in now, stuck with a boss I can't stand, is God's idea of me being a manager in His kingdom. This doesn't feel like a kingdom agenda to me."

Obviously, I can't comment on every specific job or family situation. Sometimes we get off track by taking charge of our lives, acting like owners instead of managers. But it's also possible that God has you where you are on His way to taking you where He wants you to be. If we are faithful where we are, God is free to take us to the next step.

Wherever we are on the road, the goal is for us to be able to say what Paul said at the end of his life: "I have finished the course" (2 Timothy 4:7).

## Your Future Appointment

In Hebrews 2:8, the writer said, "But now we do not yet see all things subjected to him." We still live in a sinful world, so everything is not going to be managed properly.

But in the kingdom to come, Jesus Christ is going to make sure everything is subjected to Him. And you will be appointed a place based on your faithfulness now. Then a lot of people who are now on top will be sweeping streets in the kingdom, because Jesus said the last shall be first and the first last.

So if God has you sweeping streets now, do it for His glory. When the tables get turned, you may wind up as an executive in His kingdom!

## FINDING OUR FULFILLMENT IN KINGDOM MANAGEMENT

In Ephesians 6:5–9, Paul gives us the key to finding true fulfillment as we carry out our kingdom responsibilities:

*Slaves, be obedient to those who are your masters according to the flesh, with fear and trembling, in the sincerity of your heart, as to Christ; not by way of eyeservice, as men-pleasers, but as slaves of Christ, doing the will of God from the heart. With good will render service, as to the Lord, and not to men, knowing that whatever good thing each one does, this he will receive back from the Lord, whether slave or free. And masters, do the same things to them, and give up threatening, knowing that both their Master and yours is in heaven, and there is no partiality with Him.*

If you are miserable in your work, it could be because you are working for the wrong person. What Paul said here is very important. He's telling us to go to work for the Lord on Monday morning, not just for the boss. The reason so many believers are miserable is that they are working for the wrong person.

Paul said, "Stop working for your boss, and start working for the Lord." A Christian looks at employment from a totally different perspective than the world does.

You say, "Hold it. My boss pays my salary." Not really (see v. 8). The real rewarder of your faithfulness is God Himself. When you say, "Lord, because I love You, I am going to do my work to honor You," God can begin doing something special.

He can say, "When I see you honoring Me, I get into the honoring mode too. I will honor you for your faithfulness." So the issue is, for whom do you work? Whom do you serve?

Ecclesiastes 2:24 says there's nothing better for us than to enjoy our work. There's nothing more miserable than being in a job, even a high-paying job, that you hate because it's absolutely necessary that the heart is full. The Bible says this only happens when you are working for the Lord.

And as I said above, even when you are not where you want to be and you are not where God is ultimately taking you, faithfulness is still important. If you demonstrate faithfulness now, God will be able to take you somewhere.

Right now, I am doing exactly what I want to do, what I studied and prepared to do. But along the way, I learned some valuable lessons about enjoying God where I was. And I'm still learning, just like you are.

## FINDING ULTIMATE
## FULFILLMENT IN THE KINGDOM

In Matthew 19, Jesus taught His disciples a crucial principle that we need to take note of as we close this chapter. You don't lose when you follow Christ and His alternative, even though you may give up things along the way:

> *Then Peter answered and said to Him, "Behold, we have left everything*
> *and followed You; what then will there be for us?" And Jesus said to*
> *them, "Truly I say to you, that you who have followed Me, in the*

*regeneration when the Son of Man will sit on His glorious throne,*
*you also shall sit upon twelve thrones, judging the twelve tribes of*
*Israel. And everyone who has left houses or brothers or sisters or father*
*or mother or children or farms for My name's sake, shall receive many*
*times as much, and shall inherit eternal life. But many who are*
*first will be last; and the last, first. (vv. 27–30)*

Peter asked a good business question in verse 27 after Jesus had watched the rich young man go away sadly because he refused to give up his wealth. Peter was saying, "We have committed ourselves totally to You, Jesus. We have left our security and our relatives to follow You."

Sometimes, following Christ means that you must give up earthly security. You must trade the known for the unknown. That's what missionaries do when they go out and depend on people to support them.

But look at Jesus' promise in verse 29. Now, I'm not suggesting that following Jesus is a good business deal. I'm saying that if you want fullness and fulfillment now, and in the future kingdom when Christ reigns on His throne (see v. 28), you can't do any better than to follow Him now.

Do you know why it is taking Jesus so long to return? Because He has not yet completed populating His kingdom. That means there are still key positions available! There are still some prime openings in the company.

The question is, do you want one of those slots? Then be faithful to Christ's kingdom agenda today, and He will honor you with a choice appointment in His future kingdom. (See this author's work *The Battle Is the Lord's*, Moody Publishers, for a comprehensive study on spiritual warfare and the angelic conflict.)

# The Covenants of a Kingdom Agenda

We are laying a biblical foundation for God's alternative, His kingdom agenda for His people. So far we have seen that the kingdom is God's comprehensive rule over all of His creation. He is Ruler of His kingdom, the universe is His kingdom's realm, and it operates by His rules.

Now I want to take the next step and talk about the way God governs His kingdom. Like it or not, all of us are under God's kingdom rule.

Even non-Christians are under God's rule. They are accountable to His sovereignty. They may not be in the kingdom in terms of their relationship to God, but they are under Him in terms of His position.

When it comes to the way God governs His kingdom, the word you need to grab hold of is *covenant*. God administers His kingdom through His covenants.

## THE DEFINITION OF COVENANT

First of all, let me define a covenant. It is a legally binding relationship God has ordained to administer His kingdom. We could also say that a covenant is the biblical mechanism by which God runs His alternative program.

## A Relationship of Persons

A covenant is far more than a contract. In a biblical covenant, you not only sign on the dotted line but you enter into intimate relationship with the other person or persons in the covenant.

In other words, covenants are predicated on a relationship. That's not necessarily true in a contract. You can sign a contract to buy a home and have no personal relationship at all with the seller. You may not even know or like the seller.

You can sign a business deal because the deal makes sense but have no affiliation or relationship with the other party beyond the deal itself.

Not so in a covenant. That's why, for example, marriage is called a covenant. Marriage is not only a binding agreement, but it binds the people involved in an intimate relationship.

## A Relationship of Blessing

A covenant is also a relationship of blessing. Whenever God makes a covenant, His intent is to bless the parties involved. God makes a covenant for the good of those who covenant with Him. When you enter into a covenant with God, it is so that "you may prosper in all that you do" (Deuteronomy 29:9).

Now when Moses said you would prosper, he was not only talking about your bank account. He was talking about the full intentions of God for your life.

## A Relationship of Blood

God takes His covenants very seriously, because they are the mechanism by which His kingdom functions. So whenever we see a covenant being inaugurated in the Bible, it is inaugurated by blood. Covenants were signed in blood.

Remember those old TV westerns where the Indians and the white men got ready to sign a peace treaty? Often it was sealed in blood. The two parties cut their palms then shook hands and became blood brothers. There was an exchange of blood that sealed the treaty and made it significant. It was no small thing.

So it is with God's covenants. They are so serious, significant, and meaningful that they are inaugurated by blood. Take marriage as an example again. When a husband and wife come together on the first night, if the wife is a virgin she may bleed.

Now that is not just a physiological reality but a theological reality. The wife's blood signifies the inauguration of the covenant. God has so created woman that when the marriage covenant is ratified, there can be the flowing of blood.

God's covenants are serious, and even bloody, because they are meant to make a statement about a serious relationship that has been inaugurated under His rule. You and I are part of God's kingdom, and we are there by covenant.

## THE DISTINCTIVES OF COVENANT

Let's move now from the definition of God's covenant to the distinctives of His covenants. These are the things you need to understand if you're going to live under God's covenants the way He wants you to live. Genesis 1 gives us these distinctives.

### Ordained by God

The first thing you need to understand about God's government of His kingdom through His covenant is that covenants are God-ordained, as we said in the definition above. We can see this in Genesis 1:26–28.

> Then God said, "Let Us make man in Our image, according to Our likeness; and let them rule over the fish of the sea and over the birds of the sky and over the cattle and over all the earth, and over every creeping thing that creeps on the earth." And God created man in His own image, in the image of God He created him; male and female He created them. And God blessed them; and God said to them, "Be fruitful and multiply, and fill the earth, and subdue it; and rule over the fish of the sea and over the birds of the sky, and over every living thing that moves on the earth."

You've probably heard the phrase "Let Us make man in Our image" so often that it loses its impact. But this is a very serious phrase. Creation was God's idea. He ordained it. That is important because the One who ordains something calls the shots. God was saying, "I'm in charge here." We call this attribute of God His sovereignty.

Adam and Eve existed because God said so. They functioned in an environment that God created. God set up the whole system, even the air that Adam and Eve would breathe, the life that would enable them to rule over the rest of creation. Everything was authored by God.

If you are going to come under God's rules, if you are going to serve in God's government, if you are going to be blessed as part of God's kingdom, then don't ever forget who is in charge here. Sometimes at work, the boss has to remind people who is in charge. You work at the boss's company under the boss's authority, because his or her name is on the door.

Any father of teenaged children knows there are times when you have to say, "I am the head of this home." What we do in our homes, God does in His creation.

Just ask King Nebuchadnezzar of Babylon. Nebby looked out over his balcony one day and said, "Look at this great Babylon I have built. I'm in charge here."

You may know the story in Daniel 4:28–37. God turned Nebuchadnezzar into a madman. His nails began to grow and his hair sprouted wildly, and for seven years he lived like a beast in the field. But then he came back to his senses and stood on his balcony one more time. Only this time Nebuchadnezzar said, "Let everybody in Babylon know God is in charge here."

So the question you must raise about being under God's covenant and in God's kingdom is this: Is He in charge? Or are you trying to live independently of His "in-charge-ness"? If you are, then you are in rebellion against His government through His covenant, and you are therefore an enemy of the King.

See, you are either a friend or an enemy of the King based on whether you pray "Thy will be done" or "My will be done." God says, "I am in charge here."

## Hierarchical

A second distinctive of God's covenants is that they are hierarchical. To put it another way, they are administered by His representatives. They operate by a chain of command. God mediates His covenants through people.

We just read in Genesis 1:26 that God said Adam and Eve were to rule over His creation. But that doesn't mean God abdicated His throne and turned everything over to mankind. Our authority to rule is *under* God, not apart from Him. God didn't say to Adam and Eve, "I made this for you. Rule it any way you want."

One day, my granddaughter Kariss was playing with a doll I had given her. Evidently the doll had been bad, because Kariss had the doll by the leg and was slamming its head on the floor. I said, "Kariss, stop that. Don't do that anymore."

Her answer was, "Popee, it's my doll." In other words, Kariss was claiming autonomy. She was saying, "I have the right to destroy this doll you gave me."

Not true. So I had to make my granddaughter understand something very crucial. Although I gave the doll to her, I did so with the understanding that it would be used for my intended purpose—which was for her to play with, not abuse.

How often we take the "doll" of God's goodness and kindness and slam it around with the attitude, "This is my car, my house, my job, my ability, my money. Don't tell me what to do, God." But that attitude abuses the representative nature of our authority.

Adam was to rule but not independently of the King. He was not to become autonomous. We live in a world today where men and women want autonomy. They want the right to rule apart from the One who is in charge.

In 1 Corinthians 11:3, Paul lays out this principle of God's hierarchical relationships in a much broader context: "I want you to understand that Christ is the head of every man, and the man is the head of a woman, and God is the head of Christ."

No person who names the name of Jesus Christ can claim autonomy. No man may say, "Because I am a man, I can do whatever I want." No, Christ is your head, your covering. You are answerable to Him.

Paul then said that the man is the head of "a woman." Please notice the difference here. Christ is the head of "every man," but a man is not the head of "every" woman. A man's job is not to put all women in their place.

This passage goes on to talk about the covering that God has given a woman if she is married, which is her husband. This is very important and we will deal with it in detail in a later chapter when we talk about this woman's role in the church.

My point here is that all of us are under authority. There is even a hierarchy in function within the equality of the Trinity, because Paul said, "God is the head of Christ." That's why, when Jesus was on earth, He was obedient to the Father and said He would only do the Father's will. God works through a chain of command even within Himself in order to accomplish His plan and program in history.

Why is this so crucial? Because if you rebelliously break God's chain, you automatically lose His blessing. God's covenantal blessing flows through His authorized hierarchy. If you break off and do your own thing, become your own person, then you forfeit the blessings that God designed to flow down through His chain to you. You have rebelled against God's order.

Let me show you an example of God's hierarchical blessing. Paul wrote, "The unbelieving husband is sanctified through his wife, and the unbelieving wife is sanctified through her believing husband; for otherwise your children are unclean, but now they are holy" (1 Corinthians 7:14).

So powerful is God's chain of command that even non-Christians who come under it experience its benefits. The unbelieving members of a family are blessed as the believing member comes under God's rule and exercises his or her biblical authority. So even non-Christians get the benefits of the covenant if the Christians who are under it are in right relationship with Him.

Now you can see why Satan wants to mess up the roles God has assigned us. Satan went to Eve in the garden, not because she was morally or intellectually weaker, but to bypass and mess up Adam's headship.

Eve acted independently of Adam, and Adam failed to exercise his leadership. So when Eve acted independently of her head she lost her covering, and Satan won.

This principle of representation is very strong because the Bible says in 1 Corinthians 15:22 that "in Adam all die" (see also Romans 5:12). Adam was our representative head, and when he fell, we all fell.

You may get upset and say, "I don't want Adam to represent me." Well, you may not have voted for the president in the last election, but he can still send your sons and daughters to war because he is your representative. You may not agree with everything your senators do, but they still represent you in Congress.

But praise God, you have another representative whose name is Adam too. He is the "last Adam" (1 Corinthians 15:45), Jesus Christ, who reversed the effects of the first Adam's sin (see Romans 5:21). I have decided to come under Jesus' representation so I can share in His blessing. That's the principle of representation, which is at the heart of the hierarchical aspect of each of God's covenants. That's how God's covenant flows.

## Ethical

God's covenants are also ethically established. This is their third distinctive. By ethical I mean that God's covenants have specific guidelines, or rules, that govern them. Let's go back to Genesis and the garden of Eden.

> *Then the Lord God took the man and put him into the garden of Eden to cultivate it and keep it. And the Lord God commanded the man, saying, "From any tree of the garden you may eat freely; but from the tree of the knowledge of good and evil you shall not eat, for in the day that you eat from it you shall surely die." (2:15–17)*

God gave Adam a guideline to follow. God told him, "These are the rules of My kingdom. If you are going to reign here under Me, these are the rules you must obey. If you disobey My rules, you will suffer the consequences."

God has built a cause-effect relationship into His covenant rules. If you follow His rules, you get His benefits. If you follow your way, you lose His benefits and come under His penalties. When you operate under God's covenant rules, then whatever the covenant is supposed to supply you with, it will supply.

Again, this is why Satan wanted to deceive Adam and Eve. He knew if he could lead them to violate the covenant rules, they would lose the benefits and suffer God's penalty.

So God's covenant has ethical stipulations. God told Joshua, "Be careful to do according to all the law which Moses My servant commanded you; do not turn from it to the right or to the left, so that you may have success wherever you go" (Joshua 1:7).

Joshua listened to what God told him, and he and his leaders did what God told them, and Israel gained the Promised Land. But in the very next book of the Bible, the book of Judges, the people failed to do what God said and suffered round after round of judgments.

What's true nationally is true in our lives. When we rebel against the covenant's regulations, we lose, because there is a cause-effect relationship. It has nothing to do with whether we like God's rules. It's not our kingdom.

People who want to operate by their own rules need to go out and create their own worlds. But as long as we are in God's world, where God has set the rules, we must abide by His rules or we become rebels against His kingdom government. And God always deals with rebels.

Suppose you go to the top of the Empire State Building and announce, "I don't like the rule of gravity. I'm not into gravity—never have been, never will be. Can't stand the thought of 'what goes up must come down.' So today, I am going to rebel against the law of gravity. I am serving notice that this rule isn't going to tell me what to do."

So you stand on the top of the Empire State Building and do your Superman thing. You jump from the precipice and wave your fist in gravity's face.

As they sweep you off the pavement, it will become undeniably clear that whether you buy into gravity is irrelevant. The rule is the rule, and you will pay the price for trying to break it.

## Oaths

Here's a fourth distinctive of God's covenants. They have attached to them an oath, or pledge, that you must make.

Whenever God establishes a covenant, the people who are entering it with Him must promise to obey and keep the covenant's stipulations. This pledge involves promises for obedience and penalties for disobedience. That's why the Bible says again and again that those who keep God's Word are the ones who are blessed (see James 1:25).

There's an example of this aspect of covenant in Genesis 2:23–25, where God performed the first wedding ceremony between Adam and Eve. The parties promised to leave father and mother and become one flesh, which is still the basic oath in marriage today.

The oaths that accompany God's covenants are often called sanctions, those provisions that make a law binding. The clearest example of this process of oath-taking is in Deuteronomy 27–30, when Moses had the people of Israel stand between two mountains.

One was the mountain of blessing, and the other was the mountain of cursing. Moses read the people the blessings for keeping God's law and the curses for breaking it, and the people said amen to signify that they accepted and understood these terms. Then Moses said: "I have set before you life and death, the blessing and the curse. So choose life" (Deuteronomy 30:19).

We take many kinds of oaths today. Every morning in schools across the country, kids stand and say, "I pledge allegiance to the flag . . ." That is an oath of allegiance.

When a believer comes to the water to be baptized, he or she is making a pledge, a statement of commitment to follow Jesus Christ. Baptism is an outward symbol of an inner reality. God's oaths often have symbols tied to them that are designed to reflect the intention of the oath.

The bottom line of a covenant oath is the same throughout Scripture. You are saying to God, "May good come upon me as I follow You, and may evil come upon me if I reject You." There is no such thing in the Bible as the attitude that says, "I am going to do my own thing because I am forgiven" (see Romans 6:1–5).

## Repercussions

Fifth and finally, God's covenants have continuity, or long-term repercussions. What you do affects not only you. It affects those in contact with you and those who follow you. It has to do with inheritance.

Just ask Adam and Eve. Their sin spilled over into the next generation when Cain killed Abel, ultimately leading to worldwide judgment (see Genesis 6). Many people today are undergoing things that they didn't have anything to do with personally. Mom and Dad had everything to do with the problem, and their kids are suffering the repercussions of it.

A baby who is born addicted to alcohol or suffering from drug withdrawal needs medical treatment from the moment he leaves his mother's womb because someone else broke God's law. Like all of God's principles, this principle operates on the personal, family, church, and national level.

I'm convinced that the reason the blood of violence is flowing in our streets is that we are shedding innocent blood in America's abortion mills. You cannot escape the repercussions of breaking God's law and inheriting the built-in consequences.

One reason you and I must fight to stay in God's will—and when we leave it, fight to jump back in as quickly as possible—is that life is not just about you and me. It includes many other people.

In the Ten Commandments, God said He would pass the iniquity on to "the third and the fourth generations of those who hate Me" (Exodus 20:5). And you can be sure that it will be worse for the offspring of the wicked than it is for the parents. The evil and God's judgment multiply more and more the further this thing goes.

So even if you don't care for yourself, care for others because there are long-term consequences attached to the covenant. Reflecting the fifth commandment, Paul wrote, "Children, obey your parents in the Lord, for this is right. Honor your father and mother . . . , that it may be well with you, and that you may live long on the earth" (Ephesians 6:1–3).

This doesn't mean all children who obey their parents will live to be ninety years old. It means they will live out their God-ordained days and experience His blessings as they live. We teach this truth to our children so that the continuity of God's covenant blessings may be extended to each generation.

## THE DESIGNATIONS OF COVENANT

We conclude this chapter by looking at the designations, or categories, of God's covenants.

There are four basic covenants under which God's kingdom alternative operates. We will review each of these four in a basic way here, and each of the remaining four sections of the book will focus on one of them in-depth.

### The Personal Covenant

The first covenant we need to deal with is what I call personal covenant.

When you came to know Jesus Christ, you entered into a personal covenant with Him. You turned the government, the direction of your life, over to Him. One reason you should go to church is to find out what the Governor of your life has to say to you.

Because you have entered into a personal relationship with Christ, when you stand before Him at the judgment seat it won't be a group meeting. "Each one" of us must give an account to the Lord (2 Corinthians 5:10).

Philippians 2:12 is a verse you need to read and memorize. We will deal with it in the next chapter, so let me just cite it here and move on. Paul said, "Work out your salvation with fear and trembling." Why? Because you are personally responsible to God.

The implications of this are staggering. It means we need to stop blaming everybody else for our mess. Someone may say, "But you don't know what my mama did. You don't know how my daddy failed and messed me up."

That's true. I don't know what your mama or daddy did. But the issue is, what are you going to do? We need to take personal responsibility for our lives. People want the government or the church to do it for them. But God is asking, "What about you?"

## The Family Covenant

The second covenant in God's kingdom is the family covenant, God's foundation, the institutional building block for the rest of society. Malachi 2:14 calls marriage a covenant, and that covenant is expanded through the birth and rearing of children. The family was created to uniquely model God's Trinitarian character in history and proliferate His image throughout the world (see Genesis 1:26–28).

Genesis 18:19 is a very enlightening verse in this regard. God entered into a covenant with Abraham in which He said that Abraham was to raise his family according to God's commands so that God could bring blessing to Abraham and his offspring.

Deuteronomy 6:1–9 is that great passage in which God says He is the Lord, and we are to teach our children about Him. Parents have the responsibility to get God's truth into the hearts and lives of their children, that His blessing might come to the children through their parents, as we discussed above.

God told Adam about the trees of the garden before He created Eve (see Genesis 2:16–17), so Adam's job was to tell Eve what God had said. There was to be a transfer of information from the husband to the wife—then, when they became parents, to their children.

Women have a very important role to play in the family covenant. When God calls a woman a "helper" (Genesis 2:18), how is she supposed to help? She is supposed to help her husband fulfill God's calling on their home—and dog him until he does!

Now I don't mean a wife is to nag or badger her husband. What I'm talking about is seeing her husband's strengths and weaknesses and encouraging his strengths while taking up the slack where he is weak.

I think of Moses and his wife, Zipporah, in Exodus 4:24–26, an unusual passage. God had told Moses that the sign of His covenant for the males of Israel would be circumcision. But Moses had failed to circumcise his own son, and the Bible says that God sought to put Moses to death for his rebellion against the covenant.

But Zipporah, seeing the wrath of God against her husband, took a knife and quickly circumcised their baby boy. She threw the foreskin at

Moses' feet in disgust because his failure had jeopardized their family.

Rather than fussing and cussing, Zipporah acted. And her actions caused God to back off of His intention to kill Moses. Even though the man failed, the woman took up the slack and the home was saved.

When a woman says, "My man isn't everything he is supposed to be," she needs to ask in addition, "Am I the helper God created me to be?" It may be through her that the family will be preserved.

We will get into all of these issues in much more detail later, so just note for now the importance of the family covenant. Satan is destroying families because he is out to destroy the future.

## The Church Covenant

The third covenant in God's kingdom agenda is the church covenant.

In 1 Corinthians 11:25, Paul said the church is a new covenant. It is the new arrangement by which God relates to His kingdom people. The job of the church is to manifest the ethics of the kingdom before a watching world. Paul said this in the context of the Communion service, in which we are to sit in judgment of ourselves so that God might not judge us (see 1 Corinthians 11:29–32).

We can't have it both ways. Paul also said, "You cannot drink the cup of the Lord and the cup of demons; you cannot partake of the table of the Lord and the table of demons" (1 Corinthians 10:21).

If you are going to be in God's kingdom where He rules, then you must sit at His table. Don't try to have chairs at two different tables. Don't give God Sunday and give somebody else Monday through Saturday. He is our full-time Master.

In the covenant of the church our job is to disciple the saints to live for the kingdom.

## The Civil Covenant

The fourth covenant is one that reaches beyond the individual, the family, and the church to the broadest structures of society, from the federal government to the local school board.

Romans 13 sets out the parameters of this covenant. "Let every person be in subjection to the governing authorities. For there is no authority except from God, and those which exist are established by God" (v. 1).

Now this is interesting because the ruler when this passage was written was the Roman emperor Nero. God was saying, "Even pagan rulers only rule by My permission. And when I get tired of their paganness, I will remove them."

Government is God's appointed representative. Therefore, according to verse 2, if we resist the legitimate authority of government we are "oppos[ing] the ordinance of God." We are not just fighting the government; we are fighting God.

Now, I need to point out that what God authorizes in Romans 13 is the concept of governing authority, not necessarily everything that a particular authority does. There must be a distinction.

People in a legitimate office can operate in illegitimate ways. We must oppose illegitimacy and evil no matter where they are found, but that does not negate God's establishment of government. You don't have to like the mayor or the president, but you must honor the offices of mayor and president.

The God-ordained purposes of government are to reward and promote good behavior and to restrain and punish evil behavior.

*Rulers are not a cause of fear for good behavior, but for evil. Do you want to have no fear of authority? Do what is good, and you will have praise from the same; for it is a minister of God to you for good. But if you do what is evil, be afraid; for it does not bear the sword for nothing. (vv. 3–4)*

Now the government may not do its job very well, but God still gives government tremendous authority to carry out its assignment. Romans 13:4 is, in fact, referring to capital punishment. Capital punishments it a necessary function of society to harness the evil of men. It is not always administered justly, and we must fight against and correct the injustices. But the institution of capital punishment is necessary to punish evil and help instill the fear of authority. Evildoers must be afraid of the wrath of God through government.

When children stop being afraid of disobeying their parents, the home is in trouble. When members disrespect leadership, the church is in trouble. And when citizens don't respect the law of the land, the land is in trouble.

This is why people in many cities have burglar bars on their windows and triple locks on their doors. People no longer respect authority; they have no fear of God or of punishment. Government is God's plan to manage society. It is a legitimate covenant we have to recognize and submit ourselves to.

You can rebel against God's covenant if you want to, and for a while you may seem to get away with it. But in the Bible there is a fixed law that says, "Do not be deceived, God is not mocked; for whatever a man sows, this he will also reap" (Galatians 6:7). To put it another way, what you put in the soil, you're going to see again. If you plant corn, don't look for squash. If you plant okra, don't expect green beans.

The teenagers who rebel against their parents' authority will have kids someday, and then watch out. The husband and wife who rebel against the covenant responsibilities God has set before them need not expect to hear from God on other issues in their lives. The law of the kingdom is that whatever we sow is going to come up again.

Since God governs His kingdom through His covenants, and since I am assuming that you want to experience His blessing in your life and in your family, we need to know how God's kingdom agenda operates. That's the subject we need to tackle next.

# The Government of
# a Kingdom Agenda

Over the centuries, mankind has tried a lot of options in an effort to find a means of government, a mechanism of management, that would make life livable and deal with issues such as crime, social justice, education, the environment, and so on. Let me review some of these options before we talk about God's alternative, His kingdom agenda.

Some have tried anarchy, an option that is really the absence of government. It is the rule by none. When anarchy reigns, as in times of revolution and national upheaval, chaos rules because no one is in charge. Then everyone does what is right in his or her own eyes (see Judges 21:25).

Another governmental option is oligarchy, which is rule by an elite few who sit down and decide what is good for the masses. A handful of people decide what is good and right and what is bad and ugly, usually for corrupt and selfish purposes.

Then there is monarchy, or rule by a king or queen who sits as the supreme authority in the land. When the monarchy is the absolute form of government, rather than a figurehead as it is in some countries, the monarch has the power of life and death and decides what is good or bad for the nation.

Still another form of government is what we might call "ecclesiocracy," or rule by an institutional or state church. The medieval papacy is a good example of this kind of government, although the pope wasn't the official head of state in the various countries of Europe. But the church played a dominant role, and the pope often had a hand in raising up and deposing rulers. Contemporary Islamic countries also illustrate ecclesiocracy.

Let me mention two more forms of government, the two we are most familiar with. The first is democracy, the rule by majority. That's fine if the majority is right. But if you rule by majority and the majority is wrong, the country is in trouble because the worse the majority gets, the more wrong choices they will make.

For instance, when enough people find out they have the power to vote personal benefits for themselves, they will vote for those benefits. Then the culture is in trouble when the majority of the people become selfish in their choices. That should sound very familiar to us as Americans.

The final and best form of human government I want to review is a constitutional republic. In a constitutional republic, the people rule through their chosen representatives, and those representatives must rule by law. In a republic, there is a governing document or covenant that can be appealed to that all the parties are sworn to uphold (a constitution).

This document can overrule the majority because they cannot vote out the constitution that is the governing standard for the nation. Today, America is in somewhat of a tension between democratic desires and ruling principles.

A constitutional republic is God's ideal, but only if it operates in the way God intended government in history to function, and that is under His universal governmental rule.

That form of government is, of course, the kingdom of God. In this chapter, I want to consider how God governs His kingdom. We have seen that God has four basic covenants, four mechanisms by which He rules. These are the personal, family, church, and societal covenants.

We might also call these four forms of government self-government, family government, church government, and civil government. That's how I want to refer to them throughout this chapter.

Before we go any further, I need to point out that I am using the word *government* in the biblical sense of a jurisdiction, a specific realm of authority that has been delegated to us to accomplish a given task.

This concept involves sovereignty (legitimacy to rule), representation (accountability to the rule of another), law (a moral code by which to rule), jurisdiction (authority to enforce something in the name of the ruler), and continuity (stability and longevity). Each of these is determined by the all-encompassing rule of God.

When most people hear the word *government*, all they think of is city hall downtown or Washington, D.C. But that is not the basic definition of government in the Bible. It is a sphere of delegated authority.

How do God's government entities work? How does God rule His kingdom so that life accomplishes His agenda, which is His glory? I want to suggest several things that are important here.

## GOD'S GOVERNMENT IS DECENTRALIZED

Since man was created in the image of God and government was established by God, then it serves to reason that the governments of men are to mirror (image) or pattern themselves after God. God is Trinitarian in nature. He is One (unity of being and purpose) composed of three distinct persons (diversity of function in history). Therefore, human governments are to be united by the one purpose of living under and reflecting the rule of God, while simultaneously manifesting and modeling that rule through the diversity of the three governmental institutions He has established to reflect His unified authority in history.

The first thing to understand is that God's kingdom agenda is accomplished through decentralized institutions on earth. Not in a partisan, political way, as is now being debated between Republicans and Democrats, but rather through multiple governing authorities with distinct spheres or responsibility, jurisdictions, and sanctions; and all these governing authorities are to rule under His divine authority.

This means that God doesn't want all of the power concentrated in any one governing authority. It is His intention that there be only one centralized Governor and one centralized Power in the universe, and that's Him. God is the only One who can claim absolute power in the universe. All other authorities must have checks and balances. Satan's kingdom, on the other hand, is always organized top-down and centralized. He is the consummate cosmic empire builder, which is why his kingdom only enslaves.

## The Sole Monarch

Therefore, any other person or group who claims absolute power does so in rebellion against God. Any king, any governing body, any family, or any institution that claims absolute power has rebelled against God.

How does God feel about this issue of absolute authority? He said in Isaiah:

> *"The One forming light and creating darkness, causing well-being*
> *and creating calamity; I am the Lord who does all these. . . .*
> *It is I who made the earth, and created man upon it. I stretched out*
> *the heavens with My hands, and I ordained all their host . . ."*
> *For thus says the Lord, who created the heavens (He is the God who formed the*
> *earth and made it, He established it and did not create it a waste place, but*
> *formed it to be inhabited), "I am the Lord, and there is none else." (45:7, 12, 18)*

> *"I am God, and there is no one like Me, declaring the end from the beginning*
> *and from ancient times things which have not been done, saying, 'My purpose*
> *will be established, and I will accomplish all My good pleasure.'" (46:9–10)*

One gets the impression from reading these verses that there is not a lot of room for anybody else on the throne of the universe besides God. We could find multiple passages like these, but you get the idea.

## Dealing with Autonomy

Since God has centralized all power within Himself, whenever people try to centralize power in themselves God intervenes to break up their attempts at autonomy and their "declarations of independence." Just ask the folks who gathered at the Tower of Babel (see Genesis 11:1–9).

The little project was doomed because their objective was wrong from the beginning: "Come, let us build for ourselves a city, and a tower whose top will reach into heaven, and let us make for ourselves a name; lest we be scattered abroad over the face of the whole earth" (v. 4). Man has sought to use humanly devised ingenuity (humanism) to deify himself by defying God's command to decentralize (see Genesis 9:1). So instead of being given a name by God or wearing His name, humans sought to make a name for themselves, thus establishing unity, security, and social immortality as an authority independent of God.

They sought to build a city (civilization), a tower (religious system), and a name (independence) apart from God. But God is opposed to centralism and will judge it.

God looked down and saw what the people were doing, and He didn't like what He saw. No matter how high man gets, God still must come down to him. God's concern was that the people were trying to concentrate power in their hands without God. If they succeeded, God said, "Nothing which they purpose to do will be impossible for them" (11:6). That is, they could function as their own god in history because the tower represented their religious unity, thereby erasing the Creator/creature distinction.

That was impossible for God to put up with, so He confused their language—the heart of their unity because it reflected their thinking, ideology, faith, and common confession—so that nobody could understand anybody else.

Mankind said, "Let's make ourselves a name. Let's concentrate power and build a one-world government that will rule the universe."

God said, "Not in My universe, you won't!" (see Psalms 2:1–4; 9:17–20; 33:9–12). So He segregated and decentralized the people. The Tower of Babel is a prototype of any nation that defies God and raises itself up in pride through the centralization of power. Any attempt to be autonomous from God will produce divine intervention and decentralization so that men will once again seek God (see Acts 17:24–28). God resists His creation's centralization and judges the nations that forget Him (see Romans 1:18–32). For an example of this, just look at what happened to the former Soviet Union!

## GOD'S GOVERNMENT IS PLURALIZED

This second point is a natural outgrowth of the first. God's kingdom agenda not only decentralizes power; it governs through plural institutions.

We studied Romans 13:1 in the previous chapter, so I just want to quote it here and point out one thing: "Let every person be in subjection to the governing authorities." Notice the plural here when it comes to governing *authorities*. There is more than one. The concept of multiple delegated authority is patterned after the Trinity in unity (one God) and diversity (three Persons). Each has specific tasks they accomplish in unified purpose. Divine government, then, establishes the pattern for human government. Thus the word "government" must be qualified, and not universalized.

We listed these authorities above: self-government, family government, church government, and civil government. We can boil all of life down into God's four governmental entities. The proper and successful functioning of these governments depends on the government of God, who created and rules over all things. And while these distinct authorities support, enhance, undergird, protect, and interface with one another, they are nevertheless distinct in their responsibilities and their spheres of jurisdiction. Let's talk about them in turn.

## Self-Government

Self-government means self-control of one's attitudes and actions apart from external coercion. Self-government is the foundation for leadership and every other form of government, since those who cannot govern themselves cannot properly govern others.

God's ultimate goal for mankind is self-government under Him. Why? Because as we suggested in the previous chapter, every believer will give an account to God individually. The Bible says in Romans 14:12, "Each one of us shall give account of himself to God."

Jesus said that at His return, "[I] will then recompense every man according to his deeds" (Matthew 16:27). Peter also said that each of us will give an account to God and be judged accordingly (see 1 Peter 4:5). In fact every man, including the unrighteous, will give an account to God (see Revelation 20:11–15).

When you stand before God, your family can't come along with you to support you. You can't call the elders or deacons at church to help you out. When you stand before God, you will not be able to call on the governor, the mayor, the city council, or anyone else to plead your case. You will stand alone before Christ to account for the way you governed your life under Him.

This is why I say that God's goal in life is always self-government. If you are going to live life the way life was meant to be lived in God's kingdom, you must learn to govern your life according to His rules. Personal responsibility demands self-government.

When you look at it from this standpoint, you can see that the other three forms of government are also the three primary institutions God established in His Word to help produce proper self-government: the family, the church, and the civil government, all designed to play a special and unique role in producing proper self-government under God.

The family is not supposed to govern you all your life but to raise and train you to govern yourself under God. The church is not supposed to run your life but to disciple you to govern yourself under God. And the civil government was certainly never designed to run your life but to act as God's minister in providing conditions under which you can carry out good self-government.

Now you can see why, when people lose the ability to govern themselves, they mess up the institutions God has created to help them be self-governing.

If a husband and father won't govern himself, he is going to mess up his family. If members in a church don't govern themselves, there will be chaos in the congregation. And if the citizens in a society don't govern themselves, you can't hire enough policemen to fix the crime problem that results. What we have done in this country is take the things that God meant to be decentralized and make them the primary responsibility of civil government—thus creating a mess. For example, we centralized charity in the federal government and created a well-intentioned yet wasteful and abusive system called welfare.

We have centralized one thing after another, so now we've got this huge bureaucracy that you and I have to pay for through excessive taxation. Well, if you ask the government to do it, then you have to pay the government to do it.

This concept of self-government is the cornerstone to the meaning of freedom. Freedom is essentially the release from illegitimate bondage so that a person can pursue experiencing what God created them to be.

## Family Government

By family government I mean that God has a jurisdiction of authority whereby parents are responsible for their children.

The church isn't responsible for your children. The church can help equip you and support you in raising your children, but you are responsible for your children. And Lord knows, you do *not* want the government to take responsibility for raising your children.

In biblical family government, there used to be a time when it was clear that the father was the head of this government. There used to be a time when it was understood that, like Joshua, a father's most important role was saying, "As for me and my house, we will serve the Lord" (Joshua 24:15).

Let me get specific. In biblical family government, the responsibility for educating children rested with the home. It was the duty of parents, not the state, to see to the education of their children and make sure they were raised in the "discipline and instruction of the Lord" (see Ephesians 6:4; compare with Deuteronomy 6:1–9).

The only way parents can fulfill that command is to apply God's truth to every area of a child's life and education.

But when we turn the education of our children over to the state, and the state removes biblical ethics from its curriculum, what you get is the mess we have now. What we have now in education is information devoid of godly ethics. So instead of teaching the *theory* of evolution, the public school teaches the *fact* of evolution.

Once you tell the state, "I'm going to pay you to educate my children," then the state can educate them according to the state's rules, not according to your rules. This becomes a misapplication of biblical authority and government.

Let me hit you with another big one. In the Bible, economics and charity resided in the family. You could not go to the church for money until the church first asked, "Have you gone to your parents, siblings, or other relatives for help first?" (see 1 Timothy 5:4, 8).

You couldn't skip over your family and jump to the church. And you certainly couldn't skip over the family and the church and jump to the federal government and say, "It's payday. Hand me a check." That's not the way it was meant to be.

The family—with the father as president, the mother as vice president, and both raising the children—is to be the backbone of biblical society. That is why, when family government fails, woe is everything else because everything else is predicated on the family.

That's not just theoretical. Read chapters 3–6 of Genesis and you'll see that sin, which started when Adam and Eve failed and Cain killed Abel, eventually poisoned the whole human race. God had to destroy the whole race because the failure of the family is the bottom-line cause of disintegration in the church and the government.

A man may neglect or ruin his family because he wants to be somebody in the world. He wants to be the president of the company. He wants a kingdom to rule.

My brother, God has already given you a kingdom to rule at home. Rule that well before you talk about ruling anywhere else. God has already given you a sphere of authority in which you can be president.

In fact, He has also given you a vice president to help make up for your deficiencies as president. That is your wife, who is to come alongside you and apply her strengths where you are weak.

## Church Government

The Bible says in 1 Thessalonians 5:12–13 that church leaders have charge over the flock of God. In 1 Timothy 5:17, Paul said that elders are responsible to rule. The author of Hebrews wrote that members of the church are to obey and submit to their spiritual leaders (Hebrews 13:17).

Mature, set-apart spiritual leaders are God's method of ruling in His government of the church. The church is distinct from the family and from the civil government. It is a unique governmental rule under God.

As we said above, the church's purpose is to equip you to live before God with self-government. The job of the church is not to solve all of your problems but to show you how to solve your problems under God. The church can assist you in doing that, but it cannot do it for you.

I'll have a lot more to say about the church in part 4 when we discuss the kingdom agenda and your church life.

## Civil Government

The fourth area of God's government is civil government. Jesus said in Matthew 22:21, "Render to Caesar the things that are Caesar's; and to God the things that are God's."

You have a responsibility to the government under which you live. The apostle Peter spelled it out:

> *Submit yourselves for the Lord's sake to every human institution, whether to a king as the one in authority, or to governors as sent by him for the punishment of evildoers and the praise of those who do right. For such is the will of God that by doing right you may silence the ignorance of foolish men. (1 Peter 2:13–15)*

Did you know that civil government in the Bible was designed to be small, not large? Its reach was meant to be limited, not all-encompassing. The reason is that in the Bible, civil government is not the whole show. It is only one of three God-ordained institutions, along with the family and the church.

Biblically, civil government is supposed to spend its time and energy removing tyranny from the marketplace and producing harmony in society—in other words, promoting and administering justice, protecting law-abiding citizens, and punishing the lawless.

Civil government is designed to make sure that fairness operates in such areas as business and racial relationships. Government should see to it that men are not allowed to do evil and bring injustice into society.

Let me tell you something. If the church and the family were doing their jobs—producing responsible self-government in individual lives—then the government could focus on what it needs to focus on, because people would not be looking to the government to do everything else for them. This is a biblical view of government.

If you are expecting the civil government to do for you what God says you are to do for you, that is a misuse and misappropriation of government. And if you expect Uncle Sam to do it for you, you are destined for disappointment anyway.

Since Lyndon Johnson's "Great Society" began in 1965, the government has spent five trillion dollars trying to fix our communities, raise up the poor, and take care of the infrastructure of our inner cities. Now the government is ready to reform welfare because it has finally concluded, after the monies have been spent and the well-intentioned programs have been run, that centralized welfare is not the best approach. Biblical charity is private, family oriented, local, and temporary. Thus the government is to facilitate and support this approach, not replace it.

If every church accepted its biblical responsibility for charity, the church could end welfare in five years where the government hasn't been able to do a thing with it for forty years. It would only require a church taking on one family that was willing to be responsible, assisting that family to govern itself under God, and surrounding the family with a support system until it was self-governing.

This is not hard. But it's got to be government under God's kingdom, done His way. If it is not done His way, you will wind up with a lopsided relationship in which people do not govern themselves.

The job of the civil government is to maintain justice, protect freedom, and defend its citizens. In Scripture, the government has virtually no authority in education, business, welfare, or ecclesiastical affairs, except to make sure that there are no injustices and the market is free from tyranny and discrimination.

One of the biblical things the government did do was to intervene in the injustices of racism and segregation in the South. That was a biblical role of government because injustice and tyranny were involved.

## A Biblical Example

I have tried to make it clear that each of God's governmental institutions has its own sphere of operation. Now let me illustrate that concept from 1 Corinthians 6, where Paul said it is wrong for the church to take its matters to the civil government.

I want to use the example of divorce, because this is a big issue and one on which many Christians simply ignore the church and head downtown to see the judge. They want God to join them, but they want the judge to part them. They come to the church to get married but go to the judge to get divorced.

Notice the strong language Paul uses in 1 Corinthians 6 when he comes to this issue of the church and civil government:

> *Does any one of you, when he has a case against his neighbor, dare to go to law before the unrighteous, and not before the saints? Or do you not know that the saints will judge the world? And if the world is judged by you, are you not competent to constitute the smallest law courts? Do you not know that we shall judge angels? How much more, matters of this life? If then you have law courts dealing with matters of this life, do you appoint them as judges who are of no account in the church? (vv. 1–4)*

That sounds like a different court than the one downtown, doesn't it? Paul said the judge downtown is not supposed to have authority in church matters because in the church we have our own rules.

But whenever we appeal to the civil government to deal with a church matter like divorce, we rebel against God's decentralized approach to government, and we ignore the separate spheres of His governments.

This of necessity means that the civil government should respect the church government and courts, pushing back to the church court for church matters.

America's forefathers were correct here. When they added the Bill of Rights to the Constitution, they said, "Congress shall make no law respecting an establishment of religion, or prohibiting the free exercise thereof." They recognized that church and civil governments were to be two distinct realms.

It also means that civil government is not allowed to defile the church by seeking to rule over it or in it. Such an attempt is called idolatry and makes the government and the church that allows such intrusion subject to divine judgment (Ezekiel 43:1–12). Church and state are separate but God and religion are not (Deuteronomy 17:18–20).

## GOD'S GOVERNMENT WORKS FROM THE BOTTOM UP

The government of God's kingdom is not only decentralized and pluralized. It operates from the bottom up within specific spheres of responsibility. This means that all government begins with self-government. Each one of God's governing authorities cooperates and interconnects with the others without compromising jurisdictional boundaries in order to produce accountability, responsibility, and productivity on the lowest possible level. The individual should impact and strengthen the government of the family. The family should do likewise with the church, and the church should overflow to the enhancement of every institution in society.

### Personal Responsibility

God's government always starts with personal responsibility under Him. That's the message of the Communion service. In 1 Corinthians 11:28, Paul said, "Let a man examine himself, and so let him eat of the bread and drink of the cup."

Paul was talking about spiritual self-examination, which is part of the process of self-government. Paul continued in verse 31, "If we judged ourselves rightly, we should not be judged." God's government always starts with personal responsibility at the bottom.

Let me show you another example of God's kingdom working from the bottom up. In 2 Thessalonians 3, Paul was dealing with a serious problem in the church—men who refused to work.

*Now we command you, brethren, in the name of our Lord Jesus Christ, that you keep aloof from every brother who leads an unruly life and not according to the tradition which you received from us. For you yourselves know how you ought to follow our example, because we did not act in an undisciplined manner among you, nor did we eat anyone's bread without paying for it, but with labor and hardship we kept working night and day*

*so that we might not be a burden to any of you. . . . For even when we*
*were with you, we used to give you this order: if anyone will not work,*
*neither let him eat. (vv. 6–8, 10)*

Now I know that someone will say we should feel sorry for people like this. If that's your attitude, then feel sorry enough for him to put him in your car and take him somewhere to get him a job.

If a man is not willing to take personal responsibility, then you are doing him a disservice and damage if you help him become more irresponsible. We had some people who were being irresponsible leave our church in Dallas and get mad because the church wouldn't give them money. They tried to put a guilt trip on us, but God says let a person starve long enough that he or she is willing to get up and get a job.

Until people are willing to move toward self-government and take personal responsibility, the family, the church, and the government cannot do anything constructive for them. All they can do is perpetuate the chaos in our communities.

## Family Responsibility

Only when the situation is beyond the individual's abilities to cope do we move on to the family to seek help.

Paul dealt with this in 1 Timothy 5, where he wrote: "If any widow has children or grandchildren, let them first learn to practice piety in regard to their own family, and to make some return to their parents; for this is acceptable in the sight of God" (v. 4).

Later, he said, "If any woman who is a believer has dependent widows, let her assist them, and let not the church be burdened, so that it may assist those who are widows indeed" (v. 16). Widows "indeed" were women without any family to support them; they were to come under the care of the church.

But notice it is family before church. Good parents spend all those years pouring out their hearts and souls, breaking their backs, giving all of their energy and effort to raise their kids right. The Bible says the first place these parents should go if they have needs is to their children and even grandchildren. And if a grown child has parents or grandparents who gave their lives to raise him or her, and God has given that person the means to help those older folks, it is a violation of God's Word to skip over that responsibility and send them to the church for help.

The church didn't feed and clothe that child. The church didn't have to put a roof over that child's head. The Bible says the adult child owes something to that parent. According to 1 Timothy 5:8, anyone who does not care for "his own" is "worse than an unbeliever."

## Church Responsibility

The role of the church is to disciple individuals and families in such a way that they learn how to progressively bring every area of life under the lordship of Jesus Christ. The church itself is to be viewed as an expanded household or collection of families under God's kingdom authority and truth (see 1 Timothy 3:15).

In order to achieve this goal, the church is to provide the primary collective context for its members to share in the four biblical experiences. These are worship (the celebration of God for who He is, what He has done, and what He promises to do), fellowship (the mutual sharing of the life and love of Christ among the members), education (teaching and training of a biblical worldview), and outreach (witness to the unsaved in word and deed).

The church is the place where a biblical worldview is reinforced and where the kingdom of God is corporately made manifest. The proper functioning of the church is crucial since it is the church family, not the nuclear family, that marches into eternity.

In addition, the church is to be the primary collective expression of the kingdom of God in history. It is where the principles, precepts, and values of the kingdom are put on public display for the world to observe so that if any individual or institution would like to see what God would do to address a problem or need in society, all they need to do is watch the church in action. While the church is not to impose civil religion on the culture, it is responsible for being the religious conscience of civil government so that it understands and implements the principles of the kingdom in the broader culture. In this way, the church functions as the salt of the earth and the light of the world (see Matthew 5:13–16).

## Government Responsibility

The role of the civil government is to promote justice in society so the individual, family, and church are able to fulfill their callings under God in an orderly and unencumbered manner. Civil government is to support and protect the biblical rights, freedoms, and purposes of the other divine institutions so that the atmosphere in which they function is conducive to their growth, freedom, and productivity. As such, the government is not to seek to replace, circumvent, or impede the proper functioning of the other institutional spheres through bureaucratic controls. Rather, it should assist them in whatever ways it can to enhance their ability to be more effective in accomplishing their divinely ordained purposes.

There is a great picture of this principle in action in Nehemiah 3, where Nehemiah returned to Jerusalem to rebuild the city's walls and restore community life. Nehemiah started the work from the bottom up. He started with individuals who recruited their families. Then he strategically stationed the families at a place on the wall near their own homes so that they would have a vested interest in the work (see v. 10). The priest (church) rallied, taught, and inspired the people (see 8:1–18).

The government assisted the community revitalization program by giving a grant to pay for the wood needed for the building (see 2:8) and by providing protection for the builders (see 2:7, 9). But the civil government only helped with what the individuals, families, and spiritual community was already committed to do (see 2:18). Community development took place from the bottom up, not the top down.

## GOD'S GOVERNMENT BALANCES LOVE AND DISCIPLINE

God's kingdom government works in such a way that it balances love and discipline.

Hebrews 12:6 says that God loves us but He disciplines us. Parents are to love their children enough to discipline them (see Ephesians 6:4). If you do not love your children enough to discipline them, you really do not love them at all. If little Johnny is too cute to be spanked, then little Johnny is unloved. Church leaders are called to love their flock, but they are also called to correct the flock—even to the point of excommunication of unruly members (see 2 Thessalonians 3:11–15).

The civil government is to honor and praise people who do what is right (see Romans 13:3). But the government also has the responsibility to discipline and judge citizens who break the law (see v. 4).

All of God's institutions marry love with discipline. The method of discipline for the family is the rod. The method of discipline for the church is the Communion table and excommunication. The method of discipline for the government is the sword (capital punishment). God has given each governmental institution a disciplining mechanism that people might be led to self-government under Him or else suffer the appropriate consequences.

## GOD'S GOVERNMENT WORKS TO BRING BLESSING

Here's our final principle. God's kingdom agenda operates to bring His blessing to the institutions that follow it.

In Deuteronomy 29:9, Moses told Israel, "Keep the words of this covenant to do them, that you may prosper in all that you do." The Scripture is simply saying that if you do it God's way, you'll see the benefits.

America attempted to do this in its early days. The effort was flawed because of unbiblical slavery, but apart from slavery this country attempted to operate by a decentralized government. And we prospered like no country in the history of mankind, even though not everybody at the top was a Christian.

In 3 John 2, the apostle prays that Gaius would prosper "in all respects" just as he prospered in his spiritual life. John is saying the same thing. If you do things God's way, benefit comes. And the benefit flows over into the family, the church, and the government.

This progression of blessing is laid out beautifully in Psalm 128. In verses 1–2 we see the blessing that comes from personal responsibility or self-government: "How blessed is everyone who fears the Lord, who walks in His ways, when you shall eat of the fruit of your hands, you will be happy and it will be well with you."

Then the blessing moves to the family: "Your wife shall be like a fruitful vine, within your house, your children like olive plants around your table" (v. 3). When you become responsible for yourself, your mate and your children flourish.

Next in line is the church. "The Lord bless you from Zion" (Psalm 128:5). Zion was the place of worship where the temple was located. The church—the people of God, the spiritual community—is blessed when God's government operates the way it should, since it is the New Testament expression of Zion (see Hebrews 12:22–24).

Then what happens when the individual, the family, and the church get it right? The government of the nation experiences blessing: "May you see the prosperity of Jerusalem all the days of your life.

Indeed, may you see your children's children. Peace be upon Israel!" (Psalm 128:5b–6).

When people govern themselves under God, you have peace and blessing. When people look to everything and everyone else to govern them except God, you have anarchy.

People say, "I sure wish the church or the government would do something." God says, "I sure wish *you* would do something." So let me ask you a couple of questions:

Are you governing your life according to God's Word and His principles of government? If you are, you can expect God's blessing. But if you aren't, then don't blame anybody else.

Are you governing your family under God's kingdom rule? If you are, there's blessing waiting for you again. But if you aren't, don't complain about the church or the government.

This is how God's kingdom operates: through decentralized, plural institutions, under His centralized leadership, in order to produce self-government under Him.

# CHAPTER FIVE

# The Authority of a Kingdom Agenda

When the president puts his hand on the Bible at a presidential inauguration and swears to fulfill his duties, that act reflects the fact that there is a recognized relationship between God and government.

When a witness takes the stand in a courtroom, places one hand on the Bible and lifts up the other, and answers yes to the question, "Do you swear to tell the truth, the whole truth, and nothing but the truth, so help you God?" that witness is acknowledging that there's a higher authority at work in that courtroom.

The same thing happens when a couple gets married. They stand before a preacher or a justice of the peace and state their total allegiance to each other under God. They take an oath. They make a covenant with God.

In each of these cases, the parties involved are reflecting the fact that there is a higher authority under which the agreement is made and to whom they are responsible for keeping it.

In the case of a president, a courtroom witness, or a marriage, there is the recognition that ultimate authority is based on a recorded document given by God. This document becomes the basis for the functioning of the institution of which they are a part.

## THE DIVINE STANDARD

That's not only true in these cases, of course. In every area of our lives, we must recognize that the authority under which we operate goes far beyond our own human authority. In other words, God operates His kingdom by His Word. The Bible is the authority and divine blueprint by which all of life is to be lived. It is the benchmark by which all decisions should be made.

If you and I are going to bring God's alternative into history, we must recognize and submit to the divine authority of His Word. Otherwise, we are rebels against God's kingdom.

What was the first thing Satan got Adam and Eve to do in the garden? He got them to rebel against divine authority—to challenge, question, and ultimately disobey God's revealed word. No matter how you slice it, if you or the institution of which you are a part does not submit to the authority of God's Word, you become an enemy of the King and His kingdom.

If you are going to build a structure, it is absolutely critical that you lay the right foundation. Trying to build a skyscraper on the foundation of a chicken coop won't work. God runs His kingdom by His Word, and by His Word alone. Just as a person who wants to build a building must lay the proper foundation, if you want to live and thrive in God's kingdom it must be by His blueprint.

The Bible is not the Word of God *emeritus*. It's not a book that you throw by the wayside or put on the coffee table just to look good. It is the manual of authority in God's kingdom, the Book from which our kingdom agenda is drawn. To the degree that you honor, respect, and obey the Word, you will live. To the degree that you don't, you will suffer.

The reason we need this divine document is found in Isaiah 55:8. God says, "My thoughts are not your thoughts, neither are your ways My ways." God doesn't act the way we act. He doesn't think like we think. He functions in a totally different sphere. In theological terms, we call this God's *transcendence*. He is totally distinct from and above His creation.

So if God did not reveal His will and His standard to us, we could never figure it out on our own. Often in the Bible, God makes the statement "I am not a man" (see Number 23:19). The idea is, "Then don't measure Me by your standards, because you and I are not alike."

Since God is the only true authority in His kingdom, we must live under His revealed authority. If you had a messed-up life and said, "Tony, help me with my messed-up life," I would open the Bible and show you God's standard for fixing a messed-up life.

If you came to me with a messed-up family and said, "Tony, help me with my messed-up family," I would open up the same Book and show you how the Author of the family determined the family should be run.

The same thing is true for a messed-up church. The Bible is the charter of the church, and only the Bible can fix a messed-up church.

And if the governor or the president came to me and said, "Evans, we have a messed-up state" or "a messed-up country," I wouldn't switch books. I would open up the Bible and offer the governor or the president God's solution for a broken-down world.

Even in a democracy there must be a transcendental ethical norm that must serve as the standard for making laws so that a legitimate democracy can work. Without such a standard, democracy has no anchor to hold the majority in check, lest the will of a majority lead to unrestrained national government or the uncontrolled evil desires of that majority. The Bible provides the standard.

Why would I use the same Book in all four situations? Because all four areas of kingdom life—personal, family, church, and civil government—are created by God and governed by His Word.

Now there are *Christians* who want to switch books. They want to use the Bible when it's convenient, sort of like making God a servant in His own kingdom. But it won't work. The Bible must be the authority that governs every area of life.

Since the Bible is God's rule book for life in His kingdom, let's consider how the authority of the Bible impacts the four areas of God's kingdom mentioned above. And remember as we go that no one is supreme and sovereign but Him, so He has the right to draw up the rules of kingdom life. The Word of God reveals the absolute standard to which all other standards must bow, since it is right about everything on which it speaks, and it speaks about everything.

This means we must take seriously the whole Bible, including the revelatory aspects of the Old Testament. Paul told Timothy, who did not yet have a New Testament to read, that the Scripture (Old Testament) was sufficient for all of life (see 2 Timothy 3:16–17).

The statements of particular Old Testament regulations may differ in their contemporary application. But the clear principles of Old Testament truth as they reflect the character of God and the operation of

His kingdom are applicable to us since "they were written for our instruction" (1 Corinthians 10:11), and since the typological nature of the old covenant is true of the new covenant, providing us wisdom for all of life today. Furthermore, Israel is the only government legislated by God, thus it is the only place we can look to for guidance on how government should work and reflect the character of God. This is, in fact, the effect that Israel's government was to have on other nations; to serve as a paradigm for them to emulate (see Deuteronomy 4:5–8).

## PERSONAL COMMITMENT TO BIBLICAL AUTHORITY

Let's start with the personal dimension of kingdom life, what we are calling self-government under God's authority. As I said in an earlier chapter, this is where God ultimately wants us to arrive. The place where the kingdom agenda starts is with your personal commitment to biblical authority.

Jesus said it best when He said in Matthew 4:4, "Man shall not live on bread alone, but on every word that proceeds out of the mouth of God." Life itself is tied to biblical authority. If you rebel against it, you're rebelling against life.

Moses told Israel, "All the commandments that I am commanding you today you shall be careful to do, that you may live" (Deuteronomy 8:1). Life and death in God's kingdom are tied to the issue of biblical authority. We need to know God's commandments so we can do them and live.

You may be saying, "Tony, the Bible is a big Book. It's got sixty-six smaller books inside. It takes a lifetime to understand the Bible. How can I possibly do it?"

Let me suggest that the Bible is not quite as hard as you may think. Yes, it's so inexhaustible that theologians take a lifetime to try to understand it. Yet God's Word is so clear that children can grasp it.

The Bible has relatively few core teachings. Now it may talk about them in a thousand different ways, but the Bible only has a handful of foundational truths. Let me show you what I mean.

### The "Ten Words"

Exodus 20 contains what Moses called literally the "ten words." We know them as the Ten Commandments. They are the summary of life, the foundation and essence of God's law. Now God added about 613 stipulations to break out the commandments in more detail. But these "ten words" summarize what God expects.

So if you understand the Ten Commandments, you will have the core of what God expects from His kingdom subjects. You won't have all the details, but you'll know the summary of God's law that you can build on. Let me summarize the ten words for you.

Word number one is in Exodus 20:3. It says, "You shall have no other gods before Me." If you want to live, there can be no thing or person in your life who rivals God for primacy.

If your job, money, or another person competes with God for first place in your life, then you lose God in the process. But if you are going to order your life according to God's kingdom agenda, you can't allow anything to compete with God. God will not vie with anything on earth for our loyalty.

The second command is in verses 4–6 of Exodus 20: "You shall not make for yourself an idol." This command deals with your worship. Don't conjure up anything to help you define God. Don't create anything to try to help you see God better.

Why? Because anything you make will be limited by your brain. And the best you come up with will only be glorified man. God doesn't want you to carve out anything to help you worship Him, because He does not want to be reduced to our imagination.

Have you ever gone in one of those little photo booths where you put in some money and pull the curtain? You sit down, and the camera takes four quick shots. Now those are usually bad pictures. You may have been looking pretty good on the way in, but you are ugly coming out!

But you don't fuss, because what did you expect for a dollar? Most of us wouldn't go around showing those pictures, or we would apologize for them if we did. That camera is not equipped to give you a picture that accurately represents who you are and what you look like.

God says the best picture we can come up with makes Him look ugly. So we are not to create any images or idols, because He is the invisible God. We have to know Him on His terms.

In verse 7 we find the third command: "You shall not take the name of the Lord your God in vain." That involves a lot more than just a prohibition against profanity. That's included, but there's more to it than that.

This means don't make an oath and tie God's name to it if you don't plan to keep it. To take God's name in vain is to say, "As God is my witness," and then not tell the truth. To take God's name in vain is to make Him a party to a deal or a commitment that isn't true, which means that you used God's name to endorse deceit.

Taking God's name like that is wasting it, and God's name is too precious to be wasted. His name represents His character. People would invoke the name of a god to invoke power. Don't invoke God's power if you don't intend to relate properly to His person. In other words, reverence God's name.

"Remember the Sabbath day, to keep it holy" is the fourth command or word, which is laid out in Exodus 20:8–11. The Sabbath is the seventh day, the day when God rested from His creation—not because He was sleepy, but because He wanted to enjoy what He had done.

God told Israel to set aside time for divine focus. Keeping the Sabbath doesn't mean lying in bed all day, doing nothing. The reason to stop working on the Sabbath is to reflect on who God is and what He has done to gratefully enjoy His provisions.

In the New Testament, the seventh day of the week became the first day in terms of a day set aside for God. With the resurrection of Jesus Christ on the first day, this day has become our day to celebrate God and what He has done.

But the intent of the Sabbath and the Lord's Day is the same—to enjoy God. The rhythm of life demands that we take a day to stop, reflect, give thanks, and honor God, believing that just as He brought us through last week, He'll take us through next week. Don't get so busy that you lose time with God.

The fifth command tells us, "Honor your father and your mother" (v. 12). That has to do with authority, obedience, and reverence.

This commandment reflects the fact that God has a system whereby society is to function. Children are to honor their parents—obeying them, reverencing them, and supporting them when that becomes necessary. That way, the natural system of authority that God has built into the home is honored.

Exodus 20:13 says, "You shall not murder." That's a very accurate translation, since the Hebrew word here means homicide. This command is not talking about war, self-defense, or capital punishment. This is the intentional taking of a life no one gave you authority to take.

The idea expresses the reverence for and sanctity of life. You and I are to hold life sacred. That means abortion is wrong; infanticide is wrong; physician-assisted suicide is wrong. It is wrong to act like God if you're not God. Therefore, do not take the life of another.

According to the seventh word of Moses, "You shall not commit adultery" (v. 14). Adultery in the Bible is tied to idolatry, the worship of another god. The reason is that when you commit adultery, you break covenant with God's institution of marriage.

Jesus said in Matthew 5:27–28 that adultery includes what we think, which would take in things like pornography. So the command has to do with moral purity.

Then God said, "You shall not steal" (v. 15). Honor other people's property. If it doesn't belong to you, you can't have it unless you buy it or somebody gives it to you. You can't have it just because you want it.

You have the right to what you own, but you don't have the right to take what is not yours—including the pencils and other stuff at the office. Like the other commands, this one brings things a lot closer to home than most of us like.

"You shall not bear false witness against your neighbor," the ninth command says (v. 16). This means more than swearing to tell the truth on the witness stand.

The Bible has a lot to say about gossip. Gossip is a form of false witness. In the Old Testament, if you gave a false witness, you died. Liars and gossips may not die today, but it may be why their lives are so messed up. In God's kingdom, living has to do with the quality of life and not merely existence.

The tenth and final word cautions us, "You shall not covet" (v. 17). This deals with contentment, being happy with what you have. Coveting is the attitude that says, "I wish I could have what you have. In fact, I want it so much that I might make you miserable while you try to enjoy it. And given the chance, I will take what you have from you."

## Summarizing the Law

This is a quick summary of the Ten Commandments. But maybe you are saying, "I can't remember all ten of those." Well, Jesus boiled them down even further for us in Matthew 22:36–40. A lawyer came to Jesus and asked Him a lawyer-type question: "Which is the greatest commandment in the Law?"

Jesus told him, "You shall love the Lord your God with all your heart, and with all your soul, and with all your mind. . . . The second

[commandment] is like it, 'You shall love your neighbor as yourself'"
(vv. 37, 39).

There you have the essence of God's kingdom agenda. You don't have to go to seminary. If you have the Ten Commandments, or even the two Jesus described as the first and second greatest laws, you've got the basics. It is understanding these principles that governs your personal life. In the words of Solomon, "Fear God and keep His commandments, because this applies to every person" (Ecclesiastes 12:13).

## The Motivation to Obey

Since God's Word is the authority in our personal lives and since He has specific instructions for us to keep, where do we get the motivation to keep His Word? To the unrighteous it will be fear of judgment.

The motivation for the righteous is appreciation for God's grace. You and I keep God's Word out of gratitude because we recognize that it's by His grace we are even here. All the motivation Israel needed to keep the Ten Commandments was provided back in Exodus 20:2, before the commands were given: "I am the Lord your God, who brought you out of the land of Egypt, out of the house of slavery."

If you know the Lord Jesus Christ as your Savior, He has set you free. He shouldn't be begging you to keep His commandments. You should be so glad to be free of your spiritual Egypt that you want to do ten things every day just to make God happy. It is for this reason that the more we love the Savior, the more we will obey Him (see John 14:15). His grace provides us the Holy Spirit, who enables us to obey (see John 14:16–17; Galatians 5:16).

So if you want to live out God's kingdom agenda, it starts with your obedient response to His Word. Duty should rise out of devotion.

## FAMILY COMMITMENT TO BIBLICAL AUTHORITY

The second way that biblical authority is to be made manifest in God's kingdom is through the family. It starts with the individual but moves to the family.

In Deuteronomy 4:9–10, Moses said:

> *"Give heed to yourself and keep your soul diligently, lest you forget the things which your eyes have seen, and lest they depart from your heart all*

*the days of your life; but make them known to your sons and your
grandsons. Remember the day you stood before the Lord your God at
Horeb, when the Lord said to me, "Assemble the people to Me, that I may
let them hear My words so they may learn to fear Me all the days they live
on the earth, and that they may teach their children."*

Notice the emphasis on teaching the ways and Word of God to
your children. Then in the famous passage in Deuteronomy 6 we are
told, "These words, which I am commanding you today, shall be on
your heart; and you shall teach them diligently to your sons" (vv. 6–7).

## Teaching

Do you get the message? If you have a family, you are responsible to
make sure that the truth you are learning is transmitted to your children. If you don't teach God's Word to your family, there is someone
else out there who has another word he would be glad to teach to your
kids.

Satan has his own message, his own kingdom, and his own teachers. They would be glad to teach your children for you. Some of these
teachers are on the streets, some are in the school system, and some
may even be in the church. Your child could be sitting next to another
kid whose lack of regard for God is going to rub off on your kid.

So we have to teach our children "diligently," not occasionally.
That may mean turning off the television and using the time for teaching. Whatever it may involve, you have to carve out time with your
family to teach the Word.

Neither the government nor the church has been charged to do
what parents are supposed to do. So we parents can't blame the church
or the state if our kids turn out messed up. It starts with the parents,
the family.

But if you do the job, I have good news for you. "Train up a child
in the way he should go, even when he is old he will not depart from
it" (Proverbs 22:6). Give your kids God's Word early in life, and even if
they do take a left turn, the Holy Spirit has something to hook on to
and bring them back.

## Discipline

The family is also to be the place where children are corrected based on biblical authority.

Proverbs 13:24 says, "He who spares his rod hates his son, but he who loves him disciplines him diligently." There is the same word used in connection with teaching our children. We are to be diligent in discipline too.

If Johnny's mother and father won't spank him, it's because they hate him. Anybody you love, you keep from going the wrong way.

According to Proverbs 22:15, "Foolishness is bound up in the heart of a child; the rod of discipline will remove it far from him." Children are born with foolishness in them. It takes the rod of discipline to take that mess away.

Let me give two more key verses on discipline from Proverbs. "Do not hold back discipline from the child, although you beat him with the rod, he will not die" (23:13).

Now I know that kids tell their parents, "You're killing me!" I tried that with my dad one time when he was spanking me. He said, "Die, then." He knew I wasn't going to die. Corporal punishment is supposed to hurt so the child will remember that when he thinks about doing wrong the next time.

In Proverbs 19:18, the writer said, "Discipline your son while there is hope, and do not desire his death." That's an amazing verse. If you don't discipline your children while you can, you may be sentencing them to the grave.

Why? Because they may develop a lifestyle of rebellion against God, and it could cost them their lives. The failure of parents to teach and discipline their children is at the heart of society's problems today. God's kingdom works through the family.

## Welfare

Here's one more area where the Bible is to have authority in our families. The family is the first line of responsibility for the welfare of its members.

We looked at 1 Timothy 5:8 in the previous chapter, so I won't quote it here. But the idea of the verse bears repeating, that the person who doesn't care for his or her own family is worse than an unbeliever. Even sinners know you're supposed to take care of your family.

This is God's kingdom agenda for the family. Teach your children, discipline them, and provide for them.

# THE CHURCH'S COMMITMENT TO BIBLICAL AUTHORITY

The third entity in God's kingdom is the church, which follows naturally from the individual and the family. Biblical authority expands from the person and the family to the church. God's kingdom is expanded through the influence of the church.

Let's go back to Deuteronomy 4 for an Old Testament picture of what I'm talking about:

> I have taught you statutes and judgments just as the Lord my God commanded me, that you should do thus in the land where you are entering to possess it. So keep and do them, for that is your wisdom and your understanding in the sight of the peoples who will hear all these statutes and say, "Surely this great nation is a wise and understanding people." (vv. 5–6)

## Model the Truth

Moses told the people to apply God's truth to their lives in such a way that other nations would see it and want to imitate them. The job of the church, as God's New Testament covenant people, is to model the principles of His kingdom in such a way that even the ungodly will say, "That makes sense. That's the best way to live." When the church is not the church, then society has nowhere to look for an answer since the church is uniquely the preserver and depository of divine truth (see 1 Timothy 3:14–15).

Our church in Dallas received a real honor not too long ago when the governor of Texas contacted us to say that, with our permission, he wanted to talk about the ministry of Oak Cliff Bible Fellowship in his "State of the State" address.

The governor wanted to talk about how the church should influence society; how, when the church is right, the government doesn't have to do all these things and tax people to do them, because the churches are centers of hope in every community. His office was looking for an example of that, and they chose our church.

That's what being a kingdom alternative is all about. It is about the church being the secondary tier of welfare. Welfare starts in the family, but then it goes to the church because it has to be localized where the people live.

Jesus said His people are to be "the salt of the earth" and "light of the world" (Matthew 5:13–14). The job of the church is to illuminate the truth, not just to pontificate about the truth. Our job is not just to talk about what the world should do but to illustrate before the world what the world should do.

## The Great Commission

If we are going to live under biblical authority as the church, we must obey the Great Commission (see Matthew 28:19–20). But I want to show you something about this commission you may never have seen before—something I believe the evangelical church has missed in the Great Commission.

Jesus said in Matthew 28:18–19, "All authority has been given to Me in heaven and on earth. Go therefore and make disciples of all the nations." The Greek word Jesus used for nations is *ethnos*. It means a collection of individuals who make a group.

This could be a cultural group, racial group, or a geographical group, but the word has to do with groups of people. Groups are made up of individuals, but Jesus is talking about more than individual results here.

God's idea was that the church should be so powerful and carry such impact that whole communities of people, whole races of people, whole nations of people would be affected by the disciplining ministry of the church. He wants the church to affect not just individuals but the very structures that make up society and hold people together.

This is why the church cannot be satisfied with just giving people free tickets to heaven. Now don't misunderstand. Evangelism is very important. But the church also has the responsibility to infiltrate the structures of society so that everything from the school board to the corporation to the nation is affected by people carrying the image of Jesus Christ. This is the essence of discipleship: conformity to Christ in every dimension of life.

But it has to start with the church. Second Timothy 3:16–17 says the Bible was given so that God's people would be "equipped for every good work."

If the Bible is not good enough for God's people to live by, how can it be good enough for the world? If the Bible can't straighten us out, how can it straighten out the mayor or the president? It's got to work in the family of God if it's going to work in society. We must be salt and light to the world.

## THE GOVERNMENT'S RESPECT FOR BIBLICAL AUTHORITY

A final way that God's kingdom agenda is established is by the culture's respect of biblical authority. God's words, revealed in the Bible, form the standard for not only personal righteousness but also for national obedience.

### Operating by God's Principles

Proverbs 14:34 says, "Righteousness exalts a nation, but sin is a disgrace to any people." Even non-Christian cultures can be a nice place to live if they're operating by Christian principles.

That doesn't mean every government leader has to be a Christian. That will never happen. That's why I used the word *respect* for this section instead of *commitment*. A non-Christian government will not be committed to God's Word. But there are certain principles God has established that will benefit a society if they are followed, even if the leaders don't know God.

Paul told us in 1 Timothy 2:2 to pray for our leaders and those in authority so that we might have a peaceful society. We need to pray that leaders will become sensitive to God's way of doing things, because a culture can be a reasonable place to live if it is informed by biblical principles.

The Bible says that God sets up and deposes kings (see Daniel 2:21). David said, "I will also speak of Thy testimonies before kings" (Psalm 119:46). David knew that society must run by God's rules. A nation is going to stand or fall based on whether God's rules have permeated the culture.

That's why our public education system is in trouble. It is trying to do the impossible—impart information without ethics, as we said earlier. You cannot have a separation between information and ethics, because if people do not have moral guidelines by which to measure academic data, they will create their own guidelines and inject them into the curriculum.

The issue is never teaching morality versus teaching no morality, but whose morality will be taught. The schools as a whole used to teach God's morality. That's why there used to be a time when the Ten Commandments were posted on the school wall. It was in recognition of the fact that there were basic rules of life to be honored, rules that acknowledged God's view of life.

## The Ministers of God

Governments are not merely supposed to acknowledge and honor God's principles for life. Even though many don't know it, our governmental leaders are also religious leaders. Now a politician may toss God's name into the discussion every now and then to get a vote, but that's not what I mean by saying governmental leaders are religious leaders. And I don't mean that these people are supposed to try to take over the church or anything like that. I'm talking about Paul's statement in Romans 13:4 that governmental authority is "a minister of God to you for good."

The Greek word for *minister* is a religious term. It means "one who acts on God's behalf." So although leaders serve in the civil realm, they are still God's ministers.

That is, our leaders' jobs are to uphold and carry out God's standard in the civil arena. For instance, the Bible forbids murder, as we saw above. When a murder is committed, a minister, in this case called a judge, must act and impose appropriate punishment on the murderer.

Whether or not the judge acknowledges it, the rule being imposed—"You shall not murder"—is God's rule. The reason He gave it is that we are made in His image. So when a person commits murder, he or she has in reality attacked God.

So when that happens, God has His representatives, His ministers, act on His behalf in punishing the offender. Judges may not even realize they are acting as God's ministers when they impose such a sentence, but the Bible says that's what they are doing.

## Deterring Evil

Another way rulers respect biblical authority and rule according to God's guidelines is by deterring evil. Men must fear judgment if their evil inclinations are to be kept in check. Romans 13:3 implies that officials must be able to distinguish between good and evil so they can punish the evil and reward the good.

There's only one way we can know the difference between good and evil. There must be a standard. Otherwise we're lost, because what is good and right to one person may not be good to another person. We need a guideline and a standard that will govern everybody. And since government belongs to God, it can only operate properly when it functions according to God's rules.

This is where our culture is so schizophrenic. While so many are busy trying to drive God and biblical principles out of the public arena, our culture's laws are still, for the most part, based on a biblical frame of reference.

However, many times our public officials wind up rewarding the evil and punishing or ignoring what is good. America at the beginning of the twenty-first century is a classic example of what happens in a society that rejects God's rules and tries to live by man's rules.

The result is moral and spiritual chaos. We have to live by God's Book, because if we don't, we'll live by somebody else's book. And you and I won't like the results. When governments operate under the theocratic rule of God by relecting biblical principles, they will begin to reflect already existing theocracy to their citizens. Citizens will either be ruled by the Word of God or by the work of men seeking to imitate God.

## THE NEED FOR A STANDARD

Why is it so imperative that we learn to function by biblical authority? A simple exercise will demonstrate our need.

Take a blank sheet of paper and try to draw a straight line down the middle. What will happen? It will be crooked. I don't care how steady your hand is, if you try to draw a straight line on your own there's going to be a curve in that line somewhere.

But now try drawing a straight line with a ruler. Lay a ruler next to your line and draw another line with it. The difference will be obvious.

You get the idea. When you try to live life on your own, it's going to be crooked. I don't care how much you try or how straight you are, your life is going to have lumps and bends in it because the best of us can't live a straight life on our own.

Too many of us in the kingdom of God are trying to live life on our own, and we keep messing up. But if you'll let the Word of God be your ruler and draw your life according to its standard, you'll take care of the bumps.

God's Word is the only authority that will enable us to draw a straight line in our personal life, in our family life, in the church, and in society. There's only one King in this kingdom, and He has a ruler called His Word. That's our standard, "For the Lord is our judge, the Lord is our lawgiver, the Lord is our king; He will save us" (Isaiah 33:22).

# THE KINGDOM AGENDA IN YOUR PERSONAL LIFE

# CHAPTER SIX

# The Kingdom Agenda and Your Discipleship

If I asked you to tell me who you are without giving me your name, your occupation, your title at work, or anything else like that, how would you answer?

How you answer that question says a lot about you. It lets me know if you really know who you are. In the Bible, when people came to Jesus Christ and were dead serious about following Him, when they became people of the kingdom, there was no question about who they were.

Those early disciples became known even among unbelievers as people of "the Way" (Acts 19:9), because they had chosen to walk a different path in life. They had identified themselves totally with Jesus Christ and the kingdom of God. They lived for the kingdom, and their identity was tied to the kingdom.

The great tragedy today is that we don't have enough Christians who know who they are. They may be genuine believers, but their faith is just another addition to their portfolio. When it comes to the bottom line, they define themselves in terms of their name, their job, their possessions, or the people they know.

If somebody asked you who you are and nowhere in the conversation did the name and kingdom of God come up, you are a confused

Christian. As a member of the kingdom, your identity is all tied up and wrapped up with Christ. There should be no way to talk about you and not talk about Him.

In other words, for us the term *Christian* is not just a title. It is our identification, just like our name is. Being followers of Christ is the essence of who we are.

That's why we need to understand and cultivate a kingdom mentality and a kingdom agenda. That's why we need to become mature, fully functioning men and women of the King. The process by which this is achieved is called *discipleship*. So let's talk about your discipleship in the kingdom.

## THE DEFINITION OF DISCIPLESHIP

It always helps to define where we are going. Therefore, let me give you a working definition of the spiritual process called discipleship.

When we talk about discipleship in the kingdom, we are talking about the process by which we bring all of life under the lordship of Jesus Christ. Now there is a lot to this definition, but it will give you a handle on what is involved in following Christ and being totally identified with Him. The singular, overarching goal of a disciple is to bring all of life under the lordship of Jesus Christ.

### A Learner

In Matthew 10:24–25, Jesus described what a disciple should look like. "A disciple is not above his teacher, nor a slave above his master. It is enough for the disciple that he become as his teacher, and the slave as his master."

The word *disciple* itself means "learner." It refers to a student who follows the teachings and pattern of another so closely that the student becomes a "clone" of the teacher, to use a modern-day term. We could also call a disciple an apprentice, someone who stands at the side of a skilled master in a trade to learn that trade thoroughly.

Discipleship was already a common term in the Greek world several centuries before Christ. It was used to describe the process by which the Greek philosopher Plato taught Aristotle, who then built academies to train thinkers in Greek philosophy.

These disciples would then infiltrate Greek culture and later

Roman culture, teaching what they had learned in order to pattern the world after their philosophy.

The very definition of discipleship shows that it can't be accomplished all at once, any more than a baby can become an adult overnight. Becoming a disciple is a lifelong process, but that doesn't mean we can kick back and glide for a while.

You may not be where you want to be in your spiritual growth, but you ought to be bigger spiritually this year than you were last year. You ought to be further down the road this year than you were last year. A disciple should be growing, the way children grow and mark their growth on a chart.

## Looking Like Christ

The goal of discipleship is conformity to the Savior, being transformed into the image or likeness of Christ (see Romans 8:29).

A pastor friend of mine was recently visiting a college campus. He didn't know that my son Anthony Jr. was a student there. He said he was walking across campus and saw a young man off in the distance.

My friend said he looked and then stopped dead in his tracks. "That has to be Tony Evans's son," he told himself. "He looks like Tony; he's built like Tony; he even walks like Tony."

He was right, of course. The young man he had spotted was Anthony Jr. Even though the man was a long way away, Anthony's characteristics were so obviously like mine that my friend told me, "I didn't even know Anthony was in college yet. All I knew was that nobody could look that much like you and not be yours."

Let me tell you, people ought to be able to see you from a long way off and say, "That person has to be a follower of Jesus Christ." They ought to be able to tell by the way you walk and talk, by the total orientation of your life, that you belong to Christ, because nobody could function the way you function and not know Him.

The family resemblance ought to be obvious. It ought to be clear where you stand. That is discipleship. It means to so pattern your life after Christ, to follow Him so closely, that you speak, act, and think like Him.

Failing to follow Christ as His disciple means that we will meander through a mediocre Christian life rather than living a kingdom life. We will become like the farmer who was teaching his son how to plow.

The farmer told his boy, "Now, Son, I want to plow a straight furrow from one end of this field to the other."

The son asked, "But how will I know when I am plowing it straight?"

"Do you see that cow lying down over in the next field?" the father replied. "Son, just keep your eye on that cow and plow straight toward her. You'll be fine."

The farmer came back about an hour later and saw furrows going every which way. He couldn't believe it. "Son, what in the world happened? I told you to keep your eye on the cow so you could plow a straight furrow."

"Dad, I *did* keep my eye on the cow. But the cow kept moving!"

Actually, I don't know any farmer who would advise his son to plow using a moving object. But the point is worth making. If you focus on the wrong object, your life is going to wander all over the place.

You won't have consistent spiritual victory. You'll be up one day and down the next day. But if you're following Jesus, you'll plow a straight line. He's not going anywhere. He is the same yesterday, today, and forever (see Hebrews 13:8).

## Lining Up All of Life

In terms of the four areas of kingdom life we have been talking about, a disciple is a person who lines up each area of his or her life with Jesus Christ.

Once again, it starts with the personal life, the area of self-government. There's a great example of this in Matthew 16. Jesus was telling His disciples that He was going to die, when Peter rebuked Him. "God forbid it, Lord! This shall never happen to You" (v. 22).

Jesus replied to Peter, "Get behind me, Satan! You are a stumbling block to Me; for you are not setting your mind on God's interests, but man's" (v. 23).

Peter was lining up behind the wrong object. He was sincere, but he was sincerely wrong. Being a disciple means that if you and Christ disagree, you are wrong. If your interests clash with His, you need to change interests.

Our younger son, Jonathan, is developing into a pretty good basketball player. When he first started playing at about six or seven years of age, we went to see him play a church-league game.

Jonathan stole the other team's pass and took off for the basket. But he got turned around or something and put the ball in the opponent's basket. Jonathan was sincere, but the other team got the two points.

A lot of times we say, "Well, I didn't mean any harm. I was doing what I thought was best." But that's not the point. Discipleship means following Christ and His agenda, not ours.

The same is true in family life. We have already considered Ephesians 6:1–3, which outlines the response of each family member to Christ.

Children are instructed to obey their parents "in the Lord." In other words, kids need to line up their lives on Christ. It's the parents' responsibility to set Christ's standard before their children so they can "plow a straight line." Our goal as parents is to teach our kids to think Christocentrically and bibliocentrically, a divine frame of reference.

In the church, the goal of kingdom discipleship is to "present every man complete [mature] in Christ" (Colossians 1:28). That's another way of saying that disciples need to look like Christ.

Let that sink in for a minute. It is not the church's job to make you look good but to make you look like Jesus Christ. Lots of people come to church looking real good, but if we could get behind the makeup and the fine clothes to the real person, we would see things they don't want anybody to see.

That's why the Bible tells us to be clothed with Christ (see Galatians 3:27). If we are going to put on makeup, let it be "makeup" of Jesus Christ so that we look like Him. The job of the church is to help us do that.

Finally, in the area of civil government, I would point you back to the discussion in chapter 5 about the meaning behind the word *nations* in the Great Commission (see Matthew 28:19–20). The idea is that our discipleship should affect entire nations.

I think the best biblical example of this is the preaching of Jonah that resulted in the repentance of Nineveh. Now, Jonah had a lot of personal baggage and problems to work out with the Lord, but when he finally managed to get those issues resolved, he was able to transform Nineveh by the presence of God working through him.

As disciples, we are called to bring even the nations under the lordship of Christ.

## A Process of Spiritual Growth

Discipleship is a process, not an event. Thus it demands spiritual growth. The formula is simple: Rate multiplied by time equals distance.

The speed at which you move given the time that you have been saved will determine the spiritual distance you cover. This is why you can have Christians who have been saved five years who are more spiritually mature and better disciples of Christ than others who have been Christians for twenty-five years. They have moved at a faster pace within the time period since their conversion.

The process of spiritual growth is from the inside out (see 1 Thessalonians 5:23). As the Holy Spirit empowers the human spirit, the human spirit transforms the soul (personality). The transformed soul then transforms the activity of the body, thus conforming the person's conduct to the image of Christ, which is the essence of discipleship. (See this author's work *The Promise*, Moody Publishers, for a comprehensive discussion of the person and work of the Holy Spirit in the believer's life.)

It is for this reason that there is such an emphasis on abiding in Christ. As intimacy with Christ is maintained, the transforming process is ignited and enhanced. God has provided four key resources to help us in this process. Scripture provides the authoritative, objective truth to govern our process. Scripture provides the objective truth to govern our choices and decision making. The Holy Spirit empowers Christians to accomplish the demands of Scripture as they live "under the influence," or full of the Spirit (see Ephesians 5:18), which is accomplished as we make worship a lifestyle and not just an event (see vv. 19–21). Then God uses trials to reveal to us our strengths and weaknesses so that we can tangibly see the areas that still need work. Trials, while painful, are like a good surgeon's knife, always designed to make us better (see James 1:2–5). And finally, God gives us relationships so that the spiritual passion of others keeps us spiritually hot and the discipleship process is kept on track.

The result of these divine provisions is conformity to the image of Christ, demonstrated by the reflection of the fruit of the Spirit in the life of the disciple (see Galatians 5:16–25) and a new ability to perceive and understand God's will for our life so that we can fulfill His kingdom agenda for us.

The primary context for the discipleship process to occur is the local church.

## THE DOMAIN OF DISCIPLESHIP

In Colossians 1:13–14, the apostle Paul wrote, "For He [Christ] delivered us from the domain of darkness, and transferred us to the kingdom of His beloved Son, in whom we have redemption, the forgiveness of sins."

If you are a Christian, God has transferred you to a new domain, a new dominion. You have been placed into a whole new environment, the kingdom of God's beloved Son. You can't be a disciple of the King until you first enter His realm.

## Entering the Domain

John 3 tells the familiar story of Nicodemus, whom we might call a model person. He was a Jewish Pharisee, but he had a Greek name. In that culture, giving a Jewish boy a Greek name meant that his parents were high society, "tall cotton," well cultured.

So Nicodemus had culture and wealth. As a Pharisee, he was also at the top of the pile religiously. Nicodemus had it all, but Jesus said, "You must be born again" (John 3:7).

Getting into God's kingdom has nothing to do with what side of town you live on or how often you go to church. It requires a new spiritual birth. That's the only way you get a passport to the kingdom. This spiritual rebirth only comes from placing your faith in Jesus Christ alone as your personal Sin-Bearer because of His substitutionary death on the cross and His victorious resurrection from the dead (see Romans 10:9–10).

When I travel, I have a passport that gives me access to other nations. If you have been born "from above" (a better translation than "again") by personal faith in the finished work of Jesus Christ, then your sins are forgiven and God has given you a passport into His kingdom.

That passport is the blood of Jesus, and it gets you into His domain. What's it like there? Romans 14:17 says the kingdom of God is not food and drink but "righteousness and peace and joy in the Holy Spirit." It's a spiritual realm.

Paul says we are now citizens of another kingdom, which is owned by another King (see Philippians 3:20; 1 Timothy 1:17). Our first obligation is not to this world system that leaves God out. Our first obligation and allegiance are to the kingdom of God.

Several years ago, everybody was singing, "I'm proud to be an American." Every day, schoolchildren put their hands over their hearts and recite the Pledge of Allegiance. When we go to ball games, we stand up and sing the national anthem, giving honor to our country. We do so because we are Americans.

What would people say about an American who announces, "I am not going to sing that song, recite that pledge, or honor that flag"? Most people would say that person needs to move on to another country. We do so because we are Americans.

Every day when you and I wake up we should say, "I pledge allegiance to Christ and to the cross on which He died to forgive my sin." We owe our allegiance to the kingdom of God. That's why we are trying to learn His kingdom agenda.

## Missing the Kingdom

Is it possible for believers to miss the kingdom? It is—not in terms of salvation but in terms of discipleship.

How does it happen? It happens when we become busy trying to be entertained by the world instead of setting our eyes on Christ.

Anyone who knows me can tell you that I like amusement parks with their wild rides and all of that. At the huge state fair of Texas, they have those crazy sideshows featuring all manner of oddities. We used to visit them when the kids were small.

But I don't go to the sideshows anymore, for a very simple reason. They aren't worth the price of admission. They use mirrors to make that alligator look huge, and the so-called "half man, half animal" is just a man dressed up in a crazy outfit.

That's what the world's system is like. It will promise you a great sideshow, but after you have taken a peek, you realize it isn't what was advertised. The Bible says: "Do not love the world, nor the things in the world. If anyone loves the world, the love of the Father is not in him. For all that is in the world, the lust of the flesh and the lust of the eyes and the boastful pride of life, is not from the Father, but is from the world" (1 John 2:15–16).

The world will give you a sideshow, but it won't give you life or purpose or direction because you belong to a different realm, a spiritual nation.

## Committing to the Kingdom

You may say, "Tony, I'm a Christian, but I don't have a sense that I am living in this spiritual domain." Perhaps that's because you have not fully committed yourself to your new domain.

A man once became lost in the desert. His throat was parched, and he knew he wouldn't live much longer if he didn't get some water.

Just then off in the distance he saw a little old shack. He made his way to the shack and found a pump inside with a jug of water sitting next to it. He reached for the jug to take a drink only to find this note on the jug: "The pump will give you all the water you need. But in order to prime the pump, you must pour in all the water in the jug."

This man had a dilemma. Should he drink the water in the jug and then be out of water and perhaps be unable to get more, or should he believe the note and use the water he had to prime the pump?

He began to think through his choices. "Suppose I pour all my water in the pump and nothing happens? I not only lose the water; I may lose my life.

"On the other hand, if there is a well underneath this pump and I use the water to prime it, then I can get all the water I need."

This thirsty man's dilemma is the question we have to ask ourselves as disciples. Do we get all we can get now because there might not be much later, or do we give up what we can get now because of all that's available if we are willing to take the risk of committing ourselves to Christ?

The man thought for a moment and then decided to take the risk. He poured the contents of the jug into the pump and began to work the handle. Sweat broke out on his forehead as nothing happened at first.

But as he pumped a few drops of water appeared, and then came a huge gush. He drank all he wanted, took a bath, then filled up every other container he could find in the shack.

Because he was willing to give up momentary satisfaction, the man got all the water he needed. Now the note also said, "After you have finished, please refill the jug for the next traveler." The man refilled the jug then added to the note, "Please prime the pump. Believe me, it works!"

We need to prime the pump. Some of us are half-stepping on Christ. We're trying to live in two worlds at the same time. We want to be sacred and secular, worldly and spiritual. We want to love God and love this world order. But you have to pour all the water—give God everything you have—if you want God to pour His blessings back on you. Only in the domain of the kingdom will you find God's power.

## THE DISCIPLINE OF DISCIPLESHIP

Following Jesus Christ and His kingdom agenda not only brings you into a new realm; it brings you into a new program of discipline.

There is a discipline to discipleship if you want to receive the full benefits of the kingdom. Paul advised Timothy: "Have nothing to do with worldly fables fit only for old women. On the other hand, discipline yourself for the purpose of godliness; for bodily discipline is only of little profit, but godliness is profitable for all things, since it holds promise for the present life and also for the life to come" (1 Timothy 4:7–8).

It's obvious that if you are not exercising yourself spiritually, you're not going to be in great spiritual shape. Many of us will give an hour a day to exercise and sweat for our bodies, but we aren't willing to sweat for the kingdom.

The first time kingdom work puts a little bead of sweat on our foreheads, we say, "Christianity is too hard." Of course it is hard. It wasn't supposed to be easy.

But let me tell you, if you sweat long enough and regularly enough, you'll have spiritual energy you didn't have before. You'll be in better shape than you have ever been before. You're going to look better spiritually than you ever have looked because exerting energy burns off fat and builds muscle.

But this does not come about by osmosis. It comes by discipline that transforms both this life and the life to come. It's more important for men to read their Bibles than to read the sports pages. It's more important to hit our knees than to hit a golf ball. It's more important for women to be in the presence of the Savior than to be in the mall.

But this takes discipline. It means saying yes to what is right and no to what is wrong. But people say, "I tried that, and it didn't work," or "I am not a disciplined person," or "I want to, but I don't know how to do it."

### Built-in Discipline

If you've ever said any of those things, I can help you right now! Look at Titus 2:11–13: "For the grace of God has appeared, bringing salvation to all men, instructing us to deny ungodliness and worldly desires and to live sensibly, righteously and godly in the present age, looking for the blessed hope and the appearing of the glory of our great God and Savior, Christ Jesus."

I want to share a spiritual principle here that people in my church told me was transforming once they got hold of it. Here it is: Spiritual discipline is built into the grace of God.

The basic definition of God's grace is His undeserved favor to us. It is God doing for us what we could never do for ourselves.

Now Paul said the grace of God "has appeared." That means it's here. So you say, "I am not a disciplined person." That's all right; grace has taken care of that. Grace will supply the discipline you need.

See how it works? With God's grace, He also supplies whatever you lack in order to get you where He wants you to go. God has already taken your limitations and humanity into account in supplying you with His grace. He knows your weakness and has already calculated that in. You *can* discipline yourself.

So when you say, "I can't," God says, "I have graced you with a supply of spiritual energy to say no to sin and unrighteousness and yes to righteousness." So we can't ever say we can't, because we have grace. It is the Holy Spirit's job to mediate to us the measure of grace we need to move us along toward spiritual maturity as we live in dependence on God. The Holy Spirit is a built-in "power pack" who enables and empowers us to become what God saved us to become. The Spirit's very presence within us is another provision and expression of grace.

## Pursuing a Person

Now if you're still wondering why so many Christians are still saying yes to sin even when God has supplied abundant grace, let me suggest an answer. The reason so many Christians are struggling with spiritual discipline is that they are doing a program rather than pursuing a Person.

When you read your Bible and pray because that's what good Christians ought to do, you are just fulfilling the program. But Jesus didn't die for a program, and neither is a program your Savior. Look back at Titus 2:13. What we should be looking forward to is the appearing of Jesus Christ, not the completion of a program.

Not long ago, I ran into a young woman in our church who had been on a perpetual diet. A lot of us know what that's like. She had tried one program after another. Something would work for a while, and then she would lose her discipline and her enthusiasm.

But the last time I saw her, she had lost a lot of weight. She looked great. I said, "Girl, what happened to you? You must have found the right program."

She said, "No, I found a guy. We started dating and fell in love. And in love he said to me, 'I think you need to lose some weight.'

"I found energy I never had before! It didn't matter what program I was using, because there was someone in my life I wanted to please. I can pass up any food now. Burger King can offer to do it my way, but I don't want it no way! I want to look good for my man."

When you have a passion for a person, you won't have a problem with the program. You won't read the Bible because "a verse a day keeps the Devil away" but because you want to meet the Author. You won't get on your knees because good Christians pray but because you want to talk to your divine Lover.

Pursue Christ as a Person you are in love with, and you will find the grace of God giving you power to pull off the program of God. (See this author's work *Returning to Your First Love*, Moody Publishers, for further discussion on pursuing a relationship with Christ.)

## THE DEMANDS OF DISCIPLESHIP

That leads us to the fourth and final area of discipleship: the demands. If you are going to be a part of the kingdom and carry out the kingdom agenda, you have to meet the demands.

The story is told of a farmer who put an advertisement in the classified section of the newspaper. It read, "Farmer with 160 irrigated acres wants to marry a beautiful woman with a tractor. When replying, please show a picture of the tractor." This farmer didn't want a wife to love, just one to use.

That describes the relationship a lot of Christians have with Christ. They don't really want to deal with the Savior. They just want Him to bring the goodies along. Some Christians only love Christ because of what He can supply.

But Jesus said in Revelation 3:20 that He is standing outside our door, knocking so we will open up and let Him come in and have fellowship with us. Jesus wants you to want Him because you want to be married to Him.

Jesus said in Matthew 6:33, "Seek first His kingdom and His righteousness; and all these things shall be added to you." The risen Christ warned the church in Ephesus, "But I have this against you, that you have left your first love" (Revelation 2:4).

## Putting Jesus First

If this is the kind of intimate fellowship and relationship Christ wants to have with us, we need to ask what it will take to make that a reality.

Paul answered that question in Colossians 1:18 when he said of Jesus, "He is also head of the body, the church; and He is the beginning, the first-born from the dead; so that He Himself might come to have first place in everything."

What does God demand of you if you would be His kingdom disciple? He demands that He be first in everything. Not second, not a close third, but first.

Many of God's people are spiritually anemic because Christ is not first in their lives. They will fit Him in when they have time. If they have a few extra hours on Sunday or a little money at the end of the month or whatever, they'll give Him some.

But if Christ is not first, you lose Him in terms of intimate fellowship. You cannot have the victory He supplies, the power He offers, unless He is first.

## A Transcending Relationship

In Luke 14, Jesus made a difficult statement. He turned to the large crowd that was following Him and said, "If anyone comes to Me [that's discipleship], and does not hate his own father and mother and wife and children and brothers and sisters, yes, and even his own life, he cannot be My disciple" (v. 26).

I think that means Jesus wants to be first! Now when He talked about hating people, He was not talking about your affections. He was talking about your decisions. Let me show you what I mean.

Jesus must be so important to you that He transcends your most intimate relationships. He wants to be more important to you even than *you* are to yourself. You must hate your own life.

The idea is that when you put your love for Jesus next to your love for anyone else, there should be such a big difference that the other love looks like hate. Jesus wants to know that when you have to choose between Him and everyone else, everyone else loses. This is a serious demand.

Jesus also wants to be more important to you than your own comforts. Look at Luke 14:27. "Whoever does not carry his own cross and come after Me cannot be My disciple." You must carry your cross, not Jesus' cross. He took care of His own. You need to carry your cross.

We have some messed-up ideas about what it means to carry our crosses. A physical problem, bad in-laws, or noisy neighbors—none of those things is a cross. So what does it mean to carry your cross?

The Romans invented crucifixion. When the Romans wanted to put a condemned criminal on public display to humiliate him, they paraded him down the street carrying the crossbeam of his cross. Carrying your cross to the place of execution was a public display that you were guilty of the crime you were condemned for.

To carry your cross means to bear the reproach of Jesus Christ. It is to be so identified with Him that when they accuse you of being a Christian, you say, "I am guilty." When someone accuses you of being His disciple, you say, "You got me."

To carry your own cross is to admit publicly that you are guilty of the crime of being committed to Christ, guilty of placing Him first. Guilty!

Carrying your cross is when a girl tells her boyfriend, "I can't sleep with you because I am a Christian." It's when a businessman says, "I can't do that unethical thing, because I am Christ's disciple. I am living by a different agenda." Carrying your cross is dying to yourself and what you want and putting Jesus first.

It's not comfortable to carry a cross. When you admit to the "crime" of being a committed Christian, people may want to punish you. They may want to take out their anger against you. That's not comfortable—but Jesus must be more important than your comfort.

He also must be more important than your possessions. "No one of you can be My disciple who does not give up all his own possessions," Jesus said (Luke 14:33).

This always upsets people. "You mean I have to give up my car, my house, my 'money, honey'?" Yes.

Did you expect me to say no? I say yes, we must give up these things if they become possessions. The problem is not in having something. The problem is in possessing it. To possess it means that I hold on to it so tightly even God can't pry it loose from me.

Some people would gladly give up certain family members. They might even say, "I'll go along with the idea of carrying my cross. But don't be touching my stuff."

A boy once got his hand caught in a vase. His parents kept trying to get it out, but they couldn't pull his hand out of the vase. They told him, "Son, we're going to have to break this vase to get your hand out."

The boy replied, "Mom, would it help if I let go of the penny I'm holding on to?"

You cannot possess your possessions and expect to possess Christ too. It's OK to have things, but you can't let them become possessions, because then they possess you.

## COUNTING THE COST
## OF DISCIPLESHIP

In Luke 14:31–32, Jesus said, in essence, "Count the cost of being a kingdom disciple." He then told about a king who sat down to count the cost of going into battle. Now let me throw you a little twist here. I think we've been preaching and teaching this verse wrong.

This is usually presented as the disciple counting the cost to see whether he or she has what it takes to be a disciple. But the king is the one counting the cost here, not the army. I believe this is God counting the cost of making us His disciples, not our counting the cost of following Him.

In other words, this is the King deciding whether we meet the standard to be in His army. This is the King's measurement of our commitment. Are we the kind of people He can put into the battle and get benefit from?

A teacher who wanted to teach her class a lesson got a big vase and put some rocks in it. Then she poured in gravel to fill in around the rocks.

Then this teacher asked her class, "You saw that I put in rocks, then gravel," and then she said, "Do you know why I did it this way? The lesson is if you don't put the rocks in first, you'll never be able to get them in later."

It's the same way in the spiritual realm. If you don't take care of spiritual things first but instead fill your life with gravel and sand, when you need the rock of Jesus Christ you'll have too much junk in your life to fit Him in anymore.

So we need to take out all the gravel and sand and put the Rock in first. Then we can enjoy whatever else God sends to fill in the crevices. But living by a kingdom agenda demands that we put Jesus first and follow Him as His disciples. (For a detailed discussion on discipleship and spiritual growth, see the author's work *Life Essentials*, Moody Publishers.)

# CHAPTER SEVEN

# The Kingdom Agenda and Your Calling

The thesis of this book is that God is operating His universe by His kingdom agenda. As believers, we are members of His kingdom whose assignment, whose delight, is to "log on" to that agenda and become part of the exciting, eternally significant program God has for the world and for our lives.

One major reason we need to get on board with the kingdom agenda is that our world desperately needs to hear a word from God. This world order, this system that leaves God out, desperately needs a wake-up call.

But we have a problem today—too many decaffeinated Christians. We have far too much Christianity without the caffeine. It looks like coffee, smells like coffee, but it's "unleaded." There's no buzz in it, nothing to wake us up, let alone wake up a spiritually drowsy world.

The reason for this tragedy, I believe, is that too many Christians have not found God's calling for their lives. As a result, they are living ordinary lives. Many of us who are going to experience God for eternity aren't experiencing much of Him in history. We sing the right songs and say the right words, but there is no potency in our performance.

## WHERE'S OUR SENSE OF CALLING?

Too many of us merely exist rather than live as if we are called. We work for a living but never get around to working for a life. We suffer from what I call the "same old same" disease.

Does this ever sound like you? Every morning you get up out of that same old bed. You go to that same old bathroom and look in that same old mirror at that same old face. You go to that same old closet to choose from those same old clothes.

Then you go to that same old table to eat that same old breakfast with that same old spouse. (We'll leave that one right there!) You get up and walk to that same old garage, get in that same old car, head down that same old road to arrive at that same old job. There you do that same old work for that same old pay.

At the end of the day you head back down that same old road, pull into that same old garage, and walk into that same old house to hear that same old noise from those same old kids. You sit down in that same old chair to watch those same old programs on that same old television. Or you read that same old newspaper.

At dinnertime, you pull up to that same old table and eat that same old dinner again from those same old dishes. Then you fall into that same old bed so you can wake up the next day and start that same old routine again.

Where is the sense of calling in a life like that? Where is the sense when you go to bed tonight that you are going to wake up tomorrow on the next leg of a bigger, more exciting journey than you could ever imagine yourself?

That bigger journey is the kingdom of God. The excitement is knowing that you are part of His kingdom agenda. If you settle for anything less than that, you miss God's reason for redeeming you and leaving you here.

My goal in this chapter is to put the caffeine back in your Christian cup—to help you discover God's exciting, energizing, eternally significant call on your life, because only by living out your calling will you maximize your life's potential.

## DEFINING YOUR CALLING

What do we mean by your calling? Let me give you an operating definition of *calling* in terms of God's kingdom agenda.

*Your calling is the divine mission to which God has ordained you and that He has burned into your heart and equipped you to accomplish to bring Him glory and to advance His kingdom.*

You may want to review that definition a time or two before reading on. It's not complicated, but it is foundational to everything we are going to talk about in this chapter.

A divine calling always has to do with God's glory, with fulfilling His kingdom agenda. That means if you and I are not advancing God's kingdom and bringing Him glory, we have not yet found our calling. Let's look at several aspects of a calling that will help to flesh out this definition.

## A Customized Calling

First, God's calling in your life is customized. It is uniquely designed to help you reflect God's purpose for your life. This is why everyone must "work out" his or her own salvation (see Philippians 2:12).

This means that wanting to be like somebody else is not your calling. God only has one of you. If He wanted you to copy someone else, He would have made you that person's identical twin. God has customized His calling for your life so that when you come to the end, you can say you have finished the work God gave you to do (see John 17:4).

If you find your calling—or better yet, if your calling finds you— you never have to worry about death. When it comes time to die, you'll be ready because you have finished the work God left you here to do. It is only when you have not finished your work that you are not ready to die.

## More Than Your Job

Here's another basic principle about your calling. It is more than your job or career. It may include your job, but your calling is not totally synonymous with your job. That's because your calling also includes other areas, such as your marriage and your family, that don't come under the heading of employment. Yet your employment should assist you in fulfilling aspects of your calling.

Paul was a tentmaker, yet his calling was to preach the Word. God may allow you to have a job that fulfills your calling—and in fact, it should. But your calling is more than your job; it is everything that God has in mind for you to bring Him glory and expand His kingdom.

Adam illustrates what I mean. God told him to have dominion over the rest of creation. That was his calling. We can assume that Adam did a number of specific tasks to fulfill that calling, such as tending the garden and naming the animals.

## An Encounter with God

Another thing you need to know about your calling is that it comes only in response to an encounter with the living God.

The biblical character who best exemplifies this is Moses. He's an interesting character because he had fled from Egypt after killing an Egyptian (see Exodus 2:11–15). God would call Moses to lead Israel out of Egypt (see Exodus 3), but for forty years Moses had settled for being a shepherd. He had made some mistakes, he had failed, and he had settled for hanging out with sheep on the backside of a desert.

Moses was an ordinary, "decaffeinated" believer.

So here he was, leading the sheep of his father-in-law, Jethro. (Moses had married Zipporah, an African woman. The Midianites were a north African tribe.) He came to Horeb, "the mountain of God" (Exodus 3:1). Moses was about to encounter God:

> The angel of the Lord appeared to him in a blazing fire from the midst of a
> bush; and he looked, and behold, the bush was burning with fire, yet the
> bush was not consumed. So Moses said, "I must turn aside now, and see
> this marvelous sight, why the bush is not burned up." When the Lord saw
> that he turned aside to look, God called to him from the midst of the bush,
> and said, "Moses, Moses!" And he said, "Here I am." (3:2–4)

If you want to know your calling, don't go "calling-looking." Go God-looking. God knows where He wants you, what He is calling you to do, when He wants you to do it, and how He wants it done. Therefore, if you want to find your calling, look for God. When you find God, His calling will find you.

God's calling for your life, then, will be experienced out of your relationship with Him. If there is no relationship, you will not come to know what your calling is all about.

Moses met God at a burning bush because he came to the mountain where God was hanging out. Now Moses didn't know he was going to meet God that day, but he was in God's presence.

If you want to know your calling, you have to go where God is. If you never have time to go before the face of God, you won't find your calling. If you never have time to spend in God's Word, you won't find your calling. If you never have time to be around the people of God, you will never find your calling.

We spend so much time doing things that may be OK within themselves but rob us of time in God's presence. When you encounter God, He will lead you to your calling. Your calling finds you when you find God.

I can vouch for that. As a young man I was minding my own business playing football, which is all I ever wanted to do. God found me at an evangelistic crusade when B. Sam Hart came to Baltimore. The next thing I knew I was there under the tent, asking God, "What do You want me to do?"

I was already a Christian, but I was a contented Christian, a comfortable Christian, doing my thing. But when God found me that day and called me into His service, He set into motion a series of events that would detour me radically from the direction I wanted to go. My calling found me because I was in God's presence.

At the burning bush, Moses saw God in a unique way. It was an ordinary bush, but it wasn't an ordinary day. When God shows up any old bush will do, because when God shows up, He turns the ordinary into the extraordinary. That's the essence of a calling—when God shows up in your life in an extraordinary way.

When I was under that tent, it was as if nobody else was under that tent but God and me. It was as if God called my name and pointed at me, although I didn't hear any voice. I knew that day that God was calling me into His service.

It was just an ordinary tent and an ordinary day, but it was an extraordinary moment in my life. I heard God's call because I was listening to His Word.

## THE PERSON BEFORE THE CALLING

God was about to give Moses his calling. But Moses did not get God's program until he responded to God's Person. The person precedes the program. Relationship precedes the calling.

This principle of a kingdom calling ought to sound familiar, because we touched on it in the previous chapter. Now I want to look at that lesson again through the lens of Moses' calling.

It's not enough to get on your knees and say, "Lord, show me my calling; show me Your program," when your relationship with Him is in disrepair. If you don't relate to His Person, God won't trust you with His program.

Have you ever tried to go out on a date with your spouse when the two of you aren't getting along? You are in for a miserable evening trying to accomplish a program when the relationship is ruptured. When the relationship is repaired, the program is a lot easier and a lot sweeter. God doesn't want you showing up only when you want something from Him. He wants an ongoing relationship with you.

## A Biblical Example

Luke 10:38–42 is a textbook example of what I'm talking about. It's the story of Martha and Mary and a dinner for Jesus.

Martha had a program to accomplish. She was cooking dinner for Jesus and the apostles—twelve preachers and her Lord. And she was getting upset because Mary was more interested in the person. She was sitting at Jesus' feet.

So here's Martha, cooking fried chicken—the gospel bird—for these preachers. Sweat is running down her face, and Mary is nowhere to be found. Martha goes and looks in the den, and there Mary is, sitting at Jesus' feet.

Martha blew a fuse and said, "Lord, do You not care that my sister has left me to do all the serving alone? Then tell her to help me [because I'm not talking to her right now]" (my paraphrase of v. 40).

Jesus said, "Martha, Martha."

Watch out whenever Jesus calls your name twice!

He said, "Martha, Martha, you are worried and bothered about so many things; but only a few things are necessary, really only one, for Mary has chosen the good part, which shall not be taken away from her" (Luke 10:41–42).

Jesus was saying, "Martha, a casserole will do. Just cook one dish; then come sit at My feet. Mary has chosen to make Me more important than your cooking program. She is better off out here with Me than you are there in the kitchen."

Jesus knew that if He sent Mary into the kitchen with Martha, He would have two frustrated, sweaty women on His hands. But if Mary stayed with Him, He would have somebody whose life was together.

I'll say it again. God wants a relationship with you before He is willing to give you His program.

## A Personalized Commitment

Once you get the Person ahead of the program, you get a personalized calling.

Notice back in Exodus 3 that Jesus called Moses by name. Moses' call came out of a personal commitment. Two of my favorite verses in the Bible are about this kind of commitment, and they're found in Romans 12:1–2:

> *I urge you therefore, brethren, by the mercies of God, to present your bodies*
> *a living and holy sacrifice, acceptable to God, which is your spiritual service*
> *of worship. And do not be conformed to this world, but be transformed by the*
> *renewing of your mind, that you may prove what the will of God is, that*
> *which is good and acceptable and perfect.*

These verses are saying the same thing we have been talking about. Paul said if you are going to know God's will for your life, your calling in the kingdom, then God must own all of you.

See, God is not impressed with a two-hour visit on Sunday. He wants to own your life. He wants to be in charge.

Paul said, "Present your bodies a living . . . sacrifice." That's an oxymoron; sacrifices were put to death. How can you be a living dead thing?

Paul explained in another of my favorite verses. "I have been crucified with Christ; and it is no longer I who live, but Christ lives in me; and the life which I now live in the flesh I live by faith in the Son of God, who loved me, and delivered Himself up for me" (Galatians 2:20).

Paul considered himself a living dead person, because he was dead to his own life and his plans and alive to God's. So if you asked, "Paul, what are your dreams?" he would say, "I don't know. Dead people don't dream."

"Paul, what are your goals?"

"I don't know. Dead people don't set goals."

"Paul, what about your future?"

"Dead people don't have a future."

But if you changed the question and asked, "Paul, what about God's goal for you?" he would say, "We can talk about that!" Paul had defined the totality of his life through his commitment to Jesus Christ. That's why you couldn't intimidate him.

People came to Paul one day and said, "Paul, we are going to kill you."

He answered, "That's cool. For me, to die is gain."

"All right, we're going to let you live."

"That's cool too. For me, to live is Christ."

"Well, since you're so cool about everything, we are going to beat you and make you suffer."

"That's also cool, because I consider that the suffering of this present time is not worthy to be compared with the glory that shall be revealed in me." (See Romans 8:18; Philippians 1:21.) You couldn't intimidate this guy. It didn't matter to Paul what happened to him. It was all Christ to him.

## THE CERTAINTY OF YOUR CALLING

Why does God want the totality of your life before He shows you your calling?

We have an answer in John 7:16–17, where Jesus said, "My teaching is not Mine, but His who sent Me. If any man is willing to do His will, he shall know of the teaching, whether it is of God, or whether I speak from Myself."

You must be willing to do God's will before you know His will. Many of us say to God, "Show me what You want me to do, and I will let You know whether I am into that or not. Let me know the plan, and I will tell You whether I plan to do it."

### No Negotiation

No, no. God's plan is not up for negotiation. God is only going to reveal your calling to you when you are committed to doing it ahead of time. God will not negotiate His will.

As Romans 12:1–2 says, you must give all of yourself to God and none of yourself to the world system that wants independence from God.

God says if we conform to this world, He will not reveal His calling for our lives. We must say, as Moses said to God at the burning bush, "Here I am" (Exodus 3:4). In other words, "What do You want of me, Lord? I am ready to obey."

### Saving and Losing Your Life

In Mark 8:34–36, Jesus made one of the most profoundly important statements in all of Scripture:

*If anyone wishes to come after Me, let him deny himself, and take up his cross, and follow Me. For whoever wishes to save his life shall lose it; but whoever loses his life for My sake and the gospel's shall save it. For what does it profit a man to gain the whole world, and forfeit his soul?*

We have already talked about what it means to deny yourself and carry your cross. Here, Jesus adds the teaching about saving and losing your life.

How do you save your life yet lose it? By going after the world. When you do that you forfeit your life, because life consists of more than the stuff you accumulate.

Many people have a house but no longer have a home. Many people have money but don't have peace. Many people have plans but don't have any purpose. This principle of saving and losing your life is fixed. It's another way of saying you can't find God's calling for your life when you're busy trying to save it by gaining the world.

Giving yourself totally to God is giving Him full power over your life. When you do that, you begin to live! When I committed my life to God's calling for me at the age of eighteen, I had no idea what God had in mind.

All I knew was, "Whatever You want me to do, Lord, however You want me to do it, wherever You want it done, I am Your slave." Then the Holy Ghost took over, and God began unfolding a series of events that has brought me to this point.

Jesus says the way to find your life is to lose it for His sake. When you do that, God will reveal your calling to you, and the puzzle of life will begin to come together.

My oldest daughter, Chrystal, was the puzzle lady when she was younger. She was always putting puzzles together. One day I brought home a one-thousand piece puzzle. Chrystal was excited.

She took the puzzle, went to her room, but came back a couple of hours later mad at me. "Daddy, why did you buy me this puzzle? It has too many pieces!"

Life is like that. It has too many pieces. If you try to put them together by yourself, you will only frustrate yourself. It you want to put the pieces of your life together, God must own you. If you want to see His calling for you made clear, you must be willing to yield your life to Him.

But you may say, "It's too late for me to find God's calling, Tony. I've already made too many mistakes."

Well, Moses was a murderer. I seriously doubt if you've ever killed anyone, yet God still met Moses at the burning bush. God transformed Moses and called him into His service to accomplish His will.

## GETTING STARTED ON YOUR CALLING

So now that we've defined a kingdom agenda calling and tried to put it into proper biblical perspective, how do you get started finding and fulfilling your calling? Let's talk about these two final areas in turn.

### Work Out Your Salvation

Philippians 2:12–13 is another of those seminal passages for understanding the call of God on your life. Paul wrote, "Work out your salvation with fear and trembling; for it is God who is at work in you, both to will and to work for His good pleasure."

Notice first that you have something to do when it comes to discerning God's call. You can't live off what your mother did for the Lord. You can't make it on Daddy's faith. You need to find the calling of God for your life.

Others can certainly help you in the process. Get all the information you can. But then you go on your face before God, asking Him to show you what He wants you to do. You cannot piggyback on another believer to find your calling.

### God at Work in You

But notice what else Paul said here. Your work will not be in vain because God is also at work in you.

Paul was not talking about working to become a Christian. You can't *work* to become a Christian. But once you are saved by the grace of God, He works *in* you in order to work *through* you.

So you are at work, and God is at work. Your responsibility is to commit yourself to God and seek His will.

You don't just wake up one morning and find your calling. You have to go through the process. But God meets you in the process.

### The Need to Respond

Let's go back to Moses again. He has seen an extraordinary sight:

A bush is burning, yet it is not consumed.

Read Exodus 3:3–4 again and you'll notice that when Moses stopped to look at the bush, God called to him. God didn't call him until Moses responded.

If you don't respond to what God shows you, He won't show you any more. If you don't respond to the little light He gives you, don't ask for a lot of light.

One day I gave my younger son, Jonathan, three dollars for lunch money. He lost it, so he came to me and said, "Daddy, I need five dollars for lunch."

There was something wrong here. I had given him three dollars, and he had lost it. But instead of asking me for three dollars again, he wanted five dollars. He wanted back the money that he lost—and a bonus!

You cannot waste what God gives you and then ask Him for more. Many of us go before the face of God wanting big stuff, when we have not yet said yes to the little things He has commanded us to do.

God won't be used that way. If God cannot trust us to respond correctly with what He gives us, we don't need to be asking Him for more.

We pray, "Lord, lead me in my career; show me the calling that You have for me. Give me direction in my life."

God's response is, "Are you willing to look at the bush?"

The biblical principle is this: "Whoever has, to him shall more be given; and whoever does not have, even what he thinks he has shall be taken away from him" (Luke 8:18). That's what Jesus said.

So do not shun God when He speaks to your heart, because He is preparing to take you to the next level.

## The Need for Humility

Moses responded, and then he heard the call. God's voice came from the midst of the bush, "Do not come near here; remove your sandals from your feet, for the place on which you are standing is holy ground" (Exodus 3:5).

Why did Moses have to take off his sandals? Because when you are standing in the presence of God, even a quarter-inch of leather is too high. When you come into His presence, you go as low as you can possibly get.

God demands humility if He is going to show you your calling in His kingdom. As long as you can do it all by yourself, you don't need God.

But He wants you to come before Him humbly. When you approach Him with your spiritual shoes off, admitting that you have no reason to be elevated in His sight, God will speak to you. He will lead you into your call, the mission He has divinely ordained for your life.

Let me show you how Moses' forty years of learning humility in the desert changed things for him when it came to God's calling. As Moses stood before the bush, God told him, in essence, "I am going to deliver My people Israel from Egypt, and I am sending you to Pharaoh to be their deliverer" (see Exodus 3:7–10).

Moses' response was, "Who am I, that I should go to Pharaoh, and that I should bring the sons of Israel out of Egypt?" (v.11).

Forty years earlier, Moses would have said, "You got it, Lord. Pharaoh doesn't know who he is dealing with. I am the man. I'm going to go and take God along with me, and we're going to wipe out Pharaoh." But Moses had been humbled. Now he wasn't so sure of himself.

Let me tell you a secret. God will do whatever it takes to humble you and me, even if it hurts. The hound of heaven will dog you until He humbles you, because God hates nothing more than pride. So Moses, the formerly proud man, said, "Who, me?"

## FULFILLING YOUR CALLING

Now we have a small problem. Moses has humbled himself, he has responded to God, and God has revealed Moses' calling to him.

But Moses is overwhelmed by what God is asking him to do, and he begins to back off. He feels inadequate. In Exodus 3:13, Moses asks, "I am going to the sons of Israel, and I shall say to them, 'The God of your fathers has sent me to you.' Now they may say to me, 'What is His name?' What shall I say to them?"

### A Powerful Provision

What a great answer God gave Moses: "'I AM WHO I AM'; and He said, 'Thus you shall say to the sons of Israel, "I AM has sent me to you"'" (v. 14).

That's a very powerful phrase. "I AM WHO I AM" is the personal name of God, the one we transliterate as *Yahweh*. Notice that the name is in the present tense. This is the personal God who is ever in the present tense.

Now, whenever you or I say, "I am," that only covers today. If we were talking about yesterday, we would have to say, "I was." And if we were talking about tomorrow, we would have to say, "I will be."

But not God. He is never "I was," or "I will be." He is "I AM." God has no past, no beginning. And He has no future, no ending. Everything is in the eternal present with Him.

This name means that God is self-existent and self-sufficient. When God wants help, He looks to Himself. When God wants praise, He looks to Himself. He invites us to praise Him, but He doesn't need it. When God wants to do something, He looks to Himself. He is the "self-energizer." He just keeps going and going and going. He is the great I AM.

God is saying to Moses, "You can fulfill your calling because I AM your sufficiency. I AM whatever you need. If you need a miracle, I AM your miracle. If you need help, I AM your help. If you need power, I AM your power. If you need strength, I AM your strength. I AM whatever you need."

## In Good Company

Moses is in good company here. The Bible is full of stories of men and women who were called by God to do difficult and even impossible things and found the great I AM to be sufficient.

The patriarch Joseph was called. But his calling didn't mean an easy life. He was sold into slavery in Egypt by his brothers. He was falsely accused by the wife of his Egyptian master. He was thrown into jail and languished there for years.

But if Joseph were here today, he would repeat the testimony he gave his brothers in Genesis 50:20: "You meant evil against me, but God meant it for good." God empowered Joseph to fulfill his calling, which ultimately was to save his family from death.

If John Mark were here, he would tell you about God's sufficiency to fulfill his calling. John Mark went out with Paul as an associate in the ministry, but he did a Benedict Arnold. He quit and went home when the going got tough.

Paul said, "I can't use John Mark anymore. He might go left on me." But Barnabas stepped in and gave John Mark another chance to do God's work (see Acts 15:36–40). And even though John Mark had messed up, he found grace from the Lord and became a valuable worker, even to Paul (see 2 Timothy 4:11).

John Mark—we know him just as Mark—got a second chance on

his calling, and he made good on it. So good that there's a book in the Bible that bears his name.

There was a woman called of God whose name was Esther. She was a Jewish beauty living in the Persian Empire. King Ahasuerus took one look at her and said, "Mm, mm. Girl, where have you been all my life?" So Esther became his new favorite queen.

Esther's people were exiles in Persia, and their enemy, Haman, was getting ready to annihilate them. It was time for Esther to discover her calling from God.

See, we might think God made Esther pretty so she would look good to herself in a mirror. No, God made Esther pretty so the king would choose her and marry her and establish her as his favorite wife. That way, when Haman got set to carry out the slaughter of every Jew in Persia, God would have somebody in the kingdom He could use to call for mercy on behalf of His people.

Esther's Jewish relative Mordecai knew she had been called. When Esther seemed reluctant to approach the king about her people's impending peril, Mordecai told her, "Who knows whether you have not attained royalty for such a time as this?" (Esther 4:14).

In modern terminology, Mordecai was saying, "Girl, God didn't make you pretty just to win a beauty contest. He made you pretty so you could save your people." Esther saw her kingdom calling, swallowed her fear, went to Ahasuerus with her plea, and saved the Jews from being wiped out.

The apostle Peter was called, but he denied the Lord three times. He had to get "recalled" three times into God's service (see John 21:15–17), and that time he didn't fail.

## It's God's Call

If you know Jesus Christ as Savior, God has a calling for you today.

You say, "But I don't know what my calling is." That's all right. Just go to the Caller and tell Him you're ready to be the "callee," and He will reveal your calling when it is time for you to know it. It's His call, after all.

The story is told that legendary baseball umpire Bill Klem was working behind home plate one day when a runner came sliding into home amid a huge cloud of dust. The catcher slapped the tag on the runner, and Klem jumped up to make the call.

But Klem hesitated for a second, and everyone started hollering.

The runner and his team started yelling that he was safe. The catcher and his team screamed that the runner was out. The players all crowded around Klem, yelling, "Safe!" "Out!" "Safe!" "Out!"

Klem, who was known for running a game with an iron hand, growled back, "He ain't nothing until I say what he is!"

Bill Klem was right. The call belongs to the one who is in charge. Your responsibility is to be available to God when He wants to call you. As you trust in Him instead of your own understanding (see Proverbs 3:5), He will show you step-by-step, moment by moment, what you are supposed to do and where you are supposed to do it.

I don't know what God has called you to do. But I know He wants you to come to Him and say, "Whatever You call me to do, I will do. You make the call." Do that, and then hang on for the greatest adventure of your life.

# The Kingdom Agenda
# and Your Mind

One disease becomes more unsettling to me every time I hear about it—Alzheimer's disease. Somehow, this disease causes the mind to deteriorate in such a way that the victim loses the power to think clearly and control what he or she does.

Alzheimer's sufferers become incapacitated. They lose their ability to remember and recognize familiar people and things. As the disease advances, the victim's mind loses the ability to tell the body what to do and how to function.

So the person who develops Alzheimer's is at the mercy of another person. Someone else must feed and clothe and lead the patient. One reason Alzheimer's is so terrible is that it tends to have a dehumanizing effect on its victims. The reality is that when the mind goes, virtually everything else goes with it.

## THE NEED FOR A KINGDOM MIND

A lot of believers are suffering from spiritual Alzheimer's. This malady manifests itself in a deterioration of the proper application of the mind of Christ—what we are going to call a kingdom mind—that should be operating in every believer's life. The result is a life that is no longer under Christ's control.

I remember when I was growing up, if I had done something that was unacceptable, my mother would say, "Boy, use your head for something other than a hat rack."

She was telling me to put my mind in gear. A Christian who suffers from spiritual Alzheimer's loses the ability to apply a spiritual mind to his daily life. He forgets how to think in terms of a kingdom agenda. He develops a secular mind, and when someone has a secular mind he will do secular things and develop secular habits.

A believer with a secular mind will begin to view the Christian life as impossible. He will feel that he can never meet God's holy standards. He will throw in the towel and say, "I can't" when God says, "You must." He will be at the mercy of this world's system.

We need to talk about the mind in relation to God's kingdom agenda because if we can get our minds working properly, our bodies will follow suit.

Your greatest problem, and mine, is not what we do. Our greatest problem is the way we think. In order to transform what we do, we must first transform how we think. In the words of the writer of Proverbs, "As [a person] thinks within himself, so he is" (Proverbs 23:7).

The mind is the key to our entire being, which is why the great challenge for us today is to develop a kingdom mentality: a way of thinking that is in concert with the kingdom of which we have become a part. I want to discuss four things that have to do with cultivating a kingdom mind.

## THE NECESSITY OF A KINGDOM MIND

The first thing we need to understand is the *necessity* of having a kingdom mind.

I would begin by reminding you of Isaiah 55:8, a verse we shared in an earlier chapter. It is very relevant to our topic here, so I'll give it to you again: "'My thoughts are not your thoughts, neither are your ways My ways,' declares the Lord." How far apart are the two? As far as heaven is from earth (see v. 9)!

### A Different Way of Thinking

Because God is transcendent and distinct from His creation, His way of approaching and analyzing an issue is not going to be your way.

That's why you need to develop the mind of the King. You need a kingdom mentality, a kingdom way of thinking, so that you can get God's mind on the issues of your life. Whether we are talking about marriage, sex, money, children, or any other issue, God's thinking on the subject will be different than the way this world thinks about it.

## Making the Difference

Your ability and your decision to develop a kingdom mind will also determine whether you taste victory or defeat in your daily spiritual life. Paul wrote in Romans 8:

> Those who are according to the flesh set their minds on the things of the flesh, but those who are according to the Spirit, the things of the Spirit. For the mind set on the flesh is death, but the mind set on the Spirit is life and peace, because the mind set on the flesh is hostile toward God; for it does not subject itself to the law of God, for it is not even able to do so. (vv. 5–7)

Where you set your mind will determine whether you have victory or defeat in life. What you sow in your mind will come out through your mouth, your hands, your feet. The body will express what is in the mind.

That's why we need to begin by dealing with the way we think. If we can transform our thoughts and bring our minds under the authority of Christ, we have laid the foundation for transforming our actions.

The importance of setting our minds on the things of Christ can be illustrated by what happens when we watch TV. What do we often tell ourselves when we sit down to watch TV "I'm tired. I want to give my mind a break, so I'll just 'veg out' and watch TV because I don't want to have to think."

But the problem is, we don't turn off our minds when we watch TV. The tube has a way of putting things in our minds and determining the way we think. TV is not neutral stuff for the mind. It programs the minds of those who stare at it for hours.

What draws us toward Christ will change the way we act, and what pulls us away from Christ will do the same. We can only live as Christ wants us to live when we think as He thinks. That means cultivating a kingdom mind.

## The Key to God's Will

When you develop a kingdom mind, then you will begin experiencing God's will for your life, His calling for you (see the discussion of Romans 12:2 in the previous chapter). God reveals His will to our minds.

If you want to know God's will, you need to give God your mind. He must be able to control your thought waves. The mind is to the soul what the brain is to the body—the control center.

So if I am acting like a fool, it's because I'm thinking like a fool. The same is true if I am acting ignorantly. And if I am acting "kingdomly," carrying out a kingdom agenda, it's because I am thinking with a kingdom mind.

When Lois and I first met, she didn't like me that much. But I saw her and liked her. Besides, she was cooking fried chicken that day. So I thought we had a very, very good start!

But she didn't like me. I was trying to talk to her, and she wouldn't halfway talk. She was acting hard to get and all that kind of stuff. But she didn't know who she was messing with! I knew I had to get into her mind.

So I pulled out all that ancient rap I knew from the streets of Baltimore, and I poured it on Lois. I was rapping and trying to charm her and just making up all kinds of stuff.

I remember one time we went for a walk near Lois's house and stood at a seawall with the ocean slapping up against it. It was evening, and the stars were out. I was naming stars, making up constellations, just rappin' to try to impress Lois. I remember pointing to one star and saying, "That star is probably sitting over my hometown of Baltimore, Maryland, right now."

I should be embarrassed to tell you all of this! I had no idea what I was talking about. But despite that, my relationship with Lois went from her thinking *I don't like him* to *He's all right*. So I messed with her mind a little bit more.

Then we moved from *He's all right* to *He's not that bad*. The next stage was *I kind of like him*. Then it was *I am in love with him*, and from there it was *I've got to have him*. When I got her mind I got her, and she's been by my side ever since.

My point is, when you change the mind, you can change the emotions and the actions.

So if you really want to think like God thinks, to live in victory, and to know God's will, fix your mind first. A kingdom mind is indispensable to a kingdom life.

## THE NATURE OF A KINGDOM MIND

What does a kingdom mind look like? Let's put the question under the microscope of Scripture and discover the nature of a mind that operates by a kingdom mentality:

> *Things which eye has not seen and ear has not heard,*
> *And which have not entered the heart of man,*
> *All that God has prepared for those who love Him.*
> *For to us God revealed them through the Spirit; . . . For who among men*
> *knows the thoughts of a man except the spirit of the man, which is in him?*
> *Even so the thoughts of God no one knows except the Spirit of God.*
> *(1 Corinthians 2:9–11)*

### Outside Human Limitations

Here's the first thing Paul said about a kingdom mind. It can grasp things that are outside the normal limitations of the human senses because it is illuminated by God's Spirit. God can deal with kingdom-thinking people in realms beyond what the eyes can see and the ears can hear.

In fact, when God takes possession of your mind the way He wants to and gives you a kingdom mentality, He can reveal stuff to you that would never enter a human mind left to itself.

All the good things God has prepared for us in this life are beyond our senses. His kingdom agenda reaches beyond what we can perceive or think. God sits outside of our human senses. So the mind set on Christ is not limited to what can be measured by the senses.

That doesn't mean God ignores or bypasses your human senses. What it does mean is that what you see, hear, feel, etc., is not all there is. What you think is not all there is.

There's a very good reason that the person with a kingdom mind is not bound by human limitations. It's called *revelation*. First Corinthians 2:10 says that we know the things of God because He has revealed them to us. Revelation gives us the "glasses" we need to see what is otherwise too far away for us.

Recently, I had to pay a visit to the eye doctor. I had been noticing that while I could see things clearly if they were up close, things in the distance were getting blurry. I suspected it was time for some visual assistance, so I went to see the optometrist. He confirmed my diagnosis.

Without the divine "visual assistance" called revelation, the kingdom would be very blurry for us. It wouldn't come into clear focus. Without the mind of Christ, we would live our lives only by what we see up close.

We need assistance to help us see life as it really is, so we can think kingdom thoughts and live kingdom lives.

## A Divine Viewpoint

A kingdom mind is not only outside of human limitations. It also functions the very opposite of the way a natural, or unsaved, mind functions. Paul continued in 1 Corinthians 2:

> But a natural man does not accept the things of the Spirit of God; for they are foolishness to him, and he cannot understand them, because they are spiritually appraised. But he who is spiritual appraises all things, yet he himself is appraised by no man. (vv. 14–15)

When I talk about a kingdom mind, I am talking about a mind that looks at all of reality from a spiritual or divine viewpoint. A person with a kingdom mind views life through the "glasses" of the Holy Spirit.

You have probably seen people who wear sunglasses as a fashion accent, for style only. They even have a way of putting on their shades that tells you they are merely styling when they wear them.

I'm afraid that some believers come to church for style. They're looking the part, but their divine glasses are just a fashion accent. They're not operating with a kingdom mind, so they're not pursuing a kingdom agenda.

Carrying your Bible under your arm doesn't guarantee you a kingdom mind. Neither does going through religious rituals. You know you have a kingdom mind when you sift all of your decisions through a divine mind-set.

When you have a kingdom mind and you face a decision, you raise certain questions. What does Christ think about this? How would He react to this? What does Christ want me to do here? Operating with a spiritual mentality links you up to God's "Internet" so you can tap into His thinking on your decision.

This is diametrically opposed to the way the unsaved think. Paul tells us the natural person thinks spiritual things are foolishness. The unsaved person ridicules the things of the Spirit because he cannot understand them. He doesn't have the antenna to receive them.

But since the natural mind is not our focus here, let's talk about believers. Even we who have the antenna to receive the things of the Spirit can have technical problems. And if we don't fix the problem, we can waste a lot of time and cause ourselves a lot of frustration fiddling with the wrong thing.

We were having problems with our television reception some years ago. I fooled with the buttons on the set, trying to get a good picture. I looked at the directions that came with the TV. But no matter what I did, I couldn't get clear reception.

The reason is that I was starting in the wrong place. My problem was not with the TV but on my roof. The repairman I had to call told me that my antenna had been knocked around by a recent storm. It needed to be turned back toward the signal.

Now that helped a lot, but it didn't completely fix the trouble because, as the man told me, I had a second problem. Our house is in a gully amid lots of tall trees.

The trees were interfering with the signal, so the repairman had to put an extension on our antenna to lift it above the interference so it could receive the signal clearly. Once he turned and raised the antenna, the picture was fine.

Maybe you can see where I'm heading with this. It's easy to fiddle with the buttons in our lives, trying to get a clear picture of this thing called life.

But that's starting in the wrong place. Until the antenna of your mind is turned toward the divine signal, messing with the other stuff in your life won't help. That signal is coming from a King who has a kingdom agenda for you, and when you get that signal straight, life's picture will clear up.

You say, "But, Tony, I'm really trying to develop a kingdom mind. I really believe I have my antenna turned in the right direction, but the signal doesn't seem to be coming through."

Then maybe you've got too many trees around you blocking the reception. Daily stuff like a job, finances, family problems, houses that need paint, and cars that need tires can grow up and crowd out God's signal. The answer is not to cut down the trees but to raise your antenna above them.

If you will get your mind tuned to the divine signal and lifted up above the "trees" of circumstances and other people, you will get the right picture, the divine viewpoint.

Now you can see why the unsaved person can't do either one of these things. He doesn't even have an antenna. But the problem is not just ignorance. According to Romans 1:18–23, unsaved people have corrupted their minds on purpose.

They know the truth, but they suppress it so they can sin. Genesis 6:5 says that just before the flood, every thought of men's minds was totally wicked. So God gave the unsaved over to a "depraved mind" (Romans 1:28).

## The Mind of Christ

What a contrast we see back in 1 Corinthians 2:16: "But we have the mind of Christ."

At conversion, you got a new mind. A new "diskette" with a new program on it was inserted into your soul through the life-giving work of the Holy Spirit.

But some of us have been so used to running the old program that we have problems getting the new program installed and running. The solution is to make sure your spirit is plugged into God's Spirit.

Now remember, we're not talking about salvation. We're talking about living like the kingdom people we are. Here's what I mean.

In 1 Corinthians 2:11, Paul asked, "Who among men knows the thoughts of a man except the spirit of the man, which is in him? Even so the thoughts of God no one knows except the Spirit of God." Then he said in verse 12, "Now we have received, not the spirit of the world, but the Spirit who is from God."

The idea is this: Since no one knows God's thoughts like God's Spirit, and no one knows your thoughts like your spirit, the key is to link your spirit with God's Spirit.

To put it another way, if you want your thoughts to be saturated with God's thoughts, then your spirit has to be in tune with His Spirit so that His thoughts are transferred to your thoughts.

Now, I'm not advocating some sort of mind transference. I'm talking about the way the mind of Christ is made real to you. As we said above, God wants to tie you in to His "Internet" so you can actually "download" His thinking into your life through the linkage of the Holy Spirit.

This is not automatic. It will take discipline and effort, but you can develop the mind of Christ that is in you by virtue of your salvation and the indwelling Holy Spirit.

## THE BATTLE FOR YOUR MIND

The third point I want to make about a kingdom mind is that it is a battleground. Satan is battling for your mind, not your body. Why? Because he knows that whoever wins the mind wins the body. The mind controls the body.

### Building Fortresses

If you are a Christian, Satan has already lost the war for your mind. You belong to Christ, and you will forever. But Satan can still mess you up and win a lot of battles against you by building fortresses (the King James Version translates it "strongholds") in your mind:

> For though we walk in the flesh, we do not war according to the flesh, for
> the weapons of our warfare are not of the flesh, but divinely powerful for the
> destruction of fortresses. We are destroying speculations and every lofty thing
> raised up against the knowledge of God, and we are taking every thought
> captive to the obedience of Christ. (2 Corinthians 10:3–5)

A fortress is a partition Satan can build in our minds to block spiritual thoughts and messages from invading them. It's a "lofty thing" that the Enemy raises up, a wall that Satan uses to divide your mind and block the will of God from penetrating your thinking. Then you live in spiritual defeat instead of victory.

Now, the person you would least expect to have this kind of problem was the apostle Paul. Yet he struggled with a fortress in his mind.

Paul shared his struggle with us in Romans 7 so that we might experience his problem as well as his victory. You can read the chapter for yourself, but I want you to see how Paul closes it:

> Wretched man that I am! Who will set me free from the body of this death?
> Thanks be to God through Jesus Christ our Lord! So then, on the one
> hand I myself with my mind am serving the law of God, but on the other,
> with my flesh the law of sin. (vv. 24–25)

Do you see Paul's struggle? His regenerated mind wanted to serve God, but his flesh wanted to serve sin. We said the flesh, or sin, principle that contaminates the body is controlled by the mind, so what Paul was talking about is a battle in his mind.

We will face the same battle, with Satan coming at us using one of three strategies.

## Three Strategies of Attack

*One way Satan builds his fortresses in our minds is by keeping us enslaved to the past.* You could probably go into any church in America and get a large response by asking for a show of hands of those who are still dealing today with something that happened yesterday or even years ago.

David prayed, "Do not remember the sins of my youth or my transgressions" (Psalm 25:7). We could pray the same about the sins of others committed against us.

You may have been messed over by a parent, and that abuse is ruining your life today even though that parent may be dead and gone. It could be your own past sin that is haunting you. Whatever the particulars, Satan is trying to use them to construct a fortress in your mind.

It may not be the sins of yesterday that are messing you up. *A second strategy of Satan is to lead you into sin today.* He often makes sin look pleasing enough that we plan to commit it. If you are caught up in some sin that has a controlling influence over your life, you are giving Satan enough material to build a huge fortress.

*A third battle strategy Satan uses is to get you fantasizing about sinning in the future.* These are the hidden sins because nobody knows about them but you. But they are played out in the mind.

In the Sermon on the Mount, Jesus said that if we fantasize about killing someone or committing adultery, from God's perspective, it's the same as if we committed the act (see Matthew 5:21–22, 27–28).

The point is that God not only wants to fix what you do, He wants to fix what you *think* about doing. He wants to deal with your fantasies.

That's a tough threesome, isn't it? None of us can go through that list and come away unscathed. Satan knows where to attack each one of us, but we have divine weapons that are capable of tearing down Satan's fortresses.

What God wants us to do is take every thought captive to Christ (see 2 Corinthians 10:5). Christ wants to control and possess our minds so that every thought we have is dictated by Him, dominated by Him, and directed toward Him. That's thinking with a kingdom mind.

## DEVELOPING A KINGDOM MIND

You say, "OK, Tony, I know I need to control my thought life. I know I need to bring my mind into obedience to Christ. I know I need to be renewed in my mind, to think with the mind of Christ. How do I do that?"

I want to answer that question for you from Colossians 3, a powerful chapter to conclude with because it talks about developing a kingdom mentality.

### Set Your Mind on Christ

First, you must set your mind on Christ. Colossians 3:1–2 says:

*If then you have been raised up with Christ, keep seeking the things above, where Christ is, seated at the right hand of God. Set your mind on the things above, not on the things that are on the earth.*

We talked earlier about the importance of setting our minds on the things of Christ. I want to come back to this because it is so foundational to having a kingdom mind.

Where you set your mind is so important because what you set your mind on will penetrate and dominate your thinking. Remember our illustration about what happens when you watch television? It is penetrating your thinking even when you don't think it is.

If Christ is not penetrating and dominating your thinking, then His power will not be available to you.

Setting your mind on Christ requires dedicated, sustained effort and discipline. You say, "Well, I go to church every Sunday. Isn't that good enough?"

Let me answer this way. Suppose you were to go to a cafeteria for dinner tonight. You come to the meat section and order a steak and mounds of mashed potatoes smothered in gravy. Then you get a helping of macaroni and cheese with extra cheese. And you make sure to get plenty of bread and real butter.

Next are the desserts. You get several pieces of pie à la mode and bread pudding with extra sauce.

Do you get the picture? You're carrying this high-calorie, high-fat dinner on your tray. Then, when you come to the drinks, you order a Diet Coke!

That Diet Coke may help to ease your conscience about eating all that fattening food, but that's about all it will do.

Some folks use church the same way. They want "diet worship" on Sunday after getting fat on the world all week. They come to church, saying, "Give me something to offset all this junk I have been eating all week long."

Never mind that they have been thinking junk, hanging out with junk, walking with junk, talking junk, and looking at junk all week. They want to get a diet drink on Sunday, hoping it will cancel out all the junk.

Well, I have bad news for any Christian who is a "junk-food junkie": "Diet church" on Sunday won't solve your problem. If you want to develop a kingdom mind, you must set your mind on the King and His things.

You must say, "Dear Jesus, help me to take every opportunity You give me today to think Your thoughts, to include You in my decisions, to meditate on You, to bring You to bear on my life. I need You to dominate my very brain waves today."

The Bible says that when strife occurred between the servants of Abraham and Lot, Abraham gave Lot his choice of land. Lot chose Sodom because he saw the good land and business opportunities there (see Genesis 13:10–12). Abraham took Canaan. He settled for less but wound up with more because he had set his mind to follow the Lord.

You must focus on your identity in Christ, your relationship with Christ. You're not just dropping His name but living the way Paul described in Colossians 3:3: "You have died and your life is hidden with Christ in God." He added in verse 4 that Christ is our life.

If your mind is not set on Christ, then you are not treating Him as though He *is* your life. How do you know whether Christ is your life? Well, when people start talking about the most important thing or person in their lives, they get a gleam in their eye. They get excited, because now they are talking about the thing that controls and dominates their thoughts.

God called David a man after His own heart (see Acts 13:22) because David couldn't get God off his mind. In the Psalms, David said that God was the first thing on his mind when he woke up. He couldn't get God off his mind all day. And during the night watches, when everybody else was asleep, David would wake up with thoughts of God on his mind (see Psalm 63:6).

Such passion makes a difference in the way you live. When Jesus Christ dominates your mind, your hands don't have to do what they used to do. Your feet don't have to go where they used to go. Your mouth doesn't have to say what it used to say.

Your mind doesn't have room for Christ and the world. You are either going to think about Christ or about the world. A kingdom mind is a mind firmly fixed on Christ.

## Put on New Thoughts

In Colossians 3:5–9, Paul went on to show some of the results of setting our minds on Christ. We are able to put off old practices such as greed and anger and lying because we have "laid aside the old self with its evil practices, and have put on the new self" (vv. 9–10).

When you work out or do lawn work and then take a shower, do you put your sweaty clothes back on? They were good enough to sweat in. Why aren't they acceptable now? Because you have cleaned up.

Now if you were to forget that you took a shower, then the clothes you put on may not matter that much. But once you know you are clean, you want to dress in a way that reflects your new condition.

It's the same with your mind. Once Jesus Christ has cleansed you with His blood, there's no need for you to go back and put on your old thinking patterns anymore. You *have* the mind of Christ as a believer. You just need to develop the discipline of thinking with a kingdom mind.

According to Colossians 3:15, the good news is that when you are committed to setting your mind on Christ, He will give you His peace. Even though we are engaged with the Enemy in a battle for our minds, our minds do not have to be in turmoil.

When your mind is fixed on Christ, when He is working in your life, He will give you peace about the things He wants you to do and peace about the things you can't do anything about. Your life will be in harmony when Christ rules your mind.

## Let the Word Be at Home

The final thing I want to show you is that in order to develop a kingdom mind, you must "let the word of Christ richly dwell within you" (Colossians 3:16). The Word of God must be completely at home in your heart.

That's what the word *dwell* means—"to be at home." God wants to occupy your heart and mind, and He doesn't want any rooms locked off to Him.

When guests come to our house, what do we usually tell them? "Make yourself at home." As a pastor, I have people tell me that all the time.

But they don't mean I'm free to rummage around in their bedrooms or go through their personal papers. I'm not free to take my shoes and socks off and plop my feet on the coffee table. What people usually mean is, "Within the confines of this one room I escorted you into, make yourself at home."

But God wants you to give Him access to every room in your life—including the closets, the attic, and the garage, where you have all of your junk hidden. If we will open up every room and let the Word of God do its housecleaning work, our minds and hearts will be a home where Christ will be comfortable.

Then we will be able to do everything "in the name of the Lord Jesus" (Colossians 3:17). How is it possible to do everything in the name of Jesus? When you are plugged into His kingdom agenda, thinking with a kingdom mind, what comes out of you will be pleasing to Him.

When you think with a kingdom mind, the first thing on your mind will be how your words and actions reflect on Christ. Will they make Him look good? Will they bring Him glory? When you think and act in Christ's name, you will enjoy His authority. So it's crucial that we develop kingdom minds set on God's kingdom agenda.

# The Kingdom
# Agenda and
# Your Stewardship

In chapter 2 I told you that Lois and I used to house-sit for wealthy families in Dallas when we were in seminary. It was a great way to live like kings in a kingdom for a few days.

The families usually gave us the run of the place. But while there was great opportunity for enjoyment, there were also definite limitations on that enjoyment. Each family had rules they wanted us to follow while they were away. And we agreed to follow them, because it was not our home we would be staying in.

Put in the context of this book, the home we watched over was the kingdom of the family who owned it. Lois and I were the stewards of the home, the temporary managers. It belonged to someone else, and therefore we had to function according to their agenda, not ours.

Our job was simply to manage the property of another person that had been entrusted to our care—which is the biblical definition of stewardship. A key element in carrying out God's kingdom agenda is our stewardship of His gifts. So we need to learn how to be good stewards, or managers, of what He gives us.

In Luke 19:11–27, Jesus told a powerful parable of kingdom stewardship we need to read and heed. It lays out the standards by which we, as God's stewards, are to function on His behalf in His kingdom and by which our stewardship will be evaluated. Let's unfold this important passage.

## THE MEANING OF STEWARDSHIP

The first thing I want us to consider is the meaning of stewardship:

*A certain nobleman went to a distant country to receive a kingdom*
*for himself, and then return. And he called ten of his slaves, and gave them*
*ten minas, and said to them, "Do business with this until I come back."*
*(Luke 19:12–13)*

Now it's obvious in the parable that Christ is the nobleman going away to lay claim to the kingdom He won by virtue of His victory on Calvary. The "distant country" is heaven, from which He will return one day to establish His visible kingdom in the millennium.

But in the meantime, the King has given us something to manage, and He has commanded us to manage it well until He returns.

### God Owns It All

Right away we see the first thing that stewardship means—which is that God owns it all. The nobleman gave the slaves a portion of money from his coffers. The slaves didn't contribute anything. God created it all, so it's all His (see Revelation 4:11).

Now this principle may be easy to state, but living it out is something else. The fact is, God's total ownership is inescapable. He said in the Psalms:

*Every beast of the forest is Mine, . . .*
*and everything that moves in the field is Mine.*
*If I were hungry, I would not tell you:*
*For the world is Mine, and all it contains. (50:10–12)*

God is the owner of His kingdom by virtue of the creation. Therefore, since God owns everything, everything we claim to own is only ours relatively speaking. It is not ours absolutely speaking.

The money that you have in your pocket right now was printed on paper that was ground from the pulp of trees that grew on God's property. The car that you drive was shaped out of metal whose elements were dug from God's earth. The clothes on your back are only there because God made them possible.

I remember teaching my oldest son, Anthony, about giving. I told him, "Son, whatever you get, the first 10 percent of everything goes to God. And that's just the minimum." Then I gave him five dollars for an allowance. I knew the question that was going to come next.

"Dad, that rule doesn't apply to my allowance, does it?"

I told him that it did.

"So you want me to take fifty cents out of my five dollars and give it to the Lord?"

I knew he wasn't getting the idea, so I proceeded to explain. "Son, it works like this. Where did you get the five dollars?"

"You gave it to me."

"Right. And where did I get the five dollars?"

"Well, you got it from your salary as pastor of the church."

"Right again. That five dollars came from my salary at the church, which was provided by the offerings of the congregation. Now, where did the people get the money to give so I could be paid and you could have your five dollars? They got it from their salaries at the places where they work." I was just getting warmed up!

"Now, Son, if the people got the money to give from the places where they work so they could pay me, and you could have your five dollars, then what are the things they need in order to work?"

Well, we went through the whole list: a car, clothes, a place to live, food for strength, even the air they breathe. And we traced it all back to God. So since there is nothing we have that didn't come from God, giving Him 10 percent is no big deal.

Then I asked him, "Anthony, do you have a problem with giving God fifty cents?"

He said, "No, Dad. I'll give a dollar, I guess." I think he got the message! My point is, the clearer you see God's hand in everything, the less problem you will have accepting His ownership and honoring that ownership.

Job 1:21 says you came into this world naked. The only reason you aren't going out naked is because somebody else will dress you. Death is the ultimate reminder that you own nothing. I read one time in *Jet* magazine about a woman who got buried in her Jaguar. Guess what? That Jag is still there in the grave. It's not going anywhere because we don't own anything.

The Bible says we don't even own our bodies. "You have been bought with a price" (1 Corinthians 6:20). That's why James 4:13–15 warns businesspeople not to brag with such statements as, "Today, I'm going here to cut a deal; then tomorrow I'm going there to cut a deal." We don't know whether we'll even be here tomorrow. Our lives are in God's hands.

## God Doesn't Share Ownership

Here's the corollary to point one (God owns it all): God does not share His ownership with anyone.

There was a being a long time ago who tried to share ownership with God. His name was Lucifer, the chief angel.

Lucifer wanted to turn heaven into a joint venture, to split God's throne with Him fifty-fifty. But Lucifer got booted out of heaven because God does not share His ownership with anyone.

Therefore, any attempt you and I make to share ownership with God puts us on the side of Satan, because we are operating out of the same attitude of pride.

We'll get back to Luke 19 a little later, but now I want to show you an important warning from Deuteronomy. As Israel was about to enter the Promised Land of Canaan, Moses cautioned the people:

> Beware lest you forget the Lord your God by not keeping
> His commandments and His ordinances and His statutes
> which I am commanding you today; lest, when you have
> eaten and are satisfied, and have built good houses and
> lived in them, and when your herds and your flocks multiply,
> and your silver and gold multiply, and all that you have
> multiplies, then your heart becomes proud, and you forget the
> Lord your God who brought you out from the land of Egypt,
> out of the house of slavery. . . . Otherwise, you may say in your
> heart, "My power and the strength of my hand made me this
> wealth." But you shall remember the Lord your God,
> for it is He who is giving you power to make wealth.
> (Deuteronomy 8:11–14, 17–18)

What a powerful reminder of the very essence of what it means to be a steward! The things we own are really on loan from the Lord. So we had better be careful how we treat them.

## THE RESPONSIBILITY
## OF STEWARDSHIP

A steward may not own what he has been given, but he is responsible for his management of it. This is the second principle we need to understand about stewardship.

In the parable in Luke 19, the owner gave his ten slaves a mina apiece to operate with. A mina was an amount of money worth about three months' salary for a common laborer in those days. So this was a pretty substantial allotment; these slaves definitely had something to work with.

### All Received the Same

Please note that each slave got the same amount. Why is that important? Because this parable represents something that all of us have in equal measure: what I call our "life potential."

Life potential can be divided into three categories: time, talents, and treasure. Now you may say, "Wait a minute, Tony. I can see where we're all equal in time, because everybody has the same twenty-four hours every day to use. But aren't people different in terms of their talents and treasure?"

It's true that people differ in their abilities and resources. But that's not Jesus' point here. The point is the equality of the situation. Each slave had the same amount of money, and each one had equal opportunity to do something good with his mina. God has given each of us a life potential.

### The Need to Do Business

The nobleman's command to his slaves, "Do business with this until I come back" (v. 13), gets to the heart of a steward's responsibility.

The issue is not whether you will accept your stewardship but what you will do with it. The question is, what kind of business will you do with the Lord's property?

The Greek word for *business* here is the word from which we get the English word *pragmatic*. There's nothing more pragmatic or practical in life than being a kingdom steward. Doing business for the King and His kingdom is where it's at for us, because it is using the life potential He has given us.

Now let me show you something that will encourage you in your stewardship. Jesus told this same basic story a different way in Matthew 25 in the parable of the talents.

In that parable, the three servants were given differing talents—a talent was also an amount of money—"each according to his own ability" (Matthew 25:15). This is what we referred to above, people receiving varying resources based on their abilities.

So in one sense, we don't all have the same amount of time. That is, some people will only live to be forty years old while others will live to be eighty. We don't all have the same amount of money to work with either. And we don't all have the same talents and abilities in the same area.

But as I said earlier, the key to Luke is what we might call equality of opportunity. The key in Matthew is that when the King comes back, He will only measure His servants against what He gave them. The five-talent servant had the ability to produce more talents, and he did so.

So no matter how much you have in terms of resources and abilities, no matter how long you live, the point is that Jesus Christ will not compare you to anyone else. You will only be evaluated against what He gave you.

That's why it is wrong to want what somebody else has. God is going to measure you, not you against the Joneses down the street. So if you spend all your time trying to be like the Joneses and never get around to carrying out your stewardship, you are going to come up empty-handed when the Owner returns.

## The Kind of Business to Do

What kind of business does Christ want us to conduct with the time, talents, and treasure He has entrusted to us?

In a word, we need to *invest*, not just spend. Too many of us are in debt up to our earlobes because we spend, spend, spend. So we owe, owe, owe.

If you have children, you know they would rather spend than invest any day. We don't have to teach our kids to spend. We have to teach them to save. Do you know why kids spend all the time? Because they have a wrong view of the future. Kids spend because the only day they can see is today.

My son Jonathan is a basketball player. So when the new Michael

Jordan basketball shoes came out, it was "Dad, the new Jordans just came out. I need to go buy a pair." The trouble is, when the new shoes came out endorsed by Allen Iverson, another NBA star, Jonathan wanted those too.

Given the chance to get what they want, most teenagers will get it without worrying about whether they will be broke next week. Kids don't take investing seriously because they don't take the future seriously.

Let me tell you, this is why the lives of some believers are messed up. They don't seriously believe the Owner is going to come back and ask them what they did with the time, talents, and treasure He entrusted to them as His stewards.

Now most of us prepare for the future in other areas. We have insurance policies to cover everything we have and anything that might happen to it.

In other words, we will do for ourselves what we won't do for God. We plan for what *might* happen by buying insurance. But we fail to plan for what *will* happen—the return of Jesus Christ and the evaluation of our stewardship—by wisely investing the life potential He has given us.

One day, Jesus Christ is going to look at you and me and say, "Let's see whether the agenda of My kingdom is better off because of what you did with what I gave you." A steward is responsible to manage the affairs of the King. And when the King returns, the steward will have to give an account of that responsibility.

## THE EVALUATION OF STEWARDSHIP

Everybody goes through some version of the annual review at work. Why do companies hold this review?

Because the boss wants to know how well her employees have produced. For eight hours a day, forty hours a week, those employees are on the boss's time. They are her stewards. They are on her agenda, accepting her money to produce work. So the review will give the boss a chance to find out how productive the workers have been for the company.

A time of evaluation is coming for Jesus Christ's stewards too. Let's pick up His parable in Luke 19:15. "And it came about that when [the nobleman] returned, after receiving the kingdom, he ordered that these slaves, to whom he had given the money, be called to him in order that he might know what business they had done."

## An Accounting Period

The nobleman's return is a reference to the coming of Christ, when He will call His people to account for their stewardship. Then the issue will be, "How did My company benefit by what I provided to you?"

Now, a lot of us will be able to show how God's gifts benefited *us*. But that's not the question. The issue with a steward is, how did the King's business fare under your management? Is the King better off? Was His agenda furthered? It's OK for the stewards to be better off if the King is better off, but that's a side issue.

The Bible calls this day of evaluation for kingdom stewards "the judgment seat of Christ." It is described in two key passages we need to consider now.

## Christ's Judgment Seat

The first of these important passages is in 1 Corinthians 3. I want to quote it in its entirety because it is so crucial:

> *According to the grace of God which was given to me, as a wise master builder I laid a foundation, and another is building upon it. But let each man be careful how he builds upon it. For no man can lay a foundation other than the one which is laid, which is Jesus Christ. Now if any man builds upon the foundation with gold, silver, precious stones, wood, hay, straw, each man's work will become evident; for the day will show it, because it is to be revealed with fire; and the fire itself will test the quality of each man's work. If any man's work which he has built upon it remains, he shall receive a reward. If any man's work is burned up, he shall suffer loss; but he himself shall be saved, yet so as through fire. (vv. 10–15)*

We must be careful what kind of building we construct on the foundation God gives us. This is another way of saying we must be attentive to how we carry out our stewardship.

The reason is that our stewardship will be tested one day, and it will have to withstand the fire of Christ's judgment on "that day."

Paul's reference is to the day when Christ will judge His people— not for salvation but for rewards based on our work as stewards. This day is described in 2 Corinthians 5:10–11a: "For we must all appear before the judgment seat of Christ, that each one may be recompensed for his deeds in the body, according to what he has done, whether good or bad. Therefore knowing the fear of the Lord, we persuade men."

Paul said there is a fiery judgment coming. Hebrews 10:30 says that God will judge His people. On the day of evaluation, the fire of Jesus Christ "will test the *quality* of each man's work" (1 Corinthians 3:13, emphasis mine).

## Quality—or Leftovers?

Do you appreciate sloppy work? Neither do I.

I don't know too many mothers who are satisfied when their children do the dishes or clean their rooms in a sloppy, halfhearted way. Your boss certainly doesn't want sloppy work. It's not acceptable for his secretary to say, "So what if your letter is full of errors and misspelled words? At least I typed it."

God wants quality work from His stewards too. At His judgment seat, Jesus Christ is going to evaluate how well our time, talents, and treasure were used for Him—whether they were used to produce quality work or thrown-together junk.

Many people will give their boss top-quality work when they go into the office. They won't be late, and they won't do sloppy work. Why? Because their paycheck is in the boss's pocket. They fear not getting a raise. They fear not being promoted.

If people will do that for an earthly boss, what should we do for Jesus Christ? So the question is, Are you giving God's kingdom a quality return on the time, talents, and treasure He has blessed you with? Or is God getting leftovers?

Many Christians "tip" God. By the way they live, they say, "God, whatever is left over of my time, I'll give to You. After I have spent my money on what I want, then I'll give You something. After I have used my talents to build my business, You'll get some of my time during my retirement years."

Anyone who has that attitude had better read 2 Corinthians 5:11 again. Paul called the judgment seat of Christ a thing that should cause us to fear, or be in awe. This will be a serious judgment.

The reason is that when you are dealing with something expensive, you want it done right. If it's something just thrown together, you don't care.

But if you are building an expensive house and the bricks aren't laid right, you are going to get that corrected. Let somebody even look like he's going to ding the door of your expensive car, and you flip out. You won't even park it beside other cars where it could possibly get dinged. The more something costs, the more serious you are going to be about it.

God paid a high price for you and me. We cost Him the life of His Son. Not only that, but He has entrusted us with the stewardship of His kingdom. He has given us the privilege of ruling with Him in His kingdom.

Are we going to turn around and give God sloppy work, our left-over time, talents, and treasure? Are we going to give the school district our best teaching efforts then throw something together on Saturday night to teach the kids at Sunday school?

Are we going to spend thousands of dollars on our houses and cars and clothes and then toss a little tip toward God? Are we going to spend time on ourselves and then tell God He ought to be happy we show up for two hours on Sunday?

No, God says all of this cost Him too much to let us get away with shoddy stewardship. We are going to be evaluated.

The Bible says whatever you get in time, talents, and treasure, make sure you give God His portion first. Because if you don't, you won't have any left over later.

You won't have any energy left at the end of the day. You won't have any money left at the end of the month. And you won't have any talents left over at the end of life. Be sure to take care of Jesus Christ first, so that He might have "first place in everything" (Colossians 1:18).

## THE REWARDS OF STEWARDSHIP

Once we understand what stewardship is, what our responsibilities are, and the fact that we will be tested, we are ready to talk about the rewards of stewardship.

### The Faithful Steward

We're back to the parable of Luke 19 again. The nobleman has re-turned from his journey, and he's ready to call his servants in to account for how they used their minas.

The first servant came and said, "Master, your mina has made ten minas more" (v. 16). That's a 1,000 percent increase! This man has obviously invested his master's money well. He could say, "Master, I took what you gave me and invested it, and I had fun doing it. Look at what I have for you."

What does the master, who is God, say to this man who used what he had been given so effectively for the kingdom? He receives a three-fold reward. The first reward is public recognition, the master's public announcement, "Well done" (v. 17). When you show up at His judgment seat, there will be nothing like hearing Jesus say, "Well done!" He is going to say it publicly. Millions will hear.

You may be hidden away in your work, but if you do what God has called you to do faithfully and consistently, you will be honored before all of heaven on that day.

I was talking to a relative one day, asking her why she has committed her life to certain things. Her answer was, "Because of that day. I do everything in light of the day when I will stand before Christ. I want to hear His 'Well done!'"

The second reward this faithful steward received was a kingdom inheritance. The master said, "Because you have been faithful in a very little thing, be in authority over ten cities" (v. 17).

Most people have a wrong view of the kingdom. We will not be floating around on clouds. The kingdom will be a government, which will operate in perfect righteousness. There will be people in positions of authority who were faithful servants of Jesus Christ on earth.

Just like a good worker gets a promotion, so Christ's faithful stewards will get promotions in the kingdom. Some will manage ten cities.

But this faithful steward got a third reward. It was a surprise, a bonus. You'll find it in verse 24. He got the mina that the master had originally given to the third slave. When Jesus Christ comes, He is going to look at those who were not faithful and snatch away from them what little bit they did.

You may think that's not fair. But we need to remember one thing. Christ is going to make sure His kingdom resources aren't wasted. If we fail to grasp an opportunity for kingdom service, Christ will give it to someone else and we will lose out.

## The Less Productive Steward

The second servant also had a good report, although he wasn't as productive as the first. "Your mina, master, has made five minas." So the master told him, "You are to be over five cities" (vv. 18–19).

Did you notice that this servant didn't get any public recognition? He got his five cities, but no "Well done." I believe the reason is that he was only half-faithful.

Let me explain. I think this servant represents someone who gets saved at twenty years of age but doesn't get going for the Lord until he's forty. He lives to be sixty, so he's got twenty "lost" years, in terms of kingdom reward, and twenty productive years.

Should this person say at age forty, "I've already lost twenty years. I might as well give up"? No, he should get going at forty and serve Christ effectively until he's sixty. Make sure you get your five cities.

## The Worthless Steward

Then there's the third slave. He brought his mina and said, "Master, behold your mina, which I kept put away in a handkerchief; for I was afraid of you, because you are an exacting man" (vv. 20–21).

This man said, "Master, I just want you to know I didn't lose your money. I kept it safe and sound under my mattress. I took the time, talents, and treasure you gave me and stored them away, because you are a hard master."

This guy had been playing both ends against the middle. Here was his reasoning: "I am not going to break my neck serving my master. He is going away on some long trip. He may not even come back. He may forget all about me.

"In the meantime, I've got my own business to tend to. I've got my own house to build and money to make and talents to use. But just in case he does come back, I'll make sure I don't lose what he gave me. I'll play it safe and hide his mina."

Remember the film *Lilies of the Field*, with Sidney Poitier? He was building a church for the nuns in a town and asked a local businessman to help. The man said, "I'm not really into religion. I'm not the man." But when they started building the church, he came with a hammer and nails and got up on the building and helped build the church.

Sidney Poitier asked him why he was doing this, since he wasn't a religious man. The man said, "Just in case what these nuns believe is right, I want to have something to show."

That's what this third servant was saying. "I'm not going to get fanatical about this service stuff. But just in case my master does return, I want to have something to show him. I want to have some insurance."

The master told this servant, "By your own words I will judge you,

you worthless slave" (v. 22). Then he asked him, "Why did you not put the money in the bank, and having come, I would have collected it with interest?" (v. 23). He couldn't even give this servant an *E* for effort.

I'm afraid there are many Christians who can talk about the grace and goodness of God, who can praise Him for taking them from nowhere to somewhere, but who are not giving Him a decent return on His investment in them.

These people are not only failing to return 1,000 or 500 or even 10 percent to God. Like the faithless steward, they aren't even producing the 2 or 3 percent they could get down at the local bank. The master says that stewards like that are no good to him.

So in contrast to the first servant, this steward gets a ringing condemnation. He gets no cities, and as we saw above, even the mina he has is taken away from him. He gets the same amount of credit as profit he produced for the master: none.

Notice the involvement of the "bystanders" (v. 24) in this man's judgment. I don't know how God is going to do it, but somehow the results of Christ's judgment seat will be visible to everyone. Maybe God will use a cosmic video screen. Whatever the method, others will know the results.

That means if we are simply wearing the name of Christ like a decoration instead of living it, everyone will know. If we have nothing to bring to Christ that can withstand the fire, other believers at His judgment seat will know.

That's why I think there are going to be some big surprises on that day, with people saying, "But I thought so-and-so was a good Christian. He always came to church with his Bible under his arm. He was always saying 'Praise the Lord.'" But if there is no depth to the commitment, it will become obvious on that day.

This is enough to scare me. This is enough to shake me up. I don't want my life to be put on public display and find out I came in third like the worthless servant. I don't want to see my work snatched from me. I want to be a faithful servant who makes the most of what his Master has entrusted to him. I don't want to be just a professional Christian but an authentic one.

## THE RESPONSE OF A STEWARD

Look how Jesus summarized this parable of stewardship: "I tell you, that to everyone who has shall more be given, but from the one who does not have, even what he does have shall be taken away" (Luke 19:26). We saw this in the abundant reward of the first servant and the judgment of the third servant.

## A Prayer for Faithfulness

Since this is the case, where do you start in making your stewardship productive and pleasing to God?

A good place to start is by turning the words of Hebrews 12:28 into your prayer: "Therefore, since we receive a kingdom which cannot be shaken, let us show gratitude, by which we may offer to God an acceptable service with reverence and awe."

Go to God and pray, "Lord, thank You for the certainty of Your kingdom. Help me to show my gratitude to You by serving You faithfully each day. Give me the grace I need to make the most of the time, talents, and treasure You have loaned to me. Help me use them to prioritize Your agenda over mine."

While you are praying that prayer, here's a good verse to memorize and make your daily commitment: "Be steadfast, immovable, always abounding in the work of the Lord, knowing that your toil is not in vain in the Lord" (1 Corinthians 15:58).

## Pick Up the Pace

I used to play the game of Monopoly all the time. I love to play it, because when I play Monopoly, I get to own land. I get to play Donald Trump when I play Monopoly—buying and selling property. And if you're playing with me, you'd better not let me get Boardwalk and Park Place, because if I get those two, I show no mercy.

When I get enough money, I am going to buy some little green houses for Boardwalk and Park Place. Then when I buy enough green houses, I am going to turn those bad boys in for two big red hotels.

The property value now escalates, and you'd better hope you can skip over my property and collect another two hundred dollars for passing *Go*. Because I am going to be sitting there waiting on you.

But let me tell you the hard part of playing Monopoly. It's when the game is over. Then I have to give up all my make-believe property and money, close the box, and go back to the real world.

Someday, they are going to close the box on you and me. We are going to leave this world and go to the real world, the kingdom of

God. There we will show what we really have, and the only thing that will matter on that day is not what we left behind but what we have sent on ahead.

The only "property" that will count at Christ's judgment seat is the time, talents, and treasure we invested in things of eternal value. What will matter then is what we did to make a difference for the kingdom.

You may be saying, "Tony, I want to make the most of my stewardship. I want to be an effective servant in the kingdom. But I've lost some time. I've been dragging along, shuckin' and jivin' on God. What do I do?"

You do the same thing a runner does when he or she falls behind in a race. You have to pick up the pace. You can't worry about the territory you've already covered. Yesterday is gone, but you can pick up the pace today so you can cover more territory tomorrow.

Remember what we said earlier. The kingdom of God has only one Ruler. But it has room for an unlimited number of servants. What Jesus Christ is looking for is faithful stewards who will say to Him, "Lord, You are first in my time, my talents, and my treasure. Help me to make Your kingdom agenda my agenda. And help me make an eternal difference for You."

When you're ready to pray that and live it, you're in line to hear Jesus say, "Well done!" on that day.

# CHAPTER TEN

# The Kingdom Agenda and Your Inheritance

With this chapter we will close part 2 of the book, in which we have been applying God's kingdom agenda to your personal life. We've covered a lot of territory concerning what it means to live as a kingdom person. Now I want to look ahead to where we are headed as kingdom people.

We know that the kingdom of God, which is now invisible and is being expressed in the church, will one day be made visible and cover the whole earth when Jesus returns and commences His millennial reign.

Our calling and service now are preparing us for that day. We are being fitted to inherit the kingdom. I want to consider that inheritance, both because it will be so glorious we can't even imagine it and because it will not be the same for every believer.

Our salvation is free. Our place in the kingdom is assured forever by the blood of Christ. But our inheritance in the kingdom will be determined by the degree of faithfulness with which we serve the King here and now.

We'll clarify this concept as we go along, but first let me give you a definition of a full kingdom inheritance: The inheritance is the privilege afforded to faithful Christians of enjoying all the rights and benefits of the King.

Right now, we do not experience all of our inheritance rights and benefits, just as a child does not experience all of his or her inheritance rights as long as the child's parents are still alive. But when the parents pass on—or, in our case, when Jesus comes—then the child comes into his or her full inheritance.

At Jesus' return, when He sets up His judgment seat to evaluate believers, He is going to read the "will," as it were, and determine at that time what inheritance rights we have.

## THE BOOK OF HEBREWS IS THE STAGE

I want to take you to Hebrews 4 as our main text, but I need to set the stage for you because so much in the book of Hebrews is predicated on your understanding of the Old Testament. In particular, the argument we will consider in Hebrews 4 is based on the experience of Israel in Egypt.

As you will remember, Israel was enslaved under Pharaoh in Egypt. For the author of Hebrews, this is analogous to our being enslaved to sin today. Egypt represents the world, the place of the unsaved.

But then Israel was redeemed and set free from slavery by the Passover, when the blood of the Passover lamb was shed. Similarly, you and I were set free by the blood of Jesus Christ, and we were free to leave our old lives behind, just as the Jews were free to leave Egypt.

Now Israel was not redeemed to stay in Egypt, just as we are not saved to stay in the world in terms of our lifestyle. God had prepared Canaan, the Promised Land, for Israel. To the author of Hebrews, Canaan was the Promised Land for Israel. He also regarded Canaan as equivalent to the experience of the spiritually mature Christian, what we might call the Spirit-filled life. That's the goal we're supposed to be moving toward.

But on their way from Egypt to Canaan, the people of Israel had to cross a parcel of land known as the wilderness. And instead of going straight across to Canaan and receiving what the Bible calls their full inheritance, the Israelites murmured and complained and wound up wandering around in the wilderness for forty years.

To the author of Hebrews, the wilderness represents carnal Christians: wandering around, unsettled, not having arrived at the place where God wants them to be (see Hebrews 3:7–11). The generation that came out of Egypt with Moses did not receive their inheritance, because the people stayed in a state of long-term carnality in the wilderness.

This is the scenario the book of Hebrews assumes: Egypt as the unsaved world; the wilderness as the place of carnality for Christians where they wander, not living up to their spiritual potential; and Canaan as the experience of mature, spiritual Christians who are where God wants them to be.

The problem in Hebrews is that the Jewish Christians were beginning to wander around as Israel had done, seeming to be in a spiritual wilderness rather than pressing on to "Canaan" and their inheritance.

The author wanted to let them know in no uncertain terms that we cannot stand still in the Christian life. We can't just hang out in the wilderness without slipping backward spiritually.

The Hebrews were in danger of missing their inheritance just like the Israelites did in the wilderness, so the writer wanted to address their situation. In the process, Hebrews 4 teaches us four important truths about our kingdom inheritance.

## THE INHERITANCE MEANS OWNERSHIP

The first thing we can see in Hebrews 4:1 is that an inheritance means more than making it to heaven: "Therefore, let us fear lest, while a promise remains of entering His rest, any one of you should seem to have come short of it."

### God's Rest

The key word here is *rest*. For the Jews, God's rest would be achieved when they entered Canaan and took ownership of their inheritance (see Deuteronomy 12:8–11). So God's rest was the full realization of His inheritance.

Now we need to understand that when the writer talked about coming short of God's rest, he was not talking about salvation. He was writing to saved people. Remember, the Israelites in the wilderness were already redeemed. They put the blood of the Passover lamb on the doorposts of their homes.

However, Hebrews 3:18–19 makes it clear that these Israelites became hardened by their sin and disobedience. They angered God, and He swore they would not enter His rest. But the issue was not their redemption.

This means there can be Christians who have been set free from spiritual bondage but who will never enjoy the full rights and privileges they could have inherited in the coming kingdom, what the writer of Hebrews called God's "rest." That's because these benefits accrue to believers based on their faithfulness to Christ here on earth.

This principle also holds true on your way to heaven. All Christians do not enjoy the same benefits of being saved. The same benefits are available to all Christians, but not all Christians experience them.

For example, if you don't pray, there are certain things you will never get that God had in store for you. But a Christian who prays will enjoy the privileges of answered prayer as God opens His storehouse and blesses that person in response to his obedience.

God is going to say to many believers in heaven, "Let Me show you what I had stored up for you as an inheritance that you never credited to your account by being faithful."

## Valuing Your Inheritance

Now someone may say, "I don't care about an inheritance in the kingdom, just as long as I get in."

But you will care then, and here's why. You will be a perfect person in a perfect environment, and you will feel what you missed out on more than you would here, since you are at present an imperfect person in an imperfect environment.

So inheritance involves ownership—your title deed, so to speak, to what Christ has waiting for you when He returns. The last phrase of Hebrews 4:1 suggests that it is possible for Christians to fail to gain that inheritance, to miss out on the full enjoyment of what God has for them.

We have alluded to this, but we need to explore it more directly so we can find out what could cause us to forfeit our inheritance and what it takes to gain a full inheritance.

## THE INHERITANCE IS FOR FINISHERS

In Hebrews 4:2, we find this statement: "For indeed we have had good news preached to us, just as they also; but the word they heard did not profit them, because it was not united by faith in those who heard."

## No Profit

What good news was preached to the Old Testament Israelites? Not the good news of going to heaven, but the good news of inheriting Canaan. When Israel left Egypt and came to the border of Canaan, Moses sent twelve men into Canaan to check out the land.

The spies came back and said, "It certainly does flow with milk and honey" (Numbers 13:27). Then they showed the people the incredible fruit they had gathered.

But then ten of the spies said, in effect, "We can't take the land. Too many giants, too many fortified cities" (see vv. 28–29). Only Caleb and Joshua were ready to act in faith in the good news and take the land.

But the people sided with the majority report and refused to believe God could give them the Promised Land. So God judged them (see Numbers 14), and the nation turned back into the wilderness and wandered around until everyone over twenty years old had died except Joshua and Caleb. That generation never got to taste the milk and honey of Canaan, even though God said it was theirs!

That's what Hebrews 4:2 means when it says the people did not profit from the good news of the inheritance. They failed to respond in faith and forfeited what they could have enjoyed.

## Entering God's Rest

Notice how the writer of Hebrews applies this to Christians in Hebrews 4:3–5:

> For we who have believed enter that rest, just as He has said, "As I swore in My wrath, they shall not enter My rest," although His works were finished from the foundation of the world. For He has thus said somewhere concerning the seventh day, "And God rested on the seventh day from all His works"; and again in this passage, "They shall not enter My rest."

These verses take us all the way back to creation and the beginning of the Sabbath, when God rested on the seventh day after completing His creative work (see Genesis 2:2–3).

Why did God rest on Saturday? Not because He was tired but because He was finished. He did all that He was supposed to do. Therefore, on the seventh day He sat back and enjoyed His creation. His work was completed.

In fact, God decided that a day of rest after completing one's work was such a good idea that He blessed and set aside the seventh day for mankind to rest too. The Sabbath rest became part of Israel's law (see Exodus 20:8), and the Jews were obliged to keep it throughout their history.

The idea of the Sabbath was that the people needed a day in the week to reflect on the fact that God finished His work and then rested. So the people needed to finish their work so they could also rest on the seventh day.

Why does Hebrews 4 bring up the Sabbath in a context of talking about the believers' inheritance? Because the Sabbath and all that it represented became the standard by which God would judge His people.

In other words, the fundamental question that Christ will ask every believer at His judgment seat is this: "Did you finish? Did you complete the task of living for Me that I gave you when I saved you? Were you faithful to Me?"

When you got saved, you entered into what the Bible calls "the race" (Hebrews 12:1). Your race has a finish line. That is, God has a plan for your life He wants you to complete. Many Christians will end their lives, stand before God, and say, "Look what I did!"

God is going to say, "But this is what I wanted you to do."

They will be two different things. This issue of finishing and not losing the inheritance was so important to Paul that he said in 1 Corinthians 9:27, "I buffet my body and make it my slave, lest possibly, after I have preached to others, I myself should be disqualified."

## The Real Issue

See, the issue is not just how well you are doing in your Christian race. The issue is finishing. Some of us get excited because we ran well last year. That's great—but are you a finisher?

This doesn't mean you don't ever sin. It doesn't mean you don't ever fall. But it means that when you do sin and fall, you get up and get back in the race so you can finish and enjoy all the rights and privileges of your inheritance.

If you're a parent, you know what it is to tell your kids to go back and finish the job. They do half the job and then brag on the half they did. So your teenager says, "I cleaned up my room," but he only did half the job.

Your attitude is, "You are not finished yet."

The issue of the Christian life is not how well you started but whether you do what God did when He rested on the Sabbath. He finished the job.

So the generation that came out of Egypt with Moses did not enter the Promised Land. Instead, the people wandered around in the wilderness. In your Christian life have you ever wandered around in the wilderness? Ever gone around in circles, not getting anywhere?

## Eyes on the Prize

What's the answer to wandering? Getting your eyes on the prize. Become fixated on your inheritance, on honoring Jesus Christ and living for Him, and you will stop going around in circles.

Paul told the Philippians, "Work out your salvation with fear and trembling" (2:12). That doesn't mean work your way to heaven. Paul is saying, "Now that God has saved you, get to work so that your salvation produces something. Don't take your salvation lightly. Grow in respect to your faith."

Paul had his eyes on the prize (see Philippians 3:14). When he was near death, he could say, "I have fought the good fight, I have finished the course, I have kept the faith" (2 Timothy 4:7).

What God wants you to be able to say when you get ready to die is, "This is my crowning day. This is the day I will hear, 'Well done, My good and faithful servant'"—not because you were perfect but because you finished.

# THE INHERITANCE IS A REWARD

In Hebrews 4:6–8, the writer goes back to that first generation of Israelites and reminds us that they failed to enter God's rest—their inheritance in the Promised Land—because of unbelief. Then he mentions Joshua, Moses' successor, and his leadership of the nation.

## Acting in Faith

Joshua led the people into Canaan, but remember that this was the second generation. Their parents had died in the wilderness. Let me show you how this new generation united good news with faith (see v. 2) and claimed the inheritance.

We all know that "Joshua 'fit' the battle of Jericho," and the walls tumbled down as Israel marched into Canaan and proceeded to lay claim to their inheritance (see Joshua 6).

But the key to the victory at Jericho is revealed back in Joshua 5:13–15, when the "captain of the Lord's host" appeared to Joshua. This was the preincarnate Jesus, and Joshua fell on his face in worship and said, in essence, "What do You want me to do, Lord?"

The answer was, "March around Jericho for six days, and then march around it seven times on the seventh day. Blow the trumpets, and the walls will fall down" (see Joshua 6:3–5). Joshua gave the order, the people obeyed, and they took Jericho without firing an arrow. They united the word with faith and obedience, and they gained their inheritance.

Do you know what God wants from us today? He wants some "Joshua" Christians who will obey Him and see the walls come down. If you have some walls in your life that just won't come down, it could be because you are trying to knock them down your way rather than letting God knock them down His way.

That's why you must unite the Word with faith, which means you must do what God says to do *the way* God says to do it. When you do things God's way, He says, "You're ready to earn your inheritance."

## A Greater Inheritance

Just notice in Hebrews 4:8 that Joshua couldn't give the people their permanent inheritance. That's because there is an inheritance greater than Canaan awaiting God's people, our inheritance in heaven. The writer continued in verses 9–11:

> There remains therefore a Sabbath rest for the people of God. For the one who has entered His rest has himself also rested from his works, as God did from His. Let us therefore be diligent to enter that rest, lest anyone fall through following the same example of disobedience.

The example of disobedience, of course, is Israel. The writer was urging us to finish our course, complete our work, so we can share God's rest with Him. The idea of these verses is, "Live your Christian life faithfully to the end. Don't cut it short."

The passage that validates this understanding of inheritance is Colossians 3:23–24, where Paul wrote, "Whatever you do, do your work heartily, as for the Lord rather than for men; knowing that from the Lord you will receive the reward of the inheritance. It is the Lord Christ whom you serve."

We need to work for the Lord because He's the one who holds our inheritance. That means we had better stop living to please people and start living to please God. We are His heirs, and the amount of our inheritance depends on how much we please Him.

So inheritance is earned; salvation is not. Salvation is free; inheritance costs. If you and I are going to get all that God has for us in this life and become owners in the kingdom in the next life, it will be because God gave us our inheritance, which we can only get if we finish. And you must do that by faithful obedience to God and His Word.

This orientation means you are living according to a kingdom agenda.

My four children are my heirs. But Lois and I have a special clause in our will. After we are gone, if any of our children start living in rebellion to the will and Word of God, that child's inheritance transfers to the other kids.

The rebellious child is still my heir because he or she is still my child. But it is possible for one or more of my children not to enjoy the full benefits of their inheritance because of disobedience to God. The same is true for us as Christians. We need to finish the race to enjoy the full reward.

## THE INHERITANCE WILL BE EVALUATED

If the inheritance is a reward for faithful service to Christ, then there must come a day of evaluation when what we have done will be tested. That day will be at the judgment seat of Christ, which we have already discussed.

### The Standard

What is the standard Christ will use to evaluate our service and therefore our inheritance? He will use the infallible standard of His Word:

*For the word of God is living and active and sharper than any two-edged sword, and piercing as far as the division of soul and spirit, of both joints and marrow, and able to judge the thoughts and intentions of the heart. And*

*there is no creature hidden from His sight, but all things are open and laid*
*bare to the eyes of Him with whom we have to do. (Hebrews 4:12–13)*

Only the Word of God can penetrate and judge motives. At the judgment seat of Christ, He will pass you and me through the detector of His Word the way we go through those metal detectors at the airport. If anything is wrong, there will be a beep. And wrong motive, selfish action, double standard, or whatever will be detected and exposed.

That's why the Bible says that on the day of judgment, "the last shall be first, and the first last" (Matthew 20:16). Many people we admire will be sent to the back of the line. People we don't know will be brought to the front of the line because the Word of God will judge us perfectly.

You say, "Tony, that's going to be tough. What can I do to keep from being sent to the back of the line?" Well, praise God, we don't have to wait until Christ's judgment seat to let the Word penetrate our heart and change us.

In fact, it's better to let the Word judge you now rather than to judge you then (see 1 Corinthians 11:31). Better to listen to it now than to have to listen to it then. Better to obey than to lose out then.

## Meeting the Standard

But you may come back and say, "Tony, the Word has already penetrated me, and I see my shortcomings. I need help!"

You got it. Look at Hebrews 4:12–16. Read these verses for yourself, and you'll see that we have a Great High Priest, the Lord Jesus Christ, who understands us perfectly and stands ready to help us in our time of need.

I know some people have a problem with this. They wonder how Jesus can understand our weaknesses when He never did anything wrong. How can He understand the temptations we face?

Well, a doctor doesn't have to have cancer before he or she can be a cancer surgeon. The reason Jesus can understand is because He took the full brunt of temptation without yielding to it. If He were as weak as we are, He wouldn't understand because He would have yielded before He withstood the full brunt of temptation. But because He understands, we can come to the "throne of grace" (v. 16).

*Throne* and *grace* are two great words. *Throne* means He's the King.

*Grace* means He's a benevolent dictator. *Throne* means He's sovereign. *Grace* means He cares. *Throne* means He can do anything. *Grace* means He wants to do something for us.

If you want to finish your race and receive your full inheritance, Jesus can provide you with all the grace you need. Jesus paid it all, so you have full access to God's throne room. Through His grace, you can finish and win the prize. In fact, let me show you the kind of people who finish the race and gain their inheritance in the kingdom.

For the remainder of the chapter, I want to talk about those who will share in the inheritance. The Bible calls them "partakers of Christ" (Hebrews 3:14). The word *partaker* means a "sharer." In Colossians 1:12, Paul used the same Greek word when he said God has "qualified us to share in the inheritance of the saints." So let's see who will be partakers or sharers in the inheritance of the kingdom.

## PARTAKERS ARE THE SELECT

As people who are committed to living out God's kingdom agenda, we have a great future awaiting us. I mentioned this future at the beginning of the chapter. One day the invisible kingdom will become universally visible—when Jesus Christ returns to earth and establishes His millennial reign for one thousand years (see Revelation 20:1–6). Jesus will run this planet the way it was intended to be run when God created the first Adam.

### Created to Rule

The first Adam was created to rule. That's why we humans always want to run something. But instead of Adam ruling creation, creation ruled him when sin entered the world.

But when Jesus returns as the last Adam, He will do what the first Adam did not do. He will rule the earth, and ruling with Him will be a group of people called His partakers, or sharers. They are the select of the kingdom, if you will, who will rule with Christ.

### Selecting the Rulers

Right now, God is selecting His prime ministers, governors, mayors, city council members, and so forth, faithful people who will rule with Him in His earthly kingdom. We have the opportunity now to be among these partakers.

Who will the partakers rule over? The Bible teaches that while dead believers will be resurrected and living believers changed to go into the kingdom, there will also be a whole world of people who will be on earth and move into the kingdom (see Isaiah 65:21–25).

Things will be a lot different then, because in the kingdom there will be no crime waves. Any overt sin or rebellion will be dealt with swiftly and with perfect justice. There will be an effective and efficient administration at various levels of government to carry out comprehensively the theocratical rule of God through Jesus Christ.

## A Glorious Privilege

The Bible makes it clear that ruling with Jesus Christ will be a glorious privilege for any believer. We're talking about our inheritance. Remember the servants in Jesus' parable we studied in the previous chapter? The one who was most faithful was given ten cities to rule. That's inheritance.

Anticipating Christ's future kingdom should change the way we live now. If your doctor told you that you had just one year to live, I suspect you would change some things. Places you hadn't visited you'd now want to see. Relationships that were on hold you'd probably want to fix. Your new knowledge of the future would greatly affect how you acted in the present.

As a pastor, I enjoy watching a bride and groom as they get excited about their wedding. There may be a lot to do in a short time to get ready, and the bride-to-be can get frustrated with all the details of preparation. But when the wedding comes, all of that subsides, and the joy of anticipation takes over.

You and I have a wedding to anticipate. It's called the "marriage supper of the Lamb" (Revelation 19:9), the kingdom wedding banquet of Christ and His bride, the church. Talk about a party! This party will last one thousand years (see Revelation 20:1–6).

But in order to be a full partaker, or sharer, in this marriage supper, we must be among those Christ will select to rule with Him.

## PARTAKERS ARE SERVANTS

Now, after looking at such a glorious future when we will rule with Christ in His millennial kingdom, it might be easy for us to start acting like rulers today. The Bible fixes that urge for us. I want to look at a passage of Scripture in which the mother of two of Jesus' disciples got that idea in her head for her two boys.

## Seeking the Top Spot

According to Matthew 20:20–21, the mother of James and John came and bowed down before Jesus with this request: "Command that in Your kingdom these two sons of mine may sit, one on Your right and one on Your left."

Like any good mother, she wanted her boys to reach the top. She wanted them to occupy the places of honor on either side of Jesus when He took His throne in the millennial kingdom.

But notice what Jesus said to her and the brothers. "To sit on My right and on My left, this is not Mine to give, but it is for those for whom it has been prepared by My Father" (v. 23).

What Jesus is saying is that you and I are being prepared now for the glory planned for us later. God has determined how He wants to position all of us in His kingdom. He is allowing us to experience various things in this life that will prepare us for what He has planned for us in the kingdom.

## God's Kingdom Arrangement

Now the story in Matthew 20 really gets interesting, because the other ten disciples got mad at James and John (see v. 24). They weren't upset because of what was requested but because they didn't think of it first. Wanting to be the greatest was a problem for all of them. You can see that when you compare this same story with its parallel in Mark and Luke.

But look at what Jesus did. He called the whole band together and taught them a vital lesson on servanthood:

> You know that the rulers of the Gentiles lord it over them, and their great men exercise authority over them. It is not so among you, but whoever wishes to become great among you shall be your servant, and whoever wishes to be first among you shall be your slave; just as the Son of Man did not come to be served, but to serve, and to give His life a ransom for many. (vv. 25–28)

The disciples were saying, "It sure would be nice to be like Caesar.

Then I would be boss. I could tell everyone else what to do."

But Jesus turned this kind of thinking on its head. He said if you want to be recognized as great in His future kingdom, you must be a servant in the present. If you are not a servant now (see John 13:15), you will not experience glory later. If your only agenda is, "What have You done for me lately, Lord?" then you won't merit the role of a partaker in the kingdom.

Jesus demonstrated this kind of servanthood in the upper room. The disciples all arrived with the attitude, "Where is the servant to wash our feet? We aren't about to do it. We need a slave here."

Jesus said, "We don't have a slave here today. I guess I'll be the slave." So He who was the greatest of all became the servant of all and washed the disciples' feet.

## The Reward of Service

It's not always easy to be a servant, is it? Sometimes when you serve, folks mistreat you and take advantage of you. Or they misunderstand your motives and don't appreciate what you've done.

But I've got good news for you. Jesus never misses it when you serve. He says, "Serve Me now, even if it's in secret, and someday I will reward you openly." If you are going to be a full partaker in your kingdom inheritance, you must be a servant.

There will be people at the judgment seat of Christ to whom He will say, "I just don't see anything here for Me. You served you quite well. You accomplished your agenda quite nicely. But the page marked 'For the glory of God' is blank."

Let me tell you, if you are too busy to serve now, you are too busy to be recognized then.

## PARTAKERS ARE SUFFERERS

The church at Thessalonica was a source of joy to the apostle Paul because of the way those Christians responded to the gospel and because of their steadfastness. He told them:

> We ourselves speak proudly of you among the churches of God for your
> perseverance and faith in the midst of all your persecutions and afflictions
> which you endure. This is a plain indication of God's righteous judgment
> so that you may be considered worthy of the kingdom of God, for which

*indeed you are suffering. (2 Thessalonians 1:4–5)*

## Sharing Christ's Sufferings

Notice what Paul is saying. When you suffer for the kingdom, you are counted worthy of the kingdom so that you will be rewarded in the kingdom. In other words, to be a partaker of Christ's glory in His future kingdom, you must be a partner of His sufferings here on earth (see 1 Peter 4:13).

In fact, Peter said we are to rejoice to the degree that we share in Christ's sufferings. And Paul talked about the "fellowship of His sufferings" (Philippians 3:10).

This is not the message most of us want to hear. We want to hear about reigning with Christ. We want to hear about the glory of the kingdom and the marriage supper party. Well, those are wonderful things to talk about. But the fullest inheritance goes to those who are willing to suffer for Christ now.

## Suffering and Grace

I don't know what suffering Christ is calling you to endure. But whether it's physical, emotional, spiritual, marital, or something else, He can give you the grace not only to bear up under it, but to find His joy in it.

The tragedy of many who are suffering is that they refuse to be recipients of God's grace. Remember what Hebrews 4:16 says? There is a throne of grace where we can come and obtain mercy and grace to help us. When we take our suffering to the throne, we get the grace to handle it.

That's the difference between the person who complains about a hangnail and the Christian with terminal cancer who is rejoicing in the Lord. Paul told the Thessalonians that the sufferers for Christ are the ones considered worthy of the kingdom. When you are afflicted because of your stand for God, that does not go unnoticed by heaven.

Paul knew all about suffering. His "thorn in the flesh" (2 Corinthians 12:7) was either a physical ailment or perhaps a person who was giving him grief. Whatever it was, it hurt. Paul went to God and asked Him to remove it.

No answer. So Paul prayed a second time, "Lord, please get rid of this thorn." He didn't hear anything again. So he repeated his request a third time.

Finally, God answered him, "Paul, I am not going to remove your thorn."

And then God made one of the great statements of the New Testament: "My grace is sufficient for you" (v. 9). God said to Paul, "I am not going to change your circumstances. I am going to change you in your circumstances."

That was more than good enough for Paul. He was "well content" with whatever God gave him (v. 10).

## Faithfulness in Suffering

When you go for a job interview, you're often asked, "How many years' experience do you have?" They want to know what you are bringing from your old job that will enable you to do your new job better than someone who is not experienced.

Employers know that experience is often better than degrees. People with degrees know it in their heads, but experienced people know it in their hands.

There will be a lot of people in heaven who can't show you a degree. They didn't have a lot of theology, but they had plenty of "kneeology." Their faithfulness in suffering is going to produce "an eternal weight of glory" (2 Corinthians 4:17) that will outweigh a lot of accolades and degrees.

## PARTAKERS ARE SINCERE

Here's another trademark of kingdom partakers: They are sincere in their desire to serve and please the Lord. As Paul wrote, "We have as our ambition, whether at home or absent, to be pleasing to Him" (2 Corinthians 5:9).

## Sincerity of Our Motives

Now, we know it's almost impossible for us to be completely in touch with our deepest motives all the time and to keep them completely pure all the time. But the person I'm talking about sincerely desires to please the Lord and live out His kingdom agenda.

Sincerity in our service is crucial because, as we have already seen several times, the day is coming when believers will stand before

Christ.

Paul speaks of this in the very next verse: "For we must all appear before the judgment seat of Christ, that each one may be recompensed for his deeds in the body, according to what he has done, whether good or bad" (2 Corinthians 5:10).

This judgment seat was the *bema* seat at the Isthmian Games held in Corinth, an ancient version of the Olympics in which athletes would compete and appear before the judgment seat to receive their prize.

Paul used this term to describe Christ's judgment seat. Paul's motive was to please the Lord so that he would not be disqualified from the action and miss out on the rewards of serving Christ.

## Under the Spotlight

When we stand before Christ, and the light of His blazing glory shines on our lives, we will be glad we were sincere and not deceptive in our motives. That's because Christ will evaluate the deeds we have done, the words we have said, and the motives behind all of it.

On that day, what we did and why we did it will be crystal clear. There will be no doubt or misunderstanding. It will be, in the words of famed radio commentator Paul Harvey, "the rest of the story." That's why Paul said in 1 Corinthians 3:13 that the fire of God's judgment will test our work to examine its quality.

In other words, did we do what we did for the honor of God? We can do a lot of good things for our own honor. That's a hard one to read sometimes because our motives get all twisted up, and even we aren't always able to see into our own hearts.

There will be weeping at the judgment seat of Christ when some believers see their own works burned up and see other believers receiving their full kingdom inheritance.

## PARTAKERS ARE SERIOUS

We close this chapter by returning once more to Hebrews 3, where the writer gave this exhortation:

> *Take care, brethren, lest there should be in any one of you an evil,*
> *unbelieving heart, in falling away from the living God. But encourage one*
> *another day after day, as long as it is still called "Today," lest any one*

*of you be hardened by the deceitfulness of sin. For we have become partakers*
*of Christ, if we hold fast the beginning of our assurance firm until the end.*
*(vv. 12–14)*

We referred to the first part of verse 14, above, as we introduced the section on being partakers. The rest of the verse, and the ones before it, reveal how we become partakers—by a serious commitment to persevere and hang in there for Christ.

## Partakers Persevere

Partakers are serious folks. They're serious about church, for example, because they know they can't make it on their own. They need the encouragement of other believers.

You need the rest of the body of Christ if you are going to be a partaker. Why? Because without encouragement, you will fall by the wayside. Without the encouragement of the body, you will be more susceptible to the deceitfulness of sin.

Sin is tricky. It feels good at first, but then it makes you hard. And when you get hard, you need more sin to satisfy you. Sin is so deceitful. It will make you feel like it's your best friend. Only later will you realize it was responsible for your demise.

Partakers are serious about not letting sin trick them and harden them. They are serious about persevering, holding their faith "firm until the end." Partakers are those who stay with it.

All of us have bumps in the road. God is not talking about whether you get stalled. He's talking about whether you go in reverse. That's what Israel did. The Hebrews got to the edge of the Promised Land but then threw themselves into reverse and headed back into the wilderness toward Egypt.

## What It Takes

What does it take to be serious about being a kingdom person, living on a kingdom agenda, and looking forward to a kingdom inheritance? First, it takes *dedication*. You have to set this as your goal and let nothing stop you or turn you back.

Second, it takes *discipline* to be a partaker. "Pursue righteousness," Paul told Timothy (see 1 Timothy 6:11; 2 Timothy 2:22).

God will help you, but God won't exercise discipline for you. You must say, "I am not going to let my eyes look at that which tempts me to sin. I am not going to be around that which pulls me into sin."

A third trait of partakers is *dependence*, a realization that you can't do it on your own. It's too hard for you. It's too big for you. And so every day you live, you drop to your knees before God and say, "God, I can't love this husband. I can't be patient with these children. I can't tolerate my co-workers. But I'm thankful today that You can love these people through me. I depend on You today."

Fourth and finally, partakers are *those who develop*, who keep on growing. You will never "arrive" in this life, in the sense that you will not need to grow or learn anything anymore. You may not be where you want to be right now, but you can be further down the road next year than you are now if you will allow God to keep growing you in Christ. Remember, you don't have to be perfect to be a partaker, just faithful.

# The Kingdom Agenda in Your Family Life

# CHAPTER ELEVEN

# The Kingdom Agenda
# of Husbands

Now that we have looked at a kingdom agenda in our personal lives, let's widen the focus and consider what a kingdom agenda looks like when it's applied to family life. This is a logical progression, because if the agenda is working in your own life, the most natural place it ought to show up is in your family life.

The importance of the family cannot be overstated. This is so because whoever owns the family owns the future. The family is *the* most fundamental institution in society. The story of the nation is simply the story of the family written large.

The family is also crucial because of its unique role in reflecting the unique relationship between Christ and His church. The family is also unique to history since there will be no marriage in heaven (see Matthew 22:30). You don't need an illustration when you have the real thing. Therefore, there can be no discussion of the family without linking it to the kingdom of God.

We're going to get very specific about the roles that husbands, wives, parents, children, and single people are to play in the family. I hope in the process we will become committed to reflecting God's kingdom agenda in our homes.

Whenever I deal with the husband's role in a marriage, I always think of the man who was on an airplane and noticed something unusual about the man sitting next to him. He was wearing his wedding ring on his right hand.

Somewhat curious, the first man said, "Sir, I believe you have your wedding ring on the wrong finger."

The other man said, "No, I just married the wrong woman."

There are a lot of men—and women too—who feel like they married the wrong person. They believe the biggest mistake of their lives was saying, "I do," because they don't. They simply had no idea what they were getting into.

Some men are even doubtful at the wedding. A preacher was once in the middle of the wedding ceremony and asked, "Is there anyone here who knows any reason these two should not be joined in holy matrimony?"

A voice rang out, "I do!"

The preacher said, "Hush, you're the groom."

If that's your attitude toward your marriage, or even if you feel great about the person you're married to, the Bible has some powerful and very beneficial things to say to Christian husbands.

You have probably figured out by now that I want to address the men here. But let me encourage women to keep reading also, because the principles I want to share can help a single woman know the right kind of man when she meets him or help a wife encourage her husband to be the man God wants him to be.

My brother, whether you are married, engaged, or hope to be married someday, let me address the kingdom agenda the Word of God spells out for you. People used to say a man's home was his castle. That meant he was king of his domain.

If you've always wanted to be the king of your castle, here's your chance. By living for your heavenly King as a husband, you can bring a royal presence to your home. Not because you sit on your throne and bark out orders to the wife and kids but because you reflect King Jesus.

So let's look at five ways a husband can fulfill a kingdom agenda in his marriage. I want to say up front that my purpose is not to dump on husbands, though that's popular. Instead I want to encourage you and myself to be biblical husbands.

Some of the things I'm going to share may seem hard. But husbands need to hear them because most husbands aren't going to get this stuff at work or on television or with their friends. Marriage is

God's institution, and He sets the rules. Since He created marriage, He must show us how to make it work.

Every Christian husband must recognize that he is under authority, the authority of Christ (1 Corinthians 11:3). Therefore any Christian man who refuses to submit to biblical authority regarding his submission to the lordship of Christ has forfeited his right to demand that his wife submit to him. It is his falling in line under his leader that models for his wife how she is to fall in line under him.

## LOVE YOUR WIFE

The first way a husband can reflect a kingdom agenda in his marriage is to love his wife.

I can hear some husbands saying, "That goes without saying. Move on to number two." Sorry, but we need to spend some extra time here on number one, because a lot of what goes under the name of love has little to do with true, biblical love.

The word *love* has become devalued today. People say, "I love my job. I love my home. I love chocolate cake." What they are talking about is what those things do for them. The home makes them comfortable. The work satisfies their career needs. The cake satisfies their sweet tooth.

That's fine, but that's not love. Biblical love involves the sacrifice you make for the loved one. You measure true love by sacrifice, not by enjoyment. If a husband talks about loving his wife but means by this that she does a lot of good things for him, that's not him loving her. That's her loving him.

### The Husband as Savior

What does it mean for a husband to love his wife in accordance with a kingdom agenda? The first thing it means is for the husband to be a savior for his wife.

Now I know what you're thinking. But my theology is firmly in place. Obviously, I'm not using the term *savior* in any theological sense. But I am using the word very deliberately. Let me show you what I mean.

In Ephesians 5, a classic passage on marriage, the apostle Paul said, "Husbands, love your wives, just as Christ also loved the church and gave Himself up for her" (v. 25).

How did Jesus give Himself up for the church? He died. As far as

God is concerned, to talk about marital love is to talk about a cross. To talk about love is to talk about Calvary. To talk about love is to talk about a Savior.

We have a Savior in Christ. And our wives ought to have a savior in us. We have a Deliverer in Christ. And our wives ought to have a deliverer in us. Loving your wife means carrying a cross. So if you feel like your wife is crucifying you, you have the perfect opportunity to look like Jesus.

You may know that nowhere in Scripture is a wife commanded to love her husband. She is commanded to respect him (see Ephesians 5:33). It's not that a woman shouldn't love her husband. But her love is a response to his salvation. If you and I are going to be biblical lovers as husbands, we must become biblical saviors.

That means loving as Christ loves. So a husband is called to love his wife no matter what. We can't wait until she gets everything right, just as a wife is to love her husband even when he doesn't have it all together.

This gets very practical. A husband's love cannot say, "She's meeting my needs. Therefore, I will love her." No, you love her even when she's not meeting your needs. You love her until she learns how to meet your needs.

Most men date in order to marry, when the biblical principle is marry in order to date. Most men shower a woman with love to get her to say, "I do." But the biblical ideal is to have her say, "I do," so we can spend the rest of our lives showering her with love.

Every man likes to think of himself as a lover. But the measuring rod for biblical lover is the size of the cross he is carrying. Christ loved the church to death.

When Adam was created, God opened his side and took out a rib to create Eve. Adam had to bleed to get Eve. Christ had to bleed in order to birth the church. If a wife is going to grow from where she is to where she ought to be, her husband has to take a trip to Calvary.

Now remember, I'm not talking about eternal salvation here at all. The idea is that a husband is called to give himself up for his wife. That's first on God's agenda for us husbands.

Husband, you need to decide, "I am willing to pay whatever price it takes to bring my wife to fulfillment. I am willing to go the distance to bring her from where she is to where she ought to be spiritually and every other way."

The Bible says Jacob loved Rachel so much that he worked fourteen years to gain her hand (see Genesis 29:20, 30). That's a high price to pay, but it's the price tag of love.

Too many men want to run away from their wives when there's a problem. But if there were no problems, if your wife were perfect, she wouldn't need a savior. Christ looked at us in our mess and said, "You have a Savior. Here I am."

When a man comes home, he must say, "Things may not be right. I may not like what is happening, but a savior is in the house. I am your deliverer. Whatever is wrong, I am Mr. Fix-it. Whatever price has to be paid, I will pay it."

The husband is the savior of the wife. At the heart of that is sacrifice. If there is no sacrifice, there is no love. So my question is, husband, "Do you really love your wife? If I asked her what price you are paying to love her, could she tell me? Could *you* tell me what price you are paying for her?"

When you got married, the preacher asked you up front, "Will you love this woman in sickness and in health, for richer or poorer, as long as you both shall live?" We preachers ask that because we know something. We know you haven't seen the whole deal in marriage yet, so we want an up-front commitment.

The theological equivalent of a husband's promise to love his wife no matter what, as long as he lives, is the doctrine called *eternal security*. This truth says that no matter what comes—good, bad, or ugly—because we are God's children, He is not going anywhere. We are His forever.

A husband who truly loves his wife says, "If this marriage ends, you're going to have to leave me because I'm not going anywhere. No matter how you treat me or what happens, I want you to know you have a savior." Only a man who has abandoned himself to a kingdom agenda rather than a personal one can make this level of commitment.

## The Husband as Sanctifier

Not only is a husband to be his wife's savior—if he is going to live according to a kingdom agenda, he must also be her sanctifier.

In Ephesians 5:26–27 Paul spoke of Christ and the church: "That He might sanctify her, having cleansed her by the washing of water with the word, that He might present to Himself the church in all her glory, having no spot or wrinkle or any such thing; but that she should be holy and blameless."

Now let me tell you what happens in a marriage. When a man

marries a woman, he also marries her history (this works both ways, of course). He has to accept the good parts of her past and her family as well as the bad parts. The good parts he enjoys. The bad parts he often doesn't get to see until after the honeymoon.

The husband doesn't get to see it all before the wedding. You may only get to see your future wife with her makeup on and with those eyelashes you thought were real. You only see her on her "party behavior," so it may be only after you're married that you hear yourself saying, "I didn't know you fussed like that. You didn't fuss when we were dating."

But if you love your wife, you will be her sanctifier. The word *sanctification* means "to set apart for special use." That is, to place a person in a unique category, to take her from where she is to where she needs to go. In the Bible, the process of sanctification is what we call *spiritual growth*.

A lot of men think that when they get married, the main job has been accomplished. But it's just beginning. A husband's job is to sanctify his marriage, to make it something special, something set apart. What Jesus is to the church, a husband is to his mate.

A marriage can get clogged and backed up with junk, just like the kitchen sink can back up. A lot of stuff can go hidden and undetected for a while, but it begins to build up. And when it builds up, it backs up.

At that point, husbands often get upset with their wives, looking at the emotional whirlwind swirling through her and thinking, *I didn't know you had all that stuff in there.* It was there all the time; it just hadn't backed up yet. But now it starts backing up, and the marriage gets clogged.

That's not the time to bail out. A husband needs to do what he does when the sink backs up—call a professional plumber. Then he comes out with that little snake he uses to bore through the clog and open the sink.

Husband, you're the professional. When your wife's history backs up on her, when the pressure at work backs up, when circumstances back up, you're to come in with the love "snake" and clear the backup so that everything is flowing freely once more.

What is the purpose of a sanctifier? According to Ephesians 5:26, Jesus' purpose is to cleanse the church. A husband is the wife's "cleaner-upper." His love is to be a sanctifying agent to help cleanse and heal the things she brings into the marriage that may not be right.

Maybe she was abused by her father. Or maybe she was raised by a domineering mother. That stuff won't disappear just because the husband comes on the scene. Our wives need our sanctifying love.

The result of a husband's sanctifying work is a wife who has "no spot or wrinkle" (Ephesians 5:27). These are very picturesque terms. *Spot* as it's used here represents defilement from outside. If something drops on your shirt, you get a spot.

Wrinkle has to do with internal aging. Most women are covering that up, because they don't want the wrinkles to show. Wrinkles are evidence that we're getting older.

The church has spots, the external stains of the world, and wrinkles, internal aging and decay. Jesus says, "My job is to wash off the spots and remove the wrinkles." The husband's job is to work with his wife in such a way that she begins to see a cleanup take place in her life.

What this means is that when your wife needs strength, you are her strength. When she needs encouragement, you are her encouragement. When she needs joy, you are her joy. When she needs peace, you are her peace. The result is that no matter how old she gets, your wife is kept eternally young because she's got a sanctifier in the house.

The husband says, "Well, if she hadn't screamed at me, I wouldn't have screamed at her." This is not tit for tat. What I'm talking about is showing strength. Husband, you say you're the leader. You say you're the strong one. Then be that. Be your wife's sanctifier, that she might be cleansed, for the true purpose of leadership is not domination but glorification. If it is our goal to glorify and beautify our wives, then we will not abuse them but embrace them.

## The Husband as Satisfier

The third aspect of a husband's kingdom-oriented love is that of being his wife's satisfier.

Verses 28–29 of Ephesians 5 say, "Husbands ought also to love their own wives as their own bodies. He who loves his own wife loves himself; for no one ever hated his own flesh, but nourishes and cherishes it, just as Christ also does the church."

What we need today is a group of men who know how to satisfy their wives. Now most men think *sex* when they hear that. And some men will brag about how many women they can satisfy. But any man who talks that way doesn't know what he's talking about.

A real man is one who can commit himself to his wife and love her with a steady commitment so that after fifteen, twenty, thirty, or fifty years, his wife can still say, "I'm satisfied."

Paul explains this as loving your wife the way you love your own body. So just as a man works out to make his body look good and does things to satisfy his needs, he is to help his wife look good so that she is fulfilled and satisfied.

There are too many dissatisfied wives out there because there are too many unsatisfying husbands. As I've said before, too many husbands and wives look like they were married by the secretary of war rather than the justice of the peace.

Husbands and wives in constant conflict are like the late Winston Churchill and Lady Astor in England. Lady Astor despised Winston Churchill. She said, "Winston, if you were my husband, I'd put arsenic in your tea."

Churchill responded, "Lady Astor, if I were your husband, I'd drink it."

That's the way a lot of couples live. Changing it starts with the husband. It has nothing to do with what the wife does in return, because we're talking about biblical love here. A man who is determined to satisfy his wife won't stop even if his efforts are not met with equal love. The first thing on a husband's kingdom agenda is to love his wife.

## LIVE WITH YOUR WIFE

A second way you can live out your kingdom agenda as a husband is to live with your wife.

You say, "That's easy. We're in the same house. We're still together." But there's more to it than that. The apostle Peter said, "You husbands likewise, live with your wives in an understanding way" (1 Peter 3:7).

### Live in Harmony

The Greek word for *live* means to dwell in close harmony, to be closely aligned with someone, to live together with intimacy. When somebody comes to visit and you say, "Make yourself at home," you mean more than just sit down. You mean make yourself comfortable, be joyful, be at peace.

Many men have the idea, "I'm the husband; I go out and work. You're the wife; you stay home. I do my job; you do your job."

But that's where the problem is. The home is the husband's job too. The wife is to help her husband do his job well at home, but she is not designed to replace him in the home. A husband needs to create an environment of intimacy in his home.

It is part of a husband's kingdom agenda to make sure, as much as humanly possible, that his home is a place of peace. That means he has to be present to be the leader.

## A Commitment to the Home

Remember, your wife didn't marry a paycheck, a car, or a job title. She married you. Whenever you measure the quality of your marriage by the number and size of the trinkets you own, you've missed it.

If your marriage is typical, your wife loved you when you didn't have a dime. She married you when you were just out of college, when nobody knew your name. That's the man she wants to live with. She doesn't want to trade that for a nice car or a big house.

I know we men have the responsibility to provide for our families. I'm not overlooking that. What I'm telling you is that whenever the things you do *for* your wife replace your presence *with* her, then you are not living with her in the way 1 Peter 3:7 describes.

Let me tell you, I'm as guilty as anyone else, because I know what it is to live with my job. I know what it is to spend so much time at the church that Lois is left home without anyone to talk to. In the meantime, I've got a line of people making appointments to talk with me.

I know what it is to have Lois discouraged when I come home because while I have ministered well at church, I am too tired to minister well at home. I know what it is to work twelve- and fifteen-hour days, then go home and feel like throwing in the towel because I'm so tired.

But the moment I do that, I have stopped living with my wife in an understanding way. I have started living with my ministry.

Lois didn't marry my ministry. There wasn't any Oak Cliff Bible Fellowship or The Urban Alternative when we got married. There were no church members, no pulpit, no buildings, no radio broadcast, no conferences. There was just her and me.

For a husband, making the commitment to live with his wife may mean making some hard decisions about work, hobbies, or other involvements. But imagine what it would mean to a wife to have her husband tell her, "I'm committed to you. If I have to give some things up or back off at work, I'll do it."

## A Second Job: Your Home

Obeying God's Word in this area means that when a husband goes home, he goes home to his second job. Therefore, the boss downtown can't have 100 percent of a Christian husband's time or commitment, because he has a second job.

It's commonly accepted that when a wife comes home from work, she's coming home to her second job. She's supposed to get something on the table, clean the house, and make sure everyone, including hubby, is taken care of. Then she's supposed to have enough energy to meet her husband's physical needs at night.

What I'm saying is that a wife needs a husband whose attitude also is, "This is our home. We're in this together, and I want you to know that when I come home, I come home to work." What kind of work? Whatever kind the wife needs at that time to help her out. Husbands are to outserve their wives regularly and consistently, for the essence of leadership is servanthood.

Sometimes a husband's "job" is as simple as calling his wife in the middle of the day and saying, "I can't get you off my mind today. I started to write something, and I found myself writing your name instead of what I was supposed to write."

At other times, living together with understanding means the husband dries the dishes as his wife washes them. Or maybe it's making up one side of the bed while she makes up the other side.

Brother, your wife was given to you to be your partner, not your slave. And while there is hierarchy in this partnership, it is a partnership nonetheless, and therefore she should feel infinitely valued. God wants you to live with her in the intimacy of that partnership. When you've got that thing right, there is nothing on earth more satisfying.

## KNOW YOUR WIFE

First Peter 3:7 gives us a third way a husband can fulfill his kingdom agenda in his marriage. To live with his wife in an understanding way demands that he know her intimately.

A husband needs to study two things: the Bible and his wife. Why? Because both are difficult to interpret. There are "some things hard to understand" (2 Peter 3:16) in both your Bible and your wife. Any man will testify that a woman is complex and sometimes confusing. You think she wants this, but she really wants that.

### Time to Study

That's why we have to study our wives. Now you can't study

something without giving time to it. When your wife wants to talk, she's giving you the opportunity to know her, because many times we as men are meeting needs that our wives don't have.

You say, "So how do I know what my wife's needs are?"

Ask her and then listen to the answer. She'll tell you if she knows you really want to hear the answer. Remember, God built a complex circuitry into women. That circuitry includes hormones that are on the move.

So each month, you need to be aware of what is happening to your wife. The week before her menstrual cycle, she may be a little bit more sensitive and perhaps a little more irritable, based on her temperament. During this time she may also be a little bit more frustrated, but after that she may bounce back with new energy.

A husband who really wants to know his wife will have the attitude, "I understand what's going on. So I'll be a little more understanding, a little more tender, a little more conversational. I know you're coming into a rough time, but I want you to know that I'm going to be here for you."

What a wife needs is a husband who will be there when she comes to the end of her hormonal roller-coaster ride. That doesn't mean it is always easy to be an understanding husband. But it's worth the effort, because in the process of knowing your wife, the two of you will grow closer together.

## Adjusting Your Schedule

Knowing your wife means you have to make some adjustments. You may have to give up some TV programs or get your news from somewhere besides the evening newscast.

Why? Because that time of the evening is now your time to say, "Honey, I'm ready to listen. Tell me anything you want me to know, because when I learn it, I'm going to use it to love you better. You've got my undivided attention."

Now that's a big change from reading the newspaper while you "listen" to your wife, or watching TV while she tries to tell you something. But if you want to know what makes your wife tick, you need to give her eyeball-to-eyeball attention.

When that happens, good things will start happening in your marriage, because women love to be understood. They want someone to share their fears, their cares, their hopes, and their disappointments with. When they feel loved and understood, they are better able to respond in love.

## HONOR YOUR WIFE

Here's a fourth way a husband can bring God's kingdom agenda to bear on his marriage. Peter told husbands to honor their wives.

Let's go deeper into 1 Peter 3:7: "Husbands . . . live with your wives in an understanding way, as with a weaker vessel, since she is a woman; and grant her honor as a fellow heir of the grace of life."

The word *grant* means to "assign" your wife a place of honor in your life. To put it another way, if you want to be a true "kingdom" king, treat her like your queen. She is not just another woman.

### Making Her Feel Special

The concept of honor has to do with placing your wife in a position of significance, treating her as someone very special. Does your wife feel special? Do you do things for her that let her know she is different than any other woman?

Many of us men do little courtesies for other women we don't do anymore for our wives. We used to do them. We used to open the car door every single time. We wouldn't think of letting her get in the car by herself. Now, she's lucky to get in before we drive off!

But when chivalry dies, a marriage starts to die. We need to make a commitment that other women may have to open the door for themselves, but not our wives. Your wife is your queen, so roll out the red carpet, pull out the chair, open up the door, and escort her. She *must* feel special.

You can also make your wife feel special by your words. I mentioned earlier how little time and effort it takes to pick up the phone, call your wife in the middle of the day, and tell her she's on your mind and you can't wait to see her when you get home.

There are so many other ways we can make our wives feel special. A gift for no particular reason is a great way to tell your wife she's special to you. Your time is also a gift to your wife. You don't have to give her a new car to make her feel special. Just the fact that you want to take her somewhere in the old car will do.

Have you ever written your wife a note and put it under the pillow? Write about how great it is to sleep next to her and wake up to sunshine even when the drapes are closed. Let her know you wouldn't have it any other way.

I know a lot of husbands do something special for their wives on their birthdays or anniversaries. But if those are the only times we do something special, we become too predictable. The key is to be consistent in communicating to your wife how special she is.

Just as God's loving-kindnesses are new every morning (see Lamentations 3:22–23), so we as kingdom leaders should show that same consistency to our wives.

## Recapturing the Feeling

When you were dating your wife, you didn't do special things for her only once or twice a year. You bombarded her with calls, notes, and gifts. You surprised her with stuff all the time. You were creative and spontaneous. You gave her every minute you had to spare.

She may not even have liked you when you two first met. But you kept it going, and eventually the two of you fell in love and got married.

But what happens once a man gets married? Often, he stops honoring his wife. He stops making her feel special. She has to fend for herself. Her ideas and opinions no longer matter much. Her skills are taken for granted.

I often ask husbands, "When was your last date with your wife?" Now, by a date, I'm not talking about coming home and saying, "What do you want to do tonight?"

That's not a date. A date is, "Honey, I've got this evening all planned out. All you need to do is come along. Here's what I have planned. If you want to make some adjustments, that's fine, because I want to please you. But I want to let you know I thought about this evening before it arrived."

That kind of thing communicates honor and value to your wife. It tells her you didn't just come with nothing planned and say, "What do you want to do tonight?" It tells her she's not just an afterthought to you. She is seen as significant.

## Your Spiritual Equal

Peter said we are to honor our wives because they are our "fellow heir[s] of the grace of life."

Your wife is your equal in terms of her value as a human being and her spiritual value to God. She may be called to be submissive to your leadership (see 1 Peter 3:1), but she deserves honor as your fellow heir.

She may not be as physically strong as you are, but she is worthy of your honor. Why? Because God says she is. This divine mandate must be reflected in the way you relate to your wife.

Don't misunderstand. Honoring your wife doesn't mean you two will always see eye-to-eye. You may have to make a decision she doesn't agree with.

But honoring her means you take her thoughts and feelings into account before you make that decision, because God may be showing her something you need to hear.

In fact, if you have a godly and loving wife, you need to proceed very slowly when you are facing a decision or a situation in which she is not in agreement with you. I'm not saying you have to change your decision, but it's important to take your wife's feedback seriously, because she's your partner.

And if down the line it becomes apparent that this decision is not going to be in your wife's best interest, you must be willing to reverse yourself because you don't want to do anything that's going to harm her.

Brother, if you and I will treat our wives as thoroughbreds, we won't end up with nags. You may say, "But I married the wrong woman." Then start treating her like the right woman, and she'll become the right woman. Honor your wife.

## PRAY WITH YOUR WIFE

The fifth and final way a kingdom agenda becomes real in your marriage is found in the last phrase of 1 Peter 3:7: "That your prayers may not be hindered."

This may be the last item on our list, but it's the most important. If there is no dynamic spiritual relationship between you and your wife, there won't be much dynamic to your relationship at all. If the two of you don't have a heavenly foundation, you'll wind up with a hellish relationship.

### Fellow Heirs

The key to this is found in the concept we just discussed, the fact that you and your wife are fellow heirs of God's grace. Do you know what Peter is saying? He's saying that God is not going to do anything for you if your wife can't be included.

In other words, your prayers are a waste of time if she isn't included. You don't have a singular relationship with God anymore, because you became one flesh with your wife. So if you're not treating your wife the way Peter described in this verse, God doesn't have any answers to prayer for you because He doesn't see two people anymore. He sees one person, one flesh.

Since this is true, it has to be said that one of the great sins today is that men are not praying with their wives.

Wife, if your husband is trying to pray with you, don't turn him down. He's calling on the biggest force available to save your home. Help him and encourage him. He's calling on God, because God is not going to help him, apart from you.

Husbands need to pray with their wives, so the two of them can enjoy the spiritual riches of God's kingdom plan and His kingdom inheritance together.

## The Spiritual Thermostat

Husband, you're the spiritual thermostat in your marriage and home. You control the temperature. Your wife is the thermometer. She'll tell you how it reads.

So if you have the thermostat set on 80 degrees and she's cold, your thermostat is broken. Generally, you can tell a lot about a man by looking in the face of his wife. She is his mirror.

A wife said to her husband one day, "Honey, I wish I were young again."

He said, "Why?"

"So I could live with you longer." That's what your wife ought to be saying. I pray that she *will* say it to you one day.

The question is not, will your marriage work? The question is, will you work at your marriage? If your marriage needs to be turned around, let it start with you. If you turn the right way, your wife will follow your lead.

This is the mind-set of a man who relates to his wife according to a kingdom agenda.

# CHAPTER TWELVE

# The Kingdom Agenda
# of Wives

In chapter 11 I challenged husbands to be the leaders and lovers that God's kingdom agenda demands. Now I want to turn the marriage coin over and examine the other side—I want to challenge the wives.

Men and women are ontological equals. That is, there is an equality of essence between the sexes. Women are not inferior to men. However, there is a distinction of function in God's kingdom. As Paul put it, "The man is the head of a woman" (1 Corinthians 11:3).

This is a statement of function, not of essence. A wife is required by God to function in a role that honors her husband's leadership in order to accomplish God's kingdom agenda in the home. To rebel against this assignment is to rebel against God. The challenge is how to apply this truth in such a way that women are not abused or treated as second-class citizens.

## IT TAKES TWO

It takes two people to come together as one flesh in marriage. Therefore it is not enough simply to tell the husband what he must do. The wife needs to cooperate with the agenda.

That's hard to do if your marriage is like the one I heard about recently. The minister who had married this man and his wife fifteen years earlier ran into the husband one day.

The minister was reminiscing about how he had been an hour late to the wedding that day and how everybody was hysterical. The minister never forgot it, so he said to the man, "I still feel bad about the way I scared you on your wedding day."

The husband said, "Yeah, I remember how you scared me. I've been scared ever since, because I still have her."

There are a lot of men who have great difficulty fulfilling God's kingdom calling in their marriage because their wives aren't fulfilling the other half of the agenda. Many women have taken their definition of a wife's role from *Another World*, *Days of Our Lives*, *General Hospital*, and *As the World Turns*, or the feminist movement, rather than from God's Word. That is, they got their information from the wrong source.

Some women grew up in homes where the mother ran the show. Perhaps she had to, given the nature of the father in the home. But still, that dominant attitude got transferred to the daughter. And she has brought that into her marriage.

Since God created marriage, He must define how it works. That's what we are attempting to do in these chapters by examining marriage from a biblical perspective.

One of the worst statements a woman can make is, "My mama told me." When you got married, you broke rank with your mama. Now I don't have anything against your mother, but I want you to know her opinion is no longer the reigning voice in your life.

You may say, "Yes, but you don't know my husband." Well, your husband can't be that bad. He chose you. He had enough sense to know who to marry. He was smart enough to see that you would be the woman for him. He was sharp enough to woo you and win you.

Now if something has gone wrong, a lot of the problem could be on his side. But in this chapter, our concern is to help you be the wife God wants you to be.

In the previous chapter, we gave the husband five things to consider in living out a kingdom agenda and reflecting the King in the home. But as I examine the biblical data, I think we can narrow the wife's primary task down to two areas. Let's find out what they are.

## HELP YOUR HUSBAND

The first thing a kingdom wife must do is help her husband. To be your husband's helper is not to lose or limit yourself. On the contrary, as we shall see, it is to maximize your divinely bestowed gifts, talents, skills, and training for the betterment of the home under the leadership of your husband as well as in partnership with him.

We keep going back to Adam and Eve a lot in this book, but there's a reason. Adam and Eve, in their innocence, represented marriage as it was designed to be. As God got ready to create Eve, He made that profound statement, "It is not good for the man to be alone; I will make him a helper suitable for him" (Genesis 2:18).

God was saying, "I am going to make someone to come alongside Adam, someone who will correspond to him and help accomplish the divine agenda I have given both of them."

Remember that God gave the command to manage His creation to both man and woman (see Genesis 1:28). His creation belonged to both of them. The woman is not some extra fluff on the side; she is an indispensable part of God's agenda. But in order for the agenda to be accomplished, she must be by her husband's side as his helper.

One reason so many marriages are failing is that the wife is not out to help her husband; she's using the marriage to help herself. She has a faulty view of the relationship.

Instead of being her husband's partner and coming alongside to help him, a wife who is in the situation has become part of the opposition. She has become his competitor. She is working against the program. She is not cooperating with God's kingdom agenda for the family.

When a wife loses sight of the truth that God's first expectation of her in relationship to her husband is to be his helper in the home, then a negative atmosphere is created in the home. So the question is, what does a helper look like?

I want to answer that, but first let me make one more observation by way of setting the stage. If God expects a wife to help her husband, the assumption is that he needs help. I'll be the first to admit it. We as men are not complete in and of ourselves. That's the reason God created women.

If you are finding fault with your husband, guess what your role is: to help him get better. God made the wife to be the helper because a man needs help. He needs somebody to come alongside him and be different than he is in order to complete him and help him live out the kingdom agenda of God.

So when the faults of your husband show up, they are opportunities for you to fulfill your biblical job description. If you are the complete opposite of your husband, that's wonderful. That means you can fill in all the blank spots where your husband needs help. You can cooperate with God in molding and shaping him into what God wants him to be so that together you might carry out the kingdom agenda in and through your home.

## A Real Diamond

Now we're ready to answer the question, "What does a biblical helper look like?"

We have a classic description, given in prolific detail, in Proverbs 31:10–31. God didn't go into great detail in Genesis, but in Proverbs 31 the description of a wife who fulfills her kingdom agenda is fleshed out for us.

The writer of this section begins with a question himself: "An excellent wife, who can find?" (v. 10) The Hebrew word for *excellent* means a woman of nobility, a woman of great worth. We know that because verse 10 goes on to say, "Her worth is far above jewels."

Many women have a low view of themselves, which makes for a weakness in their marriages. A woman who sees herself as an expensive diamond and is treated that way is going to act like an expensive diamond. A woman who considers herself costume jewelry is going to act like costume jewelry.

You can make jewelry that looks like the real thing, but it's plastic. Proverbs 31 is talking about a real woman, not a plastic one. The writer said that when a man finds this kind of woman, he has found something of great value.

In verse 12, this kind of wife is described as someone who "does [her husband] good and not evil all the days of her life." Here is a woman who is perpetually, ferociously, and determinedly looking out for the good of her man.

This is so crucial that it's not a stretch to say that if helping her husband is not high on a wife's agenda, she is not functioning as a Christian wife. She may do a lot of things, but a Christian wife seeks the good of her husband all the days of her life.

That is, just as a husband needs to wake up seeking how to love, honor, and cherish his wife, she needs to wake up and ask, "How can I do my husband good today?" Let's answer that from our text.

## Help Him Financially

One of the ways a wife can help her husband is financially. Look at several verses in this chapter:

> *She looks for wool and flax, and works with her hands in delight. She is like merchant ships; she brings her food from afar. . . . She considers a field and buys it; from her earnings she plants a vineyard. . . . She makes linen garments and sells them, and supplies belts to the tradesmen.*
> (vv. 13–14, 16, 24)

There's this warped view that says to be a godly Christian woman you have to check your brains at the door, throw your education in the garbage, put your skills on hold, and give up all opportunities to be productive.

That's hardly the picture here. This woman who helps her husband is skilled. She earns, saves, invests, and spends money wisely. But she's doing it for the good of her husband and her household.

This is not like a lot of women who are building their own careers and have their own money in their own bank accounts on which they write their own checks. That's not the godly woman. She uses her skills and gifts for the embellishment of her home and the enhancement of her husband, because she is kingdom oriented, not self-oriented. There is no financial competition.

If a wife loves her career so much that her husband is never benefited from the career that she loves, then she is not being a godly wife. She has bought the lie of many feminists that she's her own woman doing her own thing, and her man is an inconvenience.

The wife of Proverbs 31 has all the skills and abilities in the world. But her husband knows that every dollar she makes and every dime she spends will make their home a better place to live. But when a wife begins living for her own agenda, and the good of her husband and family is nowhere to be found, then the blessing of God will not rest on her life or her home.

When a woman begins to live her married life with little thought for the betterment of her husband, she has joined hell in helping to dissolve her marriage.

God did not give a woman a husband so she could continue living as an independent, single woman. He gave her a husband so she could partner with him, using her gifts, skills, and abilities to the fullest, so that their home is thrust forward and her husband is better off. Because he needs that help.

Don't get me wrong. I'm not saying a wife is supposed to help and better her husband while she suffers. No, when a wife is enhancing her husband, she reaps the benefit too. This thing is never meant to be one-sided.

But whenever a wife's career demands so much of her that it negates her role as wife and mother, she's in the wrong career. Someone may say, "But I love my job." That's not the first concern of a kingdom-minded woman, however.

The issue is, whenever a wife's career gets in the way of her loving and helping her husband and bettering their home, she's in the wrong job.

A wife who wants to live out a kingdom agenda must be willing to say to her husband, "Even if I have to give up this job, I won't work for another person who will be better off than you will be because of the time I spend outside this house every day."

## Help Him Parentally

Second, this wife helps her husband parentally. Proverbs 31:15 says, "She rises also while it is still night, and gives food to her household, and portions to her maidens." Then in verse 21 we read, "She is not afraid of the snow for her household, for all her household are clothed with scarlet."

This wife assists her husband by helping him with the care of the children. As we said in the previous chapter, a wife is not designed to replace her husband in the home, but to help him. Here is a woman so committed to the welfare of her household that she gets up earlier than everybody else to make sure all the bases are covered.

Why does God ask a woman to prioritize her home? Because the job of the home is to raise the next generation of godly seed. If a woman is away from home so much that she cannot assist her husband as a parent and guardian of the children, then she's not fulfilling what God has called her to do.

That's why Paul said the older women are to "encourage the young women to love their husbands, to love their children, to be sensible, pure, workers at home" (Titus 2:3–5). A woman has to take care that the pull of the outside world doesn't keep her from being an effective wife and mother as her first priority.

In other words, don't let the program downtown come into your home. Downtown must wait for your family. Your family cannot wait for downtown, because when your children go left, all downtown will do is lock them up. The world won't raise your children the way they need to be raised. If somebody has to work overtime, let it be the husband.

We have too many women working overtime outside the home and working "undertime" in the home. When that happens, what once was a godly home can become a godless home. A Christian wife helps her husband by being the manager of the home.

## Help Him Personally

A Christian wife also helps her husband by the way she takes care of her own person. Let's go back to Proverbs 31: "She girds herself with strength, and makes her arms strong. . . . She makes coverings for herself; her clothing is fine linen and purple" (vv. 17, 22). This lady is taking care of herself. She's looking good for herself and her husband. We're talking about a beautiful lady here. Her man is excited to go home.

But here's what often happens. A woman gets up every day and goes in front of the mirror because she has to go to work. She's going to look good on the job, because she knows the boss doesn't want haggard-looking people walking around the office.

So this woman makes herself look good for her boss five days a week, eight hours a day. The boss is going to see the lipstick on right and a smile on her face. The hair rollers and curling irons will be used to get the woman ready to look good on the job. And she shops until she drops looking for clothes so she can dress right at work.

And when this woman gets to the office, she's going to take care of the boss because he has her money in his pocket. She may not even like her boss, but she is still going to look good in the office eight hours a day, five days a week. Meanwhile, her husband comes home and has to fend for himself.

If a woman is giving more time and effort to present herself well before her boss than she is to present herself well before her husband, she's not helping him. She's helping her boss. Now Christians are supposed to be the best employees, but that's not what I'm talking about. I'm describing the woman who neglects her husband because the job and the boss demand all her time and her personal attractiveness.

It's OK for the office to get in on what a woman does to enhance herself for her husband, but that's secondary. A wife who wants to help her husband is committed to looking good for him, not for the man downtown. She wants to make her husband look good by making herself look good.

## Help Him Ministerially

I love this one. A Christian wife helps her husband ministerially.

Now by this I don't mean just pastors' wives. The picture here is for a wife who serves alongside her husband in their ministry for the Lord. As Proverbs 31:20, 26 puts it, "She extends her hand to the poor; and she stretches out her hands to the needy. . . . She opens her mouth in wisdom, and the teaching of kindness is on her tongue."

This woman is serving the poor and counseling those who need godly wisdom. There's nothing more beautiful than a wife who ministers alongside her husband. Nothing will draw a couple closer together than serving the Lord together.

The wife described here doesn't have time for gossip. She doesn't have time to spend all day watching soap operas. She's too busy helping her husband help others.

## Help His Reputation

We said at the beginning that a committed Christian wife does her husband good. The final thing I want you to see is just how much good she does for him. She helps him acquire a solid reputation.

According to Proverbs 31:23, "Her husband is known in the gates, when he sits among the elders of the land." What were the gates? In those days, the gates of the city were the city's downtown. It's where the elders conducted the business and government of the land. It's where this woman's husband worked.

What is the writer saying? The guys at the office should know that this man can be where he is and do what he does because he has a wife who makes it possible. Everybody knows who this man is because of his wife. When he steps out, he's the sharpest man at the office because his wife helps him get it all together.

Most of the people at our church in Dallas don't know it, but just before I go to church to preach or spend a day at the office, Lois checks me over and makes a few adjustments. If I'm looking good when I arrive, it's because I was *made* to look good.

Now I know what some women are thinking at this point. *But what about me? I don't always want to be in the background. I don't want to be hidden.* The Proverbs 31 woman wasn't an invisible person. "Her children rise up and bless her; her husband also, and he praises her" (v. 28).

Husband, you should teach your children how to praise their mother. You should teach them to say, "Thank you, Mom, that I'm warm on cold days. Thank you, Mom, for the hot food. Thank you for everything you do."

How do children learn that? By hearing Dad praise his wife. If you have a wife like this, you should talk about her all day long. You should say, "Thank you. Can't live without you. I need you . . . enjoy you . . . don't want to go to sleep without looking at you one more time. You're the first person I want to see in the morning." Go public with this woman.

But there's more to it than that. Because this woman "fears the Lord" (v. 30), because God is her motivation, "let her works praise her in the gates" (v. 31). She also has a godly public reputation. Everybody downtown understands what this woman does to help her husband and enhance her family. She makes God's kingdom agenda come alive in her home and is to receive in return the verbal praise and visible, tangible rewards that are the well-deserved fruits of her labor (see v. 31)

## REVERENCE YOUR HUSBAND

There's a second thing a woman must do to fulfill the agenda of God's kingdom for a wife.

It's found in Ephesians 5:33, where Paul wrote, "Let each individual among you also love his own wife even as himself; and let the wife see to it that she respect her husband." The word *respect* can also be translated "reverence." A wife is to reverence her husband.

### The Importance of Submission

Verses 22–24 of Ephesians 5 explains the doctrine of submission. Now this is a bad word to many women, because it has been defined so badly or used inappropriately to oppress or subjugate women. Most women hear the word *submission* and think, *Oh, no, not that. The dreaded S word.*

But submission is a biblical concept. Jesus submitted Himself to the will of the Father, so we know right off that submission has nothing to do with inferiority. Jesus is equal to God the Father (see Philippians 2:6); He is "very God of very God," as the theologians say.

So submission doesn't have to do with the wife being less than the husband. Submission has to do with accomplishing a divine agenda. Jesus submitted to the Father in order to accomplish the divine plan in our salvation.

We saw in the previous chapter that husbands and wives are equal heirs of God's grace (see 1 Peter 3:7). A wife is of the same value as her husband. Submission doesn't mean she has to be a doormat or any such thing. Any woman is equal to any man in value before God and man.

But when it comes to His kingdom agenda, a wife's submission is absolutely necessary. It means that she recognizes his position as head of the home to accomplish God's agenda in the world. Thus marriage, like the Trinity, is a *hierarchical partnership*. While all parties are equal in value, essence, and significance, there is a distinction in function (hierarchy) in order to fulfill God's kingdom agenda in history.

## The Achievability of Submission

You may say, "I can't submit to that man." Really? You may not agree with everything the boss does, but you submit. If you're hauled into court you may not like what the judge thinks, but you submit. Why? Because you're not submitting to a person. You are submitting to a position.

God has called a husband to a position as head of the home. He's not to be a dictator, but he is the head, and his job is to give direction to the body. The wife's calling is to place her strengths under the authority of her husband, to follow him as he follows Christ.

That's the key, right there in Ephesians 5:22. Wives, submit to your husbands "as to the Lord." Paul can say that because in verse 25 he calls husbands to act like Christ toward their wives.

That means when a husband leaves the Lord, he is no longer acting as his wife's proper head, and she is not obligated to submit to him in anything he wants her to do that's contrary to God's Word. A wife should never disobey the Lord to follow her husband, because her greater allegiance is to God (see Acts 5:29).

But Christian wife, if your husband is trying to serve the Lord, don't work against him. He may not be doing it perfectly, but if the man is trying to apply God's Word, hold up his hands. He needs a helper, not a hindrance; an assister, not an adversary. He needs somebody to come alongside and smooth out those rough edges.

I believe every Christian wife should say to her husband, "I recognize that God has made you the head of our home. I'm going to honor you and follow your leading. I only ask that you not lead me away from Christ."

I'm convinced one reason some Christian husbands aren't doing a better job is that they have never gotten a word of support from their wives. That's not to excuse us husbands from fulfilling our God-given agendas, but we need to hear our wives' affirmation. We need to hear you say, "I am going to reverence your position as head of our home."

If a woman can submit to a boss she doesn't like, she can submit to her husband, even if she doesn't like him at that particular moment. This is not just about liking or agreeing with someone. It's about obeying the Lord.

I've counseled enough married couples over the years to know that some wives who insist they can't submit to their husbands don't know that for a fact because they have never really tried. They have never willingly come under his authority as head and tried to motivate him to follow Christ.

Instead, they work against their husbands. They're always fussing at him. He can't do anything right. He gets beaten up outside the home all day; then he comes home to get beaten up some more. Rather than having someone at home who is going to help him, affirm him, strengthen him, and make him feel like somebody, he has another adversary across the dinner table.

As suggested above, maybe the reason a husband isn't doing so well is that he has no one to help him. Christian wife, maybe God gave your husband to you so you could smooth his rough edges.

This issue of submission hits right at the heart of what it means to be a Christian. Therefore, a wife who does not submit to her husband is not submitted to God. She can do all the spiritual stuff, but if she is not reverencing her husband as her head, she is living in carnality.

I realize this may not be a popular message today, but God did not call me to be popular. I want to encourage and affirm Christian couples as they seek to carry out God's agenda. But before we can get this thing right, we need to be honest about the problems we face. What I'm about is helping you and me face ourselves honestly in the light of God's Word.

Let me say it again. We husbands need our wives' help, and we need their support and respect. Some husbands never learned at home how to be godly men and godly husbands. It's going to take them time to learn that. But they can learn, with their wife's support. They can make it with wives who will say, "I'm going to support and reverence you, not crucify you."

## The Quietness of Submission

I want to turn now to 1 Peter 3, where the apostle Peter gave us a different slant on this matter of submission.

Peter wrote, "In the same way, you wives, be submissive to your own husbands so that even if any of them are disobedient to the word, they may be won without a word by the behavior of their wives, as they observe your chaste and respectful behavior" (vv. 1–2).

Peter raises the question a lot of women ask: "My husband isn't even a believer. What am I supposed to do?"

Well, the secular world has one answer for you. "Woman, you don't need that mess. You don't have to go through that. Leave him; walk out. Forget your husband. Look out for yourself."

But God has a better answer. He says even if your husband is not a Christlike man yet, he can still be won without a word by your godly behavior.

I know a lot of women get bent out of shape whenever someone brings up this text, but it actually takes a burden off the wife. That is, God didn't call a wife to be her husband's pastor. She doesn't have to turn up the radio so her husband can hear the preaching and get convicted. She doesn't have to pin Bible verses to his pillow or slip Christian tapes into his car's stereo.

Peter said the way a messed-up husband is won to the Lord is not be his wife's homiletics (preaching) but by her behavior.

This takes a burden off the wife because, as most women can attest, the more a wife tries to change her husband by badgering or preaching at him, the worse he usually gets.

Do you know why? Because when a woman does that, she is messing with the one thing a man will not compromise on, which is his ego. A man will let his wife mess with a lot of stuff in his life, but not his ego.

Now I'm not saying this is right. I'm just telling you that's the way it is. This is the way men are built. The man who brags about all the ladies he has is probably lying. So why does he do it? Because he has an ego, and he wants to make himself look like more of a man than he really is. If he were that much of a man, he wouldn't have to talk about his five women. But men have egos, and those egos need to come under the lordship of Christ.

God can work on a man's ego better than his wife can. So what God calls the wife to do is get out of the way so He can get to her husband. Her quiet and godly behavior makes that possible.

God can't get a husband's full attention when his wife is in the way. This does not mean that she is to be speechless in the home. It does mean that she is to honor her husband's position even when she disagrees with him.

## The Example of Submission

A wife's preaching just gets in God's way. So God says to the wife, "Be like Jesus in your home." This is the context of Peter's very first words in verse 1, "In the same way."

What way? The answer is in verses 18–25 of 1 Peter 2. The subject here is the fact that Christians have been called to suffer. The example is the way Jesus bore up under His suffering: "[He] committed no sin, nor was any deceit found in His mouth; and while being reviled, He did not revile in return; while suffering, He uttered no threats, but kept entrusting Himself to Him who judges righteously" (vv. 22–23).

Jesus did not threaten people. He didn't manipulate them by using tears, a powerful weapon some women can draw on in a heartbeat to make their husbands bend to their will. When Jesus was mistreated, He committed Himself to God the Father. He took the suffering.

What happens when a wife commits herself to God and leaves the work on her husband up to Him? Look at 1 Peter 2:25: "For you were continually straying like sheep, but now you have returned to the Shepherd and Guardian of your souls."

This is talking primarily about salvation, but the point is that when you do it God's way, He makes it work. Have you tried God's way to change your husband, or have you been fussing and nagging him? Because if you've been fussing, you're telling God, "Don't bother trying to change my husband. I'll take care of it myself."

Instead of preaching, God wants "chaste and respectful behavior" from a wife. That word *behavior* here means to stare at, to take a close look at. In other words, a Christian wife should make her husband stare at her in wonder by her attitude and reaction to him.

How can she make him stare and wonder what in the world is going on with her? By the way she reverences him and submits to him. By the way she helps and supports him.

Instead of giving her husband the leftovers of her day, her emotions, and her attention after serving and looking good for the boss all day, this kind of a wife wants to know how she can serve her man. She looks for ways to help him.

The idea is to make your husband stare, to shock him with your support and submission, to make him say, "We're going to church next week," because he likes what he sees and wants to find out what's going on.

Now, I realize some women can say, "You don't know my husband. He will take advantage of me if I do that." God says, "Leave that to Me." That may not change the situation for now. But the issue once again is, do we trust God or do we follow what our minds and emotions are telling us?

## The Adornment of Submission

Peter continues in chapter 3, verses 3–4: "Let not your adornment be merely external—braiding the hair, and wearing gold jewelry, or putting on dresses; but let it be the hidden person of the heart."

Peter is not saying, "Don't wear jewelry or nice clothes." He's saying keep these things in their proper perspective.

I hate shopping. But Lois covers every rack in the store. We're out there all day. And the salesclerks don't help, because they tell her, "Just give me what you want to try on, and I'll take it all to the changing room for you." And then some of those stores don't have a chair, so husbands can't even sit down.

Now, when it comes to fixing up the outer person, many women are meticulous. The Bible says to give that same meticulous attention to the inner person. The beauty you can buy comes and goes, but the beauty inside is going nowhere.

The word *adorned* comes from the Greek word *kosmeo*, from which comes the word *cosmetic*. This word means the opposite of *chaos*, so when a women puts on her cosmetics, she arranges chaos into order—and I'd better leave that right there! But that's what adorning means.

God says, "Glamorize the inside." Some women who come to church looking beautiful turn ugly on the inside when they get in the car with their husbands.

God wants women to be consistent. If you're going to be an ugly person, don't camouflage it with beautiful makeup. But if you are going to take the time to look beautiful on the outside, make sure your inner spirit is looking beautiful too. You do that with a "gentle and quiet spirit" (1 Peter 3:4).

This applies to your language too:

> For in this way in former times the holy women also, who hoped in God, used to adorn themselves, being submissive to their own husbands. Thus Sarah obeyed Abraham, calling him lord, and you have become her children if you do what is right without being frightened by any fear. (vv. 5–6)

Sarah reverenced Abraham. We know that because of the way she talked to him. By calling him "lord," a term of deep respect and honor, Sarah took her submission public.

The context in which Sarah called Abraham "lord" is very interesting. It's in Genesis 18, when God came to Sarah and Abraham and told them they were going to have a baby the next year.

Sarah wondered about the promise, because pregnancy was an impossible situation for her. She was ninety years old, Abe was one hundred, and there was no hope in sight. But when God saw that Sarah reverenced Abraham, suddenly Abraham was able to do things no hundred-year-old man is supposed to do. Sarah got pregnant. When she called Abraham "lord," God gave her a miracle.

What am I saying? Reverence your husband, and God can make him do things he couldn't do before. God can turn his attitude and his life around. If you as a wife will do your part and get out of the way, God can reach your husband.

So step aside and reverence your husband. Lift him up, esteem him, serve him, as he does the same to you, and you'll have a happy home because you will be fulfilling the agenda of the King.

Let me tell you what God can do when you carry out your kingdom assignment. Even if you married a fool, and the fool won't get right, live as a woman of God anyway, and God can turn your man around. You need to help him and reverence him, which you can do, and let God do the part you can't do. He will honor your reverence.

# CHAPTER THIRTEEN

# The Kingdom Agenda
# of Parents

We're dedicating an entire section of this book to God's kingdom agenda for the family for one basic reason. Every other institution in society is built and predicated upon the family. If the family breaks up, then those institutions that depend on strong families break up as well.

Once that happens, there is no law you can pass that will make up for the devastation. There is no program you can institute that will fix what happens to people's lives when a home is shattered. There is no politician you can elect who can bring harmony and social order when the family is decimated.

There's not much use in talking about the problems in Washington until we fix the problems on Main Street, because what ultimately matters is not what's happening at the White House but what's happening at your house.

So it is no wonder that Satan is attacking our families. As I said before, he knows that if he gets the family, he gets the future. If Satan can get a father out of the home, then he can raise a little girl who never knows what real love is like by the touch of a man who honors her. So she looks for love through the touches of men who don't honor her.

Or if Satan can get a father to leave his family, the Enemy can raise a boy to be an undisciplined and irresponsible man.

I know there are many people who don't have complete families and had no choice in the matter, whether through death or divorce. God cares very much for these people, but His ideal is still a father and a mother raising their children in their home, preparing them to take their place as God's kingdom representatives in their own homes someday.

Plato was right when he said, "The saga of a nation is really the saga of the family written large." That's what we are seeing in our culture. The reason America is unraveling is because our families are unraveling. That's why there is no greater effort parents can make than to keep their families together and to keep them strong.

This is getting harder to do because things have changed since the time, not too long ago, when the culture helped parents out. Back then, if a child didn't get moral instruction at home, Miss Jones at school would say, "This is right, and this is wrong." We used to be able to turn on the TV and see wholesome families. We used to live in neighborhoods made up largely of intact families.

But all of these things are rare now. Today, when your children leave home every day, there are forces at work to unravel everything you tried to teach them at home. The competition is great now.

Your children's peers are going to give them a different story than you gave them. Many of their teachers will give them a different story. The TV and the theater are certainly going to give them a different story. So if good families were very important, they're desperately important today because they're our last bastion of hope.

I don't have to tell you that raising children is a challenge. It reminds me of the lecturer whose favorite lecture was "The Ten Commandments for Parenting." Then he had his second child. Now he lectured on "Ten Suggestions for Parents." Then he had his third child—and stopped lecturing! It's a different story when you have to do it yourself.

I would like to suggest to you that if we're going to make it as parents, we need our Bibles. Because while the schools, the government, and society have changed, neither children nor God have changed.

And since children have not changed and God has not changed, we had better deal with what is unchanging and not what is fickle. The Word of God is unchanging, so let's go to the One who created families and ask Him what it takes to be godly parents.

My primary text for this chapter is one verse, Ephesians 6:4. There,

Paul wrote, "Fathers, do not provoke your children to anger; but bring them up in the discipline and instruction of the Lord."

## THE WORD TO FATHERS

Let me tell you why Paul addresses fathers primarily here and why the Bible, as a rule, addresses its child-rearing admonitions to fathers. There is a biblical, or theological, reason and a cultural reason.

First, the biblical reason: God views the father as the representative head of the home. He was the one through whom and to whom God would speak, and his job was to transfer God's teaching to his wife and children.

That's why the Devil wants to get rid of dads. When Dad is gone, the primary representative at home is gone, placing an extra burden on Mom.

As I often tell the fathers in my congregation, if you are tempted to walk out on your family, think twice. The Bible says God will visit the sins of the father on the children to the third and fourth generation (see Exodus 20:5). So when you walk out, you don't just walk out on your children. You walk out on your grandchildren and great-grandchildren—maybe even your great-great-grandchildren.

And if you think this generation of young people is bad, you haven't seen anything yet. Wait until this generation has children.

What has been lacking for so long in our culture are men in their biblical places of leadership. And while God has given women great gifts and abilities, and while we could not function in our homes without them, the great challenge for the church is to win men and call them back to their rightful place of spiritual responsibility.

So the father is the biblical representative in the home. But there is also a cultural reason that Paul addresses fathers. In ancient Rome, women did not have a lot of rights. They were a pretty subjugated group. When a baby was born, the baby would be brought to the father and placed in front of him in the basket or on the cloth or whatever.

The father would look at his son or daughter. Thumbs-up meant, "I'll keep him." Thumbs-down meant, "Put the baby out to die." A father could, with the permission of Roman law, reject a daughter, for instance, if he wanted his firstborn to be a son.

That rejected baby would be put in a public place and either left to die or maybe taken and raised in a brothel. The father had the power of life and death.

But God's Word threw out all that mess. God's Word says to fathers, "You can't turn from or deny your responsibility. You are God's representative in your home."

I know it can be hard being a parent. But God says to parents, and particularly to fathers as the representatives, "You have the power of life and death in your hands. Generations are depending on you."

So let's see what it takes to be parents who fulfill God's kingdom agenda with their children and raise up a generation who will in turn be God's representatives. There are four things we need to know about parenting from Ephesians 6:4.

## WE MUST ENCOURAGE OUR CHILDREN

The first thing we as parents must do is encourage our children. Paul stated it in the negative: "Do not provoke your children to anger." In Colossians 3:21, Paul said, "Do not exasperate your children."

In other words, we need to encourage our children, not discourage them. One thing children need to know is that no matter what anybody else may think about them, at home they are somebody.

Many young people are going after significance outside the home because they're not finding significance inside the home. They are rejected, provoked, and exasperated. So let's find out how you can encourage your kids.

### Value Our Children Equally

One way we can encourage our children is by valuing each of them equally and not playing favorites.

Parents are often tempted to show favoritism because one child has a more agreeable personality or shares the parents' likes and dislikes or is easier to discipline. A parent may also favor the child who is closest to him or her in personality.

But favoritism can be very destructive to a family. A classic biblical case of parental favoritism was Jacob, who greatly favored Joseph and made no attempt to hide it (see Genesis 37:3). He made Joseph a coat of many colors and provoked the other ten brothers' jealousy, which quickly turned to anger. They hated Joseph (see v. 4) and wanted to kill him because he was his father's favorite.

There may be one child with whom you have a greater natural affinity. But when it comes to your position as a parent, you can't afford to play favorites. God doesn't play favorites among us (see Romans 3:22; 10:12); He is not partial to some of His children. He is consistent. Favoritism will discourage your nonfavorite children.

## Prioritize Our Children

Another way to encourage your children is to make them a high priority in your life.

You do that when you let them know you want to invest in their dreams, not try to make them live out your unfulfilled dreams or what you think they ought to do.

You also prioritize your children when you put them ahead of your career. Your family is your first responsibility. If it means that you don't accept a career move upward if it will negatively impact your family, then that's the decision. That's tough to do, because some in the business world will tell you to sacrifice your family if you have to. Now, most company executives won't actually come out and say that, but that's the bottom-line effect of the way they run their companies. Their eyes are on productivity, not on their employee's families. But God says your family comes ahead of your career.

I often feel this tension myself. The demands of a growing ministry and a packed schedule, the need to serve as a counselor and to deal with problems at our church in Dallas often leave me in a catch-22.

I remember one year I promised Anthony Jr. that I would be at one of his football games. But that week, a whole bunch of problems came up. In fact, there was an emergency in Houston I had to deal with, so I had to jump on a plane to Houston the morning of Anthony's game.

As things turned out, I wouldn't be able to deal with the problem until that evening, at the exact time Anthony's game was starting. Looking at my watch, I remembered how I had already disappointed him once that year by missing a game I had told him I would attend.

So I had to make a choice—and on that particular day, I made the right choice. I don't always make the right choice concerning my family, but on that day, I made the right choice. I grabbed a flight back to Dallas, went to Anthony's game, then went right back to the airport and flew back to Houston. I had to keep my word to my son.

Sometimes we are going to be inconvenienced by making our children a priority. Encouraging rather than provoking or discouraging them is often costly to us as parents.

Another way we encourage our children is by being a positive example to them. A teacher called a father one day and said, "We're having a problem with your son."

The father asked, "What's wrong?"

"Well, he keeps stealing pencil erasers from the classroom and taking them home."

The father said, "I don't know why he would do that. I brought a whole box of erasers home from work." This kind of thing happens far too often. The idea is to give your children a positive, encouraging example they can follow.

## Bless Our Children

Another way we encourage our children is by blessing them. This is a powerful biblical concept that is being rediscovered in our day. The blessing was a key part of family life in the Old Testament. The battle between Jacob and Esau in Genesis 27 was over who would get their father Isaac's blessing.

The blessing involved a father transferring the family inheritance to his son and telling him of the future God had for him (see Genesis 49). To be blessed meant that the father recognized a child's significance. The blessing told the child that he was the future, that his father was counting on him.

The best thing we fathers can do for our sons and daughters is to put our hands on them and bless them in the name of Jesus Christ. There's no way to measure the impact that your blessing can have on your children.

The blessing is so important because we parents are so quick to curse our kids. I don't mean using profanity on them. I'm talking about the kinds of comments that slip out of our mouths so quickly and easily. "You didn't do that right." "Why don't you change this?" "How come you're not better at that?" Our kids have heard where they fall short. Have they also heard us blessing them?

The difference between encouragement and praise is important. We praise our children a lot, but we don't always encourage them. Praise focuses on what the child has accomplished.

Your son hits a home run in his baseball game, and you say, "That was great, Son. Way to go!" Your daughter gets an A on her test, and you say, "That was wonderful." That's praise, acknowledging your child's accomplishment. There's nothing wrong with praise. The only problem is, when your kids aren't doing something, they don't get any praise.

But encouragement is not related to what people achieve. It is tied to who they are. Encouragement says, "I want to affirm you as my child. You don't have to do anything spectacular. I love you because of who you are."

Have you ever seen what happens to a drooping plant when you water it? That's what encouragement does. It will take a drooping kid and make him look up. He can say, "Yeah, I am somebody. I'm special. Mom and Dad told me so."

# WE MUST NURTURE OUR CHILDREN

A second way we can fulfill our kingdom agenda as parents is to nurture our children. Ephesians 6:4 tells us to "bring them up."

This verb is the same Greek word used in Ephesians 5:29, which says, "No one ever hated his own flesh, but nourishes . . . it, just as Christ also does the church." In the same way that a husband should nourish and nurture his wife, parents need to nurture their children. The idea is to feed and care for them.

## Four Areas of Nurturing

This goes well beyond what we put on the table for the kids to eat. Luke 2:52 suggests the four areas in which children need nurturing. As a child and young person, Jesus grew intellectually, physically, spiritually, and socially.

Most of us believe passionately in our children's physical, social, and intellectual development. We make sure they have clothes and shelter. We try to see that they eat right and get enough sleep. We help them learn how to mix with other people so they don't feel odd and left out, and we monitor their friends so they aren't playing with the wrong kids. And we keep a close eye on their grades and their school so we know what they're learning.

God says we should take the same kind of care with our kids' spiritual development. We need to know how well they're being fed in church and Sunday school. We need to make sure we are giving them a regular diet of spiritual nourishment at home.

## Spiritual Training

Proverbs 22:6 gives us a comprehensive term for spiritual development: "Train up a child in the way he should go, even when he is old he will not depart from it."

A proverb is not a promise but a truism. It says, "If you will do something, this is the result you can normally expect." Let me show you how this works with Proverbs 22:6. The Hebrew word for *train* means to place something on the palate.

The picture is of a Hebrew mother who would chew her baby's food to soften it and then put the food in the baby's mouth. The presence of the food would excite the child's palate, and the child would begin eating and then would swallow the food.

Child training, therefore, involves making our teaching palatable so that our children can digest it and benefit from it. This doesn't mean soft-pedaling the truth or only saying what our kids want to hear. It does mean that we don't bulldoze them or beat them over the head with the truth.

That also rules out bribing children to get them to do what we want. Bribing says, "I will give you this to try to buy your cooperation and obedience." The opposite of bribing children is rewarding them. Rewarding says, "Because you did what I asked you to do, I want to honor you for it." Even God rewards us for our obedience.

The idea of making our teaching palatable really comes through in the middle phrase of Proverbs 22:6. The writer said we are to train a child "in the way he should go." A better translation is, "according to his way"—that is, according to each child's unique personality or bent.

The Bible is saying to parents, don't try to come up with a standard operation that you apply to each child. Since each child is different and has a unique temperament, the way you deal with your children should differ from child to child. Good parents already know that.

When we train a child well, the Bible says, "Even when he is old he will not depart from it." The Hebrew word for *old* relates to the appearance of a beard. For a boy, that could be as early as fourteen or fifteen years of age, the time when he begins the process of entering adulthood.

Many of us are where we are today because of parents or grandparents who imparted something to us that we couldn't get away from. It kept drawing us back. Your mom and dad made sure you were in church and paying attention, and now you are in church on your own. They taught you God's Word, and now that Word is deeply ingrained in your system.

That's the concept of *nurture*, training our children so that they are spiritually nourished. Now let me say something that is implicit in this verse and explicit throughout the Bible but is no longer a given in our society. This is the fact that parents are to raise their children themselves. You and I cannot delegate the nurturing of our children to others.

Neither the government, the school, nor the church is supposed to raise your child. We have parents today getting mad at the school or the church because their child went the wrong way. But if God had wanted the school or the church, He would have given that child to the school or church. Instead, He gives children to parents to raise.

Obviously, that doesn't mean you don't hold people accountable for how they impact your children. Of course, the church needs to support and reinforce the teaching children are getting at home. But nothing can replace the home.

A parent may say, "But I have too much on me." Well, a lot of parents would pick up a few hours a week just by turning off the TV. No one ever said parenting didn't take work.

It's sad to say that some people train their dogs better than they train their kids. Then they tie the dogs up at night and let the kids run loose! But kingdom parents are called to train and nurture their children to live out God's kingdom agenda.

## WE MUST DISCIPLINE OUR CHILDREN

Paul gave us a third element of kingdom parenting in Ephesians 6:4. It's centered on the word *discipline*. "Bring [your children] up in the discipline . . . of the Lord."

### Love and Sonship

Why is this so important? Because discipline is proof of two very important things. The first is love. According to Hebrews 12:6, "Whom the Lord loveth, He skinneth alive" (my paraphrase). The Lord "spanketh" those whom He loves. Love is always demonstrated by discipline.

If you love little Johnny too much to correct him, God says you hate him. "He who spares his rod hates his son, but he who loves him disciplines him diligently" (Proverbs 13:24). We'll get into the book of Proverbs in more depth below, because it is a manual on child discipline.

A second thing that discipline proves is sonship itself, the fact that a child belongs to the family. Hebrews 12:7–8 says that if God doesn't correct you, it's because you're the neighbor's kid. You don't belong in God's family at all if you aren't under His discipline.

Now I know some of us think our children are little angels. But just wait, because as their legs get longer, their wings get shorter. Children are born in sin, and all they need is time to manifest that sin.

That's why you don't have to teach your kids to be selfish. You don't have to buy them a book on how to cheat, fight, get an attitude, or throw a temper tantrum. Sin is built-in. You have to discipline them away from sin.

Children are not born with a spark of divinity in them. Instead, they are born with hell inbred in them because of Adam's sin, which has been passed down to all mankind (see Romans 5:12). So instead of trying to keep our children's wings straight, we need to challenge Satan's claim on them.

Children need discipline, but not discipline apart from love. When you discipline a child apart from love, you will do physical or emotional damage.

That's why correcting your children when you are angry is not the right time. When you explode, that is not a loving correction. It may make you feel better to let off steam, but it doesn't do anything for your kids. God disciplines us in love. We owe the same to our children.

## A Manual on Discipline

I want to do a little "Scripture search" here, using the book of Proverbs (we'll do the same in the next chapter when we focus on the kingdom agenda of children). Proverbs is a biblical manual on parenting. Let's look at some verses that spell out the responsibility and the joy involved in disciplining our children.

First of all, let me just remind you of the verse we cited above, Proverbs 13:24. I might just note here that the "rod" was not a club. It was a spanking utensil designed to sting but do no permanent damage. It would hurt but not abuse.

Proverbs 19:18 cautions us, "Discipline your son while there is hope, and do not desire his death." The ultimate result of an undisciplined life is death (see 1 Corinthians 11:29–32).

Proverbs 22 has some other great verses on parenting besides verse 6. Look at verse 15: "Foolishness is bound up in the heart of a child; the rod of discipline will remove it far from him."

The Hebrew word here means "wickedness," not just silliness. You say, "My child is bad. He's acting up, giving us a lot of grief." Well, you have a rod of discipline that is designed to drive that mess right up out of him.

We have a whole generation of kids running the streets who were never disciplined at home. Since they never got it at home, they are under nobody's authority now. Nobody can control them—not the police, the government, or anybody. Some of these young people are not even afraid to die, which makes them very dangerous.

Look at Proverbs 23:13–14. "Do not hold back discipline from the child, although you beat him with the rod, he will not die. You shall beat him with the rod, and deliver his soul from Sheol."

Now every kid who is being spanked thinks he is dying. The neighbors may think he is dying. But in reality, if you are applying loving, biblical discipline, you are actually beating *life* into your child rather than death.

Here are two more verses from the Proverbs: "The rod and reproof give wisdom, but a child who gets his own way brings shame to his mother" (Proverbs 29:15). "Correct your son, and he will give you comfort; he will also delight your soul" (v. 17).

It takes courage and commitment to discipline. It's easier to wimp out, be passive, and push the discipline of the children off onto the other spouse or someone else.

There was a little boy whose father was away on a business trip. He said to his mother at dinner, "I want to be in charge tonight, Mom."

She said, "OK, you can sit at the head of the table in your father's chair."

The boy's sister thought her brother was too young to be in charge, so, as sisters will do, she decided to challenge him. She said, "OK, if you're in charge and you're the man of the house, how much is two and two?"

The little boy looked at her and said, "Ask your mother." He had passive parenting all figured out!

## A Biblical Example

That story may make us laugh, but there's nothing funny about the real-life example of passive fathering we find in 1 Samuel. This father's name was Eli, the priest of the Lord.

Eli had two sons named Hophni and Phinehas (1 Samuel 1:3).

These boys were bad. "The sons of Eli were worthless men; they did not know the Lord" (1 Samuel 2:12). They were stealing from the Lord's house, taking meat from the sacrifices for themselves, and threatening anyone who questioned them (see vv. 13–17).

It gets worse. Hophni and Phinehas were also sleeping with the women "who served at the doorway of the tent of meeting" (v. 22). Eli did nothing to stop them except to scold them: "No, my sons; for the report is not good which I hear the Lord's people circulating" (v. 24).

In other words, all Eli did was say, "You boys stop that. Naughty, naughty. God don't like ugly." But he never tried to take a hand with them or restrain them. You can say "Naughty, naughty" to a two-year-old, but not to an eighteen-year-old.

Eli did nothing, but God got tired of these two kids real fast. In 1 Samuel 3:13, He pronounced judgment on Eli's house: "I have told him that I am about to judge his house forever for the iniquity which he knew, because his sons brought a curse on themselves and he did not rebuke them." Hophni and Phinehas were bringing death to themselves, and Eli did nothing.

What does it mean to rebuke your children? Just tell them they are doing wrong? No, Eli did that. To rebuke means to follow through on what you said, even if it means taking drastic steps.

For instance, sometimes a rebellious teenage son may be too big for his mother to handle physically. If that's the case and she's alone, she may need to get help. It may take a man or group of men to instill some respect into that boy and bring him into line.

At our church, we tell mothers to give us a call if they need that kind of help. We had just such a case recently. A single mother in our church had a big, strapping teenage son she couldn't handle. He was making her life hellish. So she brought him to the church.

My associate, Pastor Martin Hawkins, called five deacons into the room, then brought the boy and sat him down. These men looked the teenager in the eye as Pastor Hawkins said, "You will go home and study. You will obey your mother, or she will bring you back here and we will wear your backside out."

The boy went home, picked up his books, and became an A student, because for the first time in his life, he faced some men who weren't going to back down. That's what Hophni and Phinehas needed but didn't get.

The result of their sin is found in 1 Samuel 4. First, Hophni and Phinehas were killed (see v. 11). Then, when Eli heard the news, he fell over backward, broke his neck, and died (see vv. 17–18).

But it didn't stop there. Because Eli was a judge and priest in Israel, the nation suffered. The ark of the covenant was taken by the Philistines (see 1 Samuel 4:11). The ark—the glory, the presence, and the power of God—was gone.

So Eli and his sons were dead, but even then God wasn't finished. In verses 19–21, we learn that Phinehas's wife also died giving birth to a son, whom she named "Ichabod," meaning "the glory has departed from Israel" (1 Samuel 4:21).

This is what is happening in America today. The glory of the Lord is on its way out because families have decided that parents need to obey their children rather than discipline them.

## We Must Instruct Our Children

That brings us to our fourth and final piece of godly wisdom for parents from Ephesians 6:4. The Bible tells us to raise our children in the "instruction of the Lord." Make sure they are being taught the way of the Lord.

This is so clear in the great chapter on godly instruction, Deuteronomy 6. Moses told Israel, in effect, "I must teach you the commandments of God, so that you, your son, and your grandson will learn to fear the Lord and keep His commandments. Then you will live long in the land God is giving you" (see vv. 1–3). That's the background of the teaching in Deuteronomy 6:6–9.

We get upset because they have taken the Ten Commandments off the walls at school. But what I want to know is, are the commandments hanging on the walls of our homes? Are we teaching God's truth to our children?

God never commanded the school to teach your children God's Word. If the school does, that's a bonus. But we need to ask, are we doing the job at home?

Dad, if you are not sitting down with your family, opening the Word and praying with your children, then don't blame the government or the school or the streets if your kids get messed up. Their instruction is our responsibility as parents.

What are we to teach? The basics are in verses 4–5 of our text. We are to teach them that there is only one true God and that we are to love Him with all of our being. How are we to teach these truths? The text suggests several ways.

### Teach Them Convincingly

First, God's Word says to teach our children His truth in a convincing way.

Notice that before you can teach your children, God's Word must be on your own heart. You must be passionately committed to it, or you'll never convince your children that it is true.

This means that when your kids say things like, "Yeah, but Johnny's dad says this," you respond, "Well, when you start living in Johnny's house, you can follow what Johnny's dad says. But in this house, we follow the Bible."

In other words, don't acquiesce to pressure from your children, because they will test you. This doesn't mean you don't listen to your kids; it means you hear what they have to say and then guide them in the way of the Lord.

### Teach Them Consistently

We must also teach our children consistently. This is where the instruction really begins to take root and produce fruit.

Deuteronomy 6:7 shows how to teach consistently. It can happen anywhere, anytime. We know that there are times when children are especially teachable, and it's usually in the ordinary course of daily events. A consistent parent takes advantage of every opportunity to teach. Be creative.

### Teach Them Conspicuously

Finally, make your teaching conspicuous. Israel's parents were to put the Word on their hands and foreheads and on their doorposts and gates (see vv. 8–9). They memorized the Word. They made it obvious. There was nothing hidden here. No child had to guess whether his parents cared about God's truth.

## A CLOSING WORD

Let me leave you with a closing word I hope will encourage you.

You may say, "Tony, my children are grown. It's too late to do all of this. I missed it. I was working too much. I was building my business. My kids are already gone. What do I do?"

Your children may be grown, but it's never too late to pray. Psalm 127:4 says that children are like arrows in their father's hand. If you shot your "arrows" crooked, you can still get on your knees and pray for a good wind. You can ask God to catch that errant arrow and steer it back toward the target.

Even if you missed it as an earthly parent, there is still a heavenly Father who can catch that wayward arrow and bring it on home. I can't say what God will do in your case, but I know He has the power to turn your children back to Himself. So no matter whether your children are flying right or going off course right now, keep praying.

Just as God tracked you down and brought you into His kingdom after you rebelled against Him, He can certainly do the same with your children. (See the author's work *Guiding Your Family in a Misguided World*, Focus on the Family Publishing, for a more detailed discussion of biblical parenting.)

# CHAPTER FOURTEEN

# The Kingdom Agenda
# of Children

In the previous chapter, we argued for the absolute importance of family as the bedrock of instruction in society. And we talked about the indispensable role parents play in building godly families that will reflect His kingdom in the culture.

Now I want to follow that up by considering the kingdom agenda of children. It may seem unusual to you to talk about children having an agenda God wants them to follow. We tend to think of our kids as the ones being acted upon during their growing years rather than the ones doing the acting.

But the Bible is very clear on the part God calls children to play in the day-to-day operation of the family. If we are going to return the church to its rightful place as an influence and shaper of culture, we have to build strong families.

And in God's kingdom, everybody has a part to play. Children are key because they embody the essence of the kingdom. Jesus said, "Let the children alone, and do not hinder them from coming to Me; for the kingdom of heaven belongs to such as these" (Matthew 19:14).

One thing that will help us think more clearly about children's agenda in the kingdom is to remember that each one of us is somebody's child. So when we talk about a child's agenda, we don't just mean those preschoolers or elementary-aged children in your home.

We're *all* children, so the principles we are going to discuss apply in some way to all of us. As we will see, they are applied differently depending on our age and situation. But God's plan to build and display His kingdom in this world definitely includes children.

## A CULTURE OF REBELLION

A lot of what we say in this chapter will be particularly relevant to teenagers, because they are usually the ones battling through the issue of their responsibility to their parents and their place in the home.

You don't have to have teenagers to know that we are living in a day of changing values and role reversals. The culture has turned up the heat on our families. As this thing boils, what has come to the top is a very rebellious spirit that tells children to ignore, disregard, and disobey their parents—and all authority, for that matter.

Some children take this to the next level and actually abuse and mistreat their parents in some violent way that requires the intervention of the authorities to protect the parents. Cultural phenomena like rap music have also contributed to a rebellious emphasis in our day.

To give you some idea of how much things have changed, recall the days when we attended school as children. We wouldn't have dared to call our teachers anything but Mrs. Jones or Mr. Smith, because there was a general environment of respect.

But we are in a culture of rebellion. Instead of, "Children, obey your parents," we could rewrite the command today, "Parents, obey your children." It's like the father who asked another father, "Do you spank your children?"

The other father replied, "Certainly—in self-defense!"

I don't think many people will disagree with the statement that the roles of parent and child have been turned upside down in our culture. We could say that what we are seeing today is the "adultification" of children.

Even the legal structures of our society have been busy decreasing parental authority and increasing children's rights.

Now all we hear about is the rights of children in areas such as self-determination, sexual expression, and personal freedom. Children must be free to experiment sexually, the argument goes, so we adults must honor that need by passing out condoms and urging our kids to practice so-called safe sex.

So a child or teenager today is faced with a culture that says, "Rebel!" Even some people who are adults now are still living out the rebellious lifestyle they started when they were living at home. Some rebellious children of the sixties are getting a payback today in the rebellion of their own kids.

After watching a TV program about rebellious youth, a husband and wife looked at each other, and the man said, "What a mess. Where did our generation go?"

His wife said, "Well, we had children and our generation has come up again."

When children fail to live out God's kingdom agenda for them, the whole family structure is compromised. We must get this thing back on track as the people of God.

To help us do that, I want to return to the chapter we have already considered several times, Ephesians 6. As you know, this text addresses parents and children. Since we have dealt with the agenda of parents, let's back up to verses 1–3 to see the two things every child needs to give his or her parents: obedience and honor.

## Children Are to Obey Their Parents

Paul lays out the agenda for children beginning with verse 1 of Ephesians 6: "Children, obey your parents in the Lord, for this is right."

This verse always raises questions, such as, "How far does a child's obedience go?" "What if my child is not living at home?" "What happens if my child decides not to obey my instructions?"

We'll try to answer these and other questions as we go along. But first let's consider why it is so important that children obey their parents. One primary reason is that in God's kingdom, there is a fundamental distinction between children and parents.

## Parents Are the Authority

Let me show you what I'm talking about by putting this in a larger context. One of the attributes of God is His transcendence. By that we mean He is distinct from His creation. God sits outside of and above His creation, although He is involved with His creation. The problem with the New Age movement is that they want to merge men with

God, as though we were twins. But God is in a class all by Himself.

Just as God is transcendent and distinct from His creation, so parents are different from children. Our problem is that we have not maintained that crucial distinction. So we have teenagers and even children today who are trying to look and act like adults and assume adult privileges, while the adults cower and bow before their children lest they upset them or lest the kids react negatively to the parents' attempts at discipline.

As I said above, we have seriously blurred the picture. It's sometimes hard to tell who are the children and who are the parents. You can go into some homes and wonder who's in charge.

But when Paul said in Ephesians 6:1, "Children, obey your parents," he used a Greek word, *teknon*, that means "all offspring." We'll see how that applies to all of us.

The reason God gives parents to children is so that the children might have a filtered life. That is, if you are a Christian parent, your job is to filter the culture in such a way that its evil influences don't dominate your kids' lives. And you are to filter out the sinful tendencies within them in such a way that you bend their will without breaking their spirit.

Why is this necessary? Because no matter how cute your children are, they are sinfully cute. Foolishness and rebellion are built into the heart of a child (see Proverbs 22:15), as we learned in the previous chapter. That's why children must learn obedience.

## The Spiritual Thing to Do

In Ephesians 6:1, Paul gives us two excellent reasons why children are to obey their parents. The first is found in that phrase in the middle of the verse: "in the Lord." Because this verse is so familiar, we might be tempted just to rush over that phrase and miss its significance.

That would be a tragedy, because Paul is saying that for children, obedience to parents is comparable to obedience to God when what their parents are asking them to do agrees with God's instructions.

Let me say it another way. When a child rebels against his parents, God looks at that as rebellion against Himself. It is an attempted coup against the kingdom. So when a child raises his fist against his mother and father because he doesn't like their instruction and doesn't want to obey it, God looks at that as raising a fist in His face. And *no one* can raise a fist in God's face and expect to get away with it.

Ephesians 6:1 also tells us that this obedience thing is bigger than just parents and children. It has to do with the Lord. He has a deep interest in seeing that children obey.

Now of course, it's up to us parents to make sure we are raising our children "in the Lord." It's our responsibility to guide them in ways that are in harmony and not in contradiction with the Scriptures. We must give them the right target at which to aim their obedience.

I want to give you some examples from the book of Proverbs that underscore the importance of obedience. Proverbs 1:8 says, "Hear, my son, your father's instruction, and do not forsake your mother's teaching." Proverbs 3:1 is very similar: "My son, do not forget my teaching, but let your heart keep my commandments."

Proverbs 4:1–4 shows the progression of godly instruction and obedience from one generation to the next:

> *Hear, O sons, the instruction of a father, and give attention that you may gain understanding, for I give you sound teaching; do not abandon my instruction. When I was a son to my father, tender and the only son in the sight of my mother, then he taught me and said to me, "Let your heart hold fast my words; keep my commandments and live."*

Proverbs 7:1–3 is another important passage, showing how seriously God wants children to take the issue of obedience to parents:

> *My son, keep my words, and treasure my commandments within you. Keep my commandments and live, and my teaching as the apple of your eye. Bind them on your fingers; Write them on the tablet of your heart.*

The Proverbs also say that a disobedient child brings grief, unhappiness, and even destruction to his parents (see 10:1; 17:21; 19:13) and brings shame and disgrace to the whole family (see 19:26).

You get the idea. To God, obedience is no small thing. So children who are living at home under the authority of their parents must have this attitude: "Dad, Mom, unless you tell me to disobey God, I am going to obey you. I may not always like it, and I may not agree with it. But I am the child, and you are the parents. I want to please God by obeying you."

A woman was in a department store with her little girl one day. The child kept tugging at her mother and crying and whining, and the mother kept saying, "Quiet, Suzanne. Just calm yourself, Suzanne. Take it easy, Suzanne."

The salesclerk was amazed at how firmly this woman was correcting her child. He looked at the little girl and said, "So your name's Suzanne, huh?"

The mother replied, "No, her name is Joan. I'm Suzanne."

Unfortunately, that's how it happens far too often. Instead of us as parents controlling the situation, the kids control the situation. Obedience is the kingdom agenda for children, and it's a spiritual issue.

### The Right Thing to Do

Here's the second reason that children need to obey their parents. According to Paul, it is "right." That is, obedience is the righteous thing to do.

Righteousness, of course, is based on the character of God. He is the standard, and His Word reflects that standard. So when the Bible says it is right for kids to obey, God is saying that their obedience conforms to His character.

There are other reasons that make obedience right for children. The fact that parents bring children into the world and provide for their care gives them a priority call on their children's obedience. God has the same right to make this demand on us because He gave us life and sustains us every day.

Another thing that makes obedience right is the fact that parents have been around longer than their children and know more about life. So it is to the children's advantage to listen to their parents and follow their guidance.

I think you'll agree that obedience—and the submission it calls for—is not a popular topic. As I said earlier, the idea today seems to be, "Parents, obey your children, for in this way you will keep the peace in your home."

But the issue is not, is your home peaceful? The issue is, is your home operating on biblical principles? And if the only way we as parents can have peace is by yielding to our children, then we are going to have messed-up homes.

### A Sticky Question

Obedience to parents raises a very sticky question for adult children.

Let's define *adult* as anyone over eighteen who has his or her own family, job, schedule, or whatever. The question is, how long do we have to obey our parents?

Someone might say, "I haven't lived at home for years, but my parents are still trying to tell me what to do." Another person might ask, "I still live at home for economic reasons, but I'm an adult. Are you saying I still have to obey my parents?" Let's examine this issue.

The first thing to note is that the context of Ephesians 6 is the nuclear family: father, mother, and their children. This implies that children are the parents' responsibility and are under the parents' care.

So we can make this statement to start with: As long as you are under your parents' roof and they are providing for you and protecting you, the Bible commands you to obey their rules. It's as simple as that.

Even if a man is thirty years old, if he's still living in Mama's house, eating Mama's food, and has a key to Mama's front door, then he is obligated to obey Mama's rules, because she is providing for him.

Someone may say, "That's ridiculous. A grown man shouldn't have to obey his parents like he was some little child." Well, if he can't or won't obey his parents, then he needs to move and start being responsible for his own provision and protection.

What about the grown child who doesn't live at home but calls Dad for a loan? Then he needs to be ready to obey his dad's guidelines pertaining to the loan. If he doesn't want to do that, then he shouldn't borrow the money.

The point is if the parents are making provision and giving protection, they have the right to say, "In my home, I want things done this way."

Let me clarify something before we go any further. I am not talking about clear-cut biblical issues here, but a parent's own preferences and rules. Any adult who is not under his parents' care is not obligated to go to bed when they say, for instance.

What about the clear biblical precepts where God demands obedience? It's obvious that parents must make sure their children at home obey God's commands. Those are nonnegotiable. For us as adult children, the issue is not what our parents say. We deal with God Himself on these things.

But let's take the case of the thirty-year-old man still living off his parents. Suppose Dad says, "Son, you're coming in so late at night that you're keeping us up and ruining our sleep. I want you to get home earlier so we can go to bed." In that case, the son has two choices:

comply with his father's demand or move out and get his own place.

My children love it when the family goes back to my parents' home in Baltimore. The reason is that when I go home, all that Pastor Evans or Dr. Evans stuff doesn't mean a thing to my mama.

When I come into the house, my mama is talking about "Boy, this" and "Boy, that." What the kids like to see, even today, is that if I don't do something my mother insists on, she pulls out a belt. The kids are saying, "Hit him, Grandma! Hit him!" And you know what? If she decided to hit me, I would have to take it. It's her home.

I shared this story over national radio, so it's safe to tell it here. I remember an incident from my childhood as if it were yesterday. I was about ten or eleven years old when my father took our family to Granddaddy's house for Thanksgiving dinner, as he did every year.

We were all sitting around the table, about to eat Thanksgiving dinner. My younger brother, Arthur, was misbehaving at the table. My father told Arthur to stop or he was going to spank him.

But Granddaddy, who was my father's father, said to my father, "You're not going to spank him."

A hush fell over the room. I remember thinking, *This I gotta see.* We were about to have a clash of generations. Arthur kept acting up, so my father disregarded *his* father's warning and slapped Arthur right there at the table. Without even blinking, Granddaddy reached over and slapped my father!

Did you follow all the action? Here were two fathers who slapped their sons because their sons disregarded their commands. Was my grandfather right to slap my father? I believe so, because we were in his house.

When that happened, my father got embarrassed and angry. Right there in the middle of Thanksgiving dinner, he got up and said, "Let's go," and our family walked out.

My point is that if you as a child are going to be at home you must either abide by the home's rules or leave.

So children must obey their parents. If you're at home, you are obligated to obey your parents' rules and preferences as well as the clear-cut commands of Scripture. But once you leave your parents' home, you are not obligated to comply with their preferences.

## CHILDREN ARE TO HONOR THEIR PARENTS

A second thing that children owe their parents is honor. The Scripture says, "Honor your father and mother (which is the first commandment with a promise), that it may be well with you, and that you may live long on the earth" (Ephesians 6:2–3).

The Greek word for *honor* means "to value highly, to hold in highest regard." This, by the way, holds true at any age. There may be some areas of controversy and disagreement when it comes to obeying parents, but children never reach an age when they don't owe their parents honor.

The reason we have so much disrespect in the streets and in the schools is that children have never learned respect in the home. If kids don't learn to respect Dad and Mom, they may never learn to respect police officers, judges, or anyone else's person or property.

Here's another reason Satan wants to destroy the home: If he can do that, he can destroy honor in the culture.

## The Importance of Honor

How important is it to God that children honor their parents? We can answer that from Exodus 21.

Verse 15 of this chapter says, "He who strikes his father or his mother shall surely be put to death." According to verse 17, "He who curses his father or his mother shall surely be put to death."

Lifting your hand against your parents or cursing them, both terrible forms of dishonor, meant the gas chamber, the electric chair, lethal injection in ancient Israel. That's how serious God is about children honoring their parents. As I said, dishonoring parents is rebellion within God's kingdom.

Do you think the children in Israeli homes took the message seriously? Well, there is no record in all of the Bible of any child or young person in Israel being put to death for dishonoring his or her parents.

Why is that? Because these kids weren't crazy. They knew this thing was real. You can believe that if they started to slide over into serious dishonor, they got things fixed up real fast. You could not abuse your parents physically or verbally in Israel and live to brag about it.

There used to be a time when, if adults were walking down the street and met a group of kids coming the other way, the kids moved over. Now *we* see kids coming and we get out of the way.

They are not afraid of us; we are afraid of them. Why? Because you don't know what these kids might do if you make them mad. Because parents don't take care of business in the home and allow their children to get away with dishonoring them, we all pay the price.

Teaching children to honor is a long-term process. It has to be enforced and reinforced every day. Teenagers who are allowed to show disrespect to their parents are on a dead-end road. And the culture will eventually feel the effects of that rebellion.

There was a little boy in a department store at Christmastime. He got on one of those mechanical horses, and his mother said, "Get off, Son." Her arms were loaded with packages, so she couldn't pick him up. The boy refused to get off the horse. So the exchange started.

"Get off the horse, Son."

"No."

"I said get off now."

"No."

"If you'll get off the horse, I'll get it for you for Christmas."

"No!"

The man playing Santa Claus was sitting right there, watching the mother sweating. So Santa walked over and whispered in the kid's ear. The boy jumped off the horse.

The mother said to Santa, "What did you promise him?"

My man Claus said, "I promised him I was going to beat his backside if he didn't get off that horse."

See, some parents promise kids the wrong stuff. "I promise I'll give you this if you do what I want." We talked about that in the previous chapter. It's called bribing children, and it doesn't work.

## Dealing with Dishonor

I want to show you a biblical case study of how God feels about dishonor and how He deals with it.

It's an unusual story, found in 2 Kings 2:23–24. Now this is not a parent-child situation, but it's an adult—the prophet Elisha—being dishonored and cursed by a group of young men:

> Then he [Elisha] went up from there to Bethel; and as he was going up by
> the way, young lads came out from the city and mocked him and said to him,
> "Go up, you baldhead; go up, you baldhead!" When he looked behind him
> and saw them, he cursed them in the name of the Lord. Then two female
> bears came out of the woods and tore up forty-two lads of their number.

The word used here indicates that these were not little kids being irresponsible. These were older boys who were, in effect, cursing God's prophet. And their disrespect brought death. The reason so many children are dying in the streets is because they never learned honor, and it's costing them their lives.

I showed you above that God takes honor very seriously. Look at another passage that spells it out in detail. What did parents in Israel do when they had a rebellious child or a young person, who refused to obey or honor them? The Mosaic law was very specific:

*If any man has a stubborn and rebellious son who will not obey his father or his mother, and when they chastise him, he will not even listen to them, then his father and mother shall seize him, and bring him out to the elders of his city at the gateway of his home town. And they shall say to the elders of his city, "This son of ours is stubborn and rebellious, he will not obey us, he is a glutton and a drunkard." Then all the men of his city shall stone him to death; so you shall remove the evil from your midst, and all Israel shall hear of it and fear. (Deuteronomy 21:18–21)*

This is not talking about misbehavior. All children are going to misbehave. This is talking about serious, deliberate, long-term rebellion.

People in the church I pastor who are dealing with a rebellious adolescent have asked me, "What should we do? Do we call the police? We don't want to see our son locked up. What do we do?"

One thing you can do if you have a rebellious child is bring him to the church. The elders of the city would be comparable to the elders of the church today. If a child is living in your house yet won't obey and honor you, the parents, you should bring the child to the church so that the church can admonish him or her on the parents' behalf.

In the previous chapter, I gave you an example of when that happened in our church in Dallas. That teenager got his act together when the deacons got involved and made him accountable to obey his mother.

Now I realize a lot of churches are not functioning in this way. And I'm not necessarily advocating a formal ministry. But when the need arises, parents ought to be able to bring their child to the church.

Then, if the child will not listen to God's covenant community, he or she is handed over to civil authorities if the case requires, so that the authorities might do with the child whatever may be necessary.

But before parents call the police or send a child to jail, they should be able to bring the child to the church for discipline, that he or she might learn how to honor the parents. The men of the church, acting on God's behalf, represent one final chance and hope for repentance and change.

Obviously, we are talking about a very serious case here. But that's just the point. How do cases in which a child dishonors his or her parents become so bad that the authorities have to step in? One answer may be that no one called this kid to account when it first happened way back when.

Children, especially teenagers, need to know that they cannot live any way they want and dishonor their parents and expect to cruise right along with no consequences. God won't allow that to happen forever. Honoring their parents is high on the kingdom agenda of children.

### How to Show Honor

How do children honor their parents? Let me suggest several ways.

First, children need to honor their parents *emotionally*. This includes spending time with them and showing them some concern and love. Some mothers and fathers are wasting away in an old folks' home for lack of attention and honor from their grown children.

Someone may say, "But you don't know about my mother. She was a terrible mother." Or, "My father was bad news." But this person is still your parent. He or she must have done something right, fed you something good, because you're still here.

I'm not saying that you have to honor what your parents did wrong. I'm saying you can still recognize and honor your parents for their position.

You can also honor your parents *verbally*. I told you about my parents' home in Baltimore. When I go home, I don't say to my father, "Hey, Art. How's it going?" It's "Yes, sir" and "No, sir."

Paul told Timothy, "Do not sharply rebuke an older man, but rather appeal to him as a father" (1 Timothy 5:1). In other words, even if he's wrong, you still speak to him with respect.

A mother and father are not, "Hey, you" to their children. Parents are to be spoken to and about with honor.

God also calls children to honor their parents *financially*. Again in 1 Timothy 5:8 Paul wrote, "If anyone does not provide for his own, and especially for those of his household, he has denied the faith, and is worse than an unbeliever." Now go to verse 16: "If any woman who is a believer has dependent widows, let her assist them, and let not the church be burdened."

As children, we have a financial responsibility for our parents when they can no longer take care of themselves. This means more than buying them a Mother's or Father's Day card. It means seeing to their well-being when they need our assistance. Maybe they cannot live with us because of the kind of medical care they need, but honor still demands that we look after their welfare.

Notice that in 1 Timothy 5:4, Paul described what we do for our parents, in this case our mothers, as making a "return" for what they have done for us. Your mother carried you for nine months. She went through painful labor to bring you into the world. She fed you.

In the case of many poor families in our generation, your mother may have boarded a bus every day to go to the other side of town and scrub other people's floors so you could eat, have clothes, and go to school. Your dad may have worked like my dad did, until he was so tired he could hardly walk home. That kind of sacrifice deserves to be honored.

The father of one of the elders in our church left his family when this elder was a child. But when this father fell ill not long ago, our elder went to the hospital regularly to be with his father, even though none of the other kids would have anything to do with him.

This elder was showing his father honor, not because he was a great dad, but because his position as father deserved respect. And who knows? This man's honor may win his father to Christ.

## The Blessing of Honor

The last thing I want you to see is that honoring parents brings blessing.

You were wondering when I was going to get to Ephesians 6:3, weren't you? What about the Bible's promise of good quality and quantity of life for those who honor their parents?

This verse says that those children who honor their parents will be blessed with a greater quantity of life. That is, they will avoid the curse of rebellion and disobedience that, as we have seen, can bring premature death.

These children will also experience God's blessing. Do you want God to hear and answer your prayers? Do you want His blessing on your education, career, choice of a mate, or other issue of life? Then honor your mother and father. Because if you don't, it won't go well with you.

Many people are messed up because they have never fixed things up with Mom and Dad. Some of us need to put this book down and go make a phone call or pay a visit or write a letter.

This principle of honoring parents was given in the Old Testament, and it carries right through to the New Testament and today. It still applies and is still a central feature for anyone who is serious about functioning in accordance with God's kingdom agenda.

Let me close by answering the obvious question. Is Ephesians 6:3 promising that every child who honors his or her parents will live to be ninety and experience only good things?

No, the idea of long life is that you will get all the life God ordained you to have. He won't have to cut you off before your time because you refuse to stop dishonoring your parents. You won't die at forty if you're supposed to live to be seventy. You'll make all your ordained days.

Children are dying today because they refuse to honor their parents. This is an issue with the power of blessing and of life and death in it. We need to make sure honoring our parents is high on our kingdom agenda.

# CHAPTER FIFTEEN

# The Kingdom Agenda
# of Singles

With this chapter we close the section on God's kingdom agenda for the family by looking at the important and unique place that single people hold in the kingdom. We will look at how, as a single person, you can find and fulfill God's calling on your life.

There is so much emphasis on marriage and family in the church that many single men and women wonder whether it is possible to be single and satisfied. Well, it is not only possible to be single and live a fulfilled life, it is sinful to be otherwise. That is, if you are single and unhappy in the role God has given you, you do yet have a complete handle on God's kingdom view of singleness.

Unfortunately, the church has helped fuel a sense of incompleteness by its great emphasis on family. There is nothing wrong with emphasizing family. There *is* something wrong with making singles feel like second-class citizens in the kingdom.

In fact, we pastors often unconsciously fuel the discontent of single believers by helping singles to cope with their singleness. God doesn't simply want single people to cope. He wants them to succeed.

Someone has said that marriage is like flies on a screen door. Those on the outside are trying to get in, and those on the inside are trying to get out.

As a pastor, I often talk to singles who are frustrated because they're not married. Then I meet with married folks who are frustrated because they're no longer single. Sometimes I wish I could create an exchange program! The point is that both single and married people need to stop trying to cope with their marital status and start living for the kingdom.

I've been married more than thirty years, so single readers might wonder how I could understand the pain and struggle they are feeling. I agree that I am not an expert on the single life, so I want to reference two people who were—the apostle Paul and Jesus Christ.

These two team up in 1 Corinthians 6–7 to give us kingdom principles that will help all singles find satisfaction—whether that person has never been married or is divorced or widowed. Let's discover God's agenda for singles.

## WAIT ON THE LORD

The first principle I want you to see is very simple. Singles need to wait on the Lord. Now, I know that doesn't sound deep. You may be saying, "I've been waiting on the Lord for fifteen years. Go on to principle two."

But wait a minute more. . . . It's been my experience that while many single people are waiting, not all of them are waiting on the Lord. There's a big difference between simply marking time and purposely waiting on God to accomplish His will in your life.

### Focus on God

First Corinthians 7 is a section of Scripture in which Paul discussed singleness in detail. Look at verse 24: "Let each man remain with God in that condition in which he was called."

Paul related your state, whether married or single, to the word *calling*, a key concept we explored in depth in an earlier chapter. Your calling has to do with the fact that when God saved you and me, He gave us a whole new direction in life. Therefore, our concern should be finding our calling, or purpose, not in trying to change our marital status.

### Find Your Purpose

One reason so many singles are dissatisfied is that they are not finding their significance in God's calling for their lives. God gives us significance regardless of our marital status. Paul said, in effect, "Look at life from the vantage point of your calling rather than as an opportunity to change your status."

A single woman went to her pastor one day to express her deep frustration with her singleness. He said, "Well, you know, God has a man for every woman, and you can't improve on that."

She replied, "Pastor, I don't want to improve on it. I just want to get in on it."

But what Paul was saying is that if God's people will view their marital status from the standpoint of His purpose for them rather than solely from the standpoint of their desires, it will help them wait on God rather than wait on a person.

If you're waiting on a person, that person may not come, or his or her arrival may prove to be a disappointment. But if you're waiting on the Lord to work His will in His time, He will never disappoint you and never arrive late.

## Analyze Your Circumstances

Here's another way singles can wait on the Lord. Paul told singles to take a good look at their circumstances:

> Concerning virgins I have no command of the Lord, but I give an opinion as one who by the mercy of the Lord is trustworthy. I think then that this is good in view of the present distress, that it is good for a man to remain as he is. (1 Corinthians 7:25–26)

Now let me clarify Paul's language here. He was not saying, "Here is my opinion, so take it for what it's worth because it's just my idea." That's not what he meant.

Instead, Paul was saying, "When Jesus was on earth, He didn't discuss this, so let me tell you what He told me to tell you." In other words, this instruction was from Paul's pen, but it was from the Lord through the inspiration of the Holy Spirit.

Notice that Paul immediately tied singleness to moral purity. The reason this is important is that if you are going to wait on the Lord then you need help from the Lord. And you won't get help from the Lord if you're compromising Him in your moral life. So as we said above, purity is high on God's kingdom agenda for singles.

In the following verses, Paul is going to argue for the benefits of singleness. He is going to make it equal to marriage and in some ways better than marriage, in terms of our ability to carry out the agenda God has for His people.

The "present distress," as best as we can determine, had to do with the persecution Christians suffered under the Roman emperor Nero. He was the archenemy of the church. This is the man who wrapped Christians up in animal skins, sprinkled blood on them, and then let wild animals loose at them. Nero would take other Christians and dip them in wax, then hang them on posts and set them afire to light his gardens.

Obviously, if you were living in that situation, it would be better to be single—not to have a family to worry about or to have a family that would worry about what might happen to you. Paul was telling the single Christians in Corinth to analyze their circumstances before they agreed to marry. He wanted them to determine, "Am I really going to be better off if I marry?"

You aren't about to be dipped in wax and set on fire, but if you are single you still need to take a serious look at your circumstances: your work situation, your finances, your level of self-control, the spiritual condition of a possible partner, and so forth.

I say that because many single people want to get married for the wrong reason. A single person may say, "I'm tired of being lonely."

Let me tell you, I know a lot of lonely married people. I have known married couples who don't even talk to each other, who sleep either in separate rooms or are clinging to the far sides of the bed. A marriage that is not orchestrated by God won't solve your loneliness.

The desire for sexual fulfillment also propels a lot of singles into marriage. But there are many married couples who barely touch each other. There are many married couples who go weeks, months, and even years without any meaningful intimacy. Paul said, in essence, "Look at your circumstances and determine whether your desire for marriage is on target."

## Let God Do Your Looking

Here's a big one for singles. Paul wrote in verse 27, "Are you bound to a wife? Do not seek to be released. Are you released from a wife? Do not seek a wife."

Paul said if you are married, be content with that. And if you are single, be content with that too. Don't go mate hunting. You say, "But how else am I going to find one?"

The same way Adam and Eve found each other. God was their matchmaker. God knew where Adam was, and He brought Eve to Adam. If you want to find a mate, you need to find somebody who knows where the right mate is. It's obvious that you don't know where that mate is, or else you would be married by now. So if you want to find a mate, you need a professional mate-finder service.

In other words, focus on the Lord and let the Lord do your looking for you. A lot of singles are frustrated because they can't find Mr. or Miss Right. So they look and say, "Yeah, that's him," or "She's the one," but then it doesn't work out and they are frustrated.

But if you will stop looking and start living out your kingdom agenda, when the divine "mate-finder" is ready He will lead you to a mate, and you won't be frustrated.

I had no idea that I would find my wife three thousand miles from home in the country of Guyana. But I was there doing ministry, and Lois's father was involved in this ministry. He invited me over for dinner one night.

So I went to his home, and here was this cute young woman cooking in the kitchen. Now I may be a preacher, but I wasn't blind. And she was a good cook too.

So Lois and I got to talk after dinner, and as I told you earlier, I was using all the charm I could muster to impress her. I was giving her my best stuff, but the point is that I did not go to Guyana looking for a wife.

Our American system of "serial dating" is not biblical. The Bible says nothing about going from person to person, dating this guy for five months and that young woman for six months and then breaking up, as we search the field for the right person today. Instead, if you're single, the Bible urges you to keep your "antenna" tuned toward the Lord and wait for His signal.

When He sends that signal, then you spend time dating, not to find the right one, but because you've found the right one and you want to get to know that person better. When your antenna is tuned toward the Lord, you don't need to call a dating service or make the rounds of the clubs to meet people.

This is the beauty of the book of Ruth. Ruth was not an Israelite, but she went back to Bethlehem with Naomi, even though Naomi practically guaranteed Ruth that she would never find a husband in Israel.

But Ruth went to Bethlehem seeking God, not seeking a husband. She dedicated herself to God's agenda even if it meant she would never marry (Ruth 1:16). And in the course of the story, God brought Boaz into her life. Ruth didn't have to go after Boaz, because God put the interest in Boaz's heart first. Then Boaz sought out Ruth.

So here was a Moabite widow who found a mate and wound up in the messianic lineage of Jesus Christ (see Matthew 1:5). Ruth was looking for the Lord, and He knew where Boaz was.

## Consider the Challenges

Paul gave another reason for singles to wait on the Lord in 1 Corinthians 7:28: "But . . . if a virgin should marry, she has not sinned. Yet such will have trouble in this life, and I am trying to spare you."

Marriage, Paul said, brings with it a whole new set of challenges. If you don't believe Paul or me, ask the next married person you meet. You think you are miserable by yourself. But you can be miserable in company.

Now please don't misunderstand me. I am not knocking marriage, and neither is Paul. I'm just telling you the truth. Most married people will tell you, "There are a lot of things about marriage I didn't know about until I got there."

I'm talking about things like the inevitable personality conflicts and adjustments demanded in marriage, the emotional conflicts, and the clash of wills that comes when two sinful people—and we're all sinners, remember?—start living under the same roof.

That's why if you are single, don't ever think you can marry to escape your problems. All you do is drag your problems into your marriage. It's easy for singles to look at married couples and get fooled, because they look so happy on the outside.

But as I said at the beginning of this section on the kingdom agenda and the family, many couples act like they were married by the secretary of war instead of the justice of the peace. If you are determined to be miserable, it's a lot easier and less painful to be miserable by yourself.

It's better to wait longer for the right person than to be stuck with the wrong person. Marriage is a big enough challenge even when you find the right person. You don't need the headache and heartache of a bad marriage. Wait on the Lord.

## Waiting and Sex

I wanted to end this portion with a crucial area of Christian singleness. Sex is so crucial because it is so intimately related to who we are. And it's the area in which many single believers find their biggest struggle.

In 1 Corinthians 6:12–20, Paul discussed sex outside of marriage. The bottom line of his argument was that sex outside of the marriage covenant is sin and is totally contrary to God's kingdom agenda for single believers. That bedrock truth never changes in any culture or any setting.

We don't have the space here to unfold this passage in detail, but I want to note some keys points with you. First, as you read through these verses, you will see a reference to each member of the Trinity. This raises the issue of extramarital sex far above Paul's simply saying, "It's not good. You ought not do it." Instead he was saying, "This thing has theological implications."

Paul was arguing that sexual purity outside of marriage is demanded because of God the Father, it's expected because of God the Son, and it's possible because of God the Spirit. Some Christian singles falter in this area because they lose sight of the theology and limit themselves to the anthropology involved.

In other words, whenever you hear someone saying, "But I'm only human," that's an anthropological argument. But as I will argue later on in this chapter, if you are a believer you are more than just a human. You are a *saved* human, and you have God's power for purity resident within you.

Some people say sex is like food. When you're hungry, you eat. No big deal. But Paul answered that in 1 Corinthians 6:13. The stomach may be for food, he said, "yet the body is *not* for immorality" (my emphasis).

If your date tells you he washed his car and bought a new suit for this date and expects something more than a good night at the door, tell him, "You washed your car? OK, I will help put the dirt back on your car. And you bought a new suit? I'll go with you while you take it back." You are far too valuable to be used by undisciplined men for their gratification.

God created your body to be used for His glory (see v. 13b), not simply to satisfy either your own or someone else's passion unless it is within the proper functioning of marriage.

See, God does not condemn sex outside of marriage because sex is bad. He condemns sex outside of marriage because it's so good when used properly within marriage.

You say, "Wait a minute, Tony. Let's get practical. I have the same passions as married people. Where do you expect me to get the ability to control my normal passions?" From God the Father. Christian singles have the same power available to them that God used when He raised Christ from the dead (see v. 14).

So a single person's ability, or lack thereof, to control his or her sexuality has to do with the lack of accessing God's power. It has nothing to do with the level of a person's passions.

Let me summarize Paul's point in 1 Corinthians 6:15–20. Sex outside of marriage is so destructive because it is far more than a physical act between two people. There is a spiritual union that takes place when two people engage in sexual intercourse. It is like a marriage in terms of the intimacy, but it is deadly because there is no marital commitment to cement the union.

So if sex is simply an act of temporary gratification, when the two people pull away from each other, a part of their spirit tears away and remains with the other person.

And for the Christian, there's more. Because we are joined to Christ, whatever we do sexually, we bring Jesus in on. So Paul's questions was, "Shall I then take away the members of Christ and make them members of a harlot? May it never be!" (v. 15).

Sex outside of marriage for a believer is such a damaging sin because our bodies are temples of the Holy Spirit (see v. 19). And Paul had warned earlier, "If any man destroys the temple of God, God will destroy him, for the temple of God is holy, and that is what you are" (1 Corinthians 3:17).

A person who engages in sex outside of marriage is like a man who robs a bank. He gets what he wants in a hurry, but when it catches up with him he has to pay for it a long time.

But the morally pure single is a depositor in the bank. She keeps saving and gaining interest so that when it comes time to make a withdrawal, she can enjoy her life's savings.

Single Christian, if you want to have a sexual "savings account" to draw on in marriage, don't spend what you have now. If your kingdom commitment is to remain abstinent, Paul gave you the solution to sexual compromise: "Flee immorality" (1 Corinthians 6:18). The Greek means "vamoose, bye-bye, get out of there." Flee to the Lord, and wait for Him. He has the kingdom plan for sex.

## WATCH FOR THE LORD

Paul also urged singles to watch for the Lord. "But this I say, brethren, the time has been shortened, so that from now on those who have wives should be as though they had none" (1 Corinthians 7:29).

Paul was not telling Christian husbands to get rid of their wives, of course. He is saying that all of us, single included, need to take a kingdom, or eternal, perspective on our lives.

### A Kingdom Perspective

In other words, since the Lord is going to return any day and usher in the kingdom, we need to be watching for Him—which means we need to be living as if He could return today.

I want to emphasize again that Paul was not just addressing single people in this text. The Bible repeatedly tells us Christians to do everything we do and weigh every decision in light of eternity. So we are not trying to lay an extra burden on singles here.

But one reason singles need to view their marital status in light of the kingdom is that marriage will die when we die. That is, marriage has no place in eternity. "In the resurrection [people] neither marry, nor are given in marriage," Jesus said (Matthew 22:30).

Marriage is only for history. It is only valuable in time. God calls us to have an eye that looks at eternity and not at time, to have an eye that sees things in terms of His kingdom.

In this warning Paul also included earthly things, such as our emotions and our finances (see 1 Corinthians 7:30). Then he said, "The form of this world is passing away" (v. 31).

What Paul advised us to do is to live life by eternal values because our time here on earth is short. That word means "condensed." Since marriage is one of those things that is passing away, Paul didn't want us to fix our whole lives on it.

God has a purpose for singleness. If you are single and spending all of your time wanting to be married, then you are missing God's purpose for you. And that means you are not getting all that God has for you in the time He's given you.

Suppose the Lord says, "After Jane has finished doing this portion of My kingdom work, I will give her a husband." But Jane never gets around to doing that portion of His kingdom work because she is too busy being frustrated over her singleness.

So Jane spends all of her time trying to get married, when God has a mate waiting for her at the end of a certain part of her kingdom work. Because God wasn't going to give Jane a mate until she finished that, she doesn't get a husband because she never got around to doing the King's business.

## A Kingdom Agenda

There's nothing wrong with marriage, emotions, or finances, but they are short-term in comparison to the kingdom. A person who is watching for the Lord can't afford to keep his or her eyes on these things too much. This person must keep his or her kingdom perspective sharp.

Many singles are not fulfilled because they limit their lives' agendas to marriage. If God's agenda for you right now is bigger than marriage, then marriage alone can't fulfill you. And if God hasn't given you a marriage partner yet but you decide to find one on your own, you will pay a high price for that marriage.

## WORK FOR THE LORD

A third way single believers can fulfill God's kingdom agenda is by working for the Lord.

First Corinthians 7:32–33 says, "I want you to be free from concern. One who is unmarried is concerned about the things of the Lord, how he may please the Lord; but one who is married is concerned about things of the world, how he may please his wife."

Then Paul brought home the point in verse 35: "And this I say for your own benefit; not to put a restraint upon you, but to promote what is seemly, and to secure undistracted devotion to the Lord."

## Undistracted Devotion

We have already established that many singles are unhappy because they don't understand why God has them single. They are asking, "Why am I still single?"

God's answer is, "If that's where I have you right now, that's where I want to use you right now."

Paul gave us one reason for singleness that applies to any single believer: undistracted devotion to Christ. He said married people have a legitimate distraction in each other. But did you know it's possible for a single person to live with the distraction of marriage? That's what happens when a single Christian fixates on marriage rather than on serving the Lord.

And when that happens, the single person squanders his or her opportunity for undistracted devotion to the Lord. And that takes us back to what we were talking about above, the failure to find and fulfill the kingdom agenda God has for you.

There is one exception I can think of to the rule that singles should not be distracted by the issue of marriage. That is prayer. A single person can pray, "Lord, I'm trusting You. I'm going to wait on You, watch for You, and work for You, and leave my marital status at Your feet. I can't do anything about it, so if I meet Mr. or Miss Right, that's up to You."

God wants undistracted devotion. He says, "I don't want to compete with anybody. I want you to see that your singleness is a unique opportunity for you to maximize your devotion to Me."

The local church, then, should receive maximum benefit from the gifts of their singles for the expansion of the kingdom, which simultaneously serves as God's spiritual covering for those singles no longer living at home.

## Using Your Singleness

Now let me ask you a question if you're single. Why does God have you single? What is He uniquely doing in you, with you, and through you that can only be done now because when you get married you won't have the time to do it?

If you can't answer that question, and you're living a life of frustration, you're not on target. God knows that once He gives you a mate, a distraction will come into your life and you'll never be able to return to your single freedom again. So He is calling on singles to use their singleness for deeper commitment to Him and greater service for Him.

Suppose God doesn't plan to give a single man a wife for ten years. Then he might as well not be upset that he has to wait ten years. He might as well use those ten years to do something significant for God with his life.

After all, if God is not going to give this guy a wife for ten years, he is not going to make it happen in eight years or six years by trying to pursue marriage on his own. And if he goes ahead and marries somebody because he didn't want to wait for God, he is going to be a miserable person.

I know what some singles say when they hear this: "But it's too slow. God is taking too long, and I'm too frustrated." Let me suggest why that may be true.

I'm sure you've had the kind of day at work where you have so much to do you feel it's about 10:00 in the morning only to look at the clock to discover it's already 3:00 in the afternoon. You wonder where the time went.

I'm confident you've also had the kind of workday where you have hardly anything to do or you dread the work you do have to do. That day you work for what seems like hours, but when you look at the clock, it's only 9:15 a.m.

What happened on those two days? Did the clock change its speed? No, you changed your speed. In the first case, you had something interesting or challenging or important to do, and the time flew by. In the second case, you were either bored or frustrated, and the time dragged by.

## Judging Time

Now apply that situation to the example of the single man above. If he gets busy fulfilling God's agenda for his life, the time will pass a lot quicker and be a lot more spiritually profitable than if he sits around bored or frustrated because he isn't married.

Some singles will make little or nothing of their lives because they are sitting in the bleachers, spiritually speaking, waiting for a marriage partner, instead of getting in the game. As they sit there waiting for someone to come by whom God may not send right away, the years go by.

A single person may object, "But I'm getting older." Well, that's relative. If you are going to be eighty years of age and you get married at the age of forty, that's forty years of marriage. But if a person gets married at twenty-five and dies at forty, that's only fifteen years of marriage. So who's older, the twenty-five-year-old or the forty-year-old? Time is relative.

The passage of time in relation to marriage was an issue in Corinth. Evidently, some Christian fathers who had unmarried daughters were strict about not letting their daughters marry because of the stressful times they were living in (remember the "present distress" mentioned in 1 Corinthians 7:26).

These men's daughters were of "full age" (v. 36), so Paul assured these fathers that it was permissible for them to allow or arrange for their daughters to get married if the desire and opportunity were present. Later marriages are perfectly acceptable in God's sight if He presents the opportunity.

## WED IN THE LORD

Here's a fourth and final way for singles to accomplish God's kingdom agenda. If and when the time comes for them to marry, they must marry "in the Lord" (v. 39).

### The Permanence of Marriage

Notice that Paul began 1 Corinthians 7:39 by saying, "A wife is bound as long as her husband lives." He went on to address the case of the widow, but what I want you to see here is the absolute permanence of marriage.

Marriage is like a violin. After the music stops, the strings are still attached. Why is it important for singles to grasp this fact? Because they need to have the mind-set that marriage is for life. Therefore they need to take their time before committing themselves to another person for life.

There is a prevalent attitude today that says, "If we don't like our marriage, we'll just get divorced." But that attitude is from Satan, not God. Marriage is meant to be permanent.

"But I didn't know she was like that when I married her," someone says. Or, "I didn't know he snored," or "I found out all that hair wasn't really hers." Too bad, because you're bound to that marriage.

As I said before, it's better to be single and miserable than married and miserable. In fact, when the disciples heard Jesus teach about the permanence of marriage, they said, "It is better not to marry" (Matthew 19:10). Jesus answered, in effect, "Better think about that." Marriage is "till death do us part."

### The Surprises of Marriage

It's interesting to watch couples in their first year of marriage, because that's when the real deal starts to come to the surface. A lot of men lie to women when they are dating, both in what they say and in what they do. When a couple is dating, he opens the car door for her every time. He jumps around to the other side of the table to pull out her chair.

Let me tell you, the brother is lying! How do I know? Because after he wins his girl, she opens her own car door—and pulls out her own chair.

When they're dating, the guy tells his girl, "You're the prettiest thing I ever saw." He's lying because he's already told that to every woman he's dated up to this one! You get the idea. But that's the way it often happens, and marriage brings out all these little surprises.

## The Necessity of Faith

When Paul said believers are to marry "in the Lord," he ruled out marrying non-Christians, no matter how handsome or beautiful they are. As someone has said, if you marry a child of the Devil, you'll have in-law problems!

A woman was waiting to fly to Canada one day when she ran into this smooth-talking dude who was on his way to Florida. He said, "Why don't you fly with me?"

"Simple. We're going in two different directions."

If you belong to Jesus Christ, you're going to heaven, not to hell. And unless the other person is willing to fly with you toward your destination, then you can't be on the same plane together. Marriage for the Christian must be "in the Lord."

# A SUCCESSFUL SINGLE

Is there an illustration in the Bible of a successful single? Yes, there is, and we are going to jump right into the middle of his story in Genesis 39. His name is Joseph.

My purpose here is not to retell the entire story of this incredible single man. I'm going to assume some knowledge on your part. Let me just say that in Genesis 39, Joseph is a slave in Egypt, having been sold into slavery by his brothers.

But notice what the Bible says. In spite of Joseph's situation, "The LORD was with Joseph, so he became a successful man" (v. 2). Single believer, while you're waiting on a mate, you can be a successful person.

"Now [Joseph's] master saw that the LORD was with him and how the LORD caused all that he did to prosper in his hand" (v. 3). Not only was God making Joseph successful, but the sinners saw that the Lord was with him. Joseph's commitment to God and His kingdom was public knowledge.

Do the unbelievers at your job know the Lord is with you? Do the unbelievers around you know that it's possible to be single and sanctified, single and satisfied? Are people blessed because of your influence? According to Genesis 39:5, God blessed everything his Egyptian master owned because of Joseph.

But trouble was brewing in the house of the master, Potiphar. Potiphar's wife looked at Joseph, who was handsome (see v. 6), and threw herself at him. But Joseph said, "How then could I do this great evil, and sin against God?" (v. 9).

What was he doing? Maintaining his moral purity. He was a handsome, well-built single man. But that did not give him a right to prey on women. If you're a single man, you may be God's gift to one woman. But until you find her, you can't mess with other women.

Even though he was good-looking and had the opportunity, Joseph was committed to godly standards for his life. So if you're a single man, don't give God this line, "Well, God, you made me a man. You know how I operate." Yes, God made you a man. And when He saved you, He made you a *Christian* man. That means you're not like other men.

Joseph got thrown into prison for maintaining his standards. But even in prison, "the Lord was with Joseph" (v. 21). Even if you're having a hard time as a single person, if the Lord is with you, He can turn a jailhouse into a party.

Joseph stayed faithful to God through two years in prison (see Genesis 41:1), and the ultimate result was that God brought him out and gave him a wife at the age of thirty and made him the second-highest ruler in Egypt (see Genesis 41:45–46). Joseph wound up running the show in Egypt because he stayed true to God in his singleness.

## A HOLDING PATTERN?

I've talked with and counseled enough individuals to know that it can be tough being single. It may mean avoiding movies or television shows that inflame your passions or feed your frustration at not being married.

But a Christian single can find fulfillment in the Lord. We've talked about how to realize that fulfillment.

Many singles feel like their lives are in a holding pattern. If you've flown very much, you have experienced a holding pattern in which the flight controller tells the pilot it isn't safe to land yet.

Now you may not be able to see the problem from thirty thousand feet. But the pilot tells you that it would be dangerous to try to land right now. So you circle the airport.

If you're single, you may feel God has you in a holding pattern right now. You may wonder why. Everything looks clear for you to "land" in a marriage. But God sees something you can't see, and if you try to land now you will crash.

So you don't know how long the Lord's going to have you circling in singleness. But you have to wait until the Holy Spirit gives you the OK to land. If you feel like you're in a holding pattern right now, there are three things you can do.

First, you can *gripe*. "God, I'm tired of this holding pattern. I'm tired of waiting for You to send me a mate."

Second, you can *grab* the next person who walks by and try to land this thing yourself by marrying outside of God's will and timing. But that's inviting a crash landing.

Third, you can *grow*. You can do what I do when my plane is put in a holding pattern. I lie back and go to sleep. I let the controllers take control and make the decision as to when we land. I let the pilot land the plane.

Single Christian, will you let God take control of your life? Will you say to Him, "God, I want You to make me like You. Use my singleness to help me accomplish Your agenda. Help me grow for Your purposes, Your glory, and Your kingdom"?

Singleness is not second-class in God's kingdom. If you're an unhappy single, get back in God's will so you can enjoy His plan!

# THE KINGDOM AGENDA IN YOUR CHURCH LIFE

# CHAPTER SIXTEEN

# The Kingdom Agenda
# of the Church

The church is the third of the four governments God has established to administer His kingdom agenda on earth. (We will look at the fourth area of God's kingdom agenda, the civil government, in the final section.) What should God's kingdom agenda look like when applied to the church?

## THE NEED FOR SELF-EXAMINATION

We in the church need to do some careful self-examination of our agenda because, historically, God's people tend to veer off into one of two extremes.

### Two Extremes

We can describe the first extreme by the well-known charge often made against believers, that they are "so heavenly minded they are no earthly good." These are people who are definitely plugged into the church, but what they take into their heads never gets down to their feet.

That is, even though these believers have the right words and the right theology and carry the right Bible translation, their faith doesn't flesh itself out in their homes, where they work, or in their communities. It doesn't make an impact for the kingdom because these people remain so insulated and isolated from the world they never really develop relationships with unbelievers. So even though these folks have their minds on heaven, they are of little practical benefit today to the King and His kingdom.

The other extreme occurs when the church not only goes out into the world but lets the world into the church. These are people who are so earthly minded they are no heavenly good.

They think like the world, so heaven can't use them. They have been co-opted by our culture and are therefore unable to reflect properly the values of God's kingdom in a secular society.

Neither of these extremes, of course, accurately reflects the agenda God has given the church. We need to find out what that agenda is, because we have a problem today.

Let me put the problem to you in the form of a question. How can we have all these churches on all these street corners, filled with all these members, led by all these preachers, elders, and deacons, and supported by all these auxiliaries and programs, and yet still have all this mess in America? Something is wrong somewhere!

The church has become marginalized in the culture, and many parachurch organizations have arisen as a result. But these groups often forget that God's primary agency in history has been the local church, so they often detract from its ministry, power, and impact.

In fact, I would go so far as to say that any parachurch organization that does not exist for the support, empowerment, and expansion of the local church is illegitimate. It is time for us to clarify our vision of the church.

## Correcting Our Vision

I would like to suggest that one reason for this problem is that we have failed to see the church in the larger context of the kingdom of God. Let me explain.

The church is not the same as the kingdom. The kingdom is bigger than the church. I need to go back to our foundational supposition, which is that the kingdom of God is His rule over all of His creation. Therefore, the church doesn't exist for itself but rather for the kingdom.

It is the failure to recognize this broader agenda that has kept churches ingrown, divided, and fragmented. Until the church begins functioning for the kingdom rather than merely for itself, it cannot have the voice and the comprehensive impact it was created to have in areas such as social justice, race relations, economics, education, and government.

When the church has the proper kingdom perspective, there is no division between sacred and secular. All of life is viewed as an extension of God's kingdom.

In this age, the church is the primary manifestation of the kingdom, and it is the primary means by which God is extending His kingdom rule in this world. Therefore, we need to see the church within the larger setting of the kingdom so we don't become myopic in our perspective.

I had always prided myself on being the one person in six in our family who did not have to wear glasses. I used to tease my kids and my wife, calling them "four eyes" and all of that stuff.

Not anymore. I had noticed that the signs were getting fuzzy as I drove down the highway, so I had my eyes examined. I told the doctor that things in the distance were getting blurry, but I assured him that I had no problem with anything close-up.

So the doctor checked out my vision and came back with the diagnosis. My blurry vision at distant objects was really just a camouflage. My eyes were trying to compensate because they are struggling to see things up close. Then he gave me the bad news.

"If I only deal with your distance vision problem, I haven't solved your problem, because your problem is that you not only need glasses, you need bifocals." The curse of middle age! But now I have my new glasses, and I can see both up close and at a distance.

The church needs bifocals too. We are not seeing ourselves up close, and we're not seeing the bigger kingdom as clearly as we should. The reason things are hazy out there in the world is that the church often misses what God's Word is saying to us up close.

So let's attempt to clear up our vision by looking at the Word and what it says about the church's agenda so we can see the kingdom of God unleashed, realized, and experienced.

## THE POWER OF THE KINGDOM

First of all, the church is to manifest the power of God's kingdom. In a very familiar text, Jesus says something profound about the way the church is supposed to operate in the world. The text is Matthew 16:16–19, in which Peter confessed Jesus as "the Christ, the Son of the living God" (v. 16), and Jesus confirmed Peter's confession (see v. 17).

Then Jesus said to Peter, "You are Peter, and upon this rock I will build My church; and the gates of Hades shall not overpower it" (v. 18).

## Making Hell Back Up

Jesus says the test of the church's power is whether hell backs up when the church shows up. Jesus is on the offensive, building His church and accomplishing His agenda. Jesus is not trying to stop the forces of Satan and hell; hell is trying to stop Him.

Too many of the saints are saying, "Well, I'm just trying to keep Satan from defeating me." That's "Backward, Christian Soldiers"! The church is to be on the offensive in the world.

So the test of our power, both individually and corporately as the body of Christ, is whether hell backs up when we show up. If hell is winning, then we are not building Christ's church. Instead, we are building our church using Christ's name!

Then Jesus told Peter in verse 19 that He was giving the keys of the kingdom to the church. Keys speak of authority and access. When you have the keys, you have access to the building. What Jesus is saying is that the church, and only the church, has access to the kingdom of God and its power.

In other words, only the church has access to the rule of God in history. Only the church has the authority to call down heaven to address issues on earth. Only the church can open the door of eternity to cause the keys, the authority, the power, and the access to operate heaven's agenda in a hellish world. And since the spiritual precedes the physical, the church, operating properly, is the primary means of bringing spiritual solutions in history to the physical manifestations that plague humanity.

In 1 Corinthians 4:20, Paul wrote, "The kingdom of God does not consist in words, but in power." So the question is, Do we just talk about kingdom power, or do we see the power of the kingdom operating in and through the church?

## Unlocking Heaven

If there's anything that seems to be missing in the church today, it is the kind of power Jesus described in Matthew 16. But if we are the church, then we have been given the keys of the kingdom. That means we can unlock heaven, where the power is. The power comes when we call down heaven to serve notice on hell that the church of the living God is taking over.

The church has been cowering in a "holy huddle." We gather every week and call nice plays, but we don't take the plays out on the field where the real game is going on. Jesus has given the church access to heaven.

As the chaplain for the Dallas Mavericks basketball team, I often get extra tickets to share with friends or staff members at church who want to attend a basketball game.

Whenever I leave tickets at the "will call" window, I tell my guests to look for special tags in their envelope along with their tickets. They need to tie those tags to their shirt or blouse button or wherever, because those tags give them special access to things besides just the game.

With those tags, they can come back to a room next to the team's locker room and eat a meal with me. The tags give my guests special access they can't get with their tickets alone. The tickets will allow them to mingle with the crowd, but the tags open up a whole different level of access.

A lot of believers have their ticket to heaven. They have accepted Christ as Savior, and nothing is going to keep them out of heaven. But like basketball fans who have tickets to the game but don't have the special tags, they miss out on the real power available when we use the keys of the kingdom to unlock heaven.

I don't know about you, but I don't just want to make it to the game. I want more than a free ticket to heaven. I want access to the power Jesus promised. I want in on the power of the kingdom. I want to see heaven brought down to earth, demonstrating the power of God in history.

So if we are Sunday-morning-only Christians, we shouldn't be surprised if we don't see kingdom power in our lives Monday through Saturday. In the kingdom of God there is power, and the church has access to it. We are to manifest the power of heaven's kingdom here on earth.

## THE PRINCIPLES OF THE KINGDOM

The church is also designed to manifest the principles of God's kingdom in the daily lives of believers. We call these principles the Beatitudes.

Jesus taught these principles at the beginning of His great kingdom sermon, the Sermon on the Mount (see Matthew 5:1–12). The Beatitudes show how we are to think and therefore how we are to live in God's kingdom. The church is responsible to hold us accountable for living kingdom lives (see 1 Timothy 3:15).

Jesus pronounced a kingdom blessing on those who keep these principles, but the blessing is supplied today through the church because the church is the manifestation of the kingdom in this dispensation. The Beatitudes are the heart of the church's kingdom agenda. We could spend a chapter on each one, but because space doesn't allow that kind of detailed analysis, I'll just survey them briefly.

## The Poor in Spirit

"Blessed are the poor in spirit," Jesus said, "for theirs is the kingdom of heaven" (Matthew 5:3). Kingdom people are humble, not prideful. Kingdom people are dependent on God, not on themselves. They are thankful for the gifts and abilities God has given them, but kingdom people are poor in spirit.

Jesus is dealing with a heart attitude that does not cause us to walk around haughty because of who we are, what we have, or what we have done.

Some years ago, a man who was a prominent leader came to our church in Dallas and said, "I want to be a leader here." I told him we had certain qualifications for leaders and a process for taking leadership, and he was welcome to apply.

He said, "I know all of that, but I am so-and-so. I sit on this board and that board in the community, and I think you would benefit from my being in the leadership of your church."

I said, "I'm sorry, but that's not how we do it here." He got mad and left. It was obvious he did not qualify, because what he wanted to do was bring his high standing in the world into the church and let it determine his standing there.

But Jesus said that unless we come to God as little children, in humble faith, we don't qualify to be kingdom people (see Matthew 18:3).

No matter who we are in the world, the church is not privileged because we are there. Let's get that straight right away. On the contrary, we are privileged that God lets us into His church and includes us in His kingdom program.

In fact, the higher your standing in the world, the more privileged you are to be chosen of God, because the Bible says not many wise or mighty or noble people are chosen. Instead, God has chosen the foolish and the weak of this world to shame the strong (see 1 Corinthians 1:26–27).

A pastor was leaving church one Sunday when one of his members came up to him and said, "Oh, pastor, you sure can preach. In fact, in my opinion you are one of the greatest expositors of the Word of God alive today."

That made the pastor's day. He got to thinking about the great preachers of the world. When he got in the car, he said to his wife, "Mrs. Jones said I am one of the greatest expositors of the Word of God alive today. I wonder how many great expositors there are today."

His wife replied, "One less than you think!"

True poverty of spirit comes when we realize that without God, we are nothing. Anything we are or have is the result of His goodness and grace to us, and there is nothing in us that caused God to show us His favor.

Kingdom people operate by a different value system. That's why Jesus said the greatest among His disciples is the one who is the "slave of all" (Mark 10:44).

## Those Who Mourn

Then Jesus said, "Blessed are those who mourn, for they shall be comforted" (v. 4). What are we supposed to mourn over? Our sin. Jesus was saying, "Blessed are the people who feel about sin the way I feel about it."

We live in a world that celebrates sin, that tries to make sin look good, that comes up with new ways to sin every day. But Jesus says the blessed people are those who hate sin, who feel sick when they see sin in their lives. If you see ugliness in your life and you are glad about it, you are not a kingdom person living by a kingdom agenda.

When we see wickedness erupt in our hearts, it ought to send a stench to our nostrils, because that's how our King feels about sin. We are to mourn over sin and repent of it. Sin is like carbon monoxide. You may not know it's there, but it will wipe you out if you keep breathing it.

The grace of God is like an exhaust system that draws away the sin and clears our spiritual breathing passages. If the church is going to manifest the kingdom of God in the midst of this evil and perverse generation, we have to take sin as seriously as God takes it.

We all sin, but the issue here is our attitude toward it. Kingdom people are broken over sin. They feel the same way about sin that God feels about it.

That is why the church must exercise church discipline for unrepentant or rebellious members (see Matthew 18:15–20; 1 Corinthians 5:1–13). In fact, any church that does not exercise discipline is not a New Testament church.

## The Gentle

The third beatitude, or kingdom principle, Jesus gave that day is found in Matthew 5:5: "Blessed are the gentle, for they shall inherit the earth."

Many people don't understand this idea of gentleness or meekness. It has nothing to do with going around with your head down and your feet dragging. Meekness has to do with your ability to be domesticated, your willingness to submit your will to the will of God.

The best example of meekness in action is the process of taming a wild stallion. The cowboy puts a saddle on this wild horse and gets on his back. The stallion bucks because he doesn't want to be ridden. The cowboy is determined to ride the stallion until he breaks him.

Is the cowboy trying to break the horse of its strength? No, he needs the horse's strength. Instead, he is trying to break the horse of its stubborn self-will. He is trying to bring the power and strength of the horse under his control, so that when the rider issues a command, the horse obeys without bucking.

A broken horse has lost none of its strength. But once it has been broken, or domesticated, the horse's strength is now available to, and under the authority of, the rider.

This is what God wants to do with you and me. He wants to bring our wills under His authority so that when He says turn left, we turn left. When He says turn right, we turn right. When He says go, we go. When He says stop, we stop.

A meek person says to God, as Jesus said, "Not my will, but Yours be done." That's meekness, the ability to submit to God's will. These are the people who will be God's inheritors, because they are the people God can trust with His kingdom.

If God can't control you, don't look for His blessing. Why? Because

He knows He won't be able to tell you what to do with what He gives you. God is looking for meek people, so He can send them out to demonstrate the power of His kingdom to the world.

## The Hungry and Thirsty

Jesus went on to say in His teaching on the kingdom, "Blessed are those who hunger and thirst for righteousness, for they shall be satisfied" (v. 6). We must have a spiritual appetite.

We have too many church folks who are spiritually anorexic, as skinny as they can be, because they are spiritually emaciated. They don't have any appetite for spiritual things.

You probably know what it feels like to be hungry. Some people hunger for a job or a raise, so they work overtime and do everything they can to achieve their goal.

Others hunger for a relationship with a certain person. They won't give up until they win the person they desire.

When you are hungry for something, you want it in a bad way. God says if we will hunger for righteousness, He will feed us all we want. Many of us pray, "Lord, change my circumstances" when God is not interested in changing our circumstances. He is interested in fattening us up spiritually.

God wants us to be so "stuffed" with Him, if you will, that even if He sends a storm into our lives, we won't blow over because we are too full to topple.

You may say, "I don't have time to get into God's Word." That is because you are not really hungry for it. When was the last time you were really hungry, and yet you said, "I don't have time to eat"?

When you are hungry, you find time to eat! You will make a way where there is no way, because hunger demands to be satisfied. Hunger won't wait.

If you want to develop a deep hunger and thirst for the things of God, hang out where there is some good spiritual cooking. Put yourself in an atmosphere where spiritual food is being served, and you'll start to nibble.

Why is it so important to develop a spiritual hunger? Because Jesus says only those who are hungry will be satisfied. If you are not hungry, He can't feed you. Our world is starving for soul nourishment. It needs to meet people who are spiritually satisfied and can tell the lost where to get a meal.

## The Merciful

"Blessed are the merciful," Jesus said, "for they shall receive mercy" (v. 7).

This is definitely a kingdom principle that flies in the face of the world's way of operating. The world is short on mercy, that is, not giving people what they deserve, because you can't be merciful and step on people to get ahead at the same time.

But the kingdom is to be a collection of people who, because they are poor in spirit, understand that they are only here by the mercy and grace of God. When you show mercy to others, you are reflecting the heart of your King. If God didn't show mercy to us, where would any of us be?

## The Pure in Heart

Here's another kingdom principle those in the church need to manifest today: "Blessed are the pure in heart, for they shall see God" (v. 8).

Blessed are the authentic, Jesus says. Purity of heart doesn't mean you are perfect. But it does mean that when you see impurity in your life, you call it what it is and deal with it. It means that your motives are as pure as you can make them. Your word is good because you mean what you say. That's being authentic.

We live in a day of rampant hypocrisy. We are so used to people not being what they appear to be that we almost expect it. But a kingdom person can afford to be transparent because his or her heart is pure.

## The Peacemakers

Jesus also says that kingdom people live by a different principle when it comes to strife and disunity. "Blessed are the peacemakers, for they shall be called sons of God" (v. 9).

That is, blessed are those who pursue unity among the body of Christ and who reject division and gossip and all kinds of confusion. Jesus prayed for unity among God's people (see John 17:21), and Paul said our job is to keep the unity of the faith that we already possess (see Ephesians 4:3).

## *The Persecuted*

The final beatitude Jesus left us is found in verse 10: "Blessed are those who have been persecuted for the sake of righteousness, for theirs is the kingdom of heaven."

Jesus expounded on this principle in verses 11–12, in which He showed that the only valid reason to be persecuted is because of Him and for His sake. When our attempts to live for Him and manifest His kingdom meet with opposition and even hostility, Jesus said we ought to rejoice because our reward will be great.

The church, then, is to teach this kingdom ethic, apply it to the lives of the congregation, and hold them patiently and lovingly accountable to live it.

## THE PRESENCE OF THE KINGDOM

A third element of the church's kingdom agenda is a logical outgrowth of the first two. If the church manifests the power and principles of the kingdom, then it will surely make the presence of the kingdom felt in this world. The church is to manifest the kingdom's presence.

## *Our Kingdom Influence*

Paul wrote that God has "put all things in subjection under [Jesus'] feet, and gave Him as head over all things to the church, which is His body, the fulness of Him who fills all in all" (Ephesians 1:22–23).

Jesus is the Head, or Ruler, over all things. This is the kingdom of God, which is defined as God's rule over the entirety of His creation. But notice that Jesus has been given only to the church, because only the church has access to Him.

So we are the presence of Christ in this world. If the world is to know the blessings of the King and His kingdom, they will be mediated to the world through the church. In other words, no church means no blessings to the culture.

Look back at our original text in Matthew 5. Immediately after announcing the principles of the kingdom, Jesus said, "You are the salt of the earth. . . . You are the light of the world" (vv. 13–14).

The world is in decay and in darkness, in desperate need of preservation and light. When it comes to spreading that salt and shedding that light, the church is it! It is in this sense that the church is the nursery of the kingdom, bringing the blessings and benefits of the kingdom to the world.

This means the culture should be better off because of the church's presence. Our neighborhoods should be better off because the church is there. This is one reason the church I pastor in Dallas is committed to getting people in our community off welfare and standing on their own. In this way, the church serves as a surrogate family to help do for the family what it cannot, as opposed to will not, do for itself.

When the powerful reality of God's kingdom is brought to bear in an environment, that environment should be in the process of being transformed, because God's kingdom institution, the church, is present in its midst, mediating the blessing of comprehensive rule to the broader society. We are the presence of the kingdom in history. (See this author's works *America's Only Hope* and *Are Christians Destroying America?* Moody Publishers, for further discussion of the role of the church in society.)

## God's Temple

The Bible says in Ephesians 2:21 that the church is a building "being fitted together [and] growing into a holy temple in the Lord."

What does a temple do? It houses God. That's what the temple did in the Old Testament, and that's where the presence and the glory of God resided. In the same way, the glory of God in this age resides in the church.

Therefore, we should be seeing society impacted because of the church. It is a faulty eschatology and ecclesiology that has a church in history having little impact on the culture. Where the glory of God is, transformation is close by.

# THE PROCLAIMER OF THE KINGDOM

The church is also to be the proclaimer of the kingdom. This is the fourth item on our kingdom agenda.

## A Unified Proclamation

The apostle Peter told us, "You are a chosen race, a royal priesthood, a holy nation, a people for God's own possession, that you may proclaim the excellencies of Him who has called you out of darkness into His marvelous light" (1 Peter 2:9). The church is to proclaim the King and His kingdom.

Notice that the word *race* here is singular. In the next section of this book, we will deal in detail with racial issues and how they impact our kingdom agenda. But let me just say here that if you belong to Christ, you are part of a brand-new race. You may have a different heritage than some other members of Christ's body, but we are all one race now in Him.

One reason I love the Olympics is that no matter whether a winning athlete from the United States is black, Hispanic, Asian, or Anglo, only one national anthem is played when that American winner is saluted on the medal stand.

It's the same way in the body of Christ. No matter what your racial or ethnic background, there is only one Savior and one body. We come together as the collective body of Christ because we are part of a bigger agenda, the proclamation of Christ.

## A Priority Proclamation

The church has a problem here too, because we have so many Christians who aren't proclaiming anything. The church is a body of people who have come face-to-face with the Lord Jesus Christ, the Ruler and Savior of the universe. How can we not open our mouths and tell the world about Him?

Have you ever noticed that some people will talk about anything and everything except Jesus Christ? We talk about people and things that have never done for us what Jesus Christ has done for us.

Proclamation has to become a priority if the church is to fulfill its kingdom agenda in history. We need to become as bold about our message as everybody else has become about theirs.

As I often say, everybody else is coming out. We might as well come out too! Every group imaginable—and some we couldn't have imagined a few years ago—is out there on the streets, shouting its message. Nobody is ashamed of anything anymore.

Stuff people used to hide is now on TV because everybody has a message to proclaim. This is no time for Christians to be hiding in the closet!

Are we saying that as people who know Jesus Christ, who are on our way to heaven with our sins forgiven, we don't have anything to proclaim? The Bible says we are to proclaim the excellencies of Christ. It has to be a priority.

Our proclamation also goes beyond what we say. In 1 Peter 2:11–12, the apostle went on to say:

> *I urge you as aliens and strangers to abstain from fleshly lusts, which wage war against the soul. Keep your behavior excellent among the Gentiles, so that in the thing in which they slander you as evildoers, they may on account of your good deeds, as they observe them, glorify God in the day of visitation.*

We have a King and a kingdom to proclaim with our mouths and our lives. "You shall be My witnesses," Jesus said (Acts 1:8). He also told us to take the message into all the world and affect entire nations for Him (see Matthew 28:19–20).

Yes, the Great Commission refers to more than just individuals being changed by our influence on them. Entire societies should be impacted and transformed by the church's presence in their midst. This is because the church's job is to produce disciples, not just members.

A disciple is a person who is progressively bringing every area of life under the lordship of Jesus Christ. Disciples are to illustrate clearly to a watching world how the King of the universe expects the world to operate by the way they apply the truth of God to the issues of everyday life. (See this author's work *What Matters Most*, Moody Publishers, for an in-depth discussion of discipleship through the local church.)

Our problem today is that while we have many Christians, we have few disciples. We have people who are spiritual on Sunday and carnal on Monday. These schizophrenic saints paint a confusing picture of Christ and His kingdom for the rest of the world. The church is to hold its members accountable to live kingdom lives so that disciples paint an accurate picture of God's agenda in the world.

## A PORTRAIT OF THE KINGDOM

Finally, the church is to be a portrait of the kingdom. People ought to see what the kingdom of God looks like by looking at the church at work. This is why it is crucial for the church to function as the epicenter of community life.

There are five very practical reasons the church should hold this strategic position. First, churches are everywhere, so almost everyone has ready access to a local fellowship. Second, because churches meet regularly, they can readily keep their congregations informed. Third, churches represent the largest potential volunteer force in a community to address needs. Fourth, churches have existing facilities that can be used for a variety of impact programs. Fifth and most important, churches exist to manifest the moral values of God's kingdom, which is the greatest need in culture today.

## A Clear Picture

Ephesians 3:10 says that the wisdom of God is made known, made visible, through the church. The church is a microcosm of the kingdom, which is the larger expression of God's rule. Our job as the church is to live in a way that shows the world a clear picture of the kingdom. The church should present to the broader culture a working illustration of God's solutions to the problems the culture faces so that the culture can replicate these solutions in society at large. People who want to see heaven at work on earth should be able to discover it in the church.

When English settlers first landed in Africa, Africans learned English ways like afternoon teatime, even though they had never been to England. That was because the English citizens who were living in Africa still lived out their English traditions even on foreign soil.

We are kingdom people on foreign soil. Our job is to reflect the kingdom in such a way that the world sees the kingdom at work. We are to a paint a picture of heaven in fulfillment of Jesus' prayer, "Thy kingdom come. Thy will be done, on earth as it is in heaven" (Matthew 6:10). Our desire is to help impress heaven's pattern on earth.

That means we must be kingdom people. And for many of us, that will mean a radical change, because we can't talk like everyone else talks. We can't act like everyone else acts. It means instead of playing the cultural games, we serve the King.

## Coming Attractions

An illustration I like to use is the preview of coming attractions they give you on TV and at the movies. When they show you clips of upcoming programs or films, they always use the best clips, scenes of the hottest action, or the most romantic moments, because they want you to tune in next week or come back to the theater.

Well, one day the biggest show of all is coming to town. God the Father is the producer, the Holy Spirit is the director, and Jesus Christ is the superstar. It will be a worldwide production called the kingdom of God.

Jesus Christ is going to break the sky open and descend from heaven with a shout, and it will be showtime. He will proclaim His kingdom, set up His rule, and run this universe as it ought to be run. That is the coming kingdom of our Lord Jesus Christ.

But in the meantime, God wants the world to see the previews of His coming attraction. You and I are those previews. We are to be the best "clips" of the coming production.

Therefore, people ought to look at our commitment, our walk, and our impact and say, "That kingdom has got to be some kind of great show because these clips are really appealing." We need to make the kingdom look so good that people will be asking us, "Where can I buy a ticket to this show?" Then we can tell them that the price has already been paid for their ticket. It's time to get the kingdom agenda of the church in full operation, because the real show is coming soon. We are privileged to be God previews.

To be part of the church is to be part of the greatest institution known to man, because only the church can call on heaven and get an answer. Only the church has the keys of the kingdom. (See the author's work *God's Glorious Church*, Moody Publishers, for a detailed discussion on the doctrine of the church.)

Let's take the keys Christ has given us and unlock the kingdom for those who need to know the King.

# CHAPTER SEVENTEEN

# The Kingdom Agenda
# of Leaders

Now that we have sketched out the kingdom agenda of the church, I want to go in close and focus on the details of that sketch. In this chapter, I want to talk about the agenda of the church's leaders.

Leadership in the church is a given. You may have good leaders or bad leaders, but having no leaders is not an option. For the church to function at all, someone has to lead, and someone else has to follow that leadership.

So we need to find out what God wants the church's leaders to do, because leadership is God's means of building His kingdom in history. Leaders are critical because they are God's representatives, and throughout history God has always worked through the principle of representation.

## LEADERS REPRESENT GOD

This principle of representation goes all the way back to the garden of Eden. Adam acted as our representative when he sinned, so the Bible says we are born in sin. And in Adam, we all die (see 1 Corinthians 15:22a).

But praise God, Jesus Christ acted as our representative when He died on the cross to pay for that sin. If you are saved and on your way to heaven, it is because you have switched representatives (see v. 22b).

## The Origin of Representation

That's why the Bible refers to the "first" and "last" Adam (see 1 Corinthians 15:45). The first Adam brought sin and eternal death in the garden of Eden. But the last Adam, Jesus Christ, brought forgiveness, righteousness, and eternal life.

I love the way Paul stated the case in Romans 5: "For as through the one man's disobedience the many were made sinners, even so through the obedience of the One the many will be made righteous" (v. 19).

The principle of representation means that the person who has been placed over you can act for you. And in that "proxy" there can be great joy or great disaster, depending on the identity of your representative.

## Leaders Intercede

We can also see this principle at work in Genesis 18:16–33, where Abraham interceded for Sodom and Gomorrah. God told Abraham that if he could find ten people who were God's representatives in that wicked culture, He would change His mind about destroying Sodom and Gomorrah.

In other words, the reason Sodom and Gomorrah were destroyed was not just that great evil was present in these cities. In light of God's conversation with Abraham, we would have to conclude that these two cities were destroyed because God could not find enough representatives through whom He could work. That's really staggering when you think about it.

## Leaders Help Bring Deliverance

Let me show you how this principle of representation works today in the church of Jesus Christ. Paul wrote these words to Timothy, his spiritual son and disciple, who was pastoring in Ephesus:

> Until I come, give attention to the public reading of Scripture, to exhortation
> and teaching. Do not neglect the spiritual gift within you. . . . Take pains
> with these things; be absorbed in them, so that your progress may be evident

*to all. Pay close attention to yourself and to your teaching; persevere in these*
*things; for as you do this you will insure salvation both for yourself and for*
*those who hear you. (1 Timothy 4:13–16)*

Paul told Timothy that his ministry will determine not only his own spiritual fate but the fate of those in his congregation. In other words, Paul was speaking representatively. Timothy was God's representative leader to the saints at Ephesus.

Paul used the word *salvation* in verse 16 but not in the narrow sense of being born again. That was already true for Timothy and the believers at Ephesus. Paul was using this word in its broader sense of deliverance. The way Timothy would deliver himself and his people from spiritual defeat or usefulness, or any other spiritual problem, was by being diligent in his ministry.

Now this is important because while all of us as Christians bear an individual relationship to the Lord, we also bear a corporate relationship to Him as the members of His body, the church. How well we fare in this relationship, and sometimes in our individual relationships to God, is dependent in part on how well our God-appointed representatives carry out their ministry.

## The Necessity of Representation

Representation also works on the individual and family levels. In 1 Corinthians 7:12–14, Paul told a married believer not to send away his or her unbelieving spouse, because the unbelieving spouse is sanctified by God's representative in the home.

God's plan for the church is that every believer be vitally connected with other believers. There is no such thing as autonomous Christianity.

When a person says, "I can be a Christian without going to church," he is half right. He doesn't need the church to be a Christian.

But he needs the church to be a Christian who obeys, pleases, and honors God. He never designed you to function all by yourself apart from His appointed representatives. The way God brings down blessing upon the church is through His identified and approved representatives.

So Paul told Timothy, "If you want to deliver yourself and your people and insure God's blessing on the church, you must make sure you are functioning properly as God's representatives through whom His blessings will flow."

As I suggested above, the representative nature of God's work in history is a staggering principle. It has huge implications at every level of life, from our personal lives to our families and on to the church and the culture at large.

As God's representatives, what we do as church leaders doesn't just impact us or the people we minister to; it has an impact on future generations and on the future of this nation and the world. God works through His representatives.

## LEADERS OVERSEE DISCIPLESHIP

Here's another way in which leaders fulfill God's kingdom agenda in the church. They are called to oversee and direct the process of discipleship.

Again, Paul wrote to Timothy, "The things which you have heard from me in the presence of many witnesses, these entrust to faithful men, who will be able to teach others also" (2 Timothy 2:2). Paul had received a body of truth from Jesus Christ. Then he turned to this younger man, Timothy, and said, "I am giving what I have received to you."

Now I need to point out that the Greek word for *men* here is not the word for males but the word for mankind, including males and females. So Timothy was to entrust the gospel to faithful people.

### Levels of Leadership

These faithful men and women include the three levels of God-ordained leadership in a local church.

The elders are a group of spiritually mature men who oversee the preservation, dissemination, and application of spiritual truth to the church body, as well as set church policy (see 1 Timothy 3:2–7; 5:17; Titus 1:7–9). They also rule on spiritual matters and see that the ministry of the church is being carried forward.

The deacons are spiritual men and women who serve the needs of the congregation through the church's ministries (see 1 Timothy 3:8–13). In most churches, deacons also take responsibility for the physical well-being of the church.

The person who leads and coordinates the ministry and who serves as the primary spiritual leader is the pastor/teacher. He is charged with teaching the Word faithfully and with leading the church to fulfill its ministry and vision from God (see 1 Timothy 3:15; 4:13; 2 Timothy 4:2; Titus 1:5; 2:1).

We will develop these functions of disseminating and applying the Word later in this chapter as we consider the ministry of Moses. But what we are talking about here is the process of discipleship in the local church, and leaders are key to making that process happen.

## Passing on the Truth

This word *entrust* means "to put something on deposit," as in a bank. There are two reasons you put your money in a bank: to gain interest on it and to hold it for safekeeping. This is the idea in 2 Timothy 1:14, where Paul instructed Timothy, "Guard, through the Holy Spirit . . . the treasure which has been entrusted to you."

The leaders are the guardians of this deposit, but that doesn't mean they have to do all of the work themselves. That's where the other faithful men and women in the church come in. When the Word of God goes out from the pulpit, it is to be taken hold of by faithful people who turn around and teach it to others.

It's like a relay race. The interesting thing about a relay is that no matter how fast the runners are, if they don't hand off the baton successfully, their speed doesn't matter. If two teammates drop the baton between them, they lose whatever ground the team may have gained up to that point in the race.

I used the analogy of a relay race one time when I was having devotions with my sons, Anthony Jr. and Jonathan. I paraphrased 2 Timothy 2:2 by saying, "The things that I have heard from my father, the truth that has been passed to me, I am passing on to you so that my grandsons, who are not yet born, can have this same body of truth passed on to them."

I went on to explain to my sons that God's truth would never get to my grandchildren unless I handed the baton of truth successfully to them. Then I took my Bible, turned to my sons, and handed them the Bible. I said, "Please don't drop the baton. Pass it on."

We passed the Bible around, and then Anthony handed it back to me. I said, "Let's make sure we get the hand-off right. Don't take my weaknesses, my inconsistencies, and my failures and hand those off to your children. But hand off the things that you have learned from me about this Word."

You can't guarantee that your children are going to grab the baton and pass it on without dropping it, but you *can* guarantee that you give them a good hand-off. What we desperately need today is a generation of leaders who will hand the baton of the Christian faith to the next generation.

The problem is that if we don't hand our children the baton of faith, someone else will hand them another baton. Then they wind up carrying the wrong baton for the opposing team.

In order to pull this off in the church, you need faithful leaders who are going to stay the course for the long haul. Faithfulness demands time. It is not a one-shot deal. A leader can't become mature overnight. Leadership is a long-term commitment.

## The Issue of Representation

A church will only be as strong as its leadership, because God will not skip over the leaders and move to the congregation. This is so because of the principle of representation we talked about above. I'm not saying that God may not bless and develop the individual believers in a church even if the leaders are not all they are supposed to be.

But a situation like that is comparable to a person who is in a miserable marriage. God can give that married person grace, but it's still going to be a miserable environment because God's representative isn't representing Him well.

By the way, the illustration of a poor marriage is another reason why believers need to be under the authority of the church. When God's leaders in the church are functioning correctly, the person whose representative is failing at home has another representative through whom blessing can come. God works through His faithful leaders in the church to provide that which does not exist for this person at home.

That's why the church is not just a preaching station. It's a place where God's leaders oversee the process of discipleship so that His Word and His blessings may flow out to the congregation at large and disseminate from them out into the community, and ultimately into the world.

## Leaders as Shepherds

Before we leave the topic of discipleship, I want to spend some time in a passage that has some great principles for leaders in the church.

In 1 Peter 5, the apostle Peter wrote, "I exhort the elders among you, as your fellow elder and witness of the sufferings of Christ, and a partaker also of the glory that is to be revealed, shepherd the flock of God among you, exercising oversight" (vv. 1–2a).

The Word of God calls a church congregation a *flock*, and the leaders are to be its *shepherds*. Now you probably already know that calling someone a sheep is not a compliment. Sheep are easily led astray. In fact, if one sheep starts walking around in circles, another sheep will come follow it and start walking around in circles too.

Too often that's the picture of the church. Some of us have been walking around in circles for years. And we have folks following us too, thinking we are going somewhere.

Another trait of sheep is their vulnerability. Sheep are an easy target for a predator. Once you become a member of God's flock, you become a target for the Enemy's attack.

See, before you came to Christ you belonged to Satan's team. So he didn't have to target you. He owned you. But when you came to Jesus Christ, you became Satan's target. Now he wants to destroy you.

That's why Paul told the elders at Miletus in Acts 20:28–29, "Be on guard for yourselves and for all the flock. . . . I know that after my departure savage wolves will come in among you, not sparing the flock."

So Peter told church leaders to shepherd God's flock because they might not know when the wolves were out there. The elders didn't know that that circumstance, that situation, was designed for their destruction. So Peter reminded them that as shepherds they needed to watch for wolves, who, as Jesus said, come in sheep's clothing (see Matthew 7:15).

Peter went on to tell leaders to shepherd the flock of God "not under compulsion, but voluntarily, according to the will of God; and not for sordid gain, but with eagerness; nor yet as lording it over those allotted to your charge, but proving to be examples to the flock" (vv. 2b–3).

Any leader who has to be begged to take a position of leadership in the church isn't really a leader. If you have to pull and drag him into the position, he won't function well as a leader. True leaders serve with the eagerness and commitment that comes from knowing they are doing God's will.

At the same time, beware of the person who is eager to assume leadership to advance his personal fortunes, advance a personal agenda, or take a power trip. True leaders are humble and others centered, not self-centered. They recognize that they are under the authority of God themselves. They are His representatives.

The tragedy of David Koresh and the Branch Davidians in Waco, Texas, illustrates very dramatically the need for leaders to be under authority. People like Koresh get away with this kind of leadership because no one in the group questions them or calls them to account for their actions.

So Koresh was free to prey on his flock. And in this case, the principle of representation worked tragically, because Koresh's follower's followed their representative to the grave.

Leaders are to protect and preserve the sheep, not destroy them. God calls leaders to shepherd His flock because we as His sheep are prone to wander and are vulnerable to attack. They also serve as role models, illustrating in their lives what they teach so that the flock can follow not only their words but also their works.

## LEADERS DEAL WITH PROBLEMS

One of the realities of life is that whenever you bring two or more people together, conflict is inevitable.

### The Inevitability of Conflict

Marriage is a great example of the inevitability of conflict. When you were living by yourself, you had your own set of problems. But then you got married and your problems doubled, because you brought that other person into your life, and a whole set of problems came along with him or her that you didn't even know existed. And when the children started coming, the conflicts multiplied.

When Lois and I married in 1970, our problems were basically limited to the two of us. Then our daughter Chrystal came along, and our conflicts increased, especially at 3:00 in the morning—when Chrystal woke up crying, and Lois and I would try to decide who was going to get up.

Then Priscilla arrived, and our conflicts multiplied again. The girls would get into arguments, and we would have to referee and render judgments.

Then when Anthony Jr. was born, the two girls picked on him. But that stopped when Anthony started getting big! Next Jonathan came, and before long, the two boys would have their conflicts. Jonathan would complain, "Anthony's wearing my socks."

That wasn't news to me. Anthony was wearing my socks too!

So even in a family, conflict is inevitable. Imagine what it was like for Moses when he led more than two million Israelites out of Egypt into the wilderness on their way to Canaan.

## An Example of Conflict

Let's look at the situation in Exodus 18, where Moses is visited by his father-in-law, Jethro. Watching Moses trying to deal with the people all by himself, Jethro made some wise suggestions that are principles we can apply to leaders in the church today. Let's pick up the story:

> *And it came about the next day that Moses sat to judge the people, and the people stood about Moses from the morning until the evening. Now when Moses' father-in-law saw all that he was doing for the people, he said, "What is this thing that you are doing for the people? Why do you alone sit as judge and all the people stand about you from morning until evening?" And Moses said to his father-in-law, "Because the people come to me to inquire of God. When they have a dispute, it comes to me, and I judge between a man and his neighbor, and make known the statutes of God and His laws." (vv. 13–16)*

Do you get the picture here? Moses is getting up every morning at dawn and working till dark, trying to render decisions for a long line of people. The people come to him with their problems, and Lord have mercy if they need a return visit! With two million people competing for one man's attention, they're going to have a long wait.

The people crowd around Moses all day because they want him to decide their conflicts. And Moses develops a bit of a "theo ego"; that is, a God complex. He feels like he has to be like God and solve all the people's problems because, after all, they are coming to him, saying, "Moses, help us!"

## The Trap of Conflict

As I read this, I began to wonder how Moses got into this mess. I wondered why he didn't just tell the people, "I can't solve all your problems." So I looked back through Exodus, and I think I know why

Moses felt like he had to make this impossible effort to settle disputes for the whole nation.

A pattern emerges. For example, if we go back to Exodus 14, we read the thrilling story of Israel's deliverance at the Red Sea. The people were trapped with their backs to the sea, and Pharaoh and his Egyptian army were coming after them.

So the Israelites got scared and cried out to Moses, "Is it because there were no graves in Egypt that you have taken us away to die in the wilderness? Why have you dealt with us in this way, bringing us out of Egypt?" (Exodus 14:11).

The people were saying to Moses, "If it weren't for you and your leadership, we wouldn't be in this mess. You're going to be the death of us out here."

That's quite an accusation against Moses. But God answered it by having Moses stretch out his staff over the Red Sea and part it so the people could pass over safely. And as you probably know, the Egyptians were drowned trying to follow them.

What a great deliverance! So what happened? When Israel saw how God worked this miracle through Moses, they "believed in the Lord and in His servant Moses" (v. 31).

In other words, now the people were saying to Moses, "Mo, you are our man! Do we ever have a leader! You are bad, Mo! You are God's man. You lead us because you have God's ear, and we are going to follow you."

So things turned around for Moses, but not for long. Just three days later (see Exodus 15:22), the people were thirsty. When they came to Marah and found they could not drink the water, they began grumbling at Moses again. Like a little kid yelling at his parents in the middle of the night, the Israelites said to Moses, "We want a drink of water!" (see v. 24).

So Moses prayed, and God gave him the solution to the problem (see v. 25). But the problems weren't over for Moses, because after they got the water the people got hungry and started griping again (see Exodus 16:2). This time they brought the "assistant pastor" into it, griping against Aaron too. You know it's bad when people complain against the assistant pastor!

It was bad. Look at what the people said: "Would that we had died by the Lord's hand in the land of Egypt, when we sat by the pots of meat, when we ate bread to the full; for you have brought us out into this wilderness to kill this whole assembly with hunger" (v. 3).

Here they were, accusing Moses of attempted murder again. These folks were sitting around talking about, "Boy, that was some good home cooking we had back there in Egypt. Sure do miss that fried chicken and Mama's homemade bread."

So Moses is on the hot seat again. The people are again accusing him of not caring about them, so God provides another miraculous provision with quail and manna—cornflakes from heaven (see Exodus 16:13–21). The people have all they want to eat.

Look at one more incident before we get back to Exodus 18. In chapter 17, the people are at Moses again, because they are thirsty again. Only this time, they hit below the belt. They accuse Moses of trying to kill not only them but their children and even their animals as well (see Exodus 17:3).

## An Impossible Assignment

So here's the picture. The people of Israel have been charging Moses with not caring about them since they left Egypt. That's why I believe Moses was wearing himself out trying to act as judge for them, because he was trying to show the people that he did care. This was one way he could prove his concern for them.

That brings us back to Exodus and Moses' explanation to Jethro for the scene Jethro was witnessing as the people flocked to Moses with their problems.

Leaders are God's representatives to His people to deal with the conflicts that will inevitably arise in the body of Christ. But the way Moses was trying to deal with Israel's problems is not the standard God has laid out for the church.

Moses was trying to do it all himself, and his primary ministry of representation was suffering. What was Moses' primary ministry, and how did he solve his leadership problem? The answers are the subject of my final two points. As we deal with them, we will answer the question of how God wants His leaders to handle conflicts in the body of Christ.

## LEADERS COMMUNICATE DIVINE TRUTH

Moses' father-in-law had some sound advice for him. In Exodus 18:17–18, Jethro told him: "The thing that you are doing is not good. You will surely wear out, both yourself and these people who are with you, for the task is too heavy for you; you cannot do it alone."

The Hebrew words for *wear out* mean "to fade away." Moses was going to put himself in the grave trying to deal with all these problems, and the people were going to suffer too. Jethro was saying, "Moses, people who are in conflict and crisis can't wait a month or two for your schedule to open up."

## Wearing Out the Pastor

Unfortunately, this is the case with too many pastors today. Some poor pastor wears himself out trying to do everything and see everybody, and then the people stand at his funeral and say, "Oh, wasn't he a good pastor? He was down there at the church every day from dawn to dusk serving us. His reward will surely be great."

That's not the way it is supposed to happen. Moses was fading away, dealing with all the problems, but even more importantly, he didn't have time to accomplish his primary ministry, which was to go before God, get His Word, and then teach it to the people. So Jethro told Moses:

> *Now listen to me: I shall give you counsel, and God be with you. You be the people's representative before God, and you bring the disputes to God, then teach them the statutes and the laws, and make known to them the way in which they are to walk, and the work they are to do. (Exodus 18:19–20)*

## A Solution to the Dilemma

Jethro's advice to Moses was godly counsel. He told Moses to bring the people's disputes before God, get God's answers for those problems, and then communicate God's Word to the people in such a way that they would know how to apply God's truth to their lives.

If this process sounds familiar, that's because it is. Today we call it expository preaching, which is expounding the Word of God in such a way that His people understand it and know how to apply it.

The difference today is that because we have the completed revelation of God, we already have His mind on things like homosexuality, divorce, marital discord, substance abuse, and other problems that are tearing people's lives apart.

So God's leaders, particularly the pastor/teacher, are charged with preaching the Word faithfully. That's what Paul told Timothy in

2 Timothy 4:1–2: "I solemnly charge you in the presence of God and of Christ Jesus . . . preach the word."

We saw at the beginning of this chapter that by carrying out his ministry, Timothy would "save" or deliver both himself and the people in the church at Ephesus. This was so important that Paul urged Timothy to be absorbed in his ministry of preaching and teaching (see 1 Timothy 4:15).

The tragedy today is that we have too many Christians who are being defeated by, not delivered through, life's problems. The reason they are being defeated is that they do not know the Word, or they do not know how to apply the Word, or they simply refuse to apply what they know.

The pastor cannot make people obey the truth. But he can ensure, to the fullest extent of his ability as an expositor, that they understand the Word and how it should work in their lives.

Jethro was telling Moses, "If you really want to help these people, don't just give them your opinion or your ideas. Give them the truth of God. If you keep doing what you are doing, you won't have enough energy left to preach the Word of God."

This has to be number one on a pastor's kingdom agenda.

## Upholding the Standard

The people in Dallas don't come to our church to hear my opinions or my viewpoints. I have abrogated my role if I leave off the exposition of the unequivocal, authoritative, inerrant Word of God.

It is the Word that will help God's people deal with their problems. It is the Word that will give them the power to solve conflicts and overcome tough situations. It is the Word that will give them the patience to hang in there when they want to give up.

The goal of the pulpit should be to preach the Bible, because the Bible alone is total truth (see John 17:17). It is the standard. Our world is in such a tragic mess today because we have lost the standard. Everyone has his or her opinion of what to do, but what people need is the standard of God's Word.

This isn't new. There is an entire book of the Bible that describes an era like this. It is the book of Judges, which describes a time of chaos and evil. Why did this happen? Because "in those days . . . everyone did what was right in his own eyes" (Judges 21:25). There was no standard from God operating in society.

The church's leaders must communicate divine truth. They must uphold the divine standard.

## LEADERS OVERSEE THE APPLICATION OF TRUTH

Here is my final point about the kingdom agenda of church leaders, and it comes from the final portion of Jethro's advice to Moses:

> *Furthermore, you shall select out of all the people able men who fear God, men of truth, those who hate dishonest gain; and you shall place these over them, as leaders of thousands, of hundreds, of fifties and of tens. And let them judge the people at all times; and let it be that every major dispute they will bring to you, but every minor dispute they themselves will judge. So it will be easier for you, and they will bear the burden with you. If you do this thing and God so commands you, then you will be able to endure, and all these people also will go to their place in peace.*
> *(Exodus 18:21–23)*

### Appointing Leaders

This is the Old Testament equivalent of Paul's instruction to Timothy to appoint elders and deacons in the church (see 1 Timothy 3:1–16; Titus 1:5).

The qualifications were much the same in each case. Leaders had to be faithful people who feared God and held to His truth, who were "able," or skilled, and who operated honestly and ethically in the marketplace.

The task of these leaders was to oversee and carry out the application of God's truth in the people's lives. Moses was to get involved if a major conflict or issue came up that needed his attention. But he was to give his primary energy to knowing and teaching the Word, and the leaders with him were to carry it out in the day-to-day lives of the congregation.

These leaders were to be skilled and committed people. Moses needed them in his day—and the crying need of the church today is still for skillful, knowledgeable, and committed leaders.

## A New Testament Example

Let me show you a wonderful New Testament example of what we have been talking about in this chapter.

In Acts 6:1–7, the young church in Jerusalem was having a conflict: "While the disciples were increasing in number, a complaint arose on the part of the Hellenistic Jews against the native Hebrews, because their widows were being overlooked in the daily serving of food" (v. 1).

The early church had a feeding program, a "Meals on Wheels" to care for widows in the church. But a problem arose. The "Hellenistic," or Greek-speaking, Jewish believers felt that they were the victims of a little classism on the part of the Jewish believers who still spoke Aramaic, a dialect of Hebrew.

So the twelve apostles called a congregational meeting and told the church:

> *It is not desirable for us to neglect the word of God in order to serve tables. But select from among you, brethren, seven men of good reputation, full of the Spirit and of wisdom, whom we may put in charge of this task. But we will devote ourselves to prayer, and to the ministry of the word.*
> *(Acts 6:2–4)*

This is the same basic situation Moses faced. And the apostles' advice was the same advice Jethro gave Moses. "Moses, you spend your time before God in prayer and in the Word; appoint leaders who can handle the everyday matters."

That's what the Jerusalem church did. They appointed seven leaders, and the apostles laid their hands on them and commissioned them for their task (see v. 6). The apostles stuck to preaching the Word, the dispute got settled, and the church continued to explode with growth.

Do you see what happens when the church has the right leadership? Conflicts are quickly resolved, unity is maintained, and its impact increases tremendously because its people are carrying out God's chosen agenda for the church. But it all begins with the leaders and flows through them to the people. If the congregation is to be unified and operate as a team, then the leaders must model that unity and oneness of purpose among themselves.

This is why churches that are serious about executing God's agenda must establish church courts, which are duly constituted to hand down binding arbitration to resolve conflicts among church members. Paul chastises the church that does not operate church courts (see 1 Corinthians 6:1–8).

At our church in Dallas, we operate church courts every Wednesday night to address conflicts. This includes everything from business to marital issues. For example, a couple in our church cannot get a divorce in civil court unless it is sanctioned in church court based on biblical grounds. If the members disregard the decision of the church court, they are subject to church discipline.

Until the church and its leadership begin to take seriously its role of applying God's Word to conflicts among the members, the church will continue to experience the conflict, disrespect, and limited cultural impact the church is now suffering.

The church must have godly leaders—capable, godly men and women who will accept responsibility and represent Jesus Christ in His church and in the larger culture.

# CHAPTER EIGHTEEN

# The Kingdom Agenda
# of Members

Let me begin this chapter with a simple but key statement: If church leaders are called to lead, then it follows that church members are called to follow.

You may need to think about that one for a minute. It may seem obvious to say that leaders have to have followers. But believe me, being in a position of leadership is no guarantee that people will follow you. Just as God has a specific agenda for His leaders in building His kingdom, so He has an agenda for members of the body of Christ at large.

The finest leadership in the world won't help folks who won't follow those leaders. So let's consider the kingdom agenda of church members, those who benefit from the ministry of a local church. What are God's expectations of the people who fill the pews in our churches?

There are five items on the agenda of church members, but let me begin by summarizing the responsibility of church members. The church only develops and grows properly when each member plays his or her individual part.

# THE IMPORTANCE
# OF CHURCH MEMBERSHIP

While church membership is not a requirement for salvation, it is a requirement for proper spiritual development. Membership is more than fellowship. You can have fellowship with those with whom you do not share membership. Membership involves accountability and responsibility. It is the commitment of a believer to identify with and be dynamically involved with a local body of people who are under the authority of Jesus Christ. The goal is for a church member to develop into a disciple of the Lord.

Discipleship is that developmental process of the local church that progressively brings unbelievers from spiritual infancy to spiritual maturity so that they are then able to repeat the process with someone else (see Matthew 10:24–39).

Membership in a local church is necessary for a believer to partake consistently of the four vital experiences of worship, fellowship, education, and outreach that are necessary for the discipleship process to occur. No church membership means limited or no discipleship and is outright rebellion against the expressed will of God.

When Jesus gave His life on the cross, He became "the mediator of a new covenant" (Hebrews 9:15) in which our sins were cleansed by His sacrifice. The church, then, is the "community of the covenant," the assembly of those who share in the sacrifice of God's Son.

It's important to understand that many of the benefits of our relationship with Christ are realized in the church. Just as children are promised a greater length and quality of life if they obey their parents (see Ephesians 6:1–3), and a husband is provided access to God in prayer based on his relationship to his wife, so some of the advantages that individual Christians enjoy can only be experienced as they relate properly to the family of God in the local church.

For example, Paul said that Christians can only experience the spiritual growth they need as they are linked with other believers (see Ephesians 4:12–16). God shows His supernatural power to meet the needs of His people as the church brings Him glory (see Ephesians 3:20–21).

In addition, there is a level of personal care and support that can only be realized in the relationships of the local church (see 1 Corinthians 12:18–20, 25). And God's power over Satan can only be fully experienced in the context of the church (see Ephesians 3:10).

On the other side of the coin, God promises to judge those who harm the church (see 1 Corinthians 3:16–18).

Here's the point of church membership: Our corporate relationship to the body of Christ is crucial to our personal relationship with God. If all of us in the body don't play the part God has called us to play, then the ministry of the church will be stymied. And to the degree that we stymie the church, accordingly we will lose God's blessing and incur His judgment (see 1 Corinthians 3:16–17).

Why? Because when it comes to the church, it really is true that no one can replace you. So let's find out what Jesus Christ has on His agenda for the members of His body.

## RELATE PROPERLY TO LEADERS

The first item on the members' agenda is to give the church's leaders the respect and cooperation they need to do their job.

Hebrews 13 contains three important principles relating to the way believers should relate to the leaders God has placed over them. The first principle is in verse 7, where the writer of Hebrews said: "Remember those who led you, who spoke the word of God to you; and considering the result of their conduct, imitate their faith."

### Remember Your Leaders

What does it mean to remember leaders? The idea is not to take them for granted, not to forget their contribution. It's a call to esteem our leaders highly rather than treat them and their leadership lightly. We can see that in a corollary passage:

> We request of you, brethren, that you appreciate those who diligently labor among you, and have charge over you in the Lord and give you instruction, and that you esteem them very highly in love because of their work. (1 Thessalonians 5:12–13)

The body of Christ needs to esteem its leaders because of the service they render to the body. Good leadership in the church is hard to come by, but it's easily taken for granted.

When I was growing up, our pastor would come over to our house every now and then. I can remember it well. I hated for the preacher to come to our house because if my mother fixed fried chicken, we had to wait until the pastor picked the best and fattest pieces of chicken. (I have never forgiven him for that, by the way!) But the point is that he was held in high esteem in our home because he was a man of God.

One of the things I do through our national ministry, The Urban Alternative, is work with churches who are looking for pastors. Some of them have been without pastors for years. When such a church contacts us, I will ask, "What's the problem?"

The answer will usually come back in this form: "We are having trouble finding the right person." What these churches are saying is that leadership is hard to come by. If your church has pastors, elders, and deacons who are faithful to the Word of God, who are committed to Christ, and who serve you well, the Bible says you are to esteem them highly.

Now, there is an extreme here that occurs when people go beyond valuing their leaders and start fixating on them. A church member said to her pastor when he announced he was moving on to another ministry, "Pastor! Pastor! There is no way in the world I'm going to make it in my Christian life if you leave as pastor of this church."

The pastor looked at her and said, "Then I'd better hurry up and get out of here so you can take your eyes off me and put them back on Jesus, where they belong."

Leaders are never to be worshiped, but they are to be valued and esteemed.

## Obey Your Leaders

In Hebrews 13:17, the writer also said to the church, "Obey your leaders, and submit to them; for they keep watch over your souls, as those who will give an account. Let them do this with joy and not with grief, for this would be unprofitable for you."

This same concept appears in Ephesians 6:1, which tells children, "Obey your parents in the Lord." In the kingdom of God, there must be a chain of command that is marked by obedience.

Why should you place yourself under the authority of your leaders? Because of God's principle of representation we talked about in the previous chapter. God's blessings flow to the individual members of the body through the leaders who shepherd the flock.

We also saw in the last chapter that a leader is not be to heavy-handed and dictatorial (see 1 Peter 5:3). A shepherd needs to be gentle with the flock, but the Bible doesn't allow for disrespect of leadership.

As long as what leaders are asking people to do is in line with the Word of God, the people owe them obedience. There is no way around it, and it is the only way the benefits of the kingdom can accrue to you as a church member.

Note that the kind of obedience God wants is not the kind a child gives when he is pouting and doesn't want to obey, but is *made* to obey. Every parent knows how hard it is when a child offers begrudging obedience, mumbling under his breath all the time. There's no joy in that.

God doesn't want reluctant, foot-dragging obedience either. Church members are to obey in such a way that it is a joy for their leaders to lead them.

Why is it important for the members to obey their leaders? Because the leaders will have to give account of their leadership. They have a lot to be responsible for, and when their people are disobedient and give them a hard time, it makes their ministry a burden instead of joy. And nobody profits from that kind of situation.

Members will give account to God too for the way they obeyed or failed to obey the Word given through their leaders. The more disobedient believers are, the less God will honor and bless them.

One reason believers may not be seeing blessings in their lives is a rebellious attitude. Disobedience is unprofitable for the people as well as for leaders. It also kills the joy of ministry on everybody's part.

When I was in college, I thought I would be an evangelist, not a shepherd of a local church. I used to preach on the streets in Atlanta. Anytime there were a few people around, I was ready to preach.

But as God worked things out in my life, I wound up becoming the founding pastor of the Oak Cliff Bible Fellowship. In one sense, it would be easier being a traveling evangelist, because then you don't have to live with the congregation members' problems, needs, and rebellion.

Sometimes being a shepherd brings grief and pain. If you don't do something the way a certain person thinks you should, that person can start a movement to discredit you.

Don't misunderstand. I love being a pastor. I am committed to the church. I'm just saying that being a pastor can be painful. But what a joy it is to see people submit to the authority of God's Word and obey Him. As one who keeps watch over people's souls, I have no greater joy than to see our people walking in the truth (see 3 John 4).

## Greet Your Leaders

The author of Hebrews included a third directive to the church concerning its leaders. "Greet all of your leaders," he wrote in 13:24.

Now this is far different from our idea of a greeting today. When we greet people, we say, "Hello. How are you?" What we often mean to add is, "Don't really answer. I'm in a hurry."

That's not what a greeting means in the Scriptures. In the Old Testament, when a Jew met a fellow Jew, he would greet him with "Shalom."

This Hebrew word means "peace"—but not as we use the word today. *Shalom* refers to the total well-being of life. So a biblical greeting was a way of saying, "I wish you total wellness." It went a lot deeper than a rushed "How are you?"

So greeting leaders means expressing sincere personal concern for them. It involves looking out for their welfare, encouraging their well-being. It's another way members can relate properly to their leaders.

## SERVE THE BODY OF CHRIST

Here's a second item on the kingdom agenda of church members. Believers are to use their God-given gifts to build up the body of Christ and serve the kingdom of God.

Ephesians 4 is a classic passage that makes this absolutely clear. Paul wrote, "And [Christ] gave some as . . . pastors and teachers, for the equipping of the saints for the work of service, to the building up of the body of Christ" (vv. 11–12).

## Every Member a Servant

Leaders are given by God to equip His people for service. There is no such thing as a Christian who does not serve the kingdom by ministering to the church. You can't build a home without all the members doing their part, and you can't build a church without all the members doing their part.

Paul went on to say:

> We are to grow up in all aspects into Him, who is the head, even Christ, from whom the whole body, being fitted and held together by that which every joint supplies, according to the proper working of each

individual part, *causes the growth of the body for the building up of itself in love. (Ephesians 4:15–16, emphasis mine)*

It only takes one part of the body to stop the show. Perhaps you have been in a church where there was a fight going on, and everyone in the church was occupied by it. It was only one issue, but it controlled everyone, and the ministry was stymied.

Every member of the body has a part to play in making the body function. The job of leaders is not to do the ministry while the people watch. That's why it is a sin for a person to benefit from the ministry of the church and yet not contribute anything.

The body of Christ already has too many people who come to church and say, "Preach to me. Sing to me. Serve me. If I'm sick, visit me. If I'm hurting, comfort me. If I need encouragement, encourage me. But don't expect me to give any of my time or ability to this work."

Such a member is a church leech, sucking the lifeblood of the church's ministry without making any meaningful contribution. That's a sin and an insult to the Father who has invited us into His family. We are not in His family because we deserve to be here. We are here by grace (see Ephesians 2:8–9).

God adopted us into His family when we had no family from a spiritual standpoint. He brought us into His glorious home called the kingdom (see Colossians 1:13). Can you imagine a person in a family like that who refuses to clean his room, who doesn't want to carry his share of the workload?

God did not call 20 percent of the church to serve the other 80 percent. He called 100 percent of us to serve each other. That's why people must agree to serve in our church in Dallas before they are accepted into the membership.

## Using Your Gift

Paul said that God gave the church its leaders to equip the people for service. God also equips His people for service by giving them spiritual gifts. The apostle Peter wrote:

> As each one has received a special gift, employ it in serving one another, as good stewards of the manifold grace of God. Whoever speaks, let him speak, as it were, the utterances of God; whoever serves, let him do so as by the

*strength which God supplies; so that in all things God may be*
*glorified through Jesus Christ, to whom belongs the glory and*
*dominion forever and ever. Amen. (1 Peter 4:10–11)*

Let me give you a definition of spiritual gifts from this passage. Spiritual gifts are divine ennoblements, empowered by the Holy Spirit, that allow God's people to glorify Him and build up His body.

Spiritual gifts are more than human talents, because while people may be multitalented, every believer only has one spiritual gift at a time. *Talents* include things like the ability to sing, speak, write, etc. One person may possess all these talents and more. But a spiritual gift is an ability sovereignly given by God that He wants the believer to focus on in a unique way, because He wants to use that gift, through the believer, in a unique way to build His kingdom and mature His body.

God may make one of your natural talents a spiritual gift or give you something totally new. The key is that this gift will be used specifically to build up His body. When God decides to change your ministry, He will supply a new gift.

The Bible is clear that every Christian has been gifted by the Holy Spirit (see 1 Corinthians 12:7). Now you may say, "Well, I don't know what my spiritual gift is, and I don't know how to find it."

If that's the case, let me help you. Even though you may not know what your gift is, God knows, and He wants to reveal it to you. But He only hits a moving target. That is, you can't just sit around doing nothing until God drops a revelation on you. Get busy serving Him with your talents in your local church, and He will make your spiritual gift very obvious to you.

It's like a student saying, "I don't know what I want to be." Well, that student needs exposure to the options for various careers. She needs to explore different things until she finds that area of study or work that arouses her interest.

You may enjoy doing a lot of things, but God will show you the area He wants you to concentrate on in a special way to bless the church and advance His kingdom agenda.

But let me remind you that serving Christ and using your spiritual gift does not mean everything will go smoothly. Whenever people are involved, as I've said before, conflict will happen and pain can result. It reminds me of the old saying, "To dwell above with saints we love, O, that will be glory! To live below with saints we know, well, that's another story!"

If we are going to serve Christ and fulfill His agenda for our lives, we must be ready to share the joys and the tears that come with being a part of the family.

## SUPPORT YOUR FAMILY

At first glance, this heading, "Support Your Family," may look like a mistake in this chapter. It sounds like I've left the subject of church members and returned to the family section of this book.

But hang on, because this issue relates directly to your kingdom agenda. For the church to function biblically, it has to be made up of strong families who contribute to the church's work rather then drain it, because the church itself is like a family.

### The Family Provider

In a very familiar verse, Paul wrote to Timothy, "If anyone does not provide for his own, and especially for those of his household, he has denied the faith, and is worse than an unbeliever" (1 Timothy 5:8).

How can a Christian be worse than a non-Christian? Because even non-Christians know people are supposed to provide for their families.

But this is not just a personal issue, as we will see. The degree to which believers care for their families has a direct impact on the church's ministry (see 1 Timothy 5:16, discussed below).

The Greek word translated *provide* means "to think ahead" or "to provide by seeing in advance." The idea is that a man, as the head of his home and chief provider, is to look down the road and plan ahead to make sure his family is provided for. This means that part of a Christian man's responsibility to his church is to make his family as solid as possible, so that his family forms part of the support structure of the church.

Certainly that involves being the breadwinner, barring disability or some other unavoidable problem. But there's more to it than that. We know from Ephesians 6:4 that fathers are charged with the primary responsibility for their children's spiritual instruction and discipline.

Since all of this is the case, it goes without saying that the government is not supposed to provide for your family. I'll have a lot to say about this in the next section of the book, so we'll leave it at that for now.

Neither is it the church's job to support families in which a man is able-bodied and capable of supporting his own (see discussion under "Family Responsibility" in chapter 4).

## A Woman's Support Role

First Timothy 5:16 makes the church connection explicit. Even in a home where a man may not be present, those women believers who had the means were responsible to care for their family members. That way, the church would be free to help those who had no family to care for them, like the widows described in Acts 6:1.

So Paul is not saying that the church should never help anyone financially. And we're not saying that the government should never help when the need is legitimate. The point is that biblically neither the church nor the government is designed to be the primary supporter of the family.

Now let me back up a couple of verses and stir things up! Because younger widows can get in trouble by themselves (see 1 Timothy 5:11–13), Paul said in verse 14, "Therefore, I want younger widows to get married, bear children, keep house, and give the enemy no occasion for reproach."

As I told our congregation in Dallas, don't get mad at me if this seems to contradict popular ideas of a woman's role in society. My job is to teach the Word, not try to be popular.

Paul said there are two ways women can help build strong families. The women in this case are widows who are still young enough to remarry and have a family, but the principle applies to Christian families in general.

The first way is by bearing children. We've got this thinking today that says, "My goodness, things are so bad we don't want to bring kids into this world." That's nonsense. The world was much worse when Paul wrote this instruction than what we are seeing today. In the Roman world, Christians' lives were on the line. Then and now, the whole point of bearing children has been to raise up a godly seed to counteract the unrighteous seed and build the kingdom of God for the next generation.

Paul also told the younger women to "keep house." We need to talk about this phrase. First, "keep house" does not necessarily equal "stay home." The idea is bigger than that.

Keeping house means that the woman is responsible to maintain a quality environment in the home. The word *keep* denotes the idea of being a manager; the woman is the manager of the home. She is to manage the affairs of the home in such a way that God's agenda for the home is accomplished.

The question that always comes up here is whether a wife and mother should work outside the home. But that's the wrong question. The right question is, can she work outside the home and still manage her home properly?

Some women feel they need to be home full-time to manage their homes the way God wants them managed. Other women are convinced they can work outside and still manage their homes. In the case of single mothers, the woman often has no choice but to work and manage her home. God knows that, and I believe He gives grace for each situation when the person's heart seeks to do His will.

But whatever path a Christian woman may choose, Paul's point is that she cannot push the care of her family onto the back burner of her life, whether for work or just for a busy social schedule.

That leads to chaos in the home and gives the Enemy an opportunity to bring reproach on Christ. And a chaotic, undisciplined Christian home weakens the church of which that family is a part.

## SUPPORT YOUR CHURCH

A fourth item on the kingdom agenda of believers is one that you knew I would get to eventually: the privilege and responsibility of supporting God's work financially.

As we look at the opening verses of 1 Corinthians 16, let's first reconsider the context. First Corinthians 15 is a great doctrinal chapter. It deals with our resurrection, which is guaranteed because Christ was raised from the dead as the "first fruits" of the resurrection (v. 20).

In other words, Christ's resurrection was the "down payment" that guarantees our resurrection to a glorious future in which "this perishable [body] must put on the imperishable, and this mortal [body] must put on immortality" (v. 53).

### Abounding in the Work

That's a glorious future, an eternity with Christ in which death has no more "sting" (v. 55). In light of what awaits us, Paul closed chapter 15 with this exhortation: "Therefore, my beloved brethren, be steadfast, immovable, always abounding in the work of the Lord, knowing that your toil is not in vain in the Lord" (v. 58).

When you know you're on the winning team, you can afford to give it everything you've got. Paul said we should always *abound* in the Lord's work. That word means to go beyond the call of duty, to do more than just what is expected. And then Paul opened chapter 16 by saying,

> *Now concerning the collection for the saints, as I directed the churches of Galatia, so do you also. On the first day of every week let each one of you put aside and save, as he may prosper, that no collections be made when I come. (vv. 1–2)*

At first, there doesn't seem to be a relationship between the doctrine of the resurrection and the offering plate. But there is a powerful connection.

Paul was saying, "If we are going to do the work of the Lord, there is a cost involved. And when it comes to meeting that cost, we should abound here too, because we are on the winning side. We can afford to go beyond just what is expected."

## A Mirror of the Heart

The fact that effective ministry comes with a price tag should not surprise you. But when it comes to money, a lot of believers flip on a different mode of thinking. That's why, when God wants to test a believer's commitment, He virtually always uses money as a measuring stick.

The reason that money is such an accurate reflection of our commitment is because a lot of people will give up everything else before they will let go of their money. How and where we spend our money is quite telling because it reveals where our hearts are, according to Jesus (see Matthew 6:19–21).

## Biblical Principles of Giving

Verses 1–2 of 1 Corinthians 16 are packed with key principles we need to understand to fulfill our kingdom responsibility in giving. Let's unpack these principles one at a time.

The first principle is this: Our giving is designed to minister to and equip the saints, and then through them to impact a world that needs Christ (see v. 1).

There is only one legitimate reason for the church to collect money—for ministry. The purpose of giving, Paul said, is to get the ministry of the church out to the people who need it. You can't minister to people whose lives are broken and who need Christ unless someone pays the bill for that ministry.

Biblical giving is a spiritual investment designed to make sure that God's ministry to people and through people never goes lacking. God's work never suffers from insufficient funds. It may suffer from insufficient *giving*, but God is not short on funds. He always pays for what He authorizes.

First Corinthians 16:2 reveals a second principle: *Biblical giving is an act of worship to God.* Paul told us to set aside our gifts on "the first day of every week."

That's Sunday. And what's special about Sunday? It is the church's day of worship. Paul said that when you go to church to worship God, make sure giving is part of your worship.

Giving is not something you just throw into a worship service. It's an act of worship to God. This means that God evaluates our giving the same way He evaluates our singing, praying, preaching, or any other element of worship.

Some people insult God when they sing. They are singing about our great God, but they hang their heads and mumble out a few words because they don't feel like singing. God's question is, "Who are you singing to?"

Other people offend God when they pray, because their prayer reveals that they really aren't all that interested in meeting with God.

It's the same with our giving. The way we give is either a blessing or an insult to God. You can insult God by not giving when you should, by not giving what you should, or by giving only after you've taken care of yourself.

The Bible says, "Honor the Lord from your wealth, and from the first of all your produce" (Proverbs 3:9). God's portion comes first. We can't give to God out of our leftovers; even if we give a lot it's unacceptable, because it came from what we had left after we spent the best part on ourselves (see Malachi 1:7–8).

Giving to God first is crucial, because it shows how much you value Him, and it expresses your faith in His ability and willingness to provide for you.

In the Old Testament, when God's people gave Him the tithe, the first 10 percent of their money and crops, they were not saying, "God, here is the 10 percent that belongs to You. The other 90 percent belongs to me."

No, they were saying, "God, I recognize that 10 percent is simply a down payment, because it all belongs to You."

That's a critical shift in emphasis from the first scenario. God wants us to give with an attitude that says, "I recognize that everything I have belongs to You, first, as an act of loving, obedient worship, and also as a testimony of my trust in Your ability to provide for me."

In other words, giving is a test of our faith. The Jewish culture was agrarian. Those people were dependent on the harvest to live. So when they gave God the first portion of their crops, they were telling Him, "I trust You to bring in the rest of my crop so I can feed my family and be charitable to others."

To be honest, not many Christians have that kind of faith today. They take care of themselves, and if there is anything left over, God gets a part of it. How else can we explain the fact that the average evangelical, Bible-believing Christian only gives about 2.9 percent of his or her income to the Lord? That's an insult to God and destructive to the expansion of His kingdom.

Many of us have been trying to fix our finances for years. Master-Card owns us, Visa owns us, or some other lender owns us. But we have never given God the ownership of our pocketbooks. When we put Him first in our finances, He makes sure the rest of the "crop" comes in.

Let me briefly highlight two more principles that don't need a lot of elaboration. One is that *giving is for everyone* (see 1 Corinthians 16:2). No believer is too young or too poor to learn how to give.

Another principle in verse 2 is captured in the phrase "put aside and save." *Biblical giving is planned, systematic giving.* It is not simply an emotional response to a sermon or a choice musical number that moved you, or a reaction to an emotional appeal.

Finally, *biblical giving is proportional*: "as [we] may prosper" (v. 2). Your giving is to reflect God's abundance in your life. That means you are not limited to the tithe. As your income increases, so should your giving.

Here's an axiom to keep in mind: Give according to your income, lest God make your income according to your giving.

## Become a Disciple

A fifth item on a church member's kingdom agenda is the need to be involved in the discipleship process of the church. Becoming a committed disciple should be a high priority for us.

In Titus 2:1–8, Paul told a young pastor that everyone in the congregation is to be included in the process of developing in the faith and becoming like Jesus Christ.

Discipleship is definitely something Paul practiced himself. Titus was Paul's "true child" in the faith (Titus 1:4). He also called Timothy his "true child in the faith" and his "beloved son" (1 Timothy 1:2; 2 Timothy 1:2). Titus and Timothy grew up spiritually under Paul's tutelage. That's discipleship.

I have other men across the country and on our staff to whom I hold myself accountable, because I am not outside of this process. No Christian is, because once you try to stand alone you are going to start sinking. Everyone, including leaders, needs to be encouraged and guided in the faith.

Paul told Titus to "speak the things which are fitting for sound doctrine" (Titus 2:1) in the church on Crete. The key word there is *sound*, which means "healthy."

How do you grow a healthy church? By giving people the truth so they can be spiritually healthy. And what does healthy teaching or doctrine include? It includes teaching the people the agenda God has outlined for them.

### The Older Men

Paul told the older men in the church to be "temperate, dignified, sensible, sound in faith, in love, in perseverance" (Titus 2:2). In every way, they are to be examples to the younger men in the congregation.

Every teenager and young man in a church, single or married, ought to have a godly older man he can look to—someone who has already been down the road and has sound advice to offer. Our culture is sadly lacking in role models. That's tragic, because people are going to follow someone.

The spiritually mature men in a church, who have been walking with God for years, ought to inspire the young men to say, "I want to be like you because you are so much like Christ."

## The Older Women

The same is true on the other side. "Older women likewise are to be reverent in their behavior, not malicious gossips, nor enslaved to much wine, teaching what is good" (Titus 2:3).

The word *gossip* is taken from a Greek word that has the same root as "devil." Anyone who has been in a church knows that gossip isn't funny or harmless; it's devilish. A gossip is someone who has an unwavering ability to pick up the telephone and create chaos in the family of God.

Instead of becoming a problem, the mature women in a congregation are to be productive disciplers by "encourag[ing] the young women to love their husbands, to love their children, to be sensible, pure, workers at home, kind, being subject to their own husbands, that the word of God may not be dishonored" (vv. 4–5).

Why is it critical that the older, spiritually mature women invest themselves in the lives of younger women? Because all young single women, wives, and mothers struggle at times. They all have times when they tell themselves, "I'm not going to make it. I can't handle the pressure. I can't love this man I'm living with. These children are driving me crazy. I don't think I will ever be a good mother."

But at times like this an older woman can come alongside her and say, "I understand. I've been where you are. But let me tell you, you can learn to love again. I did. You can learn how to be a mother. I learned how to be a mother. God did it for me, and I know He will do it for you."

Older women can help younger women "to be sensible," to make wise choices, to be "pure," which is holy living, and to be "workers at home," which as we learned above means being a good manager of the home as the first priority.

## The Younger Men

You can tell Paul was once a young man, because he only had one piece of advice for younger men: "Be sensible" (v. 6). Young men are tempted to be impetuous and headstrong, thinking they have this thing called life in their hip pockets. Since that isn't so, young men need to learn to use good judgment so they can make good decisions. There's no excuse for being young and a fool if you're a believer.

Paul included Titus himself in this process of discipleship too, urging him to be an example to the entire body in every area of life and service.

God has a specific kingdom agenda He wants His people to fulfill in order for the church to grow properly. We've looked at it from the standpoint of believers in general. Before we leave this section on the church, I want to tighten the focus once more and share the special instructions God gives to the men of the church and to the women in chapters 19 and 20.

# CHAPTER NINETEEN

# The Kingdom Agenda
# of Men

Many men today are suffering from what I call a "loser's limp." This is what happens when a guy is playing baseball and the ball is hit over his head. He knows he should make the play, but he misjudges the ball and misses the catch.

He doesn't want anyone else to know he muffed the play because of his own shortcomings, so he falls down and gets up limping. The idea is if it weren't for whatever he tripped over or the sudden cramp he got in his leg, he would have caught the ball. A loser's limp is a way of camouflaging failure.

Far too many of us Christian men are camouflaging our failure to be men of the kingdom. We give excuses: "If it weren't for the way I was raised," or "Well, my father left my mother," or "Everybody else was doing it," or "If it weren't for this woman God gave me . . ."

But whatever a man's excuses may be for failing to fulfill his agenda in God's kingdom, he doesn't get the job done. As we continue to focus more closely on the kingdom agenda in the church, I want to help encourage Christian men to be all that God has called them to be.

But before we can become kingdom men in the church, we need to realize that just being a male isn't enough to make us faithful kingdom men who are effective for Christ. It takes more to be a man than merely wearing pants with the zipper in the front and carrying your wallet in the hip pocket.

## SEE THE NEED FOR GODLY MEN

God's kingdom is desperately short of godly men. I'm thankful for movements that are calling men to faithfulness to Christ today. But the fact remains that far too many men are missing in action, and far too many women have been thrust into the dominant role of leadership at home, at school, and in the church. Too many of our men are like the abominable snowman—footprints everywhere, but you never see him.

Tonight, 41 percent of all American children will go to bed without a father to pray with them and tuck them in. In the minority community, that figure rises to 63 percent. The social, political, economic, and spiritual repercussions of the absence of men in their children's homes are staggering.

There used to be a time when there was always an older man whom a younger man could look to—someone who had been through the course and could help guide the younger man through the mazes of life. But today, mentors like that are hard to find.

Throughout the Bible, whenever Satan wanted to destroy a civilization, he went after the males. Sodom and Gomorrah perished because of the unrighteous lifestyle of its men and the absence of divine representatives in their society. You will remember that Pharaoh wanted to kill the male Hebrew children in the time of Moses, and Herod wanted to destroy male children at the birth of Christ.

It's not that the women are not important. Their value is not at issue here. What I am talking about is the spiritual fog that has descended over so many men. They say that six city blocks' worth of fog contain only about one glass of water—a lot of smoke and very little substance.

That describes the situation we are facing in the church today. But it doesn't have to be that way. God has an exciting, demanding, and fulfilling kingdom agenda for men, and I want to try to lay that out in this chapter. So let's talk about what it takes to be a kingdom man in the church.

## SEEK YOUR KINGDOM VISION

To be a kingdom man, a man must first seek God's vision for him in the kingdom. It's not that God is hiding His will from men. God is always looking for men whose hearts are faithful toward Him. The prophet Samuel told faithless King Saul, "The Lord has sought out for himself a man after His own heart" (1 Samuel 13:14).

In Jeremiah 4:25, the lament is that "there was no man" who could be found faithful to the Lord. In Jeremiah 5:1, God sends Jeremiah roaming through the streets of Jerusalem trying to find just one man "who does justice, who seeks truth."

Then God makes an astounding promise. If Jeremiah could find even one man like that, God would pardon the people! But the prophet could not find *one* man of justice and truth among the poor or the great (see vv. 4–5). Ezekiel 22:30 says that God is looking for a man to "stand in the gap."

God is always hunting for faithful men. There are plenty of males, but what He wants is a man after His heart. He wants a man who has a vision of what God can do with him.

Now the problem is that too many of us men have learned our manhood from the wrong sources. We have taken people from Hollywood and the sports world as our heroes and models. But everyone knows you can buy the jersey emblazoned with the number of your favorite player yet still be unable to perform as he does.

A kingdom vision involves two things. First, it involves the agenda that God has already laid out for men in His Word. And then it means getting a clear picture of how God wants you to carry out that agenda in your life.

## The Original Vision

Let's start by reviewing the biblical vision, or agenda, God has given to all Christian men in the church. In Genesis 1:26, God said of Adam and Eve, "Let Us make man in Our image, according to Our likeness; and let them rule over the fish of the sea and over the birds of the sky and over the cattle and over all the earth, and over every creeping thing that creeps on the earth."

We will see later that God includes the woman in this too, because the term *man* here is the term for mankind, not just the male. But Adam will be given the headship in his relationship with Eve, so he is to lead in carrying out this agenda.

And what a big vision this is! God wants man to rule and dominate the earth. The vision God gave Adam was worldwide; its dimensions were staggering. Adam, along with Eve, was not only to rule over the earth, but he was to bear and reproduce the image of God on the earth. That's bigger than any man can pull off by himself.

## Seeing Your Vision

What about you, my Christian brother? Has God called you to do something that is far too big for you to accomplish apart from His power? If so, congratulations! You have been given a kingdom-sized vision!

A lot of men are satisfied just to put in their eight hours, collect a paycheck, and go home. God gave Adam a job, but He gave him a job so he could achieve a bigger goal, a kingdom agenda. If you cannot sit in your chair right now and articulate God's kingdom call on your life, then something is missing in your life.

A vision is the ability to see beyond the immediate and the visible. A kingdom vision is a view of life that is far bigger than just getting by day by day. A kingdom vision is a calling that allows you to make an impact for eternity while you are here in history.

My brother, God has called you and me as men to something that is bigger than life. He has called us to set the pace and lead the way in the church—and ultimately in His kingdom.

So if the sum total of your life is working and then going home to read the newspaper and watch a few TV shows before going to bed, don't be surprised if life seems boring.

Even going to church in and of itself won't make much of a difference if you aren't pursuing a vision that is so big only God can give you the power to accomplish it. If you are going to be a man of the kingdom, then you must allow God to develop a kingdom vision for you.

# LEAD UNDER KINGDOM AUTHORITY

A second part of man's kingdom agenda is that he must take leadership in the church and lead as a man under kingdom authority.

## Under Christ's Authority

In 1 Corinthians 11:3, Paul made a theological statement that has wide-ranging implications. We need to talk about it here, and we'll come back to it in the following chapter when we consider the kingdom agenda of women.

The apostle wrote, "I want you to understand that Christ is the head of every man, and the man is the head of a woman, and God is the head of Christ." This is a hierarchy of function, not of essence.

Jesus is equal to God the Father in essence, because He is fully God. But He is submissive to the Father in function. All women are equal to all men in essence and value before God, but women are under the ultimate authority of their husbands in marriage and the male leadership of the church.

But notice that men are under authority too; we are under the authority of Christ. So there is a chain of command in the kingdom. Like it or not, men were created to lead. At the very least, if a man is married, he is the leader of one other person, because the husband is head of the wife (see Ephesians 5:23).

If a man is going to take the leadership he is called to take in the church, he must come under the authority of Jesus Christ in his own life through the church. To be a kingdom man means that Christ has first call on your life. And a local church should be able to verify that this is happening.

If you are the kind of man who says, "I don't want anyone telling me what to do," then you are not a kingdom man. You are only a male. Jesus Christ claims lordship over your life, which means that you do not have unlimited authority over yourself or anyone else. You have limited authority under Christ.

## Under the Church's Authority

Being subject to Christ is to be made tangible and visible in the subjection of men to the local church, since the church is the visible expression of Christ in history (see Colossians 1:18). If men expect their wives to be submissive to them, then in the same way the church should receive the submission of men as a demonstration of Christ's authority over those men.

This is evident in 1 Corinthians 5 with the unrepentant, immoral man and in 2 Thessalonians 3:10–15 with the case of a man in the church who refuses to work and support his family.

The church is called to discipline a man like this by breaking fellowship with him until he comes around. The intent is that the man responds to the discipline and begins obeying because he recognizes that he is under the authority of the church.

I remember telling Anthony Jr. one time to empty the trash, to which he responded, "I don't feel like it, Dad."

I said, "What did you say?"

"I don't feel like emptying the trash!"

What Anthony was telling me was that as my instruction hit his frontal lobe and moved through his cranial area down his central nervous system and out to the nerves that connected to the muscles attached to his skeletal frame, there was not the concomitant emotional stimulus to move his skeletal frame into a trash-emptying mode.

That's basically what my son was telling me—to which I responded, "I can change the way you feel, boy!" My instruction to Anthony to empty the trash had nothing to do with whether he was into trash emptying that day.

My instruction needed to be obeyed for one reason and one reason alone: Because Anthony Jr.'s papa said so and Anthony Jr. was under his papa's authority as leader of the house. In the same way, Christian men are under the authority of God's house, the church, and are to submit themselves accordingly.

Too many Christian men have this "feeling problem" today. They don't want to be married anymore because *they don't feel like* being faithful. They don't want to work because *they don't feel like* working. They don't want to be responsible to raise children because *they don't feel like* raising children.

My response to that is, "You felt like getting married at the time. You felt like having children at the time. So it is a moot point to say, 'I don't feel like it anymore.'" What we need is a generation of kingdom men who are responsible under God.

Any man who is not following Jesus Christ through responsible submission to the local church is living in spiritual rebellion. It takes tenacity and commitment to follow Christ, and it takes humility to submit yourself to the authority of His church. But that's the only way to fulfill the agenda He hands you. Any man can follow the crowd, but only a kingdom man can follow Christ.

## A Man's Authority

Even though a man's authority is limited and derived from another, namely, Jesus Christ, a man still has real authority.

We can see that back in the creation of Eve. I don't need to retell the story for you. Eve was created to be Adam's helper and completer (see Genesis 2:18). She was formed from Adam's flesh (see vv. 21–22).

Then God brought her to Adam, who gave this new creation the name "woman" (v. 23).

In the Bible, to name something is to have authority over it. So God created the woman in such a way that she was placed under the authority of her husband. Not so he could dominate and intimidate her, but so he could cause her to grow and flourish and become all that God meant her to be.

That is God's ideal. Sin did not erase the ideal, but it spoiled God's plan and made the ideal much more difficult to attain. A guy once said to me, "My wife is crucifying me."

My answer was, "Well, you said you wanted to be like Jesus, didn't you?" Sometimes it takes going to the cross to be a kingdom kind of man.

After he sinned, Adam ran off and hid (see Genesis 3:8). Why? Because he had failed to obey God. God had told Adam everything he needed to know and do so that he could fulfill his God-given agenda. Adam had divine instruction. He had the mind of God. God put His thoughts within Adam. Adam had the ability to think like God, but the tragedy is that he chose not to do so.

## Men Who Think Like God

We have the same tragedy happening today: Christian men who fail to think "Christianly," to think like God.

I'm not referring here to some kind of New Age stuff. I'm talking about thinking with the mind of Christ (see 1 Corinthians 2:16). Since we have the full revelation of Christ's mind in the Bible, for us today this means thinking biblically.

There's a good example of this in Matthew 19, which describes Jesus' and the Pharisees' differences over divorce. The Pharisees wanted to trap Jesus in a no-win situation, so they asked Him what they thought was a trick question about divorce. But the first thing Jesus said was, "Have you not read?" (Matthew 19:4). And then He quoted the relevant Scripture to them.

Jesus was saying to the Pharisees, "You're not thinking correctly. You of all people should know that there is a higher authority here than your sinful desires to get rid of your wives. There is an authority that should guide how you think about this issue. God has given you His mind on this question."

This is why Christian men must submit themselves to the Word in the context of the local church. They need to be held accountable to develop biblically informed minds that are transferred to their families.

## PASS ON THE KINGDOM'S VALUES

God wants Christian men to think as He does as a way of life so they can transfer biblical values to their families. That's why Paul said in 1 Corinthians 14:34–35 that if a woman has a question in the church, she should ask her husband first. He should have some answers because he is a man of the Word.

Do you know why so many people are afraid when they see a group of teenagers coming toward them on the street? Do you know why so many teachers and school administrators are reluctant to confront an unruly student, for fear of what he might pull out of his pocket? Do you know why so many people go to bed at night afraid?

It's because we have a generation of boys who think that being a male makes them a man, who don't care about themselves or anyone else, and who aren't even afraid to die. A person who doesn't care and isn't afraid to die is dangerous.

What's wrong with these young males? The problem is that they have no values, mostly because they have no man around to pass on values to them.

My brother, we have to change that if we are even going to survive as a culture, much less advance God's kingdom and His agenda. What is missing in American culture today is this transfer.

Instead of kingdom men training the next generation, the wrong males are doing the job. The result is a generation of boys and young men who have no sensitivity for spiritual values. They are afflicted with spiritual leprosy.

### Spiritual Lepers

When I was in India a number of years ago, I saw the first leper I had ever seen. His fingers were missing down to his knuckles, and half of his ear was missing.

The reason lepers lose parts of their bodies so easily is that leprosy destroys the nerve endings in the body. So a leper loses the ability to feel and sense pain. Therefore, a leper can burn himself or injure himself in some other way and not even feel it.

A doctor who was with me in India told me that the leper whose ear was partly missing had done that to himself. Because he didn't have any feeling in his hands or ears, he had inadvertently pulled so hard on his ear that he destroyed it and never felt a thing.

So the problem with leprosy is not that the disease eats away a person's limbs. Instead, it deadens a person's ability to feel so that even normal daily activities become destructive to his or her body.

Can you see why I say we have a generation of young people who are like spiritual lepers? They have lost their ability to feel anything for God, for themselves, or for anyone else, because the values of the kingdom are not being passed on to them.

## A Kingdom Transfer

What does it take to be the kind of man who is able to pass on kingdom values to the next generation? I want to answer that from Genesis 18:19, a verse we touched on briefly in an earlier chapter.

God said of Abraham, "I have chosen him, in order that he may command his children and his household after him to keep the way of the Lord by doing righteousness and justice; in order that the Lord may bring upon Abraham what He has spoken about him."

The transfer of godly values from one generation to the next is not automatic. Your children and mine were born in sin (see Psalm 51:5). They are not going to raise themselves and pick up right values on their own. Someone has to pass those values on to them.

That's what God called Abraham to do in his generation. Let's look at how God equipped Abraham for his task.

Genesis 18:19 says God chose Abraham. This man had a *destiny*. Abraham knew that God's hand was on his life. You need to know that God's hand is on your life too, if you want to be a kingdom man who has something to pass on. That means you need to get close to God and let Him reveal His purpose for your life.

Abraham also committed himself to *discipline* so that he could "command his children and his household after him to keep the way of the Lord."

My father never asked me, "Son, do you feel like going to church today?" He got me up and took me to church. Worshiping God was a fixed priority in our home. There was no negotiation. Now we have a generation of kids who tell their parents what they are going to do.

Abraham was to "command" his children; that is, he was to transmit standards that were nonnegotiable. Every Christian man needs to hang this declaration over the door of his house: "As for me and my house, we will serve the Lord" (Joshua 24:15). A kingdom man says to his family, "We do things God's way in our home because this is a kingdom home. This is where the King rules, and I am the leader under the King."

Let me show you how Abraham exercised his commitment. Back in Genesis 17:11, God told Abraham that circumcision would be the sign of the covenant between himself and God. Every male in Abraham's family and in his extended household needed to be circumcised. According to verses 26–27, Abraham followed through on God's command the same day.

Besides having a destiny and discipline, Abraham also had *dignity*. Dignity is the result of living a life of righteousness and justice. The opposite is a life of indignity, of profane language, and of shameful living.

Have you been shocked, as I have, by the language and actions of teenagers and even elementary-aged children today? Whatever happened to the common decency and respect that used to be given in our culture? You might be tempted to say, "These kids are a lost generation."

No, I think these kids are the *product* of a lost generation. Our generation has fumbled the handoff of biblical values. The church is the loser for it, along with the home, the school, and the culture at large.

Finally, Genesis 18:19 says that God gave Abraham *dominion*. Because Abraham was faithful to lead his own house, God expanded his sphere of influence.

This is what the church needs so desperately today. The church needs faithful kingdom men who will extend God's dominion into the lives of kids without a father, serving as role models, mentors, and friends to boys who have no men in their lives to show them what a real man looks and acts like.

Where men are faithfully serving in the church, the values of the kingdom are being passed on. In that way, a boy who has no man in his family can still come to the larger family of God and learn godly values from godly men.

We have asked men in our church in Dallas to carve out a few hours a month to take a small group of boys and teach them about kingdom discipline, dignity, and dominion. We have so many children who do not have fathers at home that the men of the church must rise up and say, "We will lend our influence to these children so that the values they need will be passed on to them."

# LEAD IN KINGDOM MANAGEMENT

Here's the final kingdom agenda item I want to talk about. Men are responsible to take the lead in the management of God's kingdom. His plan is that you practice good leadership at home so you can bring it to church.

That's the idea in 1 Timothy 3:4–5, where Paul told Timothy that a candidate for church leadership must be a man "who manages his own household well, keeping his children under control with all dignity (but if a man does not know how to manage his own household, how will he take care of the church of God?)."

## Start at Home

Every Christian husband is a pastor with a built-in congregation: his family. The home is the training ground for leadership in the church. The home is where a man practices for the big show. Paul said if a man can't manage three or four other people in his own house, don't let him lead in the church.

I once told a group of men I was speaking to that some of them would go crazy at Oak Cliff Bible Fellowship. We have some kids of the kingdom there who will wear you slick, just grind all your tread right off. So if a man's own two kids are getting on his nerves, he would have a major problem working with some of the youngsters at our church.

## A Bigger Agenda

Do you know why God wants a kingdom man to practice good leadership at home? One reason is to raise a godly seed, of course. But another reason is that he is preparing men for a bigger agenda than just their families.

I said before that there is no marriage in heaven, because once the reality has come, we don't need the illustration anymore. So we are not going to heaven as family units but as individual believers. That's why a man needs to look at his leadership of his family as his training ground for kingdom leadership and management.

Take the example of prayer. As a man becomes comfortable and capable in leading his family in prayer, he is better equipped to assume a role of prayer leadership at church. And that is God's expressed will, because back in 1 Timothy 2:8, Paul wrote concerning men in the church at Ephesus, "I want the men in every place to pray, lifting up holy hands, without wrath and dissension." The word *men* here is the specific term for "males."

God wants men to step forward and set the pace, to take leadership in the church. I don't apologize for that, because this is God's call, not mine or any other man's.

I also don't apologize for teaching that men need to be the heads of their homes. I often say to the men at church, "If your wife is the head of your home, brother, you are out of line. Your wife is only taking the leadership you relinquished." A leader by calling and conviction, not by permission.

Now don't misunderstand me. I am not saying that a man can bully and threaten his way into leadership. A biblical leader leads by loving and serving, not by verbal or physical violence of any kind. Any man who has to put his hand on a woman to get her to submit has no idea what it means to be a man.

## BECOME A KINGDOM MAN

Some brother may be reading this and saying, "Tony, I'm not making it as a kingdom man, but I want to. Where can I start?" Let me suggest a place.

### Start Here

If you want to be a kingdom man who hangs in there even when he feels like throwing in the towel, you need two or three "homies," fellow men of the kingdom, who will hold up your hands when you get weary.

In Exodus 17:8–16, we find the account of Israel's battle against the Amalekites. Moses sent Joshua out to lead Israel's army in the battle, while he, Aaron, and Hur went to the top of a nearby hill to oversee the battle. Let's pick up the story:

> *Moses, Aaron, and Hur went up to the top of the hill. So it came about when Moses held his hand up, that Israel prevailed, and when he let his hand down, Amalek prevailed. But Moses' hands were heavy. Then they took a stone and put it under him, and he sat on it; and Aaron and Hur supported his hands, one on one side and one on the other. Thus his hands*

*were steady until the sun set. So Joshua overwhelmed Amalek and his people with the edge of the sword. (vv. 10–13)*

Joshua and Israel were able to win the fight because, even though Moses' arms got tired, he had some brothers around him to hold up his hands.

One of the problems we men in the church have is that too many of us are "Lone Ranger" Christians. We're trying to make it all by ourselves. But I would remind you that even the Lone Ranger had a partner.

When you feel like you aren't going to make it as a dad or as a husband, or when the job is dragging you down, you need some brothers to come alongside, hold up your hands, and say, "We're going to make it together, brother. We're going to hang in there with you. We're going to prevail for God."

As you grow in the Lord, you will also be able to hold up another man's hands when he is tired. That's the ministry of the body of Christ in action. That's why we need men's fellowships in the church that go beyond playing games and talking about work, the weather, and sports.

Proverbs 27:17 is a great verse for men: "Iron sharpens iron, so one man sharpens another." Proverbs 17:17 says, "A friend loves at all times, and a brother is born for adversity." In Ecclesiastes 4:12, Solomon said, "If one can overpower him who is alone, two can resist him. A cord of three strands is not quickly torn apart."

## A Multigenerational Commitment

It's the understatement of the year to say that the church is in desperate need of men with a kingdom vision and a kingdom agenda to fulfill. The result of this kind of commitment is the blessing of God, not just in a kingdom man's own generation, but to generations after him.

Please allow me to share with you how this has worked in the Evans family. When I was ten years old, my father came to Christ. We lived in the inner city of Baltimore, a difficult place to survive. Before my dad became a Christian, he and my mom didn't get along very well. It was violent sometimes. They were headed for divorce court.

But then Dad was gloriously saved when he was thirty years old. He made a commitment that said, "By God's grace, I am going to save my family. Even though this woman hates me, and I don't like her very much, by God's grace I am going to bring my family to Christ."

My mother made life hell on earth for him; it was a miserable existence for my dad. Every Sunday, he would go to church to gain new strength to go back to war for his family the following week.

My father was a longshoreman who worked very hard unloading and loading boats in the Baltimore harbor. He would get up at 3:00 a.m., when the house was quiet and he didn't have to worry about my mother giving him a hard time. He would go downstairs in the living room and open up his Bible, and for an hour he would pray. "Lord, please save my family; give me back my wife; deliver my children."

A year after Dad was saved, he was up one morning at 3:00, praying and reading his Bible as usual. He heard the steps creak and knew my mother was coming downstairs. He bowed his head and thought, *Oh, no, here we go again.*

But this morning was different. My mother told my father, "I have been doing everything I know to discourage you. I have tried to make your life as miserable as I could. Yet you haven't budged, so whatever this thing is in your life must be real, and I want it right now."

My father got on his knees with my mother and led her to Jesus Christ right there. Then they called me, my brothers, and my sister around the table and told us that salvation had now entered our home. My father led me to Christ, which launched me in a totally new direction than I'd been heading. Dad took us to a Bible-teaching church, where I grew up in the Word. Then I became the first person in my home to go to college.

My father was a high school dropout, but through his influence in my life I wanted to go to college. There I developed a passion for God and for ministry and wound up at Dallas Theological Seminary, where I was the first African-American to receive a doctoral degree.

Then we began a church with ten people in a living room, and the Oak Cliff Bible Fellowship was born. I've told our congregation that, from a human perspective, the reason our new sanctuary is full is not because of Tony Evans. It's because a man named Arthur Evans wouldn't give up on his family and became a faithful man of the kingdom.

Because my father wouldn't quit, I am resolved not to quit either. That's what it takes to be a man of the kingdom. (See this author's book *No More Excuses* [Crossway] for a complete analysis of the biblical role of men.)

# CHAPTER TWENTY

# The Kingdom Agenda
# of Women

We are talking about the kingdom agenda of the church and the people who make up the church.

Paul believed the way the church conducted its ministry was so important that he wrote to Timothy:

> *I am writing these things to you, hoping to come to you before long; but in case I am delayed, I write so that you may know how one ought to conduct himself in the household of God, which is the church of the living God, the pillar and support of the truth. (1 Timothy 3:14–15)*

Timothy's task as a pastor was to train the congregation in the rules of God's kingdom, which are very different than the rules of this world order. In other words, you can't bring the rules of the street, or even the rules from downtown, and try to impose them on the operation of God's kingdom. We're learning that kingdom people function differently than their counterparts in the world.

Nowhere is this difference more obvious than when it comes to the kingdom agenda of Christian women. In this final chapter on God's kingdom agenda in your church life, let's answer the question, what does God expect of kingdom women?

Now, I know that this subject will take us into areas that are difficult and, sometimes, downright controversial and divisive. I've been challenged many times for my teaching on this topic, most often because I am a man addressing issues concerning women.

My response to that is to say I didn't write the Bible! My job is to expound and teach what it says. So judge me on the basis of whether I am true to Scripture instead of the fact that I am a man. If I am accurately dividing the Word, then the objector has an argument with the Bible and therefore God, not with me.

Having said that, I want to address four items of a kingdom woman's agenda in the context of the church. To do this, I want to return to 1 Timothy, God's "manual" on how we are to function in the church as a primary expression of God's kingdom in this age.

## THE PROPRIETY OF
## A KINGDOM WOMAN

First Timothy 2:9–15 is Paul's detailed instruction on the kind of adornment and activities that should mark God's kingdom women. This is a difficult yet absolutely central text outlining the agenda that is to characterize women "making a claim to godliness" (v. 10). The first item on this agenda is a godly woman's propriety when it comes to her appearance: "I want women to adorn themselves with proper clothing, modestly and discreetly, not with braided hair and gold or pearls or costly garments" (v. 9).

Here Paul used the verb form of the same word Peter used in 1 Peter 3:3 when he wrote to women in the church, "Let not your adornment be merely external."

The word for *adorn* is the Greek verb *kosmeo*, which translates into the English word *cosmetic*. We discussed the use of this word in the chapter on the kingdom agenda of wives, so I won't repeat that discussion here other than to remind you that the word means "to arrange" or "to put in place."

God understands that women will spend time arranging themselves, putting everything in order. He knows that women give special attention to what they wear and how they look. The instruction to kingdom women is not to ignore this area or pretend it doesn't matter but to dress with modesty and good decorum as the standard.

We need to remember that many of the women coming into the

church at places like Ephesus and Corinth were coming out of pagan backgrounds. So they were coming to the church dressed like the world. They were in style with the times, but not in style with the kingdom.

Paul told Timothy, in essence, "Make sure the women in God's family understand that as kingdom women, their need for modesty and propriety in dress may mean they have to take on a different look." Modesty has to do with not drawing undue attention to yourself or being ostentatious in appearance. The issue is excess.

There were two reasons Paul had to deal with this issue. The first reason was related to morality in the church. In 1 Timothy 5:6, the apostle wrote, speaking of widows, "She who gives herself to wanton pleasure is dead even while she lives."

Then in verses 11–12 we read, "Refuse to put younger widows on the list, for when they feel sensual desires in disregard of Christ, they want to get married, thus incurring condemnation, because they have set aside their previous pledge."

Paul was stating an obvious truth. The sexual attraction between men and women is real and undeniable. When men and women are around each other, sparks begin to fly, and there is a propensity toward immorality. The point is that this attraction doesn't need any extra fuel added to it by immodest apparel.

The other problem in the early church was a disparity of wealth, much like we have today. Some women in Ephesus, where Timothy was pastoring, could afford the latest fashions, and they liked to out-dress other women (see 1 Timothy 6:17–18). In terms of propriety, the problem with this today, just as then, is that the fashion emphasis is heavy on immodesty. Too often, to dress fashionably is to dress immodestly, especially for girls and younger women.

Now I understand the fashion problem many women face. Dresses and skirts are often made to be short, and sometimes it's hard to find a modest outfit that still looks decent. It may require extra time or an extra flap of cloth to be modest, but it can be done.

## The Beauty of Modesty

I'm not being flippant when I mention an extra flap of cloth to make an outfit more modest.

Many of the things that my daughters bought to wear when they were growing up never left the house until a seamstress got hold of the garment first. That was simply because the clothes were immodest, not in keeping with kingdom propriety. Sometimes it involved letting out some of the extra material the garment maker had left in the hem.

On more than one occasion, I've also seen Lois turn down a dress or skirt she wanted to buy because it could not be lengthened and therefore would have been improper. In the little church where I grew up, the older women used to walk around with extra pieces of cloth. If a girl's or a young woman's dress came up too high when she sat down, they would spread a piece of cloth over the woman's knees.

Now you may think that's extreme. But we have gone so far to the other extreme of immodesty that I say give us some of those older ladies again! I told our church we would be willing to buy the pieces of cloth so that the women would look like kingdom women when they sat down, not just when they stood up. No one took us up on the offer.

Whenever we bring up the issue of dress, someone usually objects. "Why do you put all the responsibility on the women? Aren't men responsible to control their desires?" someone asks.

Of course they are. I'm not laying all the responsibility at the women's feet. But the fact remains that a woman's standard of dress can draw attention either to her Lord or to her body. We have enough men with wrong motives who go around looking for women they can exploit. I am responsible to control my desires as a man, but I can't control the desires of every man who walks in the door of the church.

So a kingdom woman is called of God not to dress in a way that stimulates inappropriate responses.

Paul's mention of gold and pearls and expensive clothes was a way of saying to the women in the church, "Don't look like the women out there in the street. Don't try to dazzle and impress others." Instead, there ought to be an air of dignity and respect about a kingdom woman. Corporate worship is not a fashion show or a trip to the Oscars.

Now let me say again that the Bible is not condemning beauty. We saw in Proverbs 31 that this woman was beautiful to behold. But her beauty was accomplished with propriety and modesty. I am not trying to lay down logistic rules on dress. I'm simply saying that God calls Christian mothers and daughters to dress as women of dignity and honor.

I realize that for some women, kingdom modesty in dress may mean a radical change of wardrobe. For others, it may just mean an alteration or change here and there. But whatever it takes, a woman of God needs to be modest. It should be obvious that she is a woman of the kingdom.

## A Decision for Modesty

There is another very important word relating to modesty in 1 Timothy 2:9. The word *discreetly* refers to self-control. It has to do with making a decision of discipline. In this case, it may involve a believing woman saying, "I like that dress, and it looks good on me. But I have to say no to it because it is not modest."

In case you think I've been saying it too strongly, let me point you to Isaiah 3, where the Lord addressed the immodest women of Judah. I want to pick up some key verses:

> The Lord said, "Because the daughters of Zion are proud, and walk with heads held high and seductive eyes, and go along with mincing steps, and tinkle the bangles on their feet, therefore the Lord will afflict the scalp of the daughters of Zion with scabs, and the Lord will make their foreheads bare."
> (vv. 16–17)

Read Isaiah 3:19–24, and you will see that the Lord was very specific about the various adornments these women wore to attract men. They were advertising themselves as immodest and available, and the men were taking them up on their offer.

But the whole thing made God sick. A woman is immodest if her clothes are too short or too tight, if her neckline is too low, or if her appearance is too flashy.

The challenge to kingdom women is, don't send the wrong message by the way you dress. Don't let people decide who you are by what they see, unless what they see is a woman of dignity and honor.

# THE PROFESSION OF
# A KINGDOM WOMAN

In 1 Timothy 2:9–10, Paul gave kingdom women a way to avoid spending too much time and attention on their outward appearance while ignoring what Peter called "the hidden person of the heart" (1 Peter 3:4).

## A Visible Profession

Instead of adorning themselves with gold and pearls and expensive clothes, kingdom women are to adorn themselves with "good works, as befits women making a claim to godliness," Paul said (1 Timothy 2:10). The apostle was urging women to spend more time on serving God than on giving attention to their appearance.

The time that a woman spends in front of a mirror will vary, depending on how much transformation needs to occur! Paul was not advocating that a woman never look in a mirror or take note of how she looks.

He was saying, "Make sure your good works are as visible as your makeup. Make sure that the things you do for Christ are as carefully crafted as your hairdo."

If a woman will go to great lengths and great trouble to make sure every hair is in place, a kingdom woman should be willing to go to great lengths to see that her inner life and her service are just as attractive as her appearance. Her good works or authenticity should be obvious to all.

## A Vital Profession

Anyone who knows the Bible knows that the witness and ministry of women are absolutely vital to the accomplishment of God's kingdom agenda. Unfortunately, the church has too often made it seem as if women were more on the fringe of the kingdom than part of its essence.

But Jesus' ministry was undergirded by the support of a number of faithful women (see Luke 8:1–3). The Old Testament is replete with the stories of women who were strategic to the kingdom of God. They were known by what they did, not only by how they looked.

A woman's service is vital to the ministry of the church. That's why Paul encouraged women to step beyond the surface things that capture the time and attention of so many women in the world and become a vital force in the church and in the kingdom of God it represents.

A vital profession demands energy and activity. When a Christian woman is willing to commit her life to God, there is an adornment about her spirit that is attractive to everyone who sees her.

One of the things that attracted me to Lois is that when we were dating, she told me I could never be first in her life. She said Jesus

Christ would always be first, and I would always be second. I didn't mind being number two to Him!

## THE POSITION OF A KINGDOM WOMAN

The third thing on a woman's kingdom agenda is probably the most controversial. The last five verses of 1 Timothy 2 have led to the apostle Paul being called everything from a male chauvinist to a woman hater.

### The Biblical Standard

I want to discuss verses 11–14 here, and then we will deal with verse 15 under a separate heading. We will camp on this point for a while since it encompasses Paul's most controversial teaching:

> *Let a woman quietly receive instruction with entire submissiveness. But I do not allow a woman to teach or exercise authority over a man, but to remain quiet. For it was Adam who was first created, and then Eve. And it was not Adam who was deceived, but the woman being quite deceived, fell into transgression. (1 Timothy 2:11–14)*

The first thing I want you to see is that Christianity liberated women. In the Roman world, as we saw earlier, women were little more than objects for men to use. They had very little social status, recognition, or significance.

Then Christianity came along and taught that in Jesus Christ, men and women were of equal value, that there was no male or female in Him (see Galatians 3:28). In His own ministry, Jesus treated women with dignity and honor. He reached out to them and afforded them equal spiritual standing with men. They were no longer second-class citizens.

In the words of 1 Peter 3:7, a wife was now a "fellow heir of the grace of life" with her husband. She was his partner, his spiritual equal before God.

We know from Scripture that in the beginning, it was the same way. God made Eve to be a partner to Adam, and His commission to have dominion over the earth was given to the two of them. The problem comes when people see the partnership but miss the principle of hierarchy that was also a part of creation.

Adam and Eve were a team, but the team had a leader. Each one had a specific role to play in order for the team to be most productive. Adam was not to act as if Eve did not exist, and neither was he to dominate her. He was to be her servant leader.

## The Application to the Church

The heart of what Paul said in 1 Timothy 2:11–14 is this: When the church comes together for corporate worship, the ministry of teaching is to be in the hands of the men. This illustrates and demonstrates God's hierarchy (see 1 Corinthians 11:3), just as Adam was to receive the truth of God and teach it to Eve, which he did when he taught her what God had instructed him concerning the forbidden fruit.

So even though women have equal spiritual value to men in the kingdom, there is a hierarchy, or chain of command, that God has established. In the corporate worship of the church, women are to take a position of submission. The male leadership is to receive the truth of God and proclaim it to the flock.

Paul was not being chauvinistic or anti-woman here. He was not denouncing women or denying their gifts. He was rather addressing the issue of positional hierarchy that, unlike gifts, does involve gender distinctions. He was simply saying that in the context of the church's corporate worship, a woman is not permitted to exercise final authority over a man. That is why Paul only references men when speaking about the office of overseer (see 3:1–7) yet includes women when he broadens his leadership discussion to the office of deacon (see 3:8–13), since teaching is not a part of the deacon qualifications nor is it the final authoritative office of the church.

This means, then, that a woman should not be the pastor, bishop, or elder of a church. It allows her to hold other leadership roles as approved by the final male leadership of the church. It also allows her to teach classes and lead committees under the authority of male pastors and elders, since these entities are not part of the total gathered church body, and in these roles she does not have final authority.

We know this prohibition is limited to the church's corporate worship, because this is the only context where limitations and prohibitions are prescribed.

It's not that a woman may not have the gift of proclamation or teaching. It's that a woman cannot occupy the office of elder, bishop, or pastor in the church. The simplest way I can put it is to say that a woman can do anything in the church but be in a position of final authority. She is to "remain quiet" in the sense of not teaching men or exercising undelegated authority over men. This also means that women can be legitimately ordained to ministry when such ordination *does not* include the right to function in the position of final authority in the church.

## An Important Exception

First Timothy is the prescription for a woman's conduct in the church. But there is one exception to this, which Paul explained in 1 Corinthians 11:3–10.

We have already discussed verse 3 pretty thoroughly. It describes the hierarchy in God's kingdom, which extends all the way to the Godhead itself. But if Jesus is equal to God the Father in His divine essence, how can He be under the Father's authority? Because the purpose of a hierarchy is to carry out a program, not define an essence.

Therefore, in the carrying out of God's kingdom agenda, a woman is under the leadership of a man. That's why, in 1 Corinthians 11:4–5, Paul said:

> *Every man who has something on his head while praying or prophesying, disgraces his head. But every woman who has her head uncovered while praying or prophesying, disgraces her head; for she is one and the same with her whose head is shaved.*

The key to this passage is the term *head*, which is used here to mean a person's authority. So what Paul was saying is that if a man were to wear a head covering in church, he would dishonor his head, who is Christ (see v. 3).

It's an issue of honor. Why do we take off our hats in the presence of a dignitary or when the national anthem is sung? It's a sign of respect. A man's uncovered head is a symbol of Christ's headship over him.

Now you need to understand that God's symbols always mean something. Symbols in the Bible represent something very powerful and very meaningful. That's the case with baptism and Communion—and in this case, with a head covering.

Paul said a woman who prayed or prophesied in church without a head covering was as disgraceful as a woman who had all her hair cut off (see 1 Corinthians 11:5b–6). A woman's head covering is a symbol that she recognizes she is under authority when she prays or prophesies.

I said this was an exception to 1 Timothy 2, where women are instructed to be silent in church in terms of public ministry before the whole body. Men are normally to do the public praying and prophesying, or expounding the Word. But there is one set of circumstances under which a woman can address the gathered church. It can happen when she has permission from her head (her husband) and from the leaders of the church (final authority).

Paul had to address this issue because the Corinthian church had a first-century feminist movement on its hands. It had a group of women who wanted to throw out this hierarchy, and they were causing disruption in church—so much so that Paul told all the women in the church to keep silent (see 1 Corinthians 14:34–35). Some women were bringing the rules from the street into the church, but those rules don't work in God's kingdom.

There is a legitimate exception to the general rule concerning the role of women in the church. This exception allows a woman to use her gifts in addressing the entire assembly, but it does not change her position as a person under authority.

## The Angels and Authority

Paul further developed the reason for a woman's head covering in 1 Corinthians 11:7–9, which restates the woman's position of submission to the man. Let me say again that this is not an issue of essence or spiritual worth but of function. When it comes to accomplishing God's kingdom agenda in the gathered church, a woman is under the primary functional authority of the male leadership (the pastor, bishop, and elders).

Paul then took the argument to another level with this statement in verse 10: "Therefore the woman ought to have a symbol of authority on her head, because of the angels." We may wonder what in the world angels have to do with a woman and her head covering or lack of it.

Angels have everything to do with it, because the angels also function under authority. Remember what happened when Lucifer, the chief angel, no longer wanted to function under God's authority? He got kicked out of heaven.

In the prophet Isaiah's great vision in Isaiah 6, what were the seraphim doing? They were using two of their wings to cover their faces and two to cover their feet in God's presence. In other words, angels go into God's presence covered, as a symbol of their humility and submission before Him.

So why did Paul bring this up in 1 Corinthians 11? Because in this case, the response of heaven is determined by the activity on earth.

If a woman is not under proper authority on earth, she cannot expect heaven's assistance. So when a woman calls on God for help, before God sends an angel to assist her, He is going to determine whether she is operating under the authority He established. If not, God is not going to grant the angels permission to assist her in her time of need.

The same holds true for a man, by the way. God works by a chain of authority, and when a man is not under authority before God, he cannot expect God to answer his prayers (see 1 Peter 3:7).

A woman may say, "That's all right. I don't need angels; I just need Jesus." Well, I need to explain something that Jesus said to Nathanael when He called Nathanael to be His disciple. "You shall see the heavens opened, and the angels of God ascending and descending on the Son of Man," Jesus told Nathanael (John 1:51). Jesus mediates solutions to earth's problems through the angels.

So if a woman wants to be touched by an angel, she has to be under authority. But if she is in rebellion against God's established chain of authority, she may as well get up off her knees. God is not listening.

If it seems that Paul was taking too much away from women, 1 Corinthians 11:11–12 puts this issue into perspective. "However, in the Lord, neither is woman independent of man, nor is man independent of woman. For as the woman originates from the man, so also the man has his birth through the woman; and all things originate from God."

This is a reminder of the spiritual equality we talked about earlier. Neither men nor women are free to go off and act independently of their authority. There is a chain of authority, but men and women are still of equal value before God, and they need each other.

What about the argument that all of this hierarchy and head covering and authority stuff is just cultural, unique to Paul's day and his situation? Some say these principles are no longer valid because Paul's instructions were written back in the days of the New Testament.

But Paul took this issue back a lot further than that. As we have already seen, he took it all the way back to creation (see 1 Timothy 2:13–14), staking his argument on the order of creation and the fact that Eve was the one deceived by Satan.

Why was Satan able to deceive Eve? Because she abandoned her role. Paul was not saying that women are less intelligent or more emotional than men. He was saying that Eve acted independently of her head.

And when she did that, she influenced Adam's decision, which plunged the world into sin because hell's angels took over. When you abandon biblical authority, hell always seeks to take over.

So the question for a woman is, whose angels do you want working in our life and in the church? Either God is going to send His angels to minister to you when you are under the kingdom authority He ordained, or Satan and his "angels" (demons) will be unleashed when you rebel against your position.

A kingdom woman is to find her position in God's hierarchy within the church. She is to receive instruction, unless the occasion arises in which she is designated to address the church or lead the congregation in prayer with the permission of its male leaders and under their authority, visibly symbolized by the wearing of a head covering.

## THE PRIORITY OF A KINGDOM WOMAN

We have covered some tough territory in 1 Timothy 2, and we have one more hard verse to deal with. The final verse of this chapter speaks to the priority of a kingdom woman: "But women shall be preserved through the bearing of children if they continue in faith and love and sanctity with self-restraint" (1 Timothy 2:15).

What did Paul mean by a woman being preserved? He's not talking about salvation but about a godly woman's devotion to her primary calling, the guiding and management of her home and family. Putting it in the terminology of this book, the reference is to a woman fulfilling her kingdom agenda.

### Reversing the Stigma

But I think there is something more here. What do children have to do with all of this? Everything. God is asking kingdom women to reverse the damage Satan did to them and remove the stigma he laid upon them.

What did Satan do? He induced Eve to act independently of Adam, and as a result the whole world was plunged into sin. Ever since then, woman has borne the stigma of her contribution to the fall of mankind.

But a woman can be preserved or delivered from that stigma by raising up a godly seed. God wants a woman to bear children and raise them in the discipline and instruction of the Lord so that they go out and wreak havoc on Satan's kingdom.

The entrance of sin allowed Satan to corrupt the human race through every child who would ever be born. It started with the children of Adam and Eve, when Cain killed Abel, and it's been happening ever since.

What God is looking for is a righteous seed who will react differently than the seed of Eve. God wants women to bear children who have His mark on them rather than the mark of Cain. So whenever a kingdom woman produces a righteous child she is, in a sense, getting back at Satan for what he did in the garden. By producing godly children, a godly woman serves notice on hell that although Satan may have won the first round with Eve and her kids, he is not going to take this child. A godly seed is a woman's way of saying to Satan, "You may have beaten us the first time, but you are not going to beat us this time."

## Setting Priorities

This is why the priority of a kingdom woman is her home and not her career. We discussed this in detail earlier in the book so I don't need to visit all of these issues again.

Let me just restate the basic principle that should guide the decisions of a woman who wants to accomplish her God-given kingdom agenda. Whenever a woman's work outside the home compromises her ministry inside the home, she is in the wrong job. It's time for her and her husband to sit down, examine their priorities, and do whatever reprioritizing is necessary.

This is critical, because there's more at stake here than just our own generation. If a woman's outside work keeps her from raising a godly seed in her home, she and her husband are negotiating with hell. There's no other way to say it.

Of course, there are tough situations such as single parents who have to work and have no family to help them. But even in this case, a single mother can still make her home a priority, knowing that God gives grace to each of us to deal with our daily circumstances.

I want to consider some more key passages as we wrap this chapter and this section of the book. The book of 1 Timothy addresses women's issues again in chapter 5, where Paul wrote, "I want younger widows to get married, bear children, keep house, and give the enemy no occasion for reproach; for some have already turned aside to follow Satan" (vv. 14–15).

The issue of a person's role and calling in the kingdom of God is a spiritual issue. For a woman, putting her home and family first is not just a matter of economics or scheduling. It's a spiritual issue.

The conduct of some younger widows in Ephesus was bringing reproach on the church and on the name of Christ (see 1 Timothy 5:11–13). The antidote to this was for them to remarry if they so desired and focus their attention and their energy on their homes and families. Bearing children was part of that calling.

A woman may say, "But we need the money I bring home." Obviously, no one can judge to what extent that statement may be true in every home. There are certainly homes in which the mother has to work to make ends meet. A woman in that situation may be able to find creative ways to produce income from within the home.

The point is that work outside the home should complement, not compete with, the primacy of the home.

But you and I know that in a lot of cases, the need for the extra income is simply the result of the pressures people put on themselves to acquire material possessions. But God did not call Christian husbands and wives to keep up with the Joneses. He called them to save the Joneses.

It's all right to get what money can buy as long as you don't lose what money cannot buy. Nothing can replace the value of a strong Christian heritage.

We know from 1 Timothy 5:8 that a man is called to be the primary provider for his family. That's one reason men are made physically stronger than women (see 1 Peter 3:7). A woman is given the primary assignment of being the manager of the home.

Back in Proverbs 31:11, the Bible says that the husband of a faithful woman can trust in her. This refers to more than just home management, but that certainly is included. I don't write the checks in our house and haven't done so for years. I don't need to, because Lois does a great job of managing our home.

That doesn't mean I can be oblivious to what is happening at home. I'm still responsible to be the leader at home, but I am blessed with a wife who fulfills her role very capably.

## Sharing the Blessing

The blessing a woman creates when she fulfills God's agenda reaches beyond the next generation of children she bears and raises. When her children are grown and gone, she can share the blessing with still another generation—with younger wives and mothers who are coming along behind her, and eventually, perhaps, with grandchildren.

That's the emphasis of Titus 2:3–5, a passage we studied in chapter 19, where Paul addressed older women, those who have been through the process of child-rearing and have many years' experience involving their husbands and keeping a home.

These women have a lifetime of wisdom and experience to share with younger women. One of the church's biggest challenges today is to connect godly older women with younger women who need what they have to offer. This is critical, because we now have a generation of young wives and mothers who have never learned what it means to love their husbands and children and keep a home.

In that earlier chapter, we discussed how Titus 2:4 says that biblical love can be learned, because it is a decision of the will and not simply a product of the emotions. We know love can be learned, because as believers, we are still learning what it means to love God.

I realize that little, if anything, I have said in this chapter will win me a popularity contest. I'm not looking for controversy, but my job is to be biblical, not popular. The Bible's message to women is that they are indispensable to the kingdom of God. They have an agenda to accomplish that no one else can accomplish.

My encouragement to a kingdom woman is: Maximize who you are, because you are an awesome part of God's kingdom!

# THE KINGDOM AGENDA IN YOUR COMMUNITY LIFE

# CHAPTER TWENTY-ONE

# The Kingdom Agenda
# and Justice

You probably have flown on an airplane at some time and know what happens when an airplane touches down on landing. That multiton machine is moving so fast that the only way the pilot can slow it down is to reverse the engine thrust.

There is nothing quite like that roar you hear when those jet engines are reversed. You can also feel the effect on your body as the plane is quickly slowed to a reasonable speed.

Any time you have something with that much weight behind it moving with that much speed, it takes a very powerful force to stop it. If the pilot failed to reverse the engines, in fact, the plane would probably plunge off the far end of the runway and crash.

As I look at our culture today, it reminds me of an airplane coming in for a landing. Our culture is moving in a certain direction at such a fast speed and with such force that unless we are able to throw this thing in reverse and slow it down, we are headed off the end of the runway and into a catastrophe.

It doesn't take a rocket scientist to know that our culture is in trouble. In our cities and even the suburbs, the criminals roam free while the rest of us are held prisoner behind the bars on our doors and windows.

Everyone agrees that something has to happen to get our culture back on track, and everybody has a pet idea of what needs to be done. I say why not let the Creator of culture tell us how to fix it and then how to run it?

Finding out God's agenda for society is the focus of this final portion of the book. We have talked about a kingdom agenda for our personal lives, for the family, and for the church. With each section, we have widened the focus. Now we are ready to widen it once more as we tackle the issue of God's kingdom agenda for our communities and for society at large.

That means we have some more tough topics to consider. This chapter is one of those tough topics, because few issues are more difficult to deal with than the complex issue of social justice. But we need to tackle it, and I want to begin by talking about the very concept of justice itself.

## THE CONCEPT OF JUSTICE

Everybody wants justice, but the question is, Whose definition of justice are we going to accept? The abortion controversy is a good example. On one side, a woman says, "This is my body, and it's unjust to force me to carry a child I don't want." The other side says, "But it's unjust to deprive an unborn child of life simply because you don't want him or her."

We could discuss multiple examples like this, because our society is divided down the middle on a whole range of issues. But we need a framework from which to discuss the subject, so let's begin with a basic, biblical definition of social justice.

### The Definition of Justice

Simply stated, social justice is the rule of God's moral law in society. The only way social justice can become a reality is when God's standard prevails in a society.

This means that in order to be just and right, the laws of men must testify to and reflect the truth of God. When human law differs from God's law, you may have human justice, but you won't have divine justice.

The problem with human justice is that it is flawed justice because human beings are sinful by nature and their standards are ever changing.

However, God's moral law, enshrined in the Ten Commandments, is eternal and unchanging. The entire Bible is built on it. These laws are God's stated will, the way He wants His kingdom and His universe to operate. This is what I mean when I say that human laws must mirror God's law in order for justice to prevail.

The word *justice* means to prescribe the right way, to do things in an appropriate way. Deuteronomy 1:17 is a good expression of the concept. Moses said, "You shall not show partiality in judgment; you shall hear the small and the great alike. You shall not fear man, for the judgment is God's."

Justice has to do with equity in judgment without regard for a person's status. It is equitable application of God's moral law to all people without partiality (see Numbers 15:16).

Throughout Scripture, God has declared that He does not show partiality in His judgments (see Romans 2:11) and is no respecter of persons (see Acts 10:34; Ephesians 6:9). Paul wrote earlier in Romans 2 that when it comes to the judgment, God will "render to every man according to his deeds" (v. 6).

Hebrews 2:2–3 also reminds us that no one will escape God's justice. He is the righteous Judge whom every person must ultimately face (see Romans 12:19).

## The Demonstration of Justice

We live in a society that has been called post-Christian. So how is our society going to know what God's law is and how it is supposed to function?

Let me answer that from Scripture. In Deuteronomy 4:5–6, Moses cautioned the Israelites that when they entered Canaan, they were to obey God's "statutes and judgments" as given to Moses.

By so doing, Israel would be a testimony to the unbelieving nations around them, who would look at Israel and say, "Surely this great nation is a wise and understanding people" (v. 6c).

Then Moses went on to explain why the nations would say this: "For what great nation is there that has a god so near to it as is the Lord our God whenever we call on Him? Or what great nation is there that has statutes and judgments as righteous as this whole law which I am setting before you today?" (Deuteronomy 4:7–8).

Unbelievers will know what true justice looks like when the people of God demonstrate His moral law in society. This is one aspect of our kingdom agenda in relation to the secular culture around us.

## The Standard of Justice

The prophet Habakkuk understood the need for a fixed standard of justice in society. He lived in a day when "destruction and violence are before me; strife exists and contention arises" (Habakkuk 1:3).

What was the problem? "The law is ignored and justice is never upheld. For the wicked surround the righteous; therefore, justice comes out perverted" (v. 4).

Because the people of God had spurned His law, the wicked were in control and were making up their own rules about what is fair, a society is in trouble for the reason I mentioned earlier: We are sinful people by nature, so our laws are going to be flawed.

Therefore, in order to have a just society, we must be able to appeal to a standard of justice and morality that is outside of and higher than human experience, one that does not flutter and fluctuate with every change in the wind of opinion. The only standard that meets this qualification is the Bible, because it is the authoritative, inerrant Word of God.

Now the moment you say this, someone always objects with, "You can't legislate morality."

Let me correct that. Morality, the standard for measuring what is right and wrong, is the only thing you can legislate. Our laws against murder are moral legislation because murder is a moral issue, not just a criminal issue. The law that says a person cannot break into your house and steal what belongs to you is a statement of moral value based on the command, "You shall not steal" (Exodus 20:15).

Don't let anyone give you that nonsense about not legislating morality. The only way you can have an ordered society is to base it on a moral code. And the only One qualified to set such a code is God, because He is the ultimate Lawgiver (see James 4:12).

Only God can decide what is just, because if God doesn't decide, a Hitler or a Stalin might decide. Reject God's standard, and you wind up with chaos in society, because everyone does what is right in his or her own eyes.

Or you wind up with a despot on the throne who says, "This is right because I say so." Whenever a human being comes to believe there is no higher authority to whom he is responsible, we are in trouble.

Biblical justice is not only impartial, it is predictable. That is, the standard doesn't change from person to person. God does not look at a person's skin color, address, or checkbook to determine what kind of justice he or she will receive.

Do you realize that the greatest statement of justice in all the Bible is the doctrine of hell? Hell is an awful place, but its existence is evidence that we live in a universe governed by a just God. Everyone in hell will receive exact and perfect justice for what he or she has done, no more and no less. Hell is necessary because of God's just nature.

Righteousness is the cornerstone of justice (see Deuteronomy 32:3–4; Psalm 89:14). So if you want a just society, there must be a standard to determine what is right and wrong.

God's Word is the standard, so the only way to have a just society is to govern society by a moral law that reflects the moral law and character of the cosmic Lawgiver, God.

This means that the aspects of God's law that reflect His truth and righteousness must be applied today. So we must take seriously the examples of social justice set forth in the Old Testament as illustrations for us today, even though we may differ in the methods of applying justice (such as lethal injection versus stoning).

## THE CONCERN OF JUSTICE

Here's one implication of the fact that biblical social justice, if followed today, would set our criminal justice system on its ear—actually it would set it back upright. The concern of biblical social justice is *always* restitution to the victim of a crime or wrongdoing.

You may need to read the previous sentence again and think about it. God's concern is that the offender repay the victim.

See, we're off the mark here. The foundational idea in American criminal justice is that of paying one's debt to society through the punishment of the offender. But in biblical justice, the idea is to pay one's debt to the victim. When a criminal is simply locked up for twenty years, what he or she did to the victim never really gets addressed.

That is a foreign concept in God's agenda for His kingdom and His universe. The Bible says nothing about incarcerating an offender for a certain period of time, then releasing him to go free. God had three ways of dealing with crime in the Bible: capital punishment (or restitution), corporal punishment, and economic punishment.

## Capital Restitution

Capital restitution, or capital punishment, answers the objection that is often raised against a biblically based justice system that does not include prison.

The objection is this: If you don't have prisons, how do you protect society from truly dangerous criminals such as murderers, rapists, and kidnappers?

The answer from Scripture is that if anyone committed a heinous crime such as murder, that person suffered the death penalty. There was no provision for simply locking up a person for life just to keep him or her off the streets.

In the Bible, death was the nonnegotiable sentence for willful, deliberate murder. Why? Because in a murder, there is no restitution the offender can make to his human victim. Thus, God exacts restitution on behalf of the victim, because mankind is created in God's image (see Genesis 9:6).

When a murder occurs, then, God becomes the ultimate "victim" who must be repaid, because the human victim was the bearer of God's image. Human life is therefore so valuable and so precious to God that the only way a criminal can pay for the crime is to forfeit his or her own life.

This is not a legal treatise, so I can't cover every nuance of every issue. Let me just say that the Bible makes a clear distinction between accidental death, or manslaughter, and premeditated murder. Our legal system does the same, which shows how much of our Western system of justice is based on Scripture.

Let me hasten to add that the death penalty has to be applied justly, that is, without respect of persons. The unjust application of the death penalty means that those who knowingly helped to pervert justice must suffer the same penalty themselves (see Deuteronomy 19:15–21).

In other capital crimes such as rape and kidnapping, in which the human victim remains alive, the maximum penalty is death. But the victim has the option of commuting the sentence in favor of another form of restitution, as we shall see below.

## Corporal Restitution

A second form of biblical restitution or punishment is what I call corporal punishment, or physical pain. Many people would rather go to jail than suffer physical pain for their crimes.

Actually, corporal punishment includes capital punishment, which is the ultimate form of physical restitution. But in this case I want to focus on the lesser forms of physical punishment, those that stop well short of the death penalty.

This area brings us to the *lex talionis*, the so-called law of retaliation. It is stated in Exodus 21:22–25:

> *If men struggle with each other and strike a woman with child so that she has a miscarriage, yet there is no further injury, he shall surely be fined as the woman's husband may demand of him; and he shall pay as the judges decide. But if there is any further injury, then you shall appoint as a penalty life for life, eye for eye, tooth for tooth, hand for hand, foot for foot, burn for burn, wound for wound, bruise for bruise.*

This principle has been so badly misquoted, misunderstood, and misapplied that we need to step back and take a look at what it actually teaches.

There's no denying that this law does indeed talk about a person suffering physical loss as restitution for causing another person's physical loss. But this has a deterrent value. If a criminal knew he was going to suffer a physical loss for injuring someone else, he might think twice about committing a crime.

But if he knows that the worst he will get is a place to sleep, free medical care, and three meals a day, then what he does to his victim doesn't really matter that much.

People say the law of retaliation was brutal and vengeful and has no place in a civil society. But that is a false conclusion. The reason is that the law of retaliation actually limited vengeance. In other words, God was saying that if a person knocks out your tooth, you cannot go after his eye. If a person puts out your eye, you cannot take his life.

The law of retribution limited the punishment to the extent of the infraction. It spelled out the maximum penalty the court could impose for a specific crime. Because of our sinful nature, our tendency is to return two blows for every one we receive. The law prohibited that kind of revenge. This was neither brutality nor vengeance, but exacting justice.

Let me show you how the Bible prevented brutality in the application of the law of retaliation:

*If an ox gores a man or a woman to death, the ox shall surely be stoned and its flesh shall not be eaten; but the owner of the ox shall go unpunished. If, however, an ox was previously in the habit of goring, and its owner has been warned, yet he does not confine it, and it kills a man or a woman, the ox shall be stoned and its owner also shall be put to death. If a ransom is demanded of him, then he shall give for the redemption of his life whatever is demanded of him. (Exodus 21:28–30)*

The owner of the ox was under a potential death penalty for allowing his ox to get out and kill someone. However, since the ox and not the owner actually killed the person, this was not premeditated murder in the sense described above. So the death penalty did not automatically apply. Provision was made for a lesser penalty (see v. 30). The ox's owner could work out a financial compensation with the family of the person who was killed.

The principle I want you to see is that the law of retaliation recognized extenuating circumstances and allowed for the parties involved to negotiate less than the maximum penalty prescribed. But there had to be some form of restitution to the victim or his family, not to some vague entity called "society."

## Economic Restitution

Economic restitution is the third form of repayment that biblical justice makes provision for, not only in civil but in criminal cases as well.

This makes so much sense when you read it that you wonder why it isn't part of the criminal justice system today. Yet this is a foreign concept to our society. Putting economic justice into effect would be one way to reverse the engines of culture we talked about at the beginning and get this problem turned around.

Economic restitution is described in Exodus 22. "If a man steals an ox or a sheep, . . . he shall pay five oxen for the ox and four sheep for the sheep" (v. 1). Verse 3 prescribes the punishment for the thief who cannot reimburse his victim: "If he owns nothing, then he shall be sold for his theft."

In Exodus 23:3, the law specified that a person could not use his economic status to pervert justice: "Nor shall you be partial to a poor man in his dispute." A person could not say, "Because I am poor, you cannot hold me responsible." Remember, God is not a respecter of persons on either side of the economic equation. His agenda is justice all across the board.

## A Modern Application

Now, in case you think this is something that worked in Bible days but couldn't work now, let me show you how the application of biblical economic justice could solve one of the stickiest economic and social justice problems in our society. I'm talking about the controversy over affirmative action.

The lines in this case are pretty clearly drawn. Those on one side of the political spectrum say we still need affirmative action. They argue that since people have been held back, we should give them special opportunities. As President Lyndon Johnson once said, you can't win a race when you have been hampered from the starting line.

On the other side, people argue that this system has to end somewhere. They say that the original purpose of affirmative action has been served, that enough has been done to compensate those who were unfairly disadvantaged, that parity has been achieved.

Christians are divided down the middle on this one. But for us the issue is not what the politicians or social activists say. The issue is, what does God say? Let's unravel this controversy and look at it step-by-step.

God has said if people have been mistreated, restitution must be made to the victims that is both just and predictable—that is, it has predefined boundaries and limitations. As we saw above, the thief who stole a sheep paid back four sheep. When that was done, the case was closed.

Therefore, no person or group of people can say, "Recompense me forever, world without end." There is no predictability in that. In biblical justice, the person or people who committed the wrong acknowledge that what they did was wrong, that it was sin, and that restitution needs to be made.

Then, once a fair compensation has been agreed on, the compensation is paid and the case should be closed.

In Leviticus 6:1–7, the Bible makes it clear that once the specified restitution has been made for a wrong committed, guilt is removed and the offended party can no longer say, "Keep paying me; it's not enough; I want more quotas," etc.

How does all this apply to a modern economic and social justice issue like affirmative action? Let me draw some conclusions.

Affirmative action is fair in that it recognizes that an evil that was perpetrated against a group of people has had ongoing negative consequences. The problem now is that since no fixed standards of compensation were ever established, no one knows when the debt has been fully paid. All we have is the two sides arguing and disagreeing about it.

Without fixed standards, there can be no biblical justice. So our society is torn apart on this issue because we do not operate according to biblical standards. We have abandoned God's moral law, so every man does what is right in his own eyes (see Judges 21:25).

How then do we now address the issue of affirmative action? Since the direct victims of slavery are no longer alive, personal restitution is not possible. However, since the effects of slavery are still with us, some action is appropriate.

The federal government should establish a fixed restitution goal to be collectively applied to the African-American community as a group (not individual restitution) for past injustices. When this goal is met, then affirmative action should be formally discontinued. There should also be a fixed standard of restitution established to fairly compensate any future victims of racism as well as the provision of incentives for those organizations and institutions that practice and promote empowerment and diversity (e.g., enterprise zones).

Given these fruits of repentance, the black community should extend forgiveness to the nation and then move on.

Unless an option like this is taken, the debate will never end. If biblical restitution had been part of the Great Society's plan, we would not be experiencing the chaos we are experiencing over such issues.

## THE COMPASSION OF JUSTICE

We have already seen that compassion was built into biblical social justice, even though the primary emphasis was on restitution to the victim. The ox owner whose animal killed someone could appeal for mercy to the victim's family and offer restitution instead of paying with his life.

### The Appeal for Mercy

Our system also recognizes that justice needs to be tempered with mercy. But there is an important difference between our system and the biblical system.

You have heard the familiar phrase, "I throw myself on the mercy of the court." That is the plea of a convicted person as he appeals to the state for mercy. This is in keeping with the American idea that a crime is committed against the "people" or the state, not just against an individual victim.

The difference is that in the Bible the criminal appealed for mercy, not to a big, impersonal system, but to his victim. There were appointed officials to manage the system, to see that justice and restitution were carried out properly. But the real confrontation was between the criminal and the victim.

The cross of Jesus Christ is the greatest example of an appeal for mercy, although in this case it was the victim, not the criminal, who asked for mercy. Jesus asked His Father to forgive the people who were nailing Him to the cross (see Luke 23:34).

Jesus was praying that these men might not get what they deserved. That is the definition of mercy. By the way, we can all be glad that God's justice allows for mercy. If He gave all of us justice, if we got what we so rightly deserve, none of us would be here. We would all be condemned in hell.

But God has shown us mercy in not giving us what we deserve. And He has gone much further than that by giving us grace, which is getting what we do not deserve—forgiveness and eternal life!

## An Example of Mercy

Matthew 18:21–35 is also a great example of the compassion of justice. Notice Peter's question, which triggered the story Jesus told of forgiveness and the extension of mercy:

> "Lord, how often shall my brother sin against me and I forgive him? Up to seven times?" Jesus said to him, "I do not say to you, up to seven times, but up to seventy times seven." (Matthew 18:21–22)

Then Jesus proceeded to tell the familiar story of two slaves who owed other people money.

The first slave owed his king a small fortune. The king demanded payment and threatened to have the slave and his family sold to repay the debt. The slave threw himself down before the king and begged for more time. The king did better than that. He "felt compassion and released him and forgave him the debt" (Matthew 18:27).

So that slave received mercy instead of justice. But then he went out and found a fellow slave who owed him some pocket change in comparison to what the first slave had owed the king. The forgiven slave demanded payment, and the other slave also fell down on his face and begged for mercy.

But the first slave refused to show compassion and had the other guy tossed into prison. Word of this slave's cruelty got back to the king, who promptly rescinded his grant of mercy and handed the unmerciful slave over to "the torturers" (Matthew 18:28–34).

Then Jesus stated the principle He was teaching: "So shall My heavenly Father also do to you, if each of you does not forgive his brother from your heart" (v. 35). That is, if you ever need mercy, God is going to look at how much mercy you have granted to others.

## Justice and Mercy

So if you are one of these hard hearts who can never forgive anybody, and one day you are in a mess that you need God to get you out of, God is going to say, "I am checking the books here, and I noticed that when your brother needed mercy, you gave him the maximum penalty. I have no basis for giving you mercy."

So while God demands justice, He also encourages mercy. That is what Jesus extended on the cross to those who were crucifying Him, and that's what God has extended to us.

One person who understood this was Joseph, the husband of Mary. When Joseph found out that Mary was pregnant, and before he knew who this baby was, he could have thrown the book at Mary. He could have sought to have her stoned as an adulteress.

But the Bible says that Joseph was a "righteous man" who did not want to disgrace Mary. So he sought to "put her away secretly" and not take her to court (see Matthew 1:18–19). In other words, Joseph granted mercy to Mary. He could have called for the maximum penalty, but he chose not to. Compassion was part of biblical justice.

## THE COMMUNICATION OF JUSTICE

Here is the final point I want to make about social justice in its relation to a kingdom agenda. Part of God's agenda for us is to make known the means by which His justice can be obtained.

Jesus did this in Luke 4 when He came back to His hometown of Nazareth. He went into the synagogue one Sabbath and read from the scroll of Isaiah:

> The spirit of the Lord is upon Me, because He anointed Me to preach the gospel to the poor. He has sent Me to proclaim release to the captives, and recovery of sight to the blind, to set free those who are downtrodden, to proclaim the favorable year of the Lord. (Luke 4:18–19)

Jesus said He came to proclaim liberty and freedom, to announce God's justice being satisfied through what He called "the favorable year of the Lord."

This was the Old Testament Year of Jubilee, a special year observed every fifty years in which God set society back in order. During Jubilee, slaves were released, debts were canceled, and land that had been sold reverted back to its original owner. Imagine what this did to achieve justice and restore justice to Israeli society.

## Atonement Before Justice

But there's something else here I want you to see. According to Leviticus 25:8–9, Israel could not have Jubilee until the people first observed the Day of Atonement. In other words, they could not have true justice on the human level until they got right with God on the vertical level. As long as people were not right with God, they could not enjoy the good news of Jubilee.

Do you see how it all comes together? We're right back where we started this chapter. You cannot have social justice until the people in a society get right with God. Everybody wants a better society, but nobody wants to bow before God and His moral code. But you can't have one without the other.

So our society is wasting its time seeking justice without God, because things will continue to deteriorate in proportion to the rate at which God is dismissed from the culture.

The Bible is absolutely clear that when a society marginalizes God, then God allows and even causes that society to experience revolution. It begins to self-destruct (see 2 Chronicles 15:3–6; Psalm 9:17; Romans 1:18–32).

According to 1 Timothy 1:9–19, law is needed to hold the unrighteous in check. But if those laws are not righteous laws, if they are not based on a fixed moral code, they cannot hold evil people in check.

As long as the best idea we can come up with for dealing with crime is to warehouse criminals in prison, we won't get anywhere. Why? Because we will never be able to tax the public enough to build enough warehouses. And even when we build them, they are ineffective in solving the problem because the people in them simply learn how to be better criminals.

But if a murderer knew ahead of time he would automatically and quickly forfeit his life, if a rapist knew he would face castration, if a thief knew he would have to repay his victim four- or fivefold the amount he stole, things would be different.

So how do we reverse the engines of our culture and slow this thing down before we crash off the end of the runway? Here are some kingdom agenda ideas in each of our four categories.

## Personal Justice

In Micah 6:8, the prophet asked, "What does the Lord require of you but to do justice, to love kindness, and to walk humbly with your God?"

That's a great statement of your personal responsibility and mine when it comes to justice in society. We are to uphold the divine standard, to act justly. For example, whenever you reject a person based on the color of his or her skin, you have become a respecter of persons and have acted unjustly. We'll talk more about this in a future chapter.

## Family Justice

When it comes to the family, I would refer you back to a verse we have already looked at several times, Genesis 18:19.

This was God's command to Abraham to raise his family in such a way that his descendants practiced justice. Children must learn early that sin bears consequences.

This is why you are to spank your children when they need it. You spank them now in your home so the police won't have to spank them later down at the jail.

God tells parents to raise their children so that they know there is a divine standard to which they are answerable. They need to understand that even if God lets them off now, He won't let them off in eternity.

## Church Justice

James 2:1–9 is the classic statement of social justice in the church. The apostle laid down the principle in verse 1: "My brethren, do not hold your faith in our glorious Lord Jesus Christ with an attitude of personal favoritism."

James then described a scenario where a rich man came into the assembly dressed in gold and expensive clothes, and the ushers fell all over themselves giving him the best seat in the house. Then a poor man in rags came in the back door, and the ushers made him stand against the back wall or sit on the floor.

James said this is the worst form of classism and has no place in the church. It doesn't matter which side of town you live on when you come into the family of God. James said favoritism is evil (see v. 4). It's a form of injustice. And there ought to be no injustice in the church.

This means that members of the church who practice any form of discrimination must be lovingly confronted and, if they remain unrepentant, publicly condemned.

Another illustration of what the church can do was demonstrated when one of our young men stole $1,500 from his employer. After being apprehended, he was sentenced to three years in prison. We shared with the judge the biblical principle of restitution. We explained how this young man would cost the taxpayer more than $18,000 annually for a $1,500 crime, which would not pay back the victim and only place this young man in an environment where he would simply learn how to become a better criminal.

We challenged the judge to turn the young man over to our church. We would get him a job, garnish his wages, and pay back his employer with interest. We would also give him a responsible male mentor to hold him accountable, rebuild this young man's value system, and show the judge a brand-new kid in six months.

The judge consented. We did all we promised and brought back a brand-new young man. The judge asked if we would take twenty more! Today the young man is a dynamic part of our church with a family of his own.

This is one example of how the church can promote social justice, using biblical principles. Of equal importance is that the courts recognized and respected the church's system of justice.

## State Justice

Finally, how does a kingdom agenda of social justice work itself out in society? Psalm 72 says:

> *Give the king Thy judgments, O God, and Thy righteousness to the king's son. May he judge Thy people with righteousness, and Thine afflicted with justice. . . . May he vindicate the afflicted of the people, save the children of the needy, and crush the oppressor. (vv. 1–2, 4)*

The job of government is to function as an instrument of God's justice. But once government no longer sees itself as God's agent under His authority, it becomes its own humanistic institution. Then whatever the majority thinks guides the decisions, or else decisions are made by those who have the most power. In either case, the result cannot be a just society.

That is why we need Christians running for government office. I'm not just talking about people who are saved and on their way to heaven but people who have developed a theistic worldview, a God-centered orientation they bring to every area of public life.

We also need committed young Christians in fields such as law; we need honest people who hold to God's standard of truth and justice and will do things God's way, not necessarily the American way.

We need people in places of influence who can bring divine justice to bear on this society. When unrighteous people rule, there is no moral law. When there is no moral law, there is no presence of God. And when there is no presence of God, there is chaos in society.

When Anthony Jr. was small, I bought him one of those punching bags that was anchored at the bottom with a heavy weight. You may remember those from your childhood. No matter how hard a kid punches it, the thing pops right back up.

God's moral law is the weight, the anchor, of the culture. Satan is trying to knock our culture over and out. But as long as the weight is there, culture can come back up. As long as Christians are manning their posts based on God's standard, we can get this culture back on its feet. When the righteous are nowhere to be found, however, the punching bag will stay down.

That is why fulfilling our kingdom agenda as Christians has to do with more than just being in church. It has to do with how we as Christians perform on the job, the standard we uphold in the marketplace. It has to do with our influence at the local PTA, the stand we take at the city council meeting, the letters we write to our representatives, our participation on boards, committees, and many other ways of leveraging our influence. Being a kingdom Christian means bringing the presence, precepts, and power of God to bear on society, pulling society back into an upright position.

# CHAPTER TWENTY-TWO

# The Kingdom Agenda
# and Economics

You may have heard the story of the man who stole some money but was captured by the authorities. He didn't have the money with him, so they asked him where he hid it.

But it turned out the man spoke another language, so they had to send for an interpreter. When the interpreter came, the authorities said, "Ask him where he hid the money."

So the interpreter asked the thief the question in his own language, and the thief replied. "What did he say?" the authorities wanted to know.

"He said he's not telling."

The authorities insisted. "Tell him we want to know where the money is, and we want to know *now*."

The interpreter repeated the question to the thief and got the same answer. "He says he isn't going to tell you."

The head of the authorities thought he would try to scare the thief into telling, so he said to the interpreter, "Tell him that if he doesn't tell us where the money is, we are going to blow his brains out!"

The interpreter repeated the threat to the thief, who got scared and told the interpreter step-by-step exactly where he could find the money.

The authorities listened to the conversation and then asked the interpreter, "Well, what did he say?"

"He said he isn't going to tell you anything," the interpreter then answered.

When it comes to the issue of money, I'm afraid our interpretations—and our motives—sometimes get mixed up. But money is part of God's kingdom agenda for us, and you knew we would not be able to talk about the business of the kingdom without dealing with the economics of the kingdom.

In fact, I hope you are getting the message by now that nothing sits outside the scope of God's kingdom. Economic issues are just as much a part of our kingdom work as anything else we could name. Let's see what it means to operate economically on a kingdom agenda.

## THE FOUNDATION
## OF KINGDOM ECONOMICS

The foundation of an economic view grows out of God's kingdom agenda for His people and His world. This foundation reveals how God empowers His people for the righteous use of the earth's resources for profitably (and morally) conducting business as His stewards.

### A Matter of Ownership

Let me start laying that foundation with a critical text on the subject of economics and wealth.

In Deuteronomy 8, Moses was addressing the Israelites on the eve of their entrance into Canaan. He recounted God's goodness to them all the way from their departure from Egypt to the present moment, which was almost forty years later, and he warned them not to forget who provided for them.

Beginning in Deuteronomy 8:11, we discover the reason for Moses' concern. He feared that once the people got settled in Canaan and started living the "good life" in the burbs, they would get proud. Then they would forget that they used to be slaves and that the only reason they weren't slaves now was that God gave them everything they had (see vv. 11–14).

Then Moses brought the message home and laid down an absolutely foundational principle of divine economics. The Israelites needed to keep their economics in focus because,

*Otherwise, you may say in your heart, "My power and the strength*
*of my hand made me this wealth." But you shall remember the*
*Lord your God, for it is He who is giving you power to make wealth,*
*that He may confirm His covenant which He swore to your fathers,*
*as it is this day. (vv. 17–18)*

The principle is simply this: Any discussion of economics that does not include God is a travesty, because He is the Author of all wealth. God owns it all. As the psalmist said, "The earth is the Lord's, and all it contains, the world, and those who dwell in it" (Psalm 24:1). Communism teaches that the government owns everything. Capitalism teaches that the individual owns everything. Christianity teaches that God owns everything.

God puts it on the line in Psalm 50:10, 12 as well: "Every beast of the forest is Mine, the cattle on a thousand hills. . . . If I were hungry, I would not tell you; for the world is Mine, and all it contains." And Haggai 2:8 reminds us, "'The silver is Mine, and the gold is Mine,'" declares the Lord of hosts."

All of this means that economics is a spiritual issue. It cannot be called secular when the owner of everything is God. Like the Israelites, everything we have is rooted in the goodness of God. We cannot discuss economics on any level, from personal to national, without putting God's perspective first.

Since God is the starting and ending point of all economic discussion, we need to find out what is on His kingdom agenda for the resources He has entrusted to us.

## The Purpose of Wealth

Let's start revealing that agenda with a pretty basic question: What is God's purpose for wealth?

The answer is found at the very end of Deuteronomy 8:18, quoted above. Moses said it was God who was giving the Israelites the power to gain wealth, "that He may confirm His covenant which He swore to your fathers, as it is this day."

God gives wealth that it might be used to fulfill His divine purposes, in this case His covenant with Israel. God made a covenant with Abraham, that through Abraham "all the families of the earth shall be blessed" (Genesis 12:3).

Therefore, the only legitimate use of wealth is when it is used to be a blessing to somebody else. Jesus Himself said, "It is more blessed to give than to receive" (Acts 20:35).

God uses wealth as a channel through which His benefits will flow to others. Therefore, if all you can see is your car and your house and your wardrobe . . . if you cannot point to the ways God's blessings in your life are flowing out in blessings to others, then God has no reason to give you wealth.

And if God has no reason to give you wealth, then the only way you can get it is apart from Him. But if you get it apart from Him, you will pay a heavy price for going after it. God gives His economic blessings to accomplish His purposes.

## Setting the Rules

Since God owns all the wealth of the world and has a clear purpose for it, He gets to set the rules of who will get it and how it will be used.

First Samuel 2:7–8 makes it very clear that it is God who makes people rich or poor, in essence saying, "I set the rules. If you follow My rules, you get My results. If you follow your rules, you get your results."

God told His people Israel in Deuteronomy 28:12 that if they would obey His rules, He would make them a lender nation instead of a debtor nation. When you use wealth God's way, it eliminates rather than accumulates debt.

Now don't misunderstand. I am not talking about a "name it, claim it" theology here. Bringing all of your bills in a wheelbarrow to somebody's meeting so he can pray over them is not what this is about. You can't manipulate God into making you rich. Having said that, however, it is important to understand that God is not against wealth. If God chooses to materially bless an individual, family, church, or nation that is operating on a kingdom agenda, there need be no feelings of false guilt for what God has given.

God is more concerned with how you got what you have and how you use what you have than He is with how much you have. Now if the wealth you have is gained illegitimately, you have reason to feel guilty. But if not, then God does not heap guilt on you. He can trust some of His children with millions.

## Subverting God's Rules

But whenever God sets down the rules, we as sinful people have a way of subverting those rules and setting up our own. And we lose big-time when we do this.

Our first parents found that out the hard way. Adam and Eve challenged God's ownership in the garden of Eden and made up their own rules. They decided they were going to operate independently of God's economy. But they wound up with less—far less—rather than more.

Ever since then, individuals have been cursed financially because they refuse to do things God's way. Many families are in financial disarray because they are not operating on God's economic agenda. Many churches have to resort to unbiblical means to accumulate money because they are not doing it God's way. And Lord have mercy on a government and society that is several trillions of dollars in debt.

It's amazing what people will do to shift the blame and point the finger anywhere but at their own sins. This is what's behind the false claim that the earth is overpopulated and we need to have fewer children.

I'm told that all five billion people on earth could stand within the city limits of Jacksonville, Florida, with each person having 2.6 square feet of space to stand in. Overpopulation as a reason for our economic troubles is a lie. We do not have a population problem; we have a sin problem.

The problem is also not a lack of resources on the earth. God has packed this earth with raw materials and resources beyond our wildest imagination. Mankind was designed to cultivate and develop this wealth under God's direction and blessing, because Adam was given dominion over the earth. The failure to do this is because of sin, not because the earth is tapped out.

Economics is a matter of sin and righteousness. It is a spiritual issue. But because people think our problems are merely economic, they don't see the solutions to our problems that God is addressing in His Word.

The foundation of economics is theological. If we would return to God on a personal, family, church, and national level, we would witness the kind of proper economic development our communities need so badly. But people have established their own rules, and we are all paying a high price for this disobedience.

## THE HINDRANCES
## TO KINGDOM ECONOMICS

If God is the foundation of a kingdom economic agenda, what are the hindrances that are keeping this agenda from being realized? Why can't we see kingdom-based economic development in our communities? There are a number of reasons.

## Greed

One hindrance to the development of kingdom economics is the attitude of greed. Greed is the desire to have money and material things for their own sake. A person is greedy when what he or she wants is not tied to a legitimate purpose.

So is it greedy to want a better job or a nicer car? Not necessarily. It depends on the motive that is driving the desire for these things. There is nothing wrong with wanting to better yourself if it is done legitimately.

One question that always comes up here is whether Christians should play the lottery. Well, let's say the lottery jackpot one week is ten million dollars. You are wondering whether you should try for it. I would ask you, Is there an agenda that God has set before you that requires you to win ten million dollars?

I suspect the answer would be no. You want the ten million because it's a lot of money, and you would be set for life. What I'm saying is that playing the lottery is not tied to any legitimate goal. Winning the money is an end in itself, and that is evil.

It is equally evil for a government to prey on the greed of its citizens by attempting to derive through gaming the productivity of its citizens or what it could not legitimately expect its citizens to pay in fees and taxes.

The Bible makes it clear that you and I are not to be involved in any scheme in which we try to get rich quick and bypass the process of productive work. Instead of praying that we win the lottery, here's what we should be asking God for:

> Keep deception and lies far from me, give me neither poverty nor riches; feed
> me with the food that is my portion, lest I be full and deny Thee and say,
> "Who is the Lord?" Or lest I be in want and steal, and profane the name
> of my God. (Proverbs 30:8–9)

I call this a "middle-class prayer." The writer asked for neither riches nor poverty, but for his portion. Having too much and having too little can both lead to greed.

## Envy

Envy is another sinful attitude that hinders kingdom economic development.

Envy goes on a step further than jealousy. Jealousy says, "I am upset because you have something that I don't have." Envy says, "Not only am I upset about what you have, but since I don't have it, I will either make sure you don't have it or at least you will not enjoy it."

Envy sets in motion a whole string of events that try to deny people the legitimate ownership of what they have, and it creates all manner of accompanying sin. Envy is clearly an illegitimate passion in the Bible. Paul said that the wicked are marked by envy (see Romans 1:29), among other things, and he added that envy must not characterize the people of God (see Romans 13:13).

Envy is actually a theological problem because it stems from a false view of God. When we are envious, we are saying that God is either not sovereign or not good because in our view He failed to give us what we think we ought to have. Therefore, we are envious if someone else has it. The root of envy is a faulty, weak view of God.

## Laziness

The Bible recognizes that some people are poor because they are lazy (see Proverbs 10:4, 5; 12:24; 13:4, 11). It is clear that if people wish to prosper they must be willing to work hard, and if they are unwilling to work, they should not eat (see 2 Thessalonians 3:10). Lazy people are present—rather than future—oriented and must begin taking responsibility for themselves and their families. When the lazy poor can receive handouts that require little or no productivity on their part, then we aid and abet their economic deterioration, as well as our own.

## Exhortation and Corruption

There are unrighteous attitudes that hinder kingdom economics, and there are also unrighteous practices.

Nehemiah 5 records a case of extortion among the Jews who came back under this great leader. The people cried out to Nehemiah for relief because they were being mistreated economically.

Some of the people were just plain poor (see Nehemiah 5:2).

Others were losing ownership of their property because they had to mortgage it to buy food (see v. 3). Still others were having to borrow money to pay their taxes (see v. 4). Worst of all, some of God's people were being sold into slavery to pay their bills (see v. 5), which meant they could leave no legacy to their children.

When Nehemiah heard all of this, he got very angry because he discovered that "the nobles and the rulers" (v. 7) were extorting money from their fellow Jews. Those in power were ripping off the people. They were charging the people heavy interest rates to borrow the money they needed to live.

In other words, systems were in place to make sure all of the money went to those at the top. None of it was filtering down. People could borrow money, but they had to sell their children into slavery to do it. This was systemic economic injustice, which is evil at its core because God curses ungodly structures (see Proverbs 13:23) and because it robs people of the fruit of their labor. Such injustice must be challenged precisely as Nehemiah challenged it.

Notice what he did. He called for a march (v. 7, "great assembly"), addressed the spiritual issues involved (see vv. 8–9), and set up a system of restitution (see vv. 10–13). The result was the restoration of justice and a renewed opportunity for people to benefit from their labor. In addition, a mountain of debt was removed in one day.

God hates unjust systems and practices. He made His attitude clear in James 5:1–6, which speaks to the unjust employer who withheld his workers' wages because he was interested only in his own profits.

Economic injustice can also be built into a governmental system, such as communism, which prevents people from reaping the maximum fruit of their labor. Communism establishes a hierarchy in which the leaders, like a Big Brother, tell the people they will work for the state and only get from their work what the government decides they will get.

This is one reason that communist regimes ultimately cannot stand. Once people wake up to the fact that they are being systematically ripped off, they demand more. Of course, the bigger reason these regimes fall is that they deny God's existence and try to rule Him out of life. The underlying problem with communism is a theological problem. Even capitalism, when it permits monopolies to be built with unjust wages and labor laws, reflects another form of economic injustice.

## Unjust Taxation

I am going out on a limb here, but I believe that another hindrance to God's economic agenda occurs when a government overtaxes its people. We are talking about democratic governments here too.

Whenever the government taxes you more than 10 percent of your income, it commits a systemic evil. When Israel first demanded a king, Samuel warned the people that if they got a king he would take the best of their produce for his court and impose heavy taxes on them (see 1 Samuel 8:10–18). High taxation, then, is an indication of divine judgment.

Samuel was saying that the king would demand more of the people than they were obligated to give to God Himself. God required 10 percent, the tithe, as the basic financial obligation for His people.

The king would demand more than that, Samuel told the Israelites. He was saying that no government should demand more from its people than the person who owns it all, who is God.

There should be only one tax in America, a consumption or sales tax of not more than 10 percent. All business transactions should be taxed, which would bring the government more than three trillion dollars annually. This is far more than is required to operate all levels of government and would render the wasteful bureaucracy of the International Revenue Service unnecessary.

It is also unthinkable for the government to steal a family's wealth through an inheritance tax or to tax its citizens for property they own.

So whenever a government, even a democratic government, taxes its people more than 10 percent of their income, it is committing an injustice. We are under that evil, but it is also partly our fault. We have asked the government to do things that government was never meant to do, and the government is charging us for those services at a much higher rate than would be necessary if we were properly decentralized.

Because Christians have robbed God of His tithe, we are paying much more than that amount (up to 40 percent) in unjust taxation as God's judgment on our spiritual theft.

Once we ask the government to take over things like charity, medical care, and education, government is going to tax us excessively to pay for all of those systems. And when government begins performing illegitimate functions, it becomes spiritually bankrupt—because, remember, economics is a spiritual issue.

The existence of government-sponsored lotteries is an example of how spiritually bankrupt government can become. Many of our state governments have come to the conclusion that they cannot be productive enough through legitimate efforts to raise the money they need to operate. So they lay an unofficial tax on their people by setting up a lottery in which luck is substituted for productive work.

So the people, primarily poor people who can't afford it, are enticed to try to luck their way into riches while the state gathers in illegitimate income.

Of course, the reality is a person has a better chance of finding oil in his backyard than of winning the lottery. People would be better off digging for oil! Unjust taxation stems from an unbiblical view of life. It's another form of theft. I am not an accountant or an economist, but I know who owns it all.

## THE PROCESS OF ECONOMIC DEVELOPMENT

We're ready now to talk about the process that brings about the realization of a kingdom economic agenda.

Proverbs 13:22 says, "The wealth of the sinner is stored up for the righteous." We need to understand that although wicked people have all this stuff while the righteous may have little, God has a way of transferring the resources of the wicked to their legitimate owners, the righteous, to be used and developed for kingdom purposes. What the righteous need to do is start acting righteously.

Now this is a heavy concept, so I want to develop it. Let's first understand the theology behind this concept.

### Understanding the Theology

Let me begin by giving you several illustrations of this Proverbs 13:22 principle.

The Egyptians held the children of Israel in slavery. The Israelites had nothing, but they finally made contact with God. He afflicted Egyptian society with so many plagues that Pharaoh agreed to let the people go.

God had told the Israelites that when the time came to leave, they were to ask their Egyptian neighbors for silver and gold (see Exodus 11:1–2). The Israelites did as they were told, and the Egyptians were only too glad to give God's people anything they asked. "Thus they plundered the Egyptians" (Exodus 12:36). So the Israelites left Egypt with millions of dollars' worth of Egyptian gold and silver.

God then told the Israelites to take some of that wealth and build Him a tabernacle where they could worship Him. And God was not finished yet. He had a land for the Israelites to possess, a good land "flowing with milk and honey" (Exodus 3:17).

The only problem was that the unrighteous lived in Canaan. But guess what God did? He told the unrighteous, "Build some nice houses over here, develop the neighborhoods, and cultivate the fields for My people, because they are coming." And when Israel arrived, God took care of the unrighteous. He told Israel to take the land of Canaan and do His kingdom business with it (see Psalm 105:43–45).

That was a theological transaction. It was the same with Nehemiah when he heard in Persia that the walls of Jerusalem were broken down and the city of God was in disgrace.

The first place Nehemiah went was to God in prayer (see Nehemiah 1:11). Then he approached Artaxerxes, the ungodly king he served. Nehemiah told the king that God was leading him to go back to rebuild the city of his fathers (see 2:1–10). Artaxerxes not only gave Nehemiah permission to go, but the king gave Nehemiah everything he asked for and then some.

So God moved a pagan government to support His kingdom man doing His kingdom business. Artaxerxes had so much confidence in Nehemiah's ability that the king saw even this far-off building project as an asset to his kingdom. So God transferred the wealth of the un-righteous to the righteous. Again, this was a theological deal because God's man understood how God operates—namely, that everything belongs to Him so that He will even take from pagans to give to us if we are conducting kingdom business.

## Leveraging the Influence

Once we understand the theology of the kingdom economic process, we need to leverage our kingdom influence.

Allow me to give you an example from the experience of our church in Dallas. When we were ready to build our church's Family Life Center, we went to the bank we dealt with for the financing, but the bank denied our application.

I said to the banker, "I don't understand. How can you deny us when we have been depositing in your bank all these years?"

The answer was, "We don't want to take the risk."

What the banker was telling me was that he didn't want to loan us a portion of the bank's resources so we could do kingdom business. I was sitting there dumbfounded when I think the Holy Spirit must have given me a thought. So I took a risk myself.

"I see," I said to the banker. "Then what I need to do is go back to the church and ask how many of our people are doing business with your bank.

"Then I will have to tell everyone who has deposits in your bank that you don't think our church is worth the risk so we can do God's kingdom business on our property. Then I will ask all of those families and individuals to withdraw their money from your bank and move it to your competitor."

I didn't even know if that would work, but the bankers went back, held another meeting, and came out with another decision. It was a matter of influence, because when you understand the theology of kingdom economics, you can leverage the influence of kingdom economics.

## Building for Today

Here is another important item on the agenda of kingdom economic development. We need to prepare for life, because we might be here for a while.

There's a great example of this in Jeremiah 29:4–7. The Jews were now exiles in Babylon. A false prophet had come and told the people that they would be out of there and back home within two years (see Jeremiah 28:11). So they didn't need to worry about any economic issues.

But God had a different message. He told Jeremiah to tell the people, "Build houses and live in them; and plant gardens, and eat their produce" (29:5). In other words, start economic development, because you are going to be here a long time. Don't sit back and depend on government charity to take care of you when you retire.

Building houses and planting vineyards suggests ownership, a key element of a kingdom economic strategy. And ownership always requires some sort of investment.

## Investing for Tomorrow

Do you know why so many of us kingdom people are in debt up

to our ears? Because the culture has taught us to spend, while God teaches us to invest.

In Luke 19:11–27, Jesus told a classic parable of the need to invest for the future. The master in the parable gave each of his slaves a different amount of money and told them to invest it so that he would have a profit when he returned.

Now most of us would have spent the money we got if that happened to us. It would have been gone, because we do not understand that God does not give us money just to spend but to invest.

Before commercial seed became widely available, a farmer who ate all of his crops would not have any crops the next year. He always left some seeds to put back into the ground so he would have new crops the next year. You and I must invest if we are going to be a kingdom-oriented people.

There is no such thing, by the way, as equality of opportunity, so you can forget that. We are all born with different talents in different situations that offer different levels of opportunity. But there is such a thing as maximizing what God has given us.

Nehemiah 11:1–2 is a good example of what I'm talking about. After the walls of Jerusalem were rebuilt, Nehemiah got the people to invest in the future of their community:

> *The leaders of the people lived in Jerusalem, but the rest of*
> *the people cast lots to bring one out of ten to live in Jerusalem,*
> *the holy city, while nine-tenths remained in the other cities.*
> *And the people blessed all the men who volunteered*
> *to live in Jerusalem.*

Nehemiah brought people from the burbs back into Jerusalem so they could invest in the community and build it up. Before, there were no walls, no businesses, no community—just chaos. By getting the people to invest in their own future, Nehemiah raised the standards of the community.

And when you raise the standards, then everything in a community goes up with it. Property values go up because the businesses are going up. There is stability in the community.

We have the power to do that in our communities if we would get serious about fulfilling the economic agenda of God's kingdom.

## THE RESPONSIBILITY
## OF KINGDOM ECONOMICS

The final aspect I want us to consider is the responsibility that a kingdom economic agenda entails. Let's take it through each of the four areas that make up the divisions of this book.

### Personal Responsibility

The place to start is with yourself. You must prepare yourself individually to live on a kingdom economic plan.

Many years ago, Lois and I sat under the biblical teaching of a respected Christian financial counselor. We were earning just a little bit of money in those days, but we learned how to apply God's principles where we were, and it revolutionized our financial life. We have been virtually free of debt ever since.

You need a plan. You cannot luck your way into a kingdom economic way of life. The Bible advises us to consider the ant, who stores up for the future while things are good (see Proverbs 6:6–11). If you are not operating financially by a clear plan, you are gambling with the resources God gives you.

You may say, "I don't have any money, so I don't need a plan." No, you don't have any money *because* you don't have a plan. Know where you are financially (see Proverbs 27:23), and then decide where you want to go.

Now let me give you three words that can change your life.

The first word is *give*. Always honor God with the "first fruits" of your income. If you want God's blessing, then you need to honor Him first, because He is the Owner of it all.

So if you are robbing God of His tithes to the church and offerings to eliminate the emergency needs of the poor, forget the rest of it (see Malachi 3:8–9). Even when we try to withhold from God, He has a way of making sure something is always breaking down so that we pay up anyway. So give God His portion first.

The second word is *save*. After you pay the Lord, pay yourself next. We just talked about this, so I'll leave it at that.

The third word is *spend*. There's nothing wrong with spending. But it needs to come third in your financial priorities, not first. If MasterCard is the only one enjoying the fruit of your work, if American Express is the only one who loves to see you get paid, something is wrong. You are being owned by this world order.

The order here of these three little words is all-important. But we mess it up because too many of us spend faithfully, save occasionally, and give sporadically.

So enjoy what you have to spend, but don't rob God and cheat yourself to do it. In order to do that, you must begin getting out of debt now. It's like getting off drugs. It may be hard at first, but it will be worth it when you're free.

## Family Responsibility

The Bible says in Proverbs 13:22, "A good man leaves an inheritance to his children's children."

If you have nothing to leave to your family when you die because you failed to save and plan ahead, that is wrong. You need to help your children get a start in life, but not so they can simply take their inheritance and use it for a life of laziness and lack of productivity.

How do we leave our children an inheritance and yet try to make sure they know how to handle it in a righteous way? By doing more than just leaving them money. We need to teach them godly wisdom when it comes to finances. "Wisdom along with an inheritance is good," said Solomon (Ecclesiastes 7:11).

In other words, don't just give your children money. Give them a kingdom agenda mind-set about money. And if you don't have material things to leave behind, by teaching your children wisdom you can still leave them a valuable inheritance.

We need to teach our children biblical principles of finance. When my younger son, Jonathan, got his first job, he brought home one hundred dollars for the month. He thought he really had himself some serous money, but I forced him to budget the money in accordance with the principles of give, save, and spend.

He resisted at first, but now that he sees a growing bank account he appreciates the wisdom of God. But you have to start where your children are, because if they learn how to handle ten dollars or one hundred dollars, they will know what to do with one thousand dollars when they get that much.

Families should also start family businesses utilizing the gifts, talents, and training of its various members to work together for the benefit of the whole. Such an enterprise unifies the household while simultaneously bringing financial benefit.

## Church Responsibility

The church has lost much of its influence in society because it has turned its social-service calling over to the state. In an earlier chapter we discussed the church's role in helping people such as needy widows. The church's job is not only to help the responsible poor (see 1 Thessalonians 3:10) but also to empower the poor, equipping them to create wealth.

How do you empower poor people? Not just by giving them money, because if their thinking toward money is wrong, they will be back tomorrow and the day after that for more money.

People need more than money to be empowered. They also need a kingdom orientation toward money. So part of the church's agenda when it comes to economics is to give people biblical knowledge in areas such as saving, budgeting, and investing, as well as to create opportunities for self-fulfillment and employment. This means that the gifts and skills of the church membership must be enlisted to serve the kingdom in the area of economic development.

At our church in Dallas, one way we try to empower people is to hold regular seminars in biblical economics. We also help our people who have not graduated from high school to get their GED if that is their need. And we are working with a local Christian university to set up classes at Oak Cliff Bible Fellowship so that our people can pursue a college degree.

We also help train people with job skills and then network in the community to provide them with job opportunities. For those wanting to go into business for themselves, we offer an entrepreneurial program that helps them develop their business plan. Poor people need empowerment, not just a handout. This is why I say the church is the answer to welfare. If every church in America would empower one responsible welfare family a year, we could eliminate the need for welfare in five years or less. Urban and suburban churches should partner to implement programs that empower the poor in an accountable way.

One of the greatest demonstrations of the church empowering people was the African-American church during slavery. They had limited federal government help and no Great Society program. Yet they took care of their poor and met comprehensive needs. How? Because they had a kingdom view of life, and they understood the power of the church. This combination equipped them not only to survive the evil institution of slavery but to transcend it.

The church should also begin either using the same bank, or using the skills it has acquired to establish its own financial institutions. Such a concentration of wealth would almost overnight give the church a financial monopoly within the culture. This is why our church established its own Christian Credit Union.

Such power, when used righteously, would help make the church once again the dominant influence in the culture and lead to the benefit of the community. The community should be better off for the church's presence in its midst.

## Government Responsibility

The government's primary economic responsibility is to create a just and free market (which is the system the Bible argues for), not an impersonal welfare state, by removing evil and injustice from the marketplace (see Romans 13:1–4). At best the government should be a last-resort economic safety net, not an all-encompassing promoter of federal economic dependency.

That means the government is supposed to get out of the way and let people be productive. The government should be supportive and protective of the church and the family as they care for the poor in a personal way. Now, since people are sinful by nature, the government is charged with seeing that there is justice in society to go along with the opportunities. This means ensuring that people are not denied equal access to opportunity because of their class, their color, or their background.

The government is charged with removing tyranny from the marketplace and setting the borders of justice. But within those borders there is freedom of competition. The reason this works is that whoever serves the public best should make the most profit.

So if there is free competition, what I am going to do as a competitor in business is try to outserve the competition in the marketplace. That way, people are well served, and I benefit too, because I make a profit with which I can give to God, take care of my family, and meet the needs of others.

Government should not discriminate against faith-based organizations that are providing effective social services to the poor, oppressed, and needy. On the contrary, the government should cooperate with churches and faith-based organizations to financially and legislatively support and empower their efforts since they are closest to the needs of the people and provide a moral frame of reference to affect the thinking and decisions of those in need. The separation of church and state should never be equated to the separation of God and good works.

## A CLOSING WORD

I gave a kingdom challenge to our church in relation to economics. I'd like to share it with you.

You may have grown up in the ghetto, as I did, and now you are in the suburbs. Maybe you have a nice house, two cars, and good clothes, which you don't need to apologize for if you earned those possessions legitimately.

The two questions we have to ask ourselves are: First, has the blessing of God on us become a blessing to others? If not, we are not living by a kingdom economic agenda, and God's blessing can become a curse.

It has already become a curse for some of us because we are in an economic prison called deep debt. Some of us are only one paycheck away from going back to the ghetto.

The second question is, do we have inner peace? If the resources we have come from God, He always gives joy with it (see Proverbs 10:22).

We need to get on God's economic agenda in our personal and family lives. Our churches and communities need to get on God's agenda based on the absolute authority of His Word. We need to believe that the earth is the Lord's and live like we believe it.

# The Kingdom Agenda
# and Racism

B illy Graham was once asked on a network news program, "If you could eradicate any problem in America, what would it be?"

Dr. Graham answered very quickly and directly, "The racial division and strife in our nation."

There are many who share that wish. In fact, we could say that the racial division of its members and the resulting classism is the greatest problem facing the kingdom of God. This is where we need to start, because until the people of God are truly one, we cannot expect to see the healing of racial strife in the larger culture.

So it's impossible to address God's kingdom agenda for our communities and not deal with the delicate, difficult, and often traumatic issue of racism. We will do that in this chapter, but it's not enough merely to outline the problem. We also want to move to some biblical solutions that, if applied, will help bring about racial reconciliation.

Let me tell you up front that my goal is not to argue for a particular racial or political agenda. My task is to argue for the kingdom, because God has an agenda for His people to follow in the church and in society that will lead to racial reconciliation if we will be obedient to it.

God is the Creator of the only race that will matter in eternity, the human race. He is also the Creator of the races here on earth. As such, He has spoken on the subject of race, and He has not stuttered.

In this chapter I will attempt not to stutter either. I want to be as honest and direct as I can, not backing off from or negotiating the truth, but also seeking not to be unnecessarily offensive.

## A PERVASIVE REALITY

All of us—black, white, Native American, Hispanic, Asian, or whatever—have been touched directly or indirectly by racism. Although great strides have been made in some sectors of society to rectify the problem, in other ways this era seems like "it's déjà vu all over again," to borrow the classic line of former baseball great Yogi Berra.

As is the case with most African-Americans, racism has certainly been apparent to me during my lifetime. I remember one day, when I was a boy, riding in the car with my father when we passed a White Tower restaurant in Baltimore. The White Tower was famous for its hamburgers, so I said to my dad, "Why don't we stop in there and get a hamburger?"

He said, "Because we can't go there, Son. They do not allow Negroes there." That incident began a whole series of questions to my father as I tried to make sense of this new reality.

But for me, the reality of racism did not end in my childhood. It appeared again in 1969, during my college days, when a well-known church in Atlanta split when I showed up to worship there.

The issue raised its head once more in 1987, when I was told personally by a number of radio stations across the county, "We appreciate your preaching, but we are afraid that carrying your program on the air would offend too many of our listeners."

And as late as 1993, racism made an appearance in our lives when a famous Bible teacher in Dallas made the statement that the reason black people are to be slaves is because of the curse of Ham (which we will discuss shortly).

But this is more than a personal issue. All we need to do is recall the "circus" murder trial of former football star O. J. Simpson. As soon as Simpson was arrested, people lined up along racial lines to decide his guilt or innocence.

Furthermore, the problem of racism pervades our society beyond black-and-white issues. The resurgence of neo-Nazi-type groups has led to the painting of swastikas on the homes and synagogues of Jews in Dallas and elsewhere. The pain of the internment that Japanese Americans suffered in World War II has been revisited recently, and Native Americans and Hispanic Americans have had their own sets of issues to face.

No matter where we look, we can see the stain of racism on our culture, like a stubborn ink stain on a white shirt that refuses to be laundered out. To understand and deal with the problem of racism, we need to get a biblical perspective on the larger issue of race.

## The Origin of the Races

This is the place to start, because it is both the foundation of the problem and the location of the solution.

A number of views have been set forth to explain the origin of the races we have on earth. I want to deal with two popular theories of racial origins, one secular and one religious, and then try to provide a biblical answer to the question.

## The Environmental Theory

This view says that racial differences can be pretty much explained by environment or geography.

The argument is that racial distinctions did not exist until the scattering of the people at the Tower of Babel. As the people scattered to different locations, racial differences began to appear.

For instance, according to this view Anglos have light skin because they settled in Europe, where they did not experience extreme and prolonged exposure to the sun.

The people who settled in Africa were closer to the equator, where they experienced prolonged periods of exposure to intense sunlight, leading to a darkening of the skin. And brown remained in the Middle East and Asia, where the environment was sort of a halfway point between Europe and Africa. Thus these people maintained a brownish hue to their skin.

The environmental view also says that blacks have wider noses because of the need for more oxygen intake in tropical regions where the air is thinner.

That's the environmental theory in a nutshell. It's a naturalistic explanation based more on an evolutionary view of humans than a biblical view. This theory says that we are the color we are by the forces of nature. But this theory is untenable for a number of reasons.

First, it assumes that people's complexion before the scattering at Babel was fair and that dark skin came about unintentionally, assumptions not supported in Scripture. It teaches that only fair-skinned people are direct creations of God while all other races came about environmentally.

It also contradicts Scripture, which teaches that God is the Creator of all people (see Malachi 2:10) and that He is no respecter of persons (see Acts 10:34).

Furthermore, the Scripture clearly teaches that all nations were created from one man (see Acts 17:26). Racial distinctions, then, must be rooted in the creative activity of God beginning with Adam, not in accidents of nature.

## The Curse of Ham

While secular society may be content with a naturalistic explanation for racial origins, many people in the religious world have sought a theological explanation for the reality of racial differences. Some have found it in the so-called curse of Ham in Genesis 9.

Now if you know anything about the Bible and about history, you realize we are about to enter controversial territory. The reason is that the "curse-of-Ham" argument is not just an attempt to explain the origin of the races. In addition, it has served as an attempt to justify racial suppression.

This "doctrine" dominated the church in the era of slavery and is still taught in some sectors today. It was used to give biblical authenticity to and permission for the reality of the slave trade in West Africa and the practice of slavery in the Western world. This teaching gave theological legitimacy to the evil of American racism.

But since racial suppression is the second major point we will deal with, I will leave that issue alone for the time being and deal with the reasoning that has been used to validate the teaching of a curse on black people.

The story of Ham is found in Genesis 9, following the flood of Noah:

> *Then Noah began farming and planted a vineyard. And he drank of the*
> *wine and became drunk, and uncovered himself inside his tent. And Ham,*

*the father of Canaan, saw the nakedness of his father, and told his two*
*brothers outside. But Shem and Japheth took a garment and laid it upon*
*both their shoulders and walked backward and covered the nakedness of*
*their father; and their faces were turned away, so that they did not see their*
*father's nakedness. When Noah awoke from his wine, he knew what his*
*youngest son had done to him. So he said, "Cursed be Canaan; a servant of*
*servants he shall be to his brothers." (vv. 20–25)*

Let me state the thesis of the "curse-of-Ham" argument, and then we will consider the case step-by-step.

The reasoning goes that because of what happened here, Ham and his descendants were given the curse of living in perpetual slavery. And since, the argument goes, Ham is the father of black people, black people are and always have been under a divine curse of servitude. This view is still held by many today.

The implication of this position is that black people should accept their inferior position without resistance or rebellion, since it was ordained by God. And white people should not feel guilty for enslaving blacks, because slavery is their divinely appointed lot in life.

This position has so many flaws it's hard to know where to start. Let's begin with the story itself. What exactly did Ham do here?

The text says that Noah got drunk and uncovered himself in his tent. So he was lying naked in the tent, evidently passed out from drinking too much wine. Ham saw his father's nakedness, left the tent, and told his brothers.

This is the problem. What Ham did was basically to ridicule and dishonor Noah. He should have covered Noah's shame himself instead of spreading the news about it. Shem and Japheth did the right thing, refusing even to look at Noah as they covered him.

In other words, the two brothers restored Noah's honor. As you may know, in Old Testament days it could cost you your life to dishonor your parents (see Exodus 2:15, 17). Ham dishonored his father, but here's the point. The curse wasn't put on Ham, but on his son Canaan (see Genesis 9:25).

So to talk of a "curse of Ham" is to blatantly misread the biblical text. This intentional distortion of the clear statements of Scripture was used as an excuse for oppressing an entire race of people.

But let's go a step further. Ham had four sons (see Genesis 10:6), but the curse was directed only at Canaan. So even though Ham is the father of African people, the claim that the curse extends to all people of African descent is impossible. If the curse were on Ham, all of his sons would have been cursed, not just Canaan.

Yet only Canaan and his descendants were cursed. Ham was punished for dishonoring his father by having a son who would bring dishonor to him.

Now here's the real bottom line. The descendants of Canaan were the Canaanites—the evil, pagan people who were in the Promised Land when Israel arrived to take possession of that area.

God told Israel to subjugate and eradicate the Canaanites because they were so deep in sin they were under God's judgment (see Joshua 9:23–25; 1 Kings 9:20–21). The Israelites didn't do the job all at once, but eventually the Canaanites, as a nation, disappeared from the earth. And the curse that Noah put on them died with them.

So any attempt to hand the curse of Genesis 9 onto all people everywhere of African descent is not true to the Bible. Why then was slavery ever practiced? Because the slave marketers were interested in their profits. And the white people who owned slaves, including white Christians, were really interested in maintaining their dominant position in the prevailing social order, not in pursuing a kingdom perspective on the issue. The so-called curse of Ham does not stand up to the test of biblical accuracy.

I need to answer one lingering question, and then we can move on. Why didn't Noah curse Ham himself instead of cursing Canaan? Because God made a covenant to bless Noah and his sons (see vv. 11, 15). God cannot renege on His covenants, so He caused the curse Noah pronounced to be carried out on the generation after Ham.

This happened in the case of David and Solomon. Solomon sinned against God, and God told him He would tear the kingdom from Solomon. But then God added, "I will not do it in your days for the sake of your father David, but I will tear it out of the hand of your son" (1 Kings 11:11–12).

Thus, for the sake of His covenant with David, God did not execute judgment on Solomon. Instead, God brought judgment on Reheboam, Solomon's rebellious son (see 2 Chronicles 12:13–16).

God's law stated that He would visit the sin of the fathers on their children up to the third and fourth generations (see Exodus 20:5). I believe what happened here is that God singled out Canaan because He knew Canaan's heart would not be oriented toward Him. And the children of Canaan did in fact become a debauched people.

In closing this section, it is important to note that curses based on disobedience can be reversed when there is repentance and obedience (see Exodus 20:6). So even if the "curse-of-Ham" heresy were true, it was no justification for the Anglo Christian churches in America to endorse the enslavement of their African Christian brothers.

In reality, what we had in the "curse-of-Ham" doctrine was twisted theology employed to sustain a perverted sociology. This process is known as "sacralization," the development of theological and religious constructs to serve a particular group.

## A Biblical Answer

Now we are ready to answer the question: Where did the various races originate?

Paul said in Acts 17:26 that God made all people "from one," that is, from Adam. So we had better start by figuring out how Adam was made.

"The Lord God formed man of dust from the ground," according to Genesis 2:7. Adam's very name means "earth, ground." According to verse 13, Eden was located near the land of Cush, which is modern Egypt.

So Adam was created with color, for he was created from the soil. And he was created with the genes for color determination built into his system. Our skin color is determined by part of the genes that produces melanin. Adam's melanin was programmed into him.

Now when God made Eve, He "fashioned" her not from the ground but from Adam (Genesis 2:22). The word *fashioned* means to go into intricate detail to put something together.

Eve came from Adam, so she had color too. But she was not his clone. She was different in many details. I believe one of the details God created differently in Eve was that He put a different color code in her melanin. The result was that between them, Adam and Eve possessed in their genetic pools the potential of giving birth to different-colored children.

How does this relate to the origin of the races? We can see it back in Genesis 9 with the sons of Noah: Ham, Shem, and Japheth. After the flood, Genesis 9:19 tells us that "the whole earth was populated" from these three men.

Their names reveal that Noah's sons were of different colors. Ham means "hot, dark, burnt," referring to black people. Shem means "brownish, dusky," and Japheth means "fair, light."

How in the world could Mr. and Mrs. Noah have a dark baby, a brown baby, and a light baby? There is only one way genetically. They had to be of different colors themselves. And we know how that was possible because of the creation account in Genesis 2.

Noah and his wife were able to have three children of different colors because the melanin needed to determine color was already built into the human race. This was done by the creative genius of God through the genetic coding given to Adam and Eve at creation.

So the question of racial origins has a one-word answer: God. Racial origin wasn't the result of exposure to sunlight, and it certainly wasn't the result of a curse on one man's sin.

Japheth's descendants settled in Europe, Ham's went to Africa, and Shem's offspring settled in the Middle East and Asia. But they didn't go there to get color; they took it with them. They also took with them the physical features they inherited from the progenitors of their particular tribe.

Do you know what this means? It means your color and mine are not products of chance or of nature. God created all people from one. There are no racial mistakes. So if you are not proud of what God made you to be, take it up with Him, because He is the One responsible. (For detailed discussions of the issue of race and the Bible, see this author's books *Let's Get to Know Each Other* [Thomas Nelson], and *Beyond Roots II: If Anyone Asks You Who I Am* [Renaissance Productions].)

## THE SUPPRESSION OF THE RACES

We are all from the same root racially. God's agenda for us is that we live in harmony with one another, both in the kingdom and in the culture at large.

But when God's truth is given to sinful men, they distort it. That is true in the area of race relations, which has led to the suppression of some races by other races who believe themselves superior.

Racism may be simply defined as the discrimination of people based on skin color or ethnic origin. It involves the unrighteous use of power against people toward whom we harbor prejudice, which is the emotional foundation of discrimination. Racism is equally unrighteous whether practiced by whites toward blacks, blacks toward Hispanics, Hispanics toward Asians, or any other combination thereof. It is an affront to the character of God, and His answer to racism is never racism in reverse.

The most prevalent historical expression of this suppression is the institution of slavery in all of its forms over the centuries. Now it is not my purpose here to review the history of slavery or go into the historical debate that led to the Civil War in our nation.

Instead, I want to show you the only legitimate biblical reason given for one person holding another person in servitude.

## Indentured Servitude

*Indentured servitude* is the proper term for biblically sanctioned servitude. Leviticus 25:39–41 specified that if an Israelite became indebted to a fellow Israelite, the debtor could sell or indenture himself to his creditor to pay back the legitimate debt.

But verse 40 provided that this condition would only last until the Year of Jubilee, which we know was the year in which all debts were forgiven. And even while the debtor Israelite was in the creditor Israelite's service, the latter was not to "rule over him with severity" (Leviticus 25:43). So the idea that a master could mistreat or kill a slave at a whim was strictly prohibited.

Now, the Israelites were permitted to hold permanent slaves from the heathen nations around them (Leviticus 25:44–46). But this slavery cannot be compared at all to slavery as it was known in the later Greek and Roman world and in the West.

First, the Israelites were forbidden to go out and kidnap people to sell as slaves. Exodus 21:16 prescribed the death penalty for that. If this had been applied in Europe and America in the last three centuries, the slave traders would have been wiped out!

Second, the people enslaved were Canaanites, who were under God's judgment. They were in a different category. An Israelite who took a Canaanite into his family was doing him a favor. Also, some of these people were "sojourners" who already lived with the Israelites (Leviticus 25:45).

Third, even though these people could be made slaves, they were not to be mistreated. According to Exodus 21:20, if a slave owner brutalized his slave, he was to be punished. If he knocked out his slave's eye or tooth, for example, he had to set the slave free (see Exodus 21:26–27). God never endorses arbitrary, inhumane treatment of another person.

Back to the Israelite who sold himself into indentured servitude to another Israelite. In God's economy, this person could always work his way into freedom. The most obvious way was to work off his debt.

Leviticus 25:47–55 also provided for a servant to be redeemed by a family member who paid the fee.

So in the Bible, slavery included the possibility of freedom. In fact, during the Year of Jubilee freedom was guaranteed. And slavery was an issue of restitution, not stealing and selling other human beings for economic profit.

Let me show you one more Old Testament provision. When a servant was set free, he was not to be sent out empty-handed:

> *If your kinsman, a Hebrew man or woman, is sold to you, then he shall serve you six years, but in the seventh year you shall set him free. And when you set him free, you shall not send him away empty-handed. You shall furnish him liberally from your flock and from your threshing floor and from your wine vat; you shall give to him as the Lord your God has blessed you. And you shall remember that you were a slave in the land of Egypt, and the Lord your God redeemed you; therefore I command you this today.*
> *(Deuteronomy 15:12–15)*

This was an amazing provision to guarantee that a freed servant did not begin his freedom with two strikes against him and live in perpetual need.

## Slaves of Christ

Let's bring this over to the New Testament. Paul wrote:

> *Let each man remain in that condition in which he was called. Were you called while a slave? Do not worry about it; but if you are able also to become free, rather do that. For he who was called in the Lord while a slave, is the Lord's freedman; likewise he who was called while free, is Christ's slave. You were bought with a price; do not become slaves of men. (1 Corinthians 7:20–23)*

This really puts the situation in perspective. Here is a clear statement of a kingdom agenda that God has for all of His people. Paul is saying that it was possible even for a slave to carry out his kingdom service while in bondage.

Notice that Paul did not say the person had to remain a slave forever. The goal was always to seek freedom. But even if freedom did not come, the slave was still free in Christ. And the free person who was a believer was Christ's slave.

This is the theology of it, the key statement we need to grasp today. Everyone who names the name of Christ is His slave. Therein is our problem with slavery. Whenever one person believes that he is destined to be the master while someone else is destined to be the slave, he will mistreat that other person, thinking he is in a better position than his brother.

But the reality of Scripture is that all people everywhere owe their lives to God and are enslaved to Him and are therefore accountable to Him. This is why the Bible tells a Christian slave owner, "Grant to your slaves justice and fairness" (Colossians 4:1). God expects His people to function righteously in an unrighteous system.

In Job 31:13–15, the patriarch Job says, in effect, "If I am not just and fair to my slaves when they have a claim against me, what will happen to me when I stand before God? He created me and He created my slaves, and I am no better than they are."

It is when we think we are better than somebody else that we begin oppressing other people. But no person can assume the position of God in another person's life. There is room for only one Master in the universe. For someone to arbitrarily oppress another person is an evil that must be condemned by the church.

## THE RECONCILIATION OF THE RACES

Like a cancer, the problem of racism has metastasized and invaded the very structures of American life, making the source almost impossible to trace and deal with.

Every attempt to address this evil leads to the frustration of seeing it pop up somewhere else. Countless workshops, seminars, and symposia have not led to a cure for this cultural cancer.

Why has this evil been so difficult to eradicate? Because racism is not first and foremost a skin problem. It is a *sin* problem.

That's actually good news, because that means the problem can be fixed. As long as we make racism a problem of skin, it will never be fixed.

See, when you believe that racism is a skin problem, you can take three hundred years of slavery, court decisions, marches, and the federal government involvement and still not get it fixed right.

But once you admit that racism is a sin problem, you are obligated as a believer to deal with it right away. As long as the issue of race is social and not spiritual, it will never be dealt with in any ultimate sense.

## The Need for Reconciliation

Scripture shows us how the problem of racism can be fixed immediately when it is dealt with as a sin problem rather than a skin problem, as a spiritual and theological issue rather than merely a social and political issue.

The solution to the sin of racism is in Galatians 2, the well-known incident in which Peter decided it was OK to hang out with Gentile believers . . . until the boys from his Jewish hood showed up.

We need to go to Acts 10:9–15 to see the background of this occasion. Peter was in Joppa staying with Simon the tanner. Peter was having devotions on Simon's rooftop when he saw a vision of a sheet coming down from heaven. On it were all these unclean animals.

God told Peter to kill and eat the animals, but Peter refused. "How can I eat this Gentile stuff?" was his basic response.

God said, "What God has cleansed, no longer consider unholy" (Acts 10:15). This happened three times, and then came the application. God sent Peter to the home of Cornelius, a Gentile, to lead Cornelius and his household to the Lord.

Peter had now crossed the railroad tracks. He began relating to people of a different race and a different culture. In fact, he got into this so much that he started eating with Gentile believers. I guess he liked those pork chops and chitterlings and hog mauls, food he previously could not eat.

So in Galatians 2, we find Peter hanging out at the "soul shack" in Antioch, sucking on those neck bones and having a good old Gentile, pork-eating time.

But then the problem developed. Some of Peter's boys from the Jewish hood in Jerusalem came down to Antioch (see v. 12). Peter had been eating with the Gentiles, but when his "homies" showed up, "he began to withdraw and hold himself aloof" from his Gentile brothers and sisters.

Why did Peter do this? Because the Jews said, "Peter, what are you doing here eating with Gentiles? Don't you know we don't do that in this city? That is against the guidelines of our race. We'll all get together in heaven, but on earth we don't have that kind of social relationship with Gentiles."

Peter stopped having fellowship with the Gentiles because he feared what his Jewish brethren would say. Then it got bad. "The rest of the Jews joined him in hypocrisy" (v. 13).

Now we find out that when Peter went to the soul shack to enjoy some food he couldn't eat before, he took the town's other Jewish Christians with him. So there they were, having a great time with their fellow believers who happened to be Gentiles.

But when the Jews questioned Peter, he got up, politely pushed back his chair, and said to the Gentiles, "Excuse me. I have to go now." And the other Jews did the same thing.

Can you imagine being one of those Gentile Christians? One minute you are good enough to eat with, and the next minute you are made to feel like you have some kind of contagious disease.

That's what happened, and even Barnabas got caught up in it. Barnabas was raised in Cyprus, a Gentile colony. He was raised with Gentiles, went to school and played with Gentiles. But that's how bad racism is. It can take a good man and make him act badly.

So Barnabas followed Peter out the door of the Gentile soul shack on the other side of the tracks in Antioch. And they would have gotten away with it if Paul had not showed up for some soul food too. He saw Peter coming out and "opposed [Peter] to his face, because he stood condemned" (v. 11).

This is the way racism needs to be addressed—as sin. We have treated racism as a cultural problem, not a sin. If the church would have treated racism like it did the sins of adultery, homosexuality, and abortion, racism would have been addressed a long time ago—along with the dismantling of its systemic and legal expressions. But in order to maintain economic advantage, social superiority, and power, this sin was ignored.

## The Road to Reconciliation

Why did Paul confront Peter? Because he saw that Peter and his Jewish pals "were not straightforward about the truth of the gospel" (Galatians 2:14).

That's the kingdom solution to racism and the key to racial reconciliation: Be committed to the truth. Paul said that Peter and the other Jewish believers got into trouble because they left the truth they knew, which was that in Christ "there is neither Jew nor Greek" (Galatians 3:28).

They left the truth, and that's our problem today. We don't have enough people today willing to speak and stand for the truth. Peter was the leader of the disciples. If the leader is not willing to live out the truth, how can we expect the followers to follow the truth?

This hits us who teach the truth of God from the pulpit. A mist in the pulpit becomes a fog in the pew. The reason racism has continued in this country is that the pulpits have been too quiet too long. White churches and denominations have taken too long to make a stand for righteousness in this area.

One reason slavery persisted in American was that the churches were too busy teaching "curse-of-Ham" theology to deal with the truth. Because the Dutch Reformed Church in South Africa refused to take a stand for what was true against what was false, its program of racial expediency maintained a system of apartheid that cost countless thousands of people their lives.

God has not called the church to make the culture feel good. God has called the church to stand on the truth of His Word. It is a matter of truth. Whenever we abandon the truth, we will never see solutions to the problems in a culture.

It is wrong, it is sinful, for people to judge other people by the color of their skin rather than the content of their character (to paraphrase Martin Luther King Jr.). I don't care what color a person is, if his character isn't right you shouldn't be hanging around with him anyhow.

Over the past few years, the number of Anglo and Hispanic members in our church in Dallas has increased, and I am delighted. They are welcome as a part of our family.

But we once had a black church member who wasn't too delighted with this. He came to me and said, "Pastor, we're getting too many white people in here. You know how they are. They'll keep coming and try to take over."

I said, "Well then, brother, you'd better do some black evangelism so we can keep outnumbering them."

But he said, "Well, I don't know if I can stay here."

I said, "Bye."

Why did I say that? Because I'm not going to hold the Bible hostage to anyone's prejudices. A black believer may say, "But you don't know what has been done to me."

Fine, let's not deny what happened. If a person has been abused or misused, that is sin and it must be dealt with. But that does not give the offended believer the right to become what he or she is condemning other people for being. Being sinned against does not give us the right to duplicate the sin.

## Two Radial Decisions

As I told our church, it is time now that we make some radical decisions about race, racism, and racial reconciliation. There are two that are especially important.

The first decision all of us need to make is to be what God made us to be. If you are black, say it loud, "I'm black, and I'm proud." If you are white, say, "That's all right."

No matter whether God made you red, brown, yellow, black, or white, you are, as the children's chorus says, "precious in His sight." If you feel any other way, you are saying God failed when He made you.

It is an indictment on God to want to paint your skin any other color than what God made it. So Anglos, get out of that sun and stay off those beaches. African-Americans, put that skin cream away. You ought to be proud of what God has made you.

Here's a second radical decision. We must decide to make our judgments according to truth, not according to skin pigment. We can make decisions based on truth because there is an objective standard of truth, God's Word, by which we can say, "This is right," and "This is wrong." Your job and mine is not to be popular but to live by the truth.

Let me illustrate what I mean. In Numbers 12, Moses married a Cushite woman. Now we know that Cush is modern-day Ethiopia, so this woman was an African.

Miriam and Aaron, Moses' siblings, got ticked at the wedding. "What in the world do you think you're doing, Moses? This woman isn't our color. And besides, she's not even an Israelite." So they got upset with Moses and started a little murmuring and rebellion over Moses' interracial marriage.

Numbers 12:4–9 says that when Miriam and Aaron went off on Moses, God went off on them, particularly Miriam. God rebuked them and then said to Miriam, in effect, "You like the lighter color, do you? Fine, we'll make you light colored, as white as snow." And God struck Miriam with leprosy (see Numbers 12:10).

God turned Miriam's color into a curse because she was making judgments predicated not upon truth but upon personal preferences. Paul was telling Peter in Antioch that because his identity was in Christ and not in race or culture, his life was measured by Christ.

Paul put it this way in my favorite verse, Galatians 2:20: "I have been crucified with Christ; and it is no longer I who live, but Christ lives in me."

Culture is valid, but it can never become more important than Christ. His Word is our reference point. The question is, what would Christ say about this person? What would Christ think about that group?

I have found it quite interesting to see some of the Anglo families leave our church when their children become teenagers to avoid the possibility of interracial dating and marriage among teens in the youth group. It is amazing how culture can dominate our commitment to Christ.

Other than the church at Jerusalem, the greatest church in New Testament times was the church at Antioch, where the incident with Peter occurred. Apparently they got their racial act together, because the leaders in that church included Simeon and Lucius, who were black Africans (see Acts 13:1–3).

## APPLYING THE TRUTH

How can we live by the truth we know? Let's take our four areas of focus and briefly consider the application of a kingdom agenda as it relates to race and reconciliation.

*On the personal level*, you can make a commitment to do what we talked about, dealing with people on the basis of their character, not by the color of their skin. Individually, we must apply God's standard to our relationships, not the stereotypes our parents or the media may give us.

In addition, we must deactivate racism both by resisting it when it rears its ugly head as well as by refusing to allow it to create in us a victim mentality that cripples us from maximizing our potential under God. Racism is powerful, but it is not omnipotent; only God is.

*When it comes to the family*, we need to train our children to think and act biblically first, not culturally first. This will require that we ourselves react biblically. Parents must also intentionally expose their children to families of other races who hold their values.

This means we must put race in its proper perspective. We must be biblical Christians first. This should lead us to functioning as righteous Americans, so then we can appreciate the diversity of culture. When this order and relationship is followed, then unity can be maintained and racial differences respected.

A lot of our problem in this country is that people are training their children to inherit their prejudices and wrong viewpoints, so the kids grow up to think just like their parents.

*What should the church do?* This one is easy to say but hard to do. The church needs to welcome anyone of any race, culture, or class who names the name of Jesus Christ and is willing to live by the truth of Scripture.

We must celebrate the variety of cultures that make up the church and hold everyone in the congregation to the same biblical standard. And our pulpits must condemn racism in all its forms because, as I said earlier, a mist in the pulpit is a fog in the pew. All denominations must take the same stand against racism that they have taken against other moral issues. Denominations should expel any church or boycott any cultural institution that sanctions and practices racism. Racism is a moral issue that must be condemned from the pulpit not only on the personal level but on the corporate and systematic level as well. Churches must partner across race, class, and cultural lines to minister together, thus demonstrating unity through good works, especially to the needs of the poor and disenfranchised.

This has been one of the failings of the religious right. It has fought aggressively to protect life in the womb, without fighting equally hard for the just treatment of minorities from the womb to the tomb. The church must promote a "whole life" agenda. This is why churches should open pregnancy centers that not only save the lives of the unborn but also provide wraparound services that offer total life direction, well-being, and empowerment for the mother and her child.

*We still have to deal with the government:* Our government should do what Israel did, which was to have one law, or standard of justice, for all the people (see Leviticus 24:22), not two standards of justice depending on a person's color, culture, class, or background. It must intervene as it did in the South during the fifties and sixties to assure the proper application of justice.

And if any of us have been practicing racism, whether on a personal, family, church, or government level, we must confess it as sin and turn from it. That means if restitution is needed because of harm done, we need to take care of it at each level.

I know the president apologized to a group of black men who were mistreated during a medical experiment in the forties, but one thing the government of the United States has never done is to document officially a confession that slavery was an evil perpetuated by law. It is time for that covenantal confession and request for forgiveness since it was a covenantal sin by one of God's covenantal institutions.

There has been no covenantal confession and no covenantal

forgiveness by duly appointed representatives. So racism continues to proliferate nationally.

It's easy to be a Christian inside the church walls. It's safe in there. But when we leave the church and go out into the world determined to act biblically when it comes to race, it's also easy to get intimidated and slip back into the old ways when our own race shows up.

When you go back to your community that has its own views on race, you can forget that you're part of a bigger family, the family of God. However, we might as well get used to each other being the color we are, because whatever color you are now, that is what you will be in heaven.

The apostle John said in Revelation 7:9 that when he looked into heaven in his vision, he saw a "great multitude . . . from every nation and all tribes and peoples and tongues, standing before the throne and before the Lamb."

Since what we will be then is what we are now, we had better learn to get along and live according to truth now. Practice makes perfect. Let's be the people of God that He has called us to be so that the broader culture has a model to look at in addressing the perpetual evil of racism.

Remember, God will not allow unity in a culture that excludes Him until there is first unity in the church (see Colossians 3:10–11). There is nothing that the president, Congress, or anyone else can do to bring long-term solutions to the racial divide.

Just as it was the church, under the leadership of Dr. Martin Luther King Jr., that brought about civil rights initiatives in the sixties, so the church today must lead the way in dismantling all forms of racism in the culture at large and in the church itself.

We may be of different colors, but we've been washed in the same red blood of the Lamb.

# The Kingdom Agenda
# and Politics

Sometimes I get criticized for being too conservative politically. Then other times I am criticized for being too liberal.

Quite frankly, I'm not interested in either donkeys or elephants. If I am going to be criticized, I want it to be for being too biblical. The kingdom of God sits above and judges the conservative and liberal orientations of men, because God is concerned about accomplishing His agenda, not mine or yours or anyone else's. He didn't come to take sides; He came to take over!

In part 5 we have already dealt with several areas of community life where accomplishing God's kingdom agenda makes for some controversy. Putting the volatile subject of politics under the lens of Scripture won't be any different.

But it must be done, not so we can decide who is right politically and who is wrong. That is not the most important question for us. The most important question is, How can we function in the political realm with a kingdom mind-set in order to accomplish a kingdom agenda?

Many people complain that because politics is dirty they can't get involved. But that's like saying because a baby's diaper is dirty you can't change it. It is because it's dirty that you need to get involved in changing it! In the same way, we need godly men and women in politics to help clean it up.

Believers may be Democrats, Republicans, or Independents. But above all, we are called to be kingdom people, those who subject the agendas of men to the agenda of God. The goal is that no matter how you and I may vote, when we come out of the voting booth we come out committed to doing kingdom work.

If God rules your life, then your life ought to be governed according to His truth. If God rules in your church, then your church should reflect His truth.

Let's talk about four distinct aspects of a kingdom agenda as it relates to politics and political action.

## THE BIBLE AND POLITICS

The first thing I want you to see is that the Bible is full of politics. You cannot read the Bible and ignore the political realm.

Let me cite several opening examples. John the Baptist condemned the immoral conduct of Herod Antipas, which led to the prophet's execution (see Mark 6:14–29).

In Thessalonica, Paul and his companions were charged with committing treason against Rome for insisting "that there is another king, Jesus" (Acts 17:7).

And in the greatest act of political and moral rebellion ever against God, the Antichrist will set up his worldwide government of pure evil, and he will rule the earth (see Revelation 13:1–10).

### God Rules and Overrules

So the Bible is full of politics for one basic reason: The universe is a theocracy.

By that I simply mean that God rules in His universe. Psalm 103:19 says it clearly: "The Lord has established His throne in the heavens; and His sovereignty rules over all." Not only does God reign over the earth, but human government is established by His will and operates by His permission (see Romans 13:1). The state has a God-ordained authority to perform kingdom activities that are related to civil affairs according to the specifics of the Scriptures. The politician, like the pastor, is to follow the Bible (Deuteronomy 17:18–20), which is why there can be no separation between religion and government, and why both are called ministers (see Mark 10:42–45; Romans 12:4).

Because God is the Sovereign of His universe, it follows that He is intimately concerned with the political affairs of the nations. Psalm 22:28 declares, "The kingdom is the Lord's, and He rules over the nations." There is nothing that happens in the governments of men that does not flow out of the sovereign rule of God. "The king's heart is like channels of water in the hand of the Lord; He turns it wherever He wishes" (Proverbs 21:1). God is sovereign over government since He raises up kings (Daniel 2:21) and His goal is that all nations should serve Him (Psalms 72:8–11).

So all through the Bible, we see God placing people strategically in the political realm. He moved Joseph into authority in Egypt (see Genesis 41:38–49) and elevated Daniel to a position of great influence in Babylon and later in Persia (see Daniel 1:8–21; 2:46–49; 6:1–3). God also placed Nehemiah in the Persian government so His kingdom purposes could be carried out (see Nehemiah 1:1–28). He also placed Esther as queen in Persia (see the book of Esther) and Deborah as judge in Israel to accomplish His agenda (see Judges 4–5).

In fact, the greatest example of God's involvement in the political affairs of a nation is Israel itself. In books such as 1–2 Samuel, 1–2 Kings, and 1–2 Chronicles, God is active on every page, setting up this king, judging that king, and deposing yet another king. There is no escaping God's political activity. This means we cannot divide life down the middle, putting God on one side and politics on the other.

Now someone may argue that while God was intimately involved in the governing of Israel, that was because God Himself established Israel as a theocracy. But when it comes to the other nations of earth, God is not that deeply involved.

I differ with that, because in Daniel 4 we see God getting very personally and very intimately involved in the life of King Nebuchadnezzar of Babylon, the greatest secular ruler in the greatest pagan kingdom of the day.

We have already looked at this account of Nebuchadnezzar's lesson in rulership. So just let me remind you that Nebby got the big head from looking in the mirror too long. He declared himself top banana in the universe, so God sent him a dream.

In the process of interpreting Nebuchadnezzar's dream, Daniel told him God had decreed that Nebuchadnezzar would be rendered insane until he "recognize[d] that the Most High is ruler over the realm of mankind, and bestows it on whomever He wishes" (Daniel 4:25).

But then Daniel told Nebuchadnezzar he would get his kingdom back when he thoroughly understood that "it is Heaven that rules" (v. 26). Whenever a government sets itself up as God, it is in for a short run, because there is only one King who reigns in power over the universe. God sits in judgment on kings and nations.

The rest of Daniel 4 records the fulfillment of Daniel's interpretation: Nebuchadnezzar was driven from his throne for seven years. I call this a heavenly political protest. God protested the unrighteousness of Nebby's government because Nebby sought to usurp the authority that belongs to God. Nebuchadnezzar wound up making the very confession God decreed he would make (see vv. 34–37).

We have seen a spectacular example of God's political activity in our own time with the amazingly rapid collapse of the Soviet Empire. An atheistic government that had been rigidly controlled and heavily centralized for seven decades was dismantled in a few years, because God will move against an unrighteous government when He so chooses.

The further a government drifts from God (which means it seeks to become its own god), the more it sets itself up for heavenly political action, as Herod could attest (see Acts 12:20–23).

## King of Kings

The greatest political statement in the Bible is the declaration of Revelation 19:16 that when Jesus Christ returns to earth to rule, He will come as "King of Kings, and Lord of Lords." Back in Revelation 1:5, John had seen a vision of the glorified Jesus, who was declared to be "the ruler of the kings of the earth."

The Bible also says that "by [Jesus] all things were created . . . whether thrones or dominions or rulers or authorities" (Colossians 1:16). And He not only created heavenly and earthly kingdoms (v. 15), they are dependent on Him to "hold together" (v. 17) and exist by Him and for Him (see v. 16).

When Jesus was on earth, He was perceived as a political threat. At one of Jesus' trials, the Jewish council brought Him to Pilate with this accusation: "We found this man misleading our nation and forbidding to pay taxes to Caesar, and saying that He Himself is Christ, a King" (Luke 23:2). The charge that Jesus forbade people to pay taxes was simply untrue, as we will see below in the discussion that includes Mark 12:13–17.

Earlier in His ministry, Jesus had called Herod a sneaky fox, protesting the evil of his reign (see Luke 13:31–32).

So to talk about the activity of God the Father and God the Son both in history and in the future is to include politics.

## THE REVELATION OF THE KINGDOM TO POLITICS

I am constantly being asked to get our church involved in this or that cause, take part in this or that movement, or be part of this or that political group. Those kinds of invitations and requests bombard us all the time.

Some of the movements or causes may be legitimate. But my passion is to pursue the agenda of the kingdom, because then you don't have to guess what is valid and what isn't. You have a worldview that addresses all of human experience and gives you a framework for relating kingdom concerns to the political realm.

### God and Caesar

We have already argued that faith and politics do mix. The question is, how do they mix?

Jesus answered that for all time in Mark 12:13–17. This is the famous incident in which the Pharisees and Herodians, normally religious and political enemies, teamed up to trap Jesus in His words.

Politics does make for strange bedfellows. The Pharisees were the religionists of the day, the ones interested in the spiritual side of life. The Herodians, on the other hand, were more politically oriented. They were concerned to keep Israel on good terms with the Roman government.

These two groups got together to ask Jesus a trick question concerning the separation of church and state. They figured Jesus had to take either God's side or Caesar's side, and either way He would get in trouble with somebody.

So they came to Jesus and asked, "Teacher, we know that You are truthful, and defer to no one; for You are not partial to any, but teach the way of God in truth. Is it lawful to pay a poll-tax to Caesar, or not? Shall we pay, or shall we not pay?" (Mark 12:14–15a).

The question was well thought through by these men. The trap was that if Jesus said, "Don't pay the tax because it is unlawful," which is what the Pharisees believed, then He would have been condemned for treason against the Roman state.

But if Jesus said, "Pay the tax," He would be siding with a foreign government that was oppressing His own people. It was a no-win situation for Jesus as far as His questioners were concerned. They thought they had Him.

## Government Is Legitimate

But Jesus answered the question perfectly and frustrated their plot. "Knowing their hypocrisy, [Jesus] said to them, 'Why are you testing Me? Bring Me a denarius to look at'" (Mark 12:15b).

Jesus asked for a common coin of the day. The Pharisees and Herodians must have wondered where this was going, but they brought Him the coin (v. 16a).

Then Jesus asked them a question. "'Whose likeness and inscription is this?' And they said to Him, 'Caesar's.'" The image on the coin was that of Caesar, and the inscription read "Tiberius Caesar Augustus."

"And Jesus said to them, 'Render to Caesar the things that are Caesar's, and to God the things that are God's.' And they were amazed at Him" (v.17).

These men thought they had Jesus in a trap, but He sidestepped their trickery by saying in effect, "I don't know why you asked Me this question. You have already submitted yourselves to the authority of the Roman government by virtue of the fact that you had a denarius to give Me in the first place."

In other words, when the Pharisees and Herodians accepted Roman coins, they were recognizing Rome's governmental authority. They were using the government's money and benefiting from the government's provision. So Jesus was saying they should not deny the government that which was within its legitimate authority to collect, which in this case was the poll tax.

## Government Is Limited

But Jesus didn't stop there. He went on to make the same requirement when it came to the things of God. So the question is, what things belong to God?

Last time I checked, *everything* belongs to God (see Psalm 24:1). So while Jesus' answer legitimized human government, it also limited human government. That is, you only give to the government that which the government legitimately deserves, basically your obedience to the law and your portion of the government's financial support.

But when it comes to giving God what is His, everything is on that list. We owe God our total obedience, for example. So when obeying the government will prevent you from obeying God, obedience to God takes precedence. We'll talk more about that below.

God deserves everything we are and have. Government is definitely limited in what it can demand from us. In fact, the government itself is under the authority of God. It operates at God's pleasure and by His permission, as we said above. So the government has no business interfering with the preeminence of God in our lives.

Today, the state often seeks to control the church by things such as threatening to revoke the church's tax-exempt status if the church "gets out of line."

But Jesus told Pilate at His trial, "You would have no authority over Me, unless it had been given you from above" (John 19:11). So even though Jesus' enemies turned Him over to Pilate, and even though Pilate had the power to sentence Jesus to death, the authorities were only doing what God allowed them to do. The state must always be submitted to God.

Now, when a government rebels against God's authority and tries to throw off His yoke, that government is going to be in trouble. When a nation's laws no longer reflect the standard of God, then that nation is in rebellion against Him.

When that happens, the people of God must take action to restore God's authority and see that His kingdom agenda is carried out. This leads us naturally to our next point of consideration.

## THE NATURE OF
## KINGDOM POLITICAL ACTION

What is biblically based kingdom political action? It is action that recognizes that since God rules over all, the political realm must be held accountable for straying from His authority and brought back into submission to Him.

This is done not by political revolution, which is a change imposed from the top down, but by transformation from the bottom up.

God is against revolution in the sense of imposing participatory governmental change from the top down, because that's what Satan sought to do. Satan tried to pull a coup d'état against God's government in heaven. He rebelled against God's leadership, but the rebellion was put down.

When a government acts unrighteous, what God wants from His people is not revolution but transformation. This involves the doctrine of interposition, which is a biblical form of protest.

## Interposition

Interposition is when righteous agents of God interpose themselves between an unrighteous government and its innocent victims in order to reflect and defend His standard publicly.

The Bible contains many examples of interposition. When God announced to Abraham that He was going to destroy Sodom and Gomorrah, Abraham interposed himself between God and Sodom and pled with the Lord to spare the city if He could find just ten righteous people in it (see Genesis 18:16–33).

Moses' wife, Zipporah, took action when God sought to kill Moses because he did not circumcise his son. Zipporah performed the circumcision, and Moses' life was spared (see Exodus 4:24–26).

After Israel built the golden calf in the wilderness, God was angry with the people and wanted to destroy the nation. But Moses interposed himself between God and the people, and God changed His mind (see Exodus 32:1–14).

We could also cite the story of Esther in Persia, who literally laid her life on the line to spare the Jews from Haman's decree that they be wiped out (see Esther 4:1–17).

But the greatest example of interposition is Jesus Christ, who interposed Himself between a holy God and sinful people. Because of His work, the judgment that was due us fell on Him, and we were saved from destruction by God's wrath.

As Christians, we are called to act whenever unrighteousness raises its head and threatens to bring the judgment of God upon society. If Christians shun politics, there will be no one to act as a watchman (see Ezekiel 33:1–9), to warn the people of danger and to hold back the judgment of God.

We need to be like Abraham, interposing ourselves between God and an unrighteous society, pleading with God to spare the innocent and deliver our communities from His judgment.

## Types of Interposition

The reason interposition is so critical in the political arena is that if righteous people do nothing, there is no reason that God should not bring judgment on a society. If His people sit on the sidelines, there are no other agents to stay the hand of God.

But God calls us to interpose ourselves in this culture, to be a voice for righteousness, to stand up for the innocent, and to uphold God's righteous standard in the community.

We are to show the world another option, what I call God's alternative. That may include protesting the evil that is being allowed to hold sway in a society.

There are a couple of ways to do that. One type of interposition is personal protest, based on biblical conviction, against unrighteous government action. Daniel did this as a young captive in Babylon, refusing to eat the king's meat because he did not want to break God's law and defile himself (see Daniel 1).

But Daniel did more than just refuse the food. He offered the chief eunuch anther option, suggesting that he allow Daniel and the other young men to eat vegetables.

What we need in politics are godly people who will offer society a divine option. We need people who will stand up and say, "Your way is wrong, but let's try this way, which is God's way, and see if it makes a difference."

We don't know what would have happened if Nebuchadnezzar's eunuch had refused Daniel's recommendation. But we do know what happened when Daniel's three Hebrew brothers refused to bow to the king's image (see Daniel 3). They were sentenced to die.

The actions of Shadrach, Meshach, and Abednego illustrate another type of interposition, one that is common to our era; protest through civil disobedience. This involves deliberate resistance to a government law or decree that violates God's standards.

There's an interesting example of this kind of interposition in Exodus 1. This concerned Pharaoh's order to the Hebrew midwives: "If [the child] is a son, then you shall put him to death; but if it is a daughter, then she shall live" (Exodus 1:16).

But the midwives decided to disobey Pharaoh's order because they "feared God" (v. 17). In other words, they recognized that God's law was higher than Pharaoh's law, so they stepped in between the innocent Hebrew children and the king.

Their civil disobedience could have cost them their lives, because Pharaoh called them to account for letting the Hebrew male babies live. Now the midwives lied about the reason (see v. 19), but God blessed them for putting His covenant above the commands of men (see v. 20). Thus, when faced with two evils we must determine what is in the best interest of God's kingdom.

Peter and John practiced civil disobedience when the government's action was in direct violation of God's command:

> *And when they [the Jewish council] had summoned them, they commanded them not to speak or teach at all in the name of Jesus. But Peter and John answered and said to them, "Whether it is right in the sight of God to give heed to you rather than to God, you be the judge; for we cannot stop speaking what we have seen and heard." (Acts 4:18–20)*

The apostles were saying, "You guys figure out the legality of this thing. We have a kingdom agenda to carry out."

The problem in our society is that most people fear the government more than they fear the Lord. That's true even for many Christians, because they fear the government's power to punish people and coerce them into compliance.

But we fear the wrong entity when we fear government above God. God not only deserves and demands our first loyalty, but we need to remember that government is extremely limited in what it can do.

See, the problem is that too many people are looking for "salvation by government." They are putting their hope in the political realm, but God warns us what happens when we put our confidence in kings (see 1 Samuel 8:9–18). There is no such thing as salvation by government (see Judges 8:22–23).

This is why Jesus refused attempts to make Him a political Savior (see John 6:15). The Democrats are looking for a Democratic savior, the Republicans are looking for a Republican savior, and the Independents are looking for an Independent savior. But God is sitting as the politician of the universe, saying, "I am the only Savior in town." As I've said before, the ultimate solutions to our culture's problems won't come in on *Air Force One*.

Peter wrote, "Fear God, honor the king" (1 Peter 2:17). That is always God's order of things. Whenever a government tries to usurp the rule of God, you have a legitimate basis for protest. Man's laws can be resisted and disobeyed when they come into direct conflict with the fundamental principles of the Word.

## Applications of Interposition

Let's look at a few modern-day situations in which people practiced the principle of interposition because they held God's law in higher esteem than man's law.

One instance was during the Holocaust. Christians were right to hide Jews from the Nazis, even though it was against the law. It was right because God's law forbids us from participating in murder. For Christians to do nothing as they watched their Jewish neighbors be taken away (which is what most Christians did) was to be an accomplice to murder. So it was right in those circumstances to obey God rather than to obey men.

The civil rights marches of the sixties were also legitimate because they sought to change unrighteous laws that usurped the rule of God about the dignity of men. Whenever you strip a human being of the dignity that is his or hers by virtue of being made in the image of God, you are violating God's standard.

The civil rights struggle was about more than just human or civil rights. It was about biblical rights.

The same arguments can be made for the right-to-life movement today. The law now says it is perfectly legal to take an unborn child's life. But that violates God's higher law that says, "You shall not murder." When government violates God's law, I have the right to interpose myself to protest that.

I need to close this section with a word about a sticky issue: the use of force in protesting wrong. Some people believe force is justifiable to right a wrong, but the Bible only sanctions force when you are protecting yourself from violence.

The use of force is to be defensive, in other words, not offensive. We are not to use or incite violence as a way of bringing about change. We should be known as peacemakers (see Matthew 5:9).

We said earlier that revolution is rebellion that seeks to change things from the top down. People always want to start with the president when it comes to protesting evil or getting unrighteous laws changed.

But the kind of change we are talking about rarely ever filters down from the White House. God works from the bottom up through transformation, which is why evangelism, which seeks to change the heart, must be at the center of the church's agenda. We must be careful not to drape the cross in the American flag, thus confusing the American dream with the kingdom of God.

## A KINGDOM COURSE OF ACTION

So if political action is valid based on the doctrine of interposition, what can you do to right a wrong?

### The Individual

The first thing you can do is to take responsibility for the courses of action that are available to you.

People often say, "What difference can one person make?" Let me ask you, what difference can one spark make in a dry forest? You can make a lot of difference.

One way you make a difference is by your vote. Christians who do not vote are shunning their responsibility to be a voice for righteousness in the public square.

Your vote can be a protest against an ungodly worldview and an endorsement of correct views. But you must be informed to cast your vote for righteousness. We have begun holding meetings in our church to inform voters of what various candidates believe so our people can vote intelligently.

I am often asked this question: "Why do I need to vote if God has already decided who is going to win or lose?"

I usually answer that by asking another question: "Why bother to pray if you know that God is going to do what He wants to do anyway?"

Of course there are things that God has decided He will do. And there are things He has decided He will not do. But in between those two lines are a whole group of things God *might* do, but He has decided that He will only do them in response to His people's prayers. So if you don't pray, you don't get them (see James 4:3).

There are also certain things that God is willing to do in a society, but He won't do them until we as Christians take up our responsibilities in that society. Our actions determine which way God will move.

Someone may say, "Well, how do I know which things God will do, won't do, or might do?" The answer is, unless the Bible specifically says, you don't know, so pray about everything! Be in contact with Him about all things. Act on your responsibility at the ballot box, and pray fervently that God's righteous standards will prevail.

Another thing we need is Christians who will pursue God's calling into the political arena. There are believers out there who should be running for office. Politics is only as dirty as the people involved. The way to clean up politics is to put righteous people into office.

This society needs people who feel God's call on their lives to serve Him in politics. Then we will have leaders like the ones Jethro told Moses to choose: "able men who fear God, men of truth, those who hate dishonest gain" (Exodus 18:21).

These are righteous politicians, people who serve God and others with integrity. What you see is what you get. We need people at all levels of government who will take office with a kingdom perspective in view and a kingdom agenda to pursue.

As I said, politics is dirty only when dirty people hold office. The institution of government itself is ordained of God. The reason we are in this mess politically is that Christians have forsaken politics.

## The Family

Second, teach your children that welfare begins at home. Short-circuit any idea of looking to the government for your family's well-being. Teach them that hard work and obedience to God are the keys to success.

Families must resist any political attempt to undermine the divinely ordained role of the family, whether it is same-sex marriage, legalized abortions, indiscriminate welfare, etc. Families must remove themselves from government dependency for support.

The Bible says in 1 Chronicles 12:32 that the sons of Issachar were "men who understood the times." Therefore, they were men "with knowledge of what Israel should do." Somebody raised those boys to understand what was going on around them, and they were ready to serve. Help your family be astute and observant concerning the times in which we live.

## The Church

Did you know that the church is supposed to be the leading university of the culture?

The church should be leading the way in educating the culture because it is the one entity that will interject a kingdom agenda into all the affairs of the culture.

At their secular schools, most of our children are learning humanism. They are being taught to look at the world through the eyes of man rather than through the eyes of God. The job of the church is to educate people to look at life from a divine kingdom perspective.

The church has to do more than make people feel good about their personal walk with God. The church must give God's people a divine orientation on every subject including politics and government. Why? Because everything the Bible speaks about, it speaks about authoritatively. And the Bible speaks to every issue of life. This means that the church should seek to reflect the kingdom of God in the realm of politics.

There is no area of life that does not have a biblical worldview attached to it. God lamented in Isaiah 5:13, "My people go into exile for their lack of knowledge."

Another thing the church should do is to create opportunities for people to become informed politically. I mentioned earlier the informational meetings we have been sponsoring in our church. We do these not to promote a political party, since the kingdom of God transcends the partisan politics of men, but to look at parties and issues from a kingdom perspective, so we can inject a kingdom agenda and consciousness into the political arena.

The church must also pray—which includes prayers that are called imprecatory. These are prayers against those who promote unrighteousness and evil in society.

Let me show you something else about prayer. One of the things we should be doing in prayer is making suggestions to God. Moses did this in Exodus 32:11–14 when he asked God not to destroy the Israelites. The great prayers in the Bible are not just, "Lord, let me suggest a course of action to You."

You say, "Why do I need to suggest things to God?" Because it means that you have thought through what you are praying about and you have some ideas about what needs to be done rather than just sitting around doing nothing, waiting for answers to drop from heaven.

Moses not only prayed; he offered suggestions to God. God may not act on your suggestions, but it is a way of offering yourself to God to take action if He chooses to empower you for that action. It was this activity of prayer that brought an end to the evil of racial segregation as the church marched in the civil rights movement. It brought an end to communism in the Soviet Union as the church sought God's face. Finally, the church must model righteous actions through good deeds so that civil government can see the kingdom of God at work.

## The Government

Because this universe is a theocracy in which God rules, our government will become great only to the extent that it is informed and dominated by a biblical worldview.

Our government is in desperate need of people who can inject righteousness into our political bloodstream, for a society can never rise above the quality of its leadership. The main thing the government itself can do to facilitate this is to give up this myth of a wall of separation between church and state.

Yes, church and state are functionally separate and distinct institutions with specific spheres of responsibility and jurisdiction (see 2 Chronicles 26:16–19). But the idea that the church has nothing to say about how society is governed is absurd, because all law has a religious foundation. There can be no separation of religion and state since civil government is answerable to God. The Declaration of Independence recognizes this connection since it bases the doctrine of "inalienable rights" on the doctrine of creation. People have been endowed with these rights by the Creator. Therefore, no Creator, no rights.

The church's job is to make sure that the state doesn't lose sight of the truth that God rules and that there is a moral standard in which the political realm must operate. The state needs to recognize and protect the church's freedom to exercise its prophetic role of being a voice for God and His righteous standards, since government is a divine institution and only God is autonomous, not civil government.

Then and only then will God's kingdom agenda for society be visualized. Accomplishing that agenda requires that all of God's people get involved politically at some level, for then we will see that "Blessed is the nation whose God is the Lord" (Psalm 33:12).

# The Kingdom Agenda
# and Education

Our final chapter deals with an area of kingdom life that may not be the most controversial but is certainly one of the most emotionally charged—the education of our youth.

America's early educational system was founded with a high commitment to Christ-centered education. From 1636, when Harvard University was founded, to 1769, when Dartmouth University was established, higher education in this country was undertaken with the understanding that there was no such thing as knowledge apart from God. Every discipline in the universities grew out of a biblical, God-centered worldview.

We are a long way from those early days. Education has taken some major left turns in the last three decades. And there are major debates going on at school boards in cities and states across this nation, as elected representatives try to figure out what in the world an education should do for our children and young people.

Do I need to say it? God has an agenda for the education of your children and mine. He is very interested in the information we put into our children's heads, because this is no small issue.

Education is staggering in its generational implications. Our kids spend many hours a day in school, where their thinking is being shaped for life. What they learn, or fail to learn, they will pass on to the next generation.

Education is significant in its financial implications. It is the second biggest industry in American next to the military. Billions of dollars are poured into education every year.

Education is also unique in its spiritual implications. As I said, God is very concerned with knowledge. The Bible is a Book of knowledge. There is no dichotomy in the Bible between being a Christian and being educated, since all true knowledge is rooted in God (see Romans 3:4). The Bible commands us to learn and condemns us when we refuse to do so (see Proverbs 1:7; 10:14).

So this is a big deal we're talking about. Since there is definitely a kingdom agenda for education, we need to find out what it is.

## THE CRISIS IN EDUCATION

The crisis in modern education is very simple to outline, but its impact is staggering.

The crisis in education today is a crisis of worldviews. A worldview is a grid, a set of presuppositions or assumptions a person holds about how the world works. We could say your worldview is the way you look at life, and it affects every aspect and dimension of life.

### Two Worldviews

There are two fundamental worldviews out there. One is a theistic, or God-centered, worldview. And the other is a humanistic, or man-centered, worldview. The problem is that all education comes with a worldview attached whether that fact is admitted or even understood by those doing the teaching. And the humanistic worldview is the dominant worldview in modern secular education, where the creature seeks to supplant the Creator.

Now, lest you think this is all just philosophical chat, understand that the worldview that prevails is the one that will set the standard for what is accepted as true. So when your student comes home from college and tells you, "I no longer believe there is such a thing as absolute truth," he or she is telling you that a humanistic worldview has been firmly implanted.

This crisis of worldview and truth is not new, by the way. The prophet Daniel faced it when he and his three Hebrew "homies" were carted off to Babylon as teenaged captives (see Daniel 1).

Daniel suddenly found himself in a secular culture that was a far cry from the God-centered culture he knew in Israel. He was immediately dropped into a state-run educational system that did not hold to a God-centered view of the world.

The crisis came when Ashpenaz, the chief of the king's officials, was ordered to give Daniel and some other choice young Hebrew men a royal diet as part of their Babylonian education. As we saw in the previous chapter, Daniel refused to submit to this part of his reeducation because it meant violating his God-centered worldview.

The agenda was, very simply, to prepare Daniel and his friends to serve in the court of Nebuchadnezzar. They were to be given a Babylonian worldview, which was essentially pagan. Their names were even changed to Babylonian names that reflected the names of pagan gods (see vv. 6–7).

Every aspect of Daniel's education was designed to remind him that he was now serving in Babylon and needed to operate from a Babylonian worldview. There were some things Daniel learned, such as the language and literature of the culture (see v. 14). But the rest of the book makes it clear that Daniel never compromised his spiritual principles.

## Three Areas of Attack

One plus one equals two whether you are a theist or a humanist. But when you start accumulating data and sifting it through your worldview, it affects what you do with the answer. In other words, your worldview determines how you use the information you have collected.

There are many areas of education today in which the battle of worldview is being fought. I want to mention three of the primary ones.

The first is the subject of *creation*, or First Cause. If you believe that mankind is the product of evolution, that will affect the value you put on human life, the way you think about the world, and your ethics. Instead of honoring mankind as a little lower than the angels, you will denigrate him as a little higher than the apes.

But if you believe that God is the Creator, that means you embrace the concept of another authority that supersedes human authority. Therefore you will not believe that man's authority is the measure of all things, and you will be governed by a standard of truth that is above and outside of man-made authority.

The issue of creation isn't just a matter of how we came to be here. It is a worldview issue, a matter of who calls the shots on this earth, man or God. Your decision on this question will impact every part of your life.

A second area of education undergoing an intense worldview battle is *sex education*. If our worldview is informed and determined by the Scriptures, then you will view sex as a God-given gift to be exercised only within marriage.

But if your worldview is basically humanistic, you will see sex as nothing more than a matter of personal choice. There can be no fixed standard for sexual behavior if sex is simply part of our evolutionary makeup and not a God-given part of our creation. So the homosexual can say, "Don't condemn me just because you're a heterosexual. That's your choice; this is my choice."

It's obvious from the statistics on AIDS, other sexually transmitted diseases, and the teenage pregnancy rate that this is not just an academic argument. Young people are ruining their lives and dying because they are applying a humanistic worldview to sex. And the message many of them are getting in school is, "Go ahead, but be safe."

The third area of the battle is *values clarification*. That simply means who decides what's right and what's wrong. The goal of much so-called values training in school is to help students decide what their values are on a particular subject, with no absolute standard against which to measure their conclusions.

In this environment, values are what is right for you at a given moment, which may differ from what is right for me in the same situation.

## Information and Ethics

What students are getting in each of these areas is information without any ethical framework around it. So they have no basis on which to make decisions except their own ideas.

Some people mistakenly believe that whenever you try to inject ethics into the debate about what schools should teach, it's an attempt to force religion into the schools and a violation of the separation of church and state.

We said earlier that the church and the state are, in fact, separate institutions with separate callings. But the idea that faith and ethics have no place in the debate is ridiculous. Our founders never intended for there to be a separation between ethics and knowledge or between information and religion.

In fact, giving schoolchildren knowledge without a fixed standard of truth is dangerous. Whenever you get information without a standard, then you determine how you use that information. That's how you come up with a Dr. Kevorkian.

The reason we are spending more money than ever on education and getting few positive results in terms of children's lives is not that the information is bad or the teachers are bad. It's that the schools are caught in a worldview crisis.

School can teach a young boy that one plus one equals two. But when he goes out on the street, a drug dealer wants to teach him how to make one plus one equal a million by selling some of his stuff. If that boy doesn't have the right worldview, he will take the knowledge from the school and apply it in the wrong way. The problem is not information but worldview.

Daniel was faced with a crisis. But he resisted the Babylonian worldview when it came to obeying God because his mind and heart had been soaked in the worldview of Scripture.

We must never divorce information from ethics. There is no such thing as a nonreligious education, because all knowledge involves values. Education, then, must not only give the mind information but must renew the mind with the right set of values so that knowledge is properly used (see Romans 12:1–2).

## THE CONTEXT OF EDUCATION

I want to establish a principle here that I'm sure is not new to you. But I want to develop it in a way that you may not have thought about before.

The principle is this: From a biblical standpoint, the total education of children belongs in the hands of their parents. Moses told Israel in Deuteronomy 6:1–2:

> Now this is the commandment, the statutes and the judgments which
> the Lord your God has commanded me to teach you, that you might
> do them in the land where you are going over to possess it, so that you
> and your son and your grandson might fear the Lord your God, to keep

*all His statutes and His commandments, which I command you,*
*all the days of your life, and that your days may be prolonged.*

You say, "Oh, yes, I have Bible study and devotions with my children." Well, that's fine. But that's not all that Moses was saying here.

## Comprehensive Education

It is the parents' responsibility to teach their children the commands and statutes of God in a comprehensive way. By that I mean not just as God's standards relate to matters of faith but also as they relate to math, science, the fine arts, the humanities, agriculture, law, or any other disciplines of study that exist.

What I'm saying is that as a parent, you are responsible for your children's science education, math education, history education, and every other element of their training. The Bible locates the comprehensive education of children in the home and lays the charge at the feet of Mom and Dad so that their children learn to think God's thoughts after Him in every area of life.

## Extensions of the Home

Now I know what you're thinking. Mom doesn't know this modern algebra. Dad can't recall his trigonometry, if he ever took it. And neither one remembers much about geography. How can parents be responsible for their children's education if they don't know the curriculum, especially as the children get older?

Being responsible doesn't mean you have to carry out your children's education yourself. But it does mean that the buck stops with you when it comes to making sure that God's kingdom agenda for education is being accomplished in your family.

Since most of us parents are not equipped to teach our children in a comprehensive way, we have turned that day-to-day task over to the schools. Ideally, your child's education at school should be an extension of the instruction he or she is receiving at home, because biblically it is the parents who should occupy the seat of power when it comes to education.

The problem is that the ideal seldom exists. Instead, what we often have in public education is the state wanting to act as a surrogate parent for our children and to ensure that they all received a uniform education.

The two primary ways the state does this are through the force of law, which says every child must go to school, and through school taxes, which we pay whether or not we send our children to public schools.

The state says, "Pay your taxes, and we will make sure that your children get an education." The problem is that most people cannot afford to pay school taxes and then pay again to send their children to a private school.

So the vast majority of Christian parents have no choice but to put their children in public schools. For many people, public education is the only option. My point is that the American educational system is not really set up to support and encourage parents in carrying out their biblical agenda to educate their children.

But the fact that public education is so pervasive does not relieve parents of their calling. They still need to find out the worldview that is being taught to their children in school.

## Taking Responsibility

You may say, "How can I know what my children are getting in school? I can't go to class with them."

There are many ways you can know. One is to look over your children's textbooks. For example, a quick reading of your child's biology textbook under "origins" will tell you the writer's worldview concerning creation.

You can also have a voice and a presence in the local school by attending the PTA and school board meetings and by taking advantage of opportunities to meet your children's teachers. You will probably discover in all this that your school doesn't operate on a kingdom agenda, but it's better to know that earlier than later.

One of the best ways to find out what your children are learning is to ask them. Dinnertime can be a great place to have these discussions. But that demands that we spend time with our children and listen to them. Unfortunately, these are two things a lot of parents don't take the time to do.

## Taking the Time

You say, "But I don't have time." Then you had better find it, because the biblical pattern for teaching children is to make it a part of your daily lifestyle.

"You shall teach [God's Word] diligently to your sons and shall talk of [it] when you sit in your house and when you walk by the way and when you lie down and when you rise up" (Deuteronomy 6:7).

Your teaching doesn't always have to be a formal occasion, as I indicated above in referring to mealtimes. The idea is that your home should be so saturated with a biblical worldview and a biblical way of thinking that it comes out in everything you do.

If we don't create Christian environments in our homes, then we can't blame anybody else if our children go off track. Your children's teachers are not responsible to give them the Christian worldview and training they are missing at home.

If a Christian teacher can impact his or her students for Christ, that's great. But the public school will never be able to supply what is lacking in a home.

The more time your children spend in a non-God-centered atmosphere at school, the more time you need to spend with them to counteract that influence and reinforce a biblical worldview.

A parent may say, "I know what you mean. That's why I make sure that my kids are in Sunday school every week, and that's why we pray at mealtimes and at bedtime."

Again, that's wonderful. But if your children are getting a secular worldview every day in school—and especially if they come home and watch a couple of hours of TV every night—Sunday school classes, mealtime blessings, and bedtime prayers alone won't cut it.

## Starting in the Home

So we've come back full circle to the home, where the kingdom agenda for education is to be carried out.

The tragedy today is that we have a generation of children who have become children of the state, because the parents have refused to make them children of the home. So the state is having its way with them.

It's no wonder, when the kids are in school seven or eight hours a day and then the average parent spends about ninety seconds a day in serious, face-to-face communication with his or her children. The Bible says in Psalm 127:4 that children are "like arrows in the hand of a warrior."

In ancient times, warriors made their own arrows. They shaped the arrows just right so they would fly straight and hit the target when released from the bow. That's what we are to do with our children—shape them and aim them in the right direction so that they hit the right target in life.

But it's pretty hard to shape and sharpen those arrows when children are absorbing thousands of hours of TV and thousands more hours listening to rock music.

Too many of our children think watching TV is a right, not a privilege. They spend so much time glued to the TV that when we try to inject time for Bible reading and prayer into the evening, it seems like an intrusion to them.

If we are going to equip our children to live in a world that is hostile to faith, there can't be much room in our agenda for time wasters like TV. We need to work at least as hard with our children as the schools are working to educate them.

If our children are given the freedom to spend all of their time in front of the "tube," if we as parents are not taking the time to turn off the TV and teach our children the things of God, then we can't blame the public school for the way the kids turn out.

## THE CENTER OF EDUCATION

The crisis in education is one of competing worldviews, of who gets to set the standards and to call the shots in the training of our children. The context of education is the home, where a biblical foundation for life is to be laid and the humanistic, man-centered philosophy that pervades public education is to be countered.

If we are going to pull off this agenda, we need to know what the center, the heart of education, really is. The center of education is God Himself.

### Knowledge Without God

We said earlier that God never intended for us to have knowledge that was separated from Him. What did Satan do the first time he came on the human scene? He tried to separate man's knowledge from God.

When Eve told Satan what God had commanded concerning the tree of knowledge, Satan replied, "You surely shall not die! For God knows that in the day you eat from it your eyes will be opened, and you will be like God, knowing good and evil" (Genesis 3:4–5).

Satan was trying to separate information from ethics. He was inviting Eve to have all the knowledge she wanted without worrying about what God thought.

Let me tell you, whenever God is left out of any field of knowledge, whether it is science or medicine or engineering, you are on your way down. God has so constructed the universe that when He is excluded, whatever you're studying is in trouble because He is no longer the center, the reference point.

## God's Truth

Make no mistake. Any truth discovered in God's world is God's truth. Much of this truth is what we call *natural revelation* (see Psalm 19:1–6). This knowledge is not exclusively written in the pages of the Bible, but it has also been discovered through the study of God's world.

The other source of truth is the Bible itself, which is called *special revelation*. But whether learned from nature or from Scripture, all truth is God's revelation. That's why Christian education should be distinct. A Christian education is anchored in God's revelation. It is based on His standards.

Suppose you were cooking a recipe that called for one cup of milk. You can't add one cup of milk unless you know how much a one-cup measure holds. There has to be a standard that is agreed upon for the recipe to work.

Too often the public schools are trying to give children a cup of education when no one agrees on what a cup should be. Nobody wants God to be the standard, yet everyone still wants to produce the right information and get the right results.

But as long as God is left out of the education "recipe," the government won't be able to spend enough to save our schools. When information is divorced from its center, from God, nothing works right. That's why Satan wants to get God out of the classroom, not just by excluding prayer or the Bible, but by excluding a divine viewpoint to knowledge.

Without God, there is no certainty. Would you take medicine from a pharmacist who said, "I *think* this is the right stuff"? Would you submit to a surgeon who said, "I'm *pretty* sure I need to cut here"? How about flying with a pilot who said, "I'm not really positive, but I *believe* I can land this plane"?

When it comes to things that matter, you want certainty. You want pharmacists, surgeons, and pilots who know what they're doing. God knows what He's doing. He's the author of natural revelation, and He's the author of special revelation. He set the standards, and to ignore them leads to chaos in education.

## Societal Breakdown

Excluding the center of education not only produces chaos in the classroom; it leads to breakdown in society.

Romans 1:18–31 describes this downward spiral. Notice how many times words such as *truth, knowledge,* and *understanding* are used to explain how people can come to the point where God gives up on them.

Paul wrote, "The wrath of God is revealed from heaven against all ungodliness and unrighteousness of men, who suppress the truth in unrighteousness" (Romans 1:18). You're in trouble when people start deliberately trying to ignore and hide the truth.

According to Romans 1:20, there is no excuse for this, because the truth about God can be "understood through what has been made." So verse 21 says, "Even though they knew God, they did not honor Him as God."

The knowledge of God is out there, accessible to everyone. Don't tell me God can't be included in the course description. When God is excluded from the conversation in a society, you wind up with talk shows, babble by the hour.

When people exclude God, they become empty-headed, "futile in their speculations" (v. 21). "Professing to be wise, they [become] fools" (v. 22). This is exactly the case in much of our education.

Schools trade "the glory of the incorruptible God for an image in the form of corruptible man" (v. 23). They substitute humanism for theism. That happens when people "exchang[e] the truth of God for a lie" (v. 25).

What happens when a society reaches this point? "God [gives] them over to degrading passions" (v. 26). Everybody's coming out of the closet these days. But when God is removed from the environment, who's to say that one person's standard is right or wrong?

Finally, Paul said in Romans 1:28, "Just as they did not see fit to acknowledge God any longer, God gave them over to a depraved mind." This is where we are today in contemporary America.

## True Knowledge

A mind is a terrible thing to waste. But when you exclude God, you have wasted your mind. Our job as parents is to make sure God is not excluded from our children's education.

The Bible declares that man's knowledge is extremely limited (see Proverbs 30:2–3). God alone can address all the categories of life because "His way is blameless; the word of the Lord is tried" (Psalm 18:30).

God can give your children what no classroom teacher can give them apart from Him, for with God comes not only information but wisdom, the ability to use the information skillfully.

People can give you knowledge, but they can't teach you how to use that knowledge in a God-honoring way. Our children need to learn how to pass life, not just pass tests. They need the ability to filter what they learn through a divine grid so they can apply it properly.

According to Isaiah 8:20, knowledge apart from God is antithetical to reality. So the education process will never get the job done until there are programs and structures in place to bring education back to its center.

## THE CURE FOR EDUCATION

That brings us to our final point. What is the cure for the malaise in education?

I can give it to you in one word: decentralization. We learned earlier in this book that God's system of government is always decentralized; it is composed of multiple governing authorities with distinct spheres of responsibility, jurisdictions, and sanctions.

When everything is centralized, a few people can control what happens and make sure that everyone says and does the same thing. Freedom is lost. This is true in education. That's why socialist countries always want centralized education, so they can teach every child the same thing and indoctrinate the upcoming generations in their dogma.

America is not socialist, but, as I said above, we do have a system of taxation that tends to force families into public schools. Now let me say again that there is nothing necessarily wrong with the public schools, and most families can't afford private school.

In a given school with a particular teacher, the public school can be a great experience for your child. Someone has said that if a child has a great teacher, he or she is in a great school.

But decentralization means we must have access to other options, such as private schools or homeschooling. It also means that control of the schools needs to be in the hands of parents and local administrators rather than having policies and curricula being dictated from above.

Now, I realize there are a lot of problems in education that need attention, and this chapter is not meant to be a detailed discussion of educational theory or philosophy.

What I want to do is give you a framework for evaluating, and perhaps changing, the way your children are being taught. And I want to give you a grid through which you can filter all areas of life. So let's look at our four areas in relation to education as we wrap things up.

## A Personal Application

What can you do personally to see that you are not being unduly influenced by the world's system?

Very simply, make sure you pass everything you see and read through the God-centered worldview we were talking about earlier. "See to it that no one takes you captive through philosophy and empty deception, according to the tradition of men," Paul warned (Colossians 2:8).

God's Word gives you a standard against which you can test any idea. But that means you must know the Word.

Parents should vote for the decentralization of education through some justly administered voucher system that allows parents to determine the education of their children. Competition in the realm of education will enhance all forms of education.

## A Family Application

What can parents do? Begin by finding out what's on the classroom menu as well as the lunchroom menu at your school.

We've already talked about the importance of being involved in your children's education through the PTA and the local school board and by meeting and talking to your kids' teachers.

Now if you have checked things out at school and are disturbed by what you found, you may need to remove your children from that school.

You may say, "I can't afford private education." That could be true, but it may also be a matter of priorities.

People will moonlight or work extra hours for a new car. We need some people who are willing to drive a used car so their children can have a quality education. The car depreciates the minute you drive it off the lot, but your children's education *appreciates* in value when you raise them in the nurture and instruction of the Lord.

Parents who simply cannot afford private school have the option of homeschooling, particularly when the children are younger. This involves sacrifice too, since one parent—usually Mom—will have to stay home and guide the process. But it can be a great "joint venture" when the parents are committed to it.

We talked above about the importance of making sure our homes are teaching and reinforcing spiritual truth. It won't do much good to take your children to Sunday school every week or send them to a Christian school if the home is undoing what the church and the school are trying to teach.

I have to say that I am amazed at what some Christian parents allow in their homes. They will watch any old thing on TV, and they allow their kids to listen to any kind of music or see any movie that comes through town.

My kids used to get ticked off because we always wanted to know the children they were playing with and hanging out with. One of my children would ask to spend the night at Jane's house, for example.

Lois and I would say, "But we don't know Jane's parents. If you want to spend the night with Jane, you and Jane had better find a way for us to hook up with her parents." We must monitor the environment our children live in.

## The Church's Assignment

There is a fourth option in education besides public schools, independent private schools, and home schools. The fourth option is church-based schools.

I know that a lot of churches can't support a school. But again, I think it's a matter of commitment. From the day Oak Cliff Bible Fellowship began with ten members, I told our people we were going to have a Christian school one day that would operate with excellence and quality. This dream has now become a reality.

The church also needs to encourage and equip godly people to go into the public schools. I hope nothing I have said in this chapter has given you the idea that Christians should just abandon public education and leave it to the humanists. That attitude has helped to get us in this mess in the first place.

Far from it. We are called to bring every area of life under the lordship of Christ. Churches should have members who are in key positions on local school boards. Our church also has a lot of public-school teachers, and we are committed to supporting them.

Not long ago I met with the principal at a local high school. We were talking about the separation of church and state. He said, "Listen, when you see the mess we have in the lives of these children, talking about the separation of church and state doesn't help much. What can we do together?"

Educators want help, and the church is in the best position to help them by preparing people who can represent God's agenda in the schools by "adopting" schools in their communities and providing tutoring, mentoring, and other support services. Many of the schools in our church's district have a church representative assigned to them. Through these representatives we serve the public schools as a community of faith.

When Paul was in Athens, he was able to talk with the philosophers on their level yet still talk to them about the "unknown God" (Acts 17:23) and introduce them to Christ.

Paul knew his subject, but he also knew the Lord. That's what we need in public education, and the church can help provide that. People who feel God's call into education are there to be His priests (1 Peter 2:5) in that world.

## The Government's Role

This is a tough one, because the goal in public education is supposed to be freedom *of* religion, not freedom *from* religion.

The government's overall calling is to maintain order and provide an environment in which its citizens are free to pursue their calling. We are not trying to say that the government should legislate public schools into Christian schools. That will never happen, and it wouldn't work anyway.

But the problem is that the government is not giving Christians a fair hearing in the public schools. We are being excluded from the discussion, on the charge that we are trying to push religion on people.

But we aren't trying to push anything on anyone. You can't coerce people to accept Christ. All we want is a level playing field, the freedom we are supposed to have to express our beliefs in the schools. It is our conviction that a Christian world- and life-view will clearly demonstrate a better life for all. The government should seek to win the educational battle based on truth, not on the power of taxation. But these days, "free and open" public education isn't really free *or* open. The government's goodies come with a hidden agenda attached. So we must constantly challenge the public schools to give equal time to the Christian perspective while simultaneously seeking a more equitable and competitive approach to all forms of education (e.g., vouchers).

Let me illustrate what I mean with a closing story. There was a man who provided wild pigs for slaughter. He was bringing them in by the thousands.

Another guy said to him, "How are you able to capture all of these wild pigs?"

The man replied, "I came up with an ingenious method. All I do is put out a big trough and fill it with food. I make the food real nice and sweet and attractive, and I get the little piglets to come.

"When the piglets come, their parents follow, because they like this free food. So while they are getting used to coming every day and enjoying the free food, one day I put up a fence on the west side of the trough.

"They come back the next day for the free food, and I put up a fence on the east side. Then I do the same thing the next day on the south side.

"Finally, as they are eating away and not paying attention to what's going on around them, I build the fence on the north side. Then all I have to do is shut the gate."

Parents, we may use the government's "free" education, but we need to keep an eye on the fences that are going up. While we're partaking at public education's "trough" with our children, we need to make sure that the fences of humanism are not being erected around us, because then all the humanists have to do is shut the gate. When that happens, it will be too late to squeal.

I believe the fences are already being erected. The world's agenda is being carried out, but we can counter that influence with a kingdom agenda if we as believers and as parents will shoulder our biblical responsibility for our children's education.

# *Epilogue*

Most major cities in our country have a freeway that loops around the city. This loop allows travelers to skirt the downtown section as they head for their destination.

This is precisely what our culture has done with God. He has been put on the "loop" of our personal, family, church, and community lives—close enough to be at hand when we need Him but far enough away that He can't invade the center of our lives.

We want a God on the loop, not the God of the Bible who comes downtown and demands to occupy the center of all of life. But the results of keeping God on the loop are terrifying, as we have seen. To reverse this downward spiral, God must exit the loop and regain His position at the center of life. This is the heart of kingdom living, God's alternative way of running life.

In Psalm 128, God summarizes in six verses what I have just spent hundreds of pages to explain. This passage lays out life as it was meant to be lived by kingdom people. It begins with a stirring challenge to us as individual believers: "How blessed is everyone who fears the Lord, who walks in His ways. When you shall eat of the fruit of your hands, you will be happy and it will be well with you" (vv. 1–2).

The first thing the psalmist wanted you to know is that if your personal life is in line with God's Word, blessing will flow out of you into your home, your church, and your community. But it all starts with you and me personally.

"How blessed," how happy, is the person who fears the Lord. To fear God simply means to take Him seriously. It has to do with holding God in awe and reverence. It means God is not to be marginalized, discounted, or put on the loop of life. Rather, He must be at the control center of your existence.

What happens when you fear God? He will take care of your fortune: "You shall eat of the fruit of your hands" (Psalm 128:2a). He will take care of your feelings: "You will be happy" (v. 2b). And He will take care of your future: "It will be well with you" (v. 2c).

But we live in a culture that does not take God seriously. Most people keep God out on the loop, the fringe, of their lives, as I said in the introduction to this book. He is always circling but never allowed to come in.

You may say, "I want to take God seriously. How can I know whether I am doing it or not?"

The psalmist answered that question in verse 1. You take God seriously when you walk in His ways, when doing what He wants done is your goal and the pattern of your life.

When you take God seriously in your personal life, the next place it shows up is in your family life. "Your wife shall be like a fruitful vine, within your house, your children like olive plants around your table. Behold, for thus shall the man be blessed who fears the Lord" (Psalm 128:3–4).

God was saying to families, "You must be rooted in Me." The writer pictured the wife as a "fruitful vine." Let me tell you three things you need to know about vines. First, a vine clings. It will take hold of whatever it is attached to and cling to it. The atmosphere in a home should be such that a wife can wrap her "branches" around her husband for stability, security, and love.

Vines not only cling, but they climb. A healthy vine will spread out and take over a whole wall of a house. In other words, when a husband is providing the right kind of atmosphere, his wife can develop her strengths and abilities. She can grow, becoming a better woman than she ever was.

If a man has a stunted, no-growing wife, the problem could be that she doesn't have what she needs to cling to. She may not be getting the spiritual nurturing and nourishment she needs. The wife of a kingdom man should be able to say, "When I cling to my husband, good things start growing out of my life that I didn't know were there."

The third thing about vines is that they produce. A grapevine will yield clusters of grapes. Grapes start budding out everywhere. Now, grapes are used to make wine. A person who drinks enough wine will start becoming intoxicated. He will act different because the wine makes him feel good.

Husband, if your wife is a clinging, climbing, and clustering fruitful vine, your family life will be a delight instead of just a duty.

The wife also has a responsibility here. She is described as the wife "within [the] house," meaning that a woman must prioritize the nurturing of her home and family above all else to be fully blessed of God and reap the full benefits of the fear of God in her home. All of her outside activity must be measured by whether it complements or conflicts with the priority of family.

But before any of that can happen, a vine has to have the right atmosphere to grow in. Don't expect a summer wife if the husband brings home stormy winter weather. Don't expect a vineyard to grow if it's snowing and hailing when he comes home.

When it comes to children, the psalmist changed the imagery from a vine to olive plants. Notice they are not trees yet but plants. Olive plants take up to fifteen years to mature, and they have to be nurtured. When they are nurtured properly they provide a multitude of benefits since olive oil was used for cooking, medicine, massage, and many other profitable opportunities.

The psalmist was saying that we must provide a nurturing environment for our children if they're going to grow up to be olive trees. The beauty of an olive tree in biblical times was that when it matured it would produce olives for another forty years. That's the picture of productive children raised in a nurturing environment.

One of the great places to do family nurturing is "around the table" (Psalm 128:3b). Mealtimes provide many great teachable moments —but Dad has to be there around the table with the kids if those moments are going to be seized for God. The man who provides this kind of climate in the home will be blessed of the Lord (see v. 4).

In verse 5, we come to the third category of life that needs to be addressed in living out a kingdom agenda: "The Lord bless you from Zion," the psalmist wrote.

Zion was the city of God, where the temple was located. It was the place where families came to worship God. The author of Hebrews picked this up when he said, "You have come to Mount Zion and to the city of the living God" (Hebrews 12:22). The very next verse in Hebrews tells us that, for us, Mount Zion is the church.

Mount Zion, the church, is the place where you meet God. The person who has God at the center of his or her life, and the family that gathers regularly with God's people to be affirmed and reaffirmed in the things of God, will be blessed.

If we are serious about fulfilling the agenda God has given us, if we are serious about passing on the faith to succeeding generations, then we had better be serious about the corporate body of Christ. The reason we have so many failing individuals and faltering families is that they're not involved in a spiritual maintenance program in the family of God with the people of God.

Fourth and finally, the writer of Psalm 128 said that when we have our personal, family, and church lives lined up with God's agenda, we will be powerful in our impact on society: "May you see the prosperity of Jerusalem all the days of your life. Indeed, may you see your children's children. Peace be upon Israel!" (vv. 5b–6).

Notice that last phrase of the psalm. Peace is shalom, well-being in the community, because individuals, families, and the church are right with God and right with each other. When you get all of that lined up properly, guess what happens: You see the prosperity of the community. You see peace take over. You see a nation recover its spiritual health.

Some of us in America won't get to see our children's children, because there's no peace. There's violence, corruption, and corrosion. The psalmist said, in essence, "If you want to fix the culture, then start with your own spheres of influence."

How are we as Christians going to help influence the leaders of our society if we're not willing to commit our personal lives to Christ, to love and nurture our families, and to serve and strengthen the church of the living God?

We live in a world that has lost its morals and its standards. Our public schools are falling apart. Criminals are dominating our neighborhoods, and we're just *having* church rather than *being* the church. That's not good enough.

We need to break the huddle and go out and let the world know that Jesus is Lord. We have too many "secret-agent" Christians. Too many spiritual CIA representatives. Too many covert operatives for the kingdom. Everybody else is coming out. We might as well come out too.

It's time for the people on your job to know where you stand. If you stand with Christ, stand up and be counted. People in your neighborhood ought to know where you stand. They ought to know that there is a standard, and God is that standard.

Our world needs truth. It needs the truth of God from people who know it. When you fear God, it rolls over to your home. And then it rolls over from there into your church.

And then we will see the betterment of the community. We will see the impact of Christ around the world. We will see the difference the cross can make.

Living out a kingdom agenda starts with your walk with God, moves to your relationship with your family, and then to your involvement in the church. And soon, your city, your state, and your nation are not the same. That's kingdom impact, and it starts with you and me. We're talking about a kingdom agenda, God's alternative. What a way to live!

# *About The Urban*
# *Alternative*

The Urban Alternative (TUA) is the national ministry of Dr. Tony Evans and is dedicated to promoting God's kingdom agenda through equipping, empowering, and uniting Christians to impact individuals, families, churches, and communities for the rebuilding of their lives from the inside out.

## THE PROBLEM

The moral fabric of America is being torn to shreds by issues such as family disintegration, crime, racial division, injustice, and countless other problems that are destroying our culture. Many solutions that have been proposed to solve these problems consistently fall short of providing real, long-term answers. This is because many of the proposed solutions address these issues from the outside in and from the top down.

## THE PHILOSOPHY

Tony Evans and The Urban Alternative believe that the real answer to solving these problems lies in a transformation that comes from the inside out and from the bottom up. As Dr. Evans states, "The core cause of the problems we face is a spiritual one, and therefore, the only successful way to address these issues is spiritually; that means the application of the Bible to the four dimensions of life, beginning with the individual then moving on to the family and then to the church, and from there overflowing into the broader society. We've tried a political agenda, a social agenda, and an economic agenda. It's time now for a kingdom agenda."

## THE PROGRAM

Today more than ever, Dr. Evans and The Urban Alternative are committed to clearly communicating the truth of God's Word through teaching, training, and mobilizing the body of Christ.

### Media

The Urban Alternative proclaims the truth of God's Word daily on over five hundred radio stations throughout the U.S. and in over forty countries worldwide. In addition, the The Urban Alternative television broadcast can be seen nationwide.

### Training

The Urban Alternative hosts two national conferences designed to train and equip church leaders for effective ministry both to their members and to their community.

### Resources

The Urban Alternative offers an array of books, audio, and video teaching series and many other ministry helps to promote a spiritual development and the Kingdom Agenda philosophy.

## National Church Adopt-A-School Initiative

The Urban Alternative developed a comprehensive community outreach strategy designed to partner church and schools to impact the lives of urban youth and their families. The comprehensive implementation toolkit and accompanying mentoring manual, along with the accompanying training that TUA offers, will equip churches to transform their community spiritually and socially through this partnership.

FOR MORE INFORMATION CONTACT:

The Urban Alternative

P.O. Box 4000

Dallas, TX 75208

1-800-800-3222

www.tonyevans.org

# General Index

# Scripture Index

# The Understanding God Series

## Totally Saved
*Understanding, Experiencing and*
*Enjoying the Greatness of Your Salvation*

Tony Evans explores justification, propitiation, redemption, reconciliation, forgiveness, and other biblical truths.

*ISBN: 978-0-8024-6824-6*

## Our God Is Awesome
*Encountering the Greatness of Our God*

*Tony Evans has done a masterful job of unfolding the rich truth about*
*God . He writes with uncommon clarity, accuracy and warmth. A trea-*
*sured resource for all who desire to know God better.*
– John MacArthur, Pastor, Grace Community Church of the Valley.

*ISBN: 978-0-8024-4850-7*

## Returning To Your First Love
*Putting God Back in First Place*

*Tony Evans has done to us all a service in focusing the biblical spot-*
*light on the absolute necessity of keeping our love of Christ as the*
*central passion of our hearts.*
– Charles Stanley, Pastor, First Baptist Church in Atlanta, Author
*ISBN: 978-0-8024-4851-4*

## The Promise
*Experiencing God's Greatest Gift—The Holy Spirit*

*Here is a book that points us to the Spirit's way to purity and power.*
*Every chapter is appropriately titled "Experiencing the Spirit's . . ."*
*May this work help all who read it to do so.*
– Dr. Charles Ryrie, Professor, Dallas Theological Seminary

*ISBN: 978-0-8024-4852-1*

## God's Glorious Church
*The Mystery and Mission of the Body of Christ*

Tony Evans shows how the church is nothing less than the ongoing
incarnation of Christ on earth—a living body with a mission,
a purpose, and an ultimate call to disciple the whole world.
*ISBN: 978-0-8024-3951-2*

## Who Is This King of Glory?
*Experiencing the Fullness of Christ's Work in Our Lives*

In this practical, biblically-based volume, Tony Evans examines Jesus, "the greatest of all subjects," from three different perspectives: His uniqueness, His authority, and our appropriate response to Him.

**ISBN: 978-0-8024-4854-5**

## The Battle Is the Lord's
*Waging Victorious Spiritual Warfare*

We're in a war, but Christ has given us the victory. In *The Battle Is the Lord's*, Tony Evans reveals Satan's strategies, teaches how you can fight back against the forces of darkness, and shows you how to find deliverance from the devil's snares.

**ISBN: 978-0-8024-4855-2**

## The Best Is Yet to Come
*Bible Prophecies Through the Ages*

Tony Evans propels you past the hype and confusion of prophecy, straight to the Source. He skillfully unlocks the secrets of the prophetic program, simultaneously unveiling the future for all to read and understand.

**ISBN: 978-0-8024-4856-9**

## What Matters Most
*Four Absolute Necessities in Following Christ*

God's goal for believers is that they become more like Christ. But what does that mean? In *What Matters Most*, Tony Evans explores the four essential elements of discipleship: worship, fellowship, education and outreach.

**ISBN: 978-0-8024-4853-8**

## The Transforming Word
*Discovering the Power and Provision of the Bible*

Maybe you read a portion of the Bible everday, or several times a week . . . but do you know the transforming power of God's revealed word? Tony Evans explains where Scripture came from and why it is so unique. You will never view the Bible the same way again.

**ISBN: 978-0-8024-6820-8**